A World of Populations

A World of Populations

Transnational Perspectives on Demography in the Twentieth Century

Edited by Heinrich Hartmann and Corinna R. Unger

berghahn
NEW YORK · OXFORD
www.berghahnbooks.com

First edition published in 2014 by
Berghahn Books
www.berghahnbooks.com

© 2014, 2017 Heinrich Hartmann and Corinna R. Unger
First paperback edition published in 2017

All rights reserved. Except for the quotation of short passages
for the purposes of criticism and review, no part of this book
may be reproduced in any form or by any means, electronic or
mechanical, including photocopying, recording, or any information
storage and retrieval system now known or to be invented,
without written permission of the publisher.

Library of Congress Cataloging-in-Publication Data

A world of populations: transnational perspectives on demography in the twentieth century / edited by Heinrich Hartmann and Corinna R. Unger.
    pages cm
ISBN 978-1-78238-427-4 (hardback: alk. paper) -- ISBN: 978-1-78533-351-4 (paperback) -- ISBN 978-1-78238-428-1 (ebook)
1. Demography--History--20th century. 2. Population. I. Hartmann, Heinrich, 1977- II. Unger, Corinna R.
HB851.W56 2014
304.609'04--dc23

2014009543

British Library Cataloguing in Publication Data
A catalogue record for this book is available from the British Library

ISBN: 978-1-78238-427-4 (hardback)
ISBN: 978-1-78533-351-4 (paperback)
ISBN: 978-1-78238-428-1 (ebook)

Contents

List of Figures   vii

Introduction. Counting, Constructing, and Controlling Populations: The History of Demography, Population Studies, and Family Planning in the Twentieth Century   1
  Corinna R. Unger and Heinrich Hartmann

Part I. Producing Demographic Subjects: Transnational Discourses

1. The View From Below and the View From Above: What U.S. Census-Taking Reveals about Social Representations in the Era of Jim Crow and Immigration Restriction   19
  Paul Schor

2. "Reproduction" as a New Demographic Issue in Interwar Poland   36
  Morgane Labbé

3. Family Planning—A Rational Choice? The Influence of Systems Approaches, Behavioralism, and Rational Choice Thinking on Mid-Twentieth-Century Family Planning Programs   58
  Corinna R. Unger

4. "Overpopulation" and the Politics of Family Planning in Chile and Peru: Negotiating National Interests and Global Paradigms in a Cold War World   83
  Jadwiga E. Pieper Mooney

5. Revisiting the Early 1970s Commoner-Ehrlich Debate about Population and Environment: Dueling Critiques of Production and Consumption in a Global Age   108
  Thomas Robertson

Part II. Demographic Knowledge in Practice: Transfers and Transformations

6 Counting People: The Emerging Field of Demography and the Mobilization of the Social Sciences in the Formation of Policy in South Korea since 1948   129
   John P. DiMoia

7 Laparoscopy as a Technology of Population Control: A Use-Centered History of Surgical Sterilization   147
   Jesse Olszynko-Gryn

8 A Twofold Discovery of Population: Assessing the Turkish Population by its "Knowledge, Attitudes, and Practices," 1962–1980   178
   Heinrich Hartmann

9 Seeing Population as a Problem: Influences of the Construction of Population Knowledge on Kenyan Politics (1940s to 1980s)   201
   Maria Dörnemann

10 Filtering Demography and Biomedical Technologies: Melanesian Nurses and Global Population Concerns   222
   Alexandra Widmer

Notes on Contributors   243
Index   247

Figures

Figure 7.1	A promotional image of Ortho's pelvic teaching model "Gynny."	153
Figure 7.2	A promotional flyer from the late 1970s for Rocket's gun-like clip applicator dramatically evokes female sterilization by the broken gender symbol for woman.	156
Figure 7.3	A world map showing the distribution of the 509 scopes purchased and distributed by USAID by 1976.	158
Figure 7.4	A promotional display of the compact KLI Laprocator system with instructional manual and reserve boxes of Falope rings.	160
Figure 7.5	Mehta's preferred operating position: though apparently sketched nude, patients remained dressed in their everyday clothing with their midriffs conventionally exposed.	162

Introduction

Counting, Constructing, and Controlling Populations

The History of Demography, Population Studies, and Family Planning in the Twentieth Century

Corinna R. Unger and Heinrich Hartmann

"Population," a topic long considered the exclusive concern of demographers and welfare politicians, has come to the attention of historians in recent years. The reasons for this new interest seem to be anchored in public discussions and societal concerns about contemporary and future demographic developments. For one, many European nations are experiencing a decrease in birth rates at a time when the influx of migrants from African and Asian countries is triggering debates about increasing religious and ethnic heterogeneity, and the social and cultural effects this has on the formerly more homogenous societies. The expectation that climate change will bring about mass migration movements in the near future adds to the perception of crisis in terms of wealth and security in many Western nations.[1] Yet it is not only the demographic consequences of these endurable changes that play a certain role in the formation of these perceptions, it is also the population as a dynamic actor in changing contexts. Some scholars, as well as some representatives of the mass media, associate high birth rates and the resulting young populations with the political and social tensions in many Arab countries, and identify them as one reason for political unrest or the rise of terrorism.[2]

Hence, demographic changes taking place in many regions of the world are inspiring new political debates. This has led a growing number of historians to turn to older debates about "overpopulation."[3] Many of those historians share a discomfort with the neglect of historical thinking in today's political use of demographic concepts. They consider it important to take into account the historical context of demographic arguments, and to be aware of the historicity of debates on population issues in general. Consequently, historians are interested in earlier discussions about demographic developments and their economic, political, and social consequences, particularly with regard to the potential effects those phenomena might have on the conceptualization of the nation state in an increasingly interconnected world, in which trans-border movements have steadily gained in frequency. The importance of the nation state in producing knowledge about demographic developments and in defining categories to describe its "population" figures prominently in many studies,[4] as do historical debates about migration restrictions and population transfers.[5] The growing interest in historical precedents for today's developments and debates is linked to the second reason why many historians have become interested in historicizing demographic discourse: the continuing fascination with transnational history, particularly with transfers and transformations across national borders, and the evolution of a sphere of international interaction parallel to the established political arena.[6] This becomes manifest in the attention historians pay to the role of demographic knowledge in the colonial context[7] as well as in development programs, and in the emphasis on birth control and family planning throughout the second half of the twentieth century.[8] This volume aims to add to debates on the genuinely transnational character of demographic discourse while also challenging some of the assumptions on which they are based. It intends to do so by scrutinizing the process of the production and transfer of demographic knowledge and population policies across the globe.[9]

In our understanding, the history of demography as an academic discipline was (and is) characterized by its close proximity to politics.[10] We assume that demographic knowledge was never purely technical and above all not "apolitical," even if many agents tried to argue that "natural" demographic patterns invariably called for specific population policies. Hence, the authors of this volume propose to probe deeper into the political processes of knowledge production and to analyze how this knowledge was mobilized to define and enact new forms of population policies. We would also like to highlight how different kinds of localities are linked in these concepts. The topic of "transnational demographics" in no way aims to replace a local level of analysis, but rather tries to point to the interconnections between the local, the national and the claims for a global dimension of demographic issues.

To do so, we follow three overarching questions: i) Is demography as a discipline different from other scientific disciplines because of its multidisciplinary, or perhaps transdisciplinary, character, and if so, how? ii) How are "populations" constructed, and how do research settings and the institutions involved contribute to produce a common understanding of what "population" is? iii) How does demographic knowledge become transformed into a scientific approach applied in practice, and how does the knowledge change when it comes into contact with local practices of speaking about populations and regulating them? Using these three questions as guidelines, the authors hope to offer new perspectives on the social and transnational history of the twentieth century. Demographic knowledge helped to shape representations of the social, and it emerged from a socially embedded background that transgressed borders, not only on the level of explicit international politics and organizations, but also through transnational communities of experts. Hence, we suggest employing a history of knowledge perspective on the history of demography, population studies, and population politics as well as a social historian's perspective on the agents involved.[11]

This perspective, as well as the co-evolution of demographic thinking and practices of the welfare state, points to a chronology that will be inherent in this volume. Many chapters explicitly or implicitly focus on the 1960s and 1970s, a time when discourses about "world population" gained importance and demographic reasoning contributed to the reorientation of social policies in different countries. Time periods like these, reflecting a particular intensification of debates, allow historians of knowledge and science to gain insight into the reasons why some approaches were more "successful" than others. However, this chronology is based on our particular methodological approach, and therefore by no means exclusive. It allows us to see demography in different time frames and to acknowledge the role of preceding developments while also taking into account more recent dynamics in the academic thinking about demography.

In the following, we will outline some of the historical and sociological perspectives that frame our interest.

Historical and Sociological Perspectives on Demographic Knowledge

For two centuries, Thomas Malthus has influenced public discourse about demographic developments like few other scholars. His sinister prediction that the globe would become overpopulated has produced anxiety in societies all over the globe, taken up time and again in public discourse.[12] The experience of counting and being counted was a necessary precondition for this seemingly uniform apocalyptic population discourse. It is in this sense, we would argue, that the history of statistical knowledge overlaps directly with the transnational history of demographic discourses. Malthus's normative way of thinking about population sizes preceded the development of a clearly defined census method, which was established at the Statistical Congress in St. Petersburg in 1872.[13] In the following years, most European states began to regularly count their populations, thereby producing reliable pools of demographic knowledge. The emergence of "population" as a political issue in the second half of the nineteenth century was intimately linked to changing conditions of policy-making in the modern era. Statistics and demographic knowledge were among the key necessities of the emerging European welfare states, linked both to bureaucrats and to new administrative institutions like private assurance companies.[14] The administrative interest in demography influenced the discipline's institutional and methodological evolution, and it accelerated technological developments in the administration of "large numbers."[15]

The practice of counting individuals, which can be understood as an instrument of modern governance in a Foucauldian sense, preceded its systematic application as a measure of statecraft. Governments were not the only ones interested in demographic statistics; however, in an age of nationalism, many industrialized societies used population sizes to define themselves, often by claiming a quantitative superiority over their neighbors. As a result of the American and European nation states' self-definition as statistical and demographic entities, professional, social, and ethnic categories that were used to describe a nation's inhabitants became entangled with each other and produced a new, highly politicized understanding of "population."[16] In recent years, many historians, social scientists, and sociologists of knowledge have embraced this constructivist perspective on demographic discourses and practices as expressions of increasingly complex regulatory requirements under the conditions of "reflexive modernity" (U. Beck).

Since the 1980s, the interplay between science and nationally anchored social phenomena has received much scholarly attention. Ian Hacking has argued that we should understand the political history of vital statistics in Europe in light of a paradigmatic shift in mathematics, the development of probability calculus.[17] In this respect, the statistically informed view on European populations shaped particular cultures of scientific evidence.[18] By installing new institutions relying on experts, a "knowledge society" came into being whose protagonists tried to foresee the future and simultaneously develop scientific methods to shape that future.[19] The notion of being able to plan society characterized much of the twentieth century and made social engineering a core element of policy making across political and ideological borders.[20] The concept of "population" played an important role in this regard. For example, communist and Keynesian regimes alike relied on empirical information about population size and constitution to formulate their economic plans.[21] The reliance on demographic data increased simultaneously with the growing possibilities of mathematical computing in the postwar era.[22]

This brings us to the modalities of demographic knowledge production. Over the last years, the role of the localities in which scientific evidence is generated has received growing attention.[23] Scholars in the history of science have focused on the laboratory to show the interrelatedness of expert networks, objects, and the social process of knowledge production. With the statistical "revolution" of the nineteenth century in mind, one might be tempted to see an analogy between the rising number of statistical offices in almost all European countries and the growing number of scientific laboratories. If we accept that the notion of population emerged from the categories developed by networks of researchers, it might be worth returning to the specific settings of their production, even by transgressing the classical *topos* of the laboratory.[24] To take the hypothesis one step further, one could argue that the statistical offices were part of a "social and cultural materiality" that provided the basis for the multiplicity of localities of modern knowledge production.[25] It seems promising to study the process of how "population" as scientific evidence started to travel from its place of production to the outside world.

The focus on the local circumstances of knowledge production has encouraged attempts to overcome the traditional dichotomy between scientific subjects and objects. The interaction between academic research and the public in censuses seem to induce what modern sociologists of knowledge refer to as looping effects.[26] Subjects being counted often understand much more about the methodology of the surveys and their underlying assumptions than statisticians suspect. Consequently they may adjust their attitudes to the categories of statistical thinking. They will respond to surveys and data-taking in accordance with their understanding of what is being searched for. This does not necessarily imply that their responses are driven by personal interest; individuals might also adopt the statistical descriptors to make sense of their own personal situation and behavior. The interplay between demographic subjects and statistical categories offers links to related discussions in the history and sociology of knowledge as well as to the construction of subjects and objects in other scientific fields.[27]

Historical research on demography has also debated the question of a particular European understanding of social engineering by numbers.[28] In spite of well-established international ties, the effort to "nationalize" demographic discourses and to interpret demographic data through the "national lens" characterized demography in much of the twentieth century. This development seems to have been related to a reinforced eugenic research agenda, which defined qualitative criteria for "desirable" national populations. Nonetheless, the eugenic movement from its inception was heavily influenced by an international community of biologists and demographers who promoted eugenics as part of the internationalization of scientific expertise.[29]

To understand the interrelatedness of national and transnational academic discourses and practices one needs to take a closer look at the field of demography in the colonial and postcolonial context. The emergence of the statistical and anthropological sciences that shaped early demographic discourses coincided with the climax of European colonial expansion overseas, and colonial experiences clearly influenced demographic practices and argumentative patterns in the

European metropoles.[30] Thus it is evident that decolonization played a major role in reshaping postwar demographic thinking.

Scholarly interest in the "globalization" of demographic expertise and population discourses in the postwar era has blossomed recently. The focus of much of the research lies in the history of demographic thinking in the context of development concepts. The complex histories of demographic transition theory cannot be summarized as a simple function of modernization theories.[31] Already in the prewar era demographic thinking provided an important antithesis to contemporary notions of modernization, and many scholars considered the nexus between modernity and demographic transition reversible. We have learned much about the role of the new nations' regimes in promoting and sometimes enforcing birth control, but comparatively little about the effects that the globalization of the political perspective had on demographic knowledge and methods. Many of the contributions in this volume aim to equilibrate these perspectives by relating "Third World" family planning programs and their often coercive character to new ways and models of analyzing data. For example, one could perhaps argue that new approaches like cybernetics not only influenced representations of the population but also had a notable effect on development programs. To better understand the issues at stake, it will be helpful to study in greater detail the infrastructure of demographic knowledge production in the postwar era. Non-governmental organizations like the International Planned Parenthood Federation (founded in 1952), institutions like the Population Council (founded in 1952) and the United Nations Fund for Population Activities (founded in 1967), as well as large international demographic conferences (starting 1954 in Rome) provided forums for international demographic experts to meet and exchange ideas. Simultaneously, immense amounts of public and private money flowed into demographic research at dozens of universities and research centers, and equally considerable sums were invested into programs to develop more effective birth control methods.[32] One could argue that together those institutions and centers constituted a globalized demographic laboratory. Studying closely the transdisciplinary research performed in the "global lab" from a history of science perspective should allow us to observe how new demographic methods affected the public perception of "population" under the conditions of decolonization, the Cold War, and accelerated globalization.

Topics in the History of Demography and Population Studies

Taking up these perspectives we can identify three broad fields that deserve systematic attention: the institutionalization and professionalization of demography as an academic discipline in the twentieth century; the application of demographic theories and approaches and the resulting construction of specific "populations";

and the translation of demographic knowledge into population policies domestically and in the international arena. The way in which the individual contributions are organized in this volume is intended to provide a degree of orientation in a very broad field. However, we want to emphasize that the contributions address a variety of questions and cannot be reduced easily to one point. Hence, in the following we do not aim to impose a "grand narrative," but to sketch overarching perspectives along the three lines of inquiry outlined above.

The first section addresses the process of the production of demographic subjects in different national and transnational contexts. Here we are particularly interested in the co-evolution of demographic discourses in scientific communities and among a wider public, and the interplay between discourses (which we define in a broad sense as acts of conscious or unconscious communication, not necessarily as a form of oral or written contribution to the advancement of demographics), nation building, and the establishment of institutions.

Paul Schor opens the section with an analysis of the American census in the second half of the nineteenth century, a time when the United States was experiencing both massive immigration and the effects of emancipation. Consequently, the census focused on questions referring to ethnic and racial difference, thereby reinforcing and sometimes challenging existing stereotypes. Enumerators' reports to the census office reflect a high sensitivity for difference, both negatively and positively described, and an understanding of individuals as representatives of their respective social or racial groups rather than of the American nation. As Schor shows, censuses did not necessarily contribute to the process of nation building in the sense of increasing national unity; a census could also help to cement differences and create a statistical image of a highly pluralistic, unequal population.

The situation was different in Latin America in the postwar period, as Jadwiga E. Pieper Mooney suggests in her chapter on family planning approaches in Chile and Peru in the 1960s. While both countries referred to global population paradigms, they did so in markedly different ways, and in response to distinct historical trajectories and political priorities. In Chile, doctors' efforts to prevent abortion together with their interest in limiting population growth resulted in the establishment of large, state-supported family planning programs. Peru, on the other hand, where eugenic elements were present in demographic debates much longer than in other Latin American countries, focused on private, decentralized activities and installed official state-sponsored family planning programs only in the 1980s. Hence, national frameworks played a decisive role in shaping demographic thinking and practices.

In the case of interwar Poland, the felt need for national self-confidence and credibility had a notable impact on Polish experts' activities in the field of demography. Morgane Labbé, in her chapter on Polish research on reproduction in the interwar period, emphasizes how closely individual biographies, personal networks and scientific approaches were linked to each other, and how they influenced each other in producing a specific understanding of demographic problems. As her research shows, paying attention to individuals and networks also helps us to better understand how demographic discourses traversed national, political, and ideological borders. This is true, for example, of Polish demographer Stefan Szulc and his reception of the work of Kuczynski and Lotka in the 1920s and 1930s. And as Thomas Robertson demonstrates in his chapter on two key figures in the debate about "overpopulation," Barry Commoner and Paul Ehrlich, the role of individuals can provide insight into why some demographic positions gained much greater public prominence than others.

Corinna R. Unger's chapter studies the rise and fall of one of these approaches to demography: behavioralism. In the 1950s and 1960s, the belief in the existence of universal laws of human behavior seemed to outweigh notions of cultural or racial difference. Against this background it seemed possible to construct a "world population," which was understood as the sum of individuals making reproductive choices. If those individual decisions could be steered in the "right" direction with the help of scientific interventions, the "population problem" identified as urgent in the 1960s could be solved, contemporaries believed.

The issue of transferring academic and institutional "models" abroad links the first to the second section, which is devoted to the question of how different kinds of demographic knowledge under various institutional, political, cultural, and geographic conditions produce demographic subjects. In his chapter on the history of demography in South Korea, for example, John P. DiMoia shows how intimately the establishment of South Korean demographic institutions was tied to the outcome of World War II, specifically the occupation by American troops. Yet he also demonstrates that it would be reductionist to consider the Republic of Korea's (ROK) demographic institutions solely a copy of American institutions. South Korea's ties to imperial and postwar Japan strongly influenced the ROK's demographic structures, as did its relations with Taiwan. Hence, regional networks overlapped or competed with international agencies and produced new institutional patterns reflecting the specific historical circumstances under which they came into existence.

Similarly, transferring a demographic discourse from one part of the world to another is a process that cannot easily be reduced to a mere spatial transposition. The complexity of this process often led actors to change their basic assumptions. Ideas shifted away from the original intentions of their social carriers and, in a different setting, had other socioeconomic effects than in the environment in which they had been developed. This phenomenon of multilayered transformation challenges the notion of a homogenous demographic "discourse." It also implies that the transfer of ideas about population was not limited to oral or written acts of communication but also took place as part of the exchange of material products and technologies.

Jesse Olszynko-Gryn, in his chapter on the history of surgical sterilization, suggests understanding the transfer of discourses as more than the pure transfer of ideas and proposes looking at the technological side of this transfer. Analyzing the introduction of the new sterilization method of laparoscopy, he describes a series of "trade-offs" this technology went through in order to create manageable and "efficient" devices for world population control. The technological bias that many family planning programs implicitly embraced undermined many of the explicit discourses about reproductive choices and women's rights. "Population control" was thus strongly materially biased.

The situation in pre- and postcolonial Vanuatu seems to point in a similar direction. Alexandra Widmer describes how everyday behavior of the population and their reproductive habits became subjects of the expertise of local nurses who introduced a "filtered" form of global knowledge about reproduction into the local setting. Widmer argues that the notion of technology needs to be broadened to be able to understand the effects of the transfer of concepts on local situations. In this perspective, midwives bringing clean sheets to villages are part of the same category of actors as reproductive experts representing New York's Population Council. Here the relational quality of knowledge bridges the classical caesura between colonial and postcolonial contexts, seeing that the carriers of local knowledge often remained the same.

Maria Dörnemann introduces readers to another issue related to the complex transfer of knowledge by studying the multifold processes of translation that led to the implementation of population programs in Kenya. For one, her chapter points to the fact that an abstract idea of economic development went hand in hand with the idea of regulating individual reproductive behavior. Yet the "development lens" was not a one-way street, and should be looked at from two sides, with Kenya being not only a respondent but a proactive producer of knowledge which Western experts and institutions took into account. The chapter also analyzes the learning processes of Kenyan officials and finds that they cannot be reduced to the taking up of demographic paradigms or abstract statistical skills. They also included appropriating statistical metaphors and strategic behavior that served to promote Kenyan institutional, academic, and political interests.

Heinrich Hartmann's analysis of population programs in Turkey supports these findings by relativizing the role of population experts and their self-declared scientocratic independence. Studying a national and an international method of conducting behavioralist programs in rural Anatolia in the 1960s and 1970s, Hartmann's chapter helps us to understand the impact of political negotiations in the transfer processes. Applying the "right" means of investigating reproduction patterns was not as neutral an activity as many experts presented it. Hence, the experts' room for maneuver was limited so long as the experts themselves aimed to implement particular programs, thereby making deliberate choices.

It is an explicit goal of this volume to open doors for a discussion of the history of demographic thinking across borders. It certainly does not claim to cover every aspect of this history or to provide a complete analysis of every macro region of the world. Instead, the volume is designed to give an overview of the major fields of interest that are linked to a transnational history of demographic discourses and practices. It might allow interested readers to find clues for further research topics or to define genuinely transnational materials and methods for a new approach to the history of demography. And, perhaps, it might convince others that the history of defining and thinking of the world's populations never was nor ever will be a purely national history.

We would like to thank Elizabeth Berg, Adam Capitanio, Owen Gurrey, Karin Hagen, and Charlotte Mosedale for their various kinds of support in putting this volume together. We are also grateful to the two anonymous reviewers for their constructive comments. Finally we would like to thank our authors for all the time and energy they have invested into their chapters.

Notes

1. R. McLeman, *Climate Change, Migration, and Critical International Security Considerations* (Geneva, 2011), http://publications.iom.int/bookstore/free/MRS42.pdf (accessed August 14, 2013); E. Piguet ed., *Migration and Climate Change* (Cambridge, 2011); G. White, *Climate Change and Migration: Security and Borders in a Warming World* (Oxford, 2011).
2. See, for example, J.A. Goldstone, "The New Population Bomb: The Four Megatrends That Will Change the World," *Foreign Affairs* 89 (2010): 31–43; A. Croissant et al., *Culture and Conflict in Global Perspective: The Cultural Dimensions of Global Conflicts 1945–2007* (Gütersloh, 2010).
3. T. Robertson, *The Malthusian Moment: Global Population Growth and the Birth of American Environmentalism* (New Brunswick, 2012); D. Hoff, *The State and the Stork: The Population Debate and Policy Making in US History* (Chicago, 2012); M. Frey, "Experten, Stiftungen und Politik: Zur Genese des globalen Diskurses über Bevölkerung seit 1945," *Zeithistorische Forschungen/Studies in Contemporary History* 4, no. 1–2 (2007), http://www.zeithistorische-forschungen.de/16126041-Frey-2-2007.
4. S. Patriarca, *Numbers and Nationhood: Writing Statistics in Nineteenth Century Italy* (Cambridge, 1996); L. Schweber, *Disciplining Statistics: Demography and Vital Statistics in France and England, 1830–1885* (Durham, 2006); P. Schor, *Compter et classer. Histoire des recensements américains* (Paris, 2009).
5. B. Lüthi, *Invading Bodies: Medizin und Immigration in den USA 1880–1920* (Frankfurt am Main, 2009); A. McKeown, *Melancholy Order: Asian Migration and the Globalization of Borders* (New York, 2008).
6. K.K. Patel, "Überlegungen zu einer transnationalen Geschichte," *Zeitschrift für Geschichtswissenschaft* 52 (2004): 626–646; P. Clavin, "Defining Transnationalism," *Contemporary European History* 14 (2005): 421–439; AHR Conversation on Transnational History, *American Historical Review* 111, no. 5 (2006); I. Tyrrell, "Reflections on the Transnational Turn in United States History: Theory and Practice," *Journal of Global History* 4 (2009): 453–474; A. Arndt et al., eds., *Vergleichen, verflechten, verwirren? Europäische Geschichtsschreibung zwischen Theorie und Praxis* (Göttingen, 2011).

7. K. Ittmann et al., eds., *The Demographics of Empire: The Colonial Order and the Creation of Knowledge* (Athens, 2010); B. Etemad, "Pour une approche démographique de l'expansion coloniale de l'Europe," *Annales de Démographie Historique* 113 (2007): 13–32; R.R. Gervais and I. Mandé, "How to Count the Subjects of the Empire? The Imperial Demography Stages in French Western Africa Before 1946," *Vingtième Siècle. Revue d'Histoire* 95 (2007): 63–74.
8. M. Connelly, *Fatal Misconception: The Struggle to Control World Population* (Cambridge, Mass., 2008); S. Engh, *Population Control in the 20th Century: Scandinavian Aid to the Indian Family Planning Programme* (D. Phil. thesis, University of Oxford, 2005); J. Sharpless, "Population Science, Private Foundations, and Development Aid: The Transformation of Demographic Knowledge in the United States, 1945–1965," in *International Development and the Social Sciences: Essays on the History and Politics of Knowledge*, F. Cooper and R. Packard eds. (Berkeley, 1997), 176–200.
9. P. Overath, "Bevölkerungsprognosen und das Antlitz Europas im 20. und 21. Jahrhundert," in *Die Vergangene Zukunft Europas: Bevölkerungsforschung und -prognosen im 20. und 21. Jahrhundert*, P. Overath ed. (Köln, 2011), 7–26.
10. Cf. S. Greenhalgh, "The Social Construction of Population Science: An Intellectual, Institutional, and Political History of Twentieth Century Demography," *Comparative Studies in Society and History* 38, no. 1 (1996): 26–66; S. Szreter, "The Idea of Demographic Transition and the Study of Fertility Change: A Critical History," *Population and Development Review* 19, no. 4 (1993): 659–701; D. Hodgson, "Demography as Social Science and Policy Science," in *Population and Development Review* 9, no. 1 (1983): 1–34.
11. For a detailed outline of how we frame the history of demography as a history of knowledge see H. Hartmann and C.R. Unger, "Bevölkerung – Geschichte eines Konzepts," *European History Online* (EGO). Arguing for a new conceptual history of knowledge approach in the social sciences: C. Camic, N. Gross, and M. Lamont, "The Study of Social Knowledge Making," in *Social Knowledge in the Making*, C. Camic, N. Gross, and M. Lamont eds. (Chicago, 2011), 1–40.
12. See, among others, F. Ronsin, *La grève des ventres: Propagande néo-malthusienne et baisse de natalité en France, 19e-20e siècles* (Paris, 1980); P.R. Ehrlich, *The Population Bomb* (New York, 1968).
13. H. Alterman, *Counting People: The Census in History* (San Diego, 1969).
14. J. Yates, *Structuring the Information Age: Life Insurance and Technology in the Twentieth Century* (Baltimore, 2005); G. Eghighian, *Making Security Social: Disability, Insurance, and the Birth of Social Entitlement State in Germany* (Ann Arbor, 2000); P.V. Dutton, *Origins of the French Welfare State: The Struggle for Social Reform in France 1914–1947* (New York, 2002); F. Ewald, *L'Etat providence* (Paris, 1986); T.M. Porter, *Trust in Numbers: The Pursuit of Objectivity in Science and Public Life* (Princeton, 1995), 89–113.
15. A. Desrosières, *La politique des grands nombres: Histoire de la raison statistique* (Paris, 1993), 203–258.
16. See, for example, P. Axelsson, "Abandoning the 'Other': Statistical Enumeration of Swedish Sami, 1700 to 1945 and Beyond," *Berichte zur Wissenschaftsgeschichte* 33, no. 3 (2010): 263–279; R. Necochea López, "Demographic Knowledge and Nation-Building: The Peruvian Census of 1940," *Berichte zur Wissenschaftsgeschichte* 33, no. 3 (2010): 280–296. More generally, see M. Geyer, "Die Gegenwart der Vergangenheit: Die Sozialstaatsdebatten der 1970er Jahre und die Umstrittenen Entwürfe der Moderne," in *Der Sozialstaat in der Krise: Deutschland im internationalen Vergleich*, F. Boll and A. Kruke eds. (Bonn: Dietz, 2008), 47–95.
17. I. Hacking, *The Taming of Chance* (Cambridge, 1990).
18. Porter, *Trust in Numbers*.
19. H. Hartmann and J. Vogel, eds., *Zukunftswissen: Prognosen in Wirtschaft, Politik und Gesellschaft seit 1900* (Frankfurt am Main, 2010); R. Heilbroner, *Visions of the Future: The Distant Past,*

Yesterday, Today, Tomorrow (Oxford, 1995); L. Hölscher, Die Entdeckung der Zukunft (Frankfurt, 1999), 219–221. For a sociological approach to expert knowledge see A. Abbott, The System of Professions: An Essay on the Division of Expert Labor (Chicago, 1988); P. Weingart, Die Stunde der Wahrheit? Zum Verhältnis der Wissenschaft zu Politik, Wirtschaft und Medien in der Wissensgesellschaft (Weilerswist, 2001); S. Fisch and W. Rudloff, eds., Experten und Politik: Wissenschaftliche Politikberatung in geschichtlicher Perspektive (Berlin, 2004).

20. D. van Laak, "Planung: Geschichte und Gegenwart des Vorgriffs auf die Zukunft," Geschichte und Gesellschaft 34 (2008): 305–326; D. van Laak, "Technokratie im Europa des 20. Jahrhunderts – eine einflussreiche 'Hintergrundideologie'," in Theorien und Experimente der Moderne: Europas Gesellschaften im 20. Jahrhundert, Lutz Raphael ed. (Köln, 2012), 101–128; A. Döring-Manteuffel, "Konturen von 'Ordnung' in den Zeitschichten des 19. Jahrhunderts," in Die Ordnung der Moderne: Social Engineering im 20. Jahrhundert, Thomas Etzemüller ed. (Bielefeld, 2009), 41–64.

21. M. Lengwiler, Risikopolitik im Sozialstaat: Die schweizerische Unfallversicherung 1870–1970 (Köln, 2006); J.A. Tooze, Statistics and the German State: The Making of Modern Economic Knowledge, 1900–1945 (Cambridge, 2001).

22. P. Erickson, "Mathematical Models, Rational Choice, and the Search for Cold War Culture," Isis 101, no. 2 (2010): 386–392; J. Cohen-Cole, "Cybernetics and the Machinery of Rationality," British Journal for the History of Science 41 (2008): 109–114.

23. K. Knorr-Cetina, Epistemic Cultures: How the Sciences Make Knowledge (Cambridge, 1999); B. Latour and S. Woolgar, Laboratory Life: The Social Construction of Scientific Facts (Beverly Hills, 1979).

24. G. Gooday, "Placing or Replacing the Laboratory in the History of Science?," Isis 99, no. 4 (2008): 783–795.

25. R.E. Kohler, "Lab History: Reflections," Isis 99, no. 4 (2008): 761–768; S.E. Igo, "Subjects of Persuasion: Survey Research as a Solicitous Science; or, The Public Relations of the Polls," in Social Knowledge in the Making, ed. Camic, Gross, and Lamont, 286–306, 287.

26. S. Beck and J. Niewöhner, "Somatographic Levels of Complexity," BioSocieties 1 (2006): 219–227; I. Hacking, The Social Construction of What? (Cambridge, Mass., 2000).

27. B. Latour, Nous n'avons jamais été modernes: Essai d'anthropologie symétrique (Paris, 1991), 33–46.

28. T. Etzemüller, Die Romantik der Rationalität. Alva & Gunnar Myrdal – Social Engineering in Schweden (Bielefeld, 2010).

29. A. Bashford and P. Levine, The Oxford Handbooks of the History of Eugenics (Oxford, 2012); I. Dowbiggin, The Sterilization Movement and Global Fertility in the Twentieth Century (Oxford, 2008); S. Kühl, Die Internationale der Rassisten: Aufstieg und Niedergang der Internationalen Bewegung für Eugenik und Rassenhygiene im 20. Jahrhundert (Frankfurt am Main, 1997).

30. E. Collingham, Imperial Bodies: The Physical Experience of the Raj, c. 1800–1947 (Cambridge, 2001); C.R. Paligot, La république raciale: Paradigme racial et idéologie républicaine (1860–1930) (Paris, 2006), 221–275; K. Kateb, Européens, "Indigènes" et Juifs en Algérie (1830–1862): Représentations et réalités des populations (Paris, 2001); C. Bruns, "Wilhelminische Bürger und 'germanische Arier' im Spiegel des 'Primitiven' – Ambivalenzen einer Mimikry an die kolonialen 'Anderen'," Comparativ 19 (2009): 15–33. Also see K. Raj, "Colonial Encounters and the Forging of New Knowledge and National Identities: Great Britain and India, 1760–1850," in Nature and Empire: Science and the Colonial Enterprise, Roy MacLeod ed., Osiris 15 (2001): 119–134.

31. Szreter, The Idea of Demographic Transition; G. Weisz and J. Olszynko-Gryn, "The Theory of Epidemiologic Transition: The Origins of a Citation Classic," Journal of the History of Medicine and Allied Sciences 65, no. 3 (2010): 287–326.

32. B. Duden, "Population," in The Development Dictionary: A Guide to Knowledge as Power, Wolfgang Sachs ed. (Johannesburg, 1993), 146–157.

Bibliography

Abbott, A., *The System of Professions: An Essay on the Division of Expert Labor* (Chicago, 1988).
AHR Conversation on Transnational History, *American Historical Review* 111, no. 5 (2006).
Alterman, H., *Counting People: The Census in History* (San Diego, 1969).
Arndt, A., et al., eds., *Vergleichen, verflechten, verwirren? Europäische Geschichtsschreibung zwischen Theorie und Praxis* (Göttingen, 2011).
Axelsson, P., "Abandoning the 'Other': Statistical Enumeration of Swedish Sami, 1700 to 1945 and Beyond," *Berichte zur Wissenschaftsgeschichte* 33, no. 3 (2010): 263–279.
Bashford, A., and Levine, P., *The Oxford Handbooks of the History of Eugenics* (Oxford, 2012).
Beck, S., and Niewöhner, J., "Somatographic Levels of Complexity," *BioSocieties* 1 (2006): 219–227.
Bruns, C., "Wilhelminische Bürger und 'germanische Arier' im Spiegel des 'Primitiven' – Ambivalenzen einer Mimikry an die kolonialen 'Anderen'," *Comparativ* 19 (2009): 15–33.
Camic, C., Gross, N., and Lamont, M., "The Study of Social Knowledge Making," in *Social Knowledge in the Making*, C. Camic, N. Gross, and M. Lamont eds. (Chicago, 2011), 1–40.
Clavin, P., "Defining Transnationalism," *Contemporary European History* 14 (2005): 421–439.
Cohen-Cole, J., "Cybernetics and the Machinery of Rationality," *British Journal for the History of Science* 41 (2008): 109–114.
Collingham, E., *Imperial Bodies: The Physical Experience of the Raj, c. 1800–1947* (Cambridge, 2001).
Connelly, M., *Fatal Misconception: The Struggle to Control World Population* (Cambridge, Mass., 2008).
Croissant, A., et al., *Culture and Conflict in Global Perspective: The Cultural Dimensions of Global Conflicts 1945–2007* (Gütersloh, 2010).
Desrosières, A., *La politique des grands nombres: Histoire de la raison statistique* (Paris, 1993).
Döring-Manteuffel, A., "Konturen von 'Ordnung' in den Zeitschichten des 19. Jahrhunderts," in *Die Ordnung der Moderne: Social Engineering im 20. Jahrhundert*, Thomas Etzemüller ed. (Bielefeld, 2009), 41–64.
Dowbiggin, I., *The Sterilization Movement and Global Fertility in the Twentieth Century* (Oxford, 2008).
Duden, B., "Population," in *The Development Dictionary: A Guide to Knowledge as Power*, Wolfgang Sachs ed. (Johannesburg, 1993), 146–157.
Dutton, P.V., *Origins of the French Welfare State: The Struggle for Social Reform in France 1914–1947* (New York, 2002).
Eghighian, G., *Making Security Social: Disability, Insurance, and the Birth of Social Entitlement State in Germany* (Ann Arbor, 2000).
Ehrlich, P.R., *The Population Bomb* (New York, 1968).
Engh, S., *Population Control in the 20th Century: Scandinavian Aid to the Indian Family Planning Programme* (D. Phil. thesis, University of Oxford, 2005).
Erickson, P., "Mathematical Models, Rational Choice, and the Search for Cold War Culture," *Isis* 101, no. 2 (2010): 386–392.
Etemad, B., "Pour une approche démographique de l'expansion coloniale de l'Europe," *Annales de Démographie Historique* 113 (2007): 13–32.
Etzemüller, T., *Die Romantik der Rationalität. Alva & Gunnar Myrdal – Social Engineering in Schweden* (Bielefeld, 2010).
Ewald, F., *L'Etat providence* (Paris, 1986).
Fisch, S., and Rudloff, W., eds., *Experten und Politik: Wissenschaftliche Politikberatung in geschichtlicher Perspektive* (Berlin, 2004).
Frey, M., "Experten, Stiftungen und Politik: Zur Genese des globalen Diskurses über Bevölkerung seit 1945," *Zeithistorische Forschungen/Studies in Contemporary History* 4, no. 1–2 (2007), http://www.zeithistorische-forschungen.de/16126041-Frey-2-2007.

Gervais, R.R., and Mandé, I., "How to count the subjects of the empire? The imperial demography stages in French Western Africa before 1946," Vingtième Siècle. Revue d'Histoire 95 (2007): 63–74.
Geyer, M., "Die Gegenwart der Vergangenheit: Die Sozialstaatsdebatten der 1970er Jahre und die Umstrittenen Entwürfe der Moderne," in Der Sozialstaat in der Krise: Deutschland im internationalen Vergleich, F. Boll and A. Kruke eds. (Bonn: Dietz, 2008), 47–95.
Goldstone, J.A., "The New Population Bomb: The Four Megatrends That Will Change the World," Foreign Affairs 89 (2010): 31–43.
Gooday, G., "Placing or Replacing the Laboratory in the History of Science?," Isis 99, no. 4 (2008): 783–795.
Greenhalgh, S., "The Social Construction of Population Science: An Intellectual, Institutional, and Political History of Twentieth Century Demography," Comparative Studies in Society and History 38, no. 1 (1996): 26–66.
Hacking, I., The Social Construction of What? (Cambridge, Mass., 2000).
Hacking, I., The Taming of Chance (Cambridge, 1990).
Hartmann, H., and Unger, C.R., "Bevölkerung – Geschichte eines Konzepts," European History Online (EGO).
Hartmann, H., and Vogel, J., eds., Zukunftswissen: Prognosen in Wirtschaft, Politik und Gesellschaft seit 1900 (Frankfurt am Main, 2010).
Heilbroner, R., Visions of the Future: The Distant Past, Yesterday, Today, Tomorrow (Oxford, 1995).
Hodgson, D., "Demography as Social Science and Policy Science," in Population and Development Review 9, no. 1 (1983): 1–34.
Hölscher, L., Die Entdeckung der Zukunft (Frankfurt am Main, 1999).
Hoff, D., The State and the Stork: The Population Debate and Policy Making in US History (Chicago, 2012).
Igo, S.E., "Subjects of Persuasion: Survey Research as a Solicitous Science; or, The Public Relations of the Polls," in Social Knowledge in the Making, ed. Camic, Gross, and Lamont, 286–306.
Ittmann, K., et al., eds., The Demographics of Empire: The Colonial Order and the Creation of Knowledge (Athens, 2010).
Kateb, K., Européens, "Indigènes" et Juifs en Algérie (1830–1862): Représentations et réalités des populations (Paris, 2001).
Knorr-Cetina, K., Epistemic Cultures: How the Sciences Make Knowledge (Cambridge, 1999).
Kohler, R.E., "Lab History: Reflections," Isis 99, no. 4 (2008): 761–768.
Kühl, S., Die Internationale der Rassisten: Aufstieg und Niedergang der Internationalen Bewegung für Eugenik und Rassenhygiene im 20. Jahrhundert (Frankfurt am Main, 1997).
Laak, D. van, "Planung: Geschichte und Gegenwart des Vorgriffs auf die Zukunft," Geschichte und Gesellschaft 34 (2008): 305–326.
Laak, D. van, "Technokratie im Europa des 20. Jahrhunderts – eine einflussreiche 'Hintergrundideologie'," in Theorien und Experimente der Moderne: Europas Gesellschaften im 20. Jahrhundert, Lutz Raphael ed. (Köln, 2012), 101–128.
Latour, B., Nous n'avons jamais été modernes: Essai d'anthropologie symétrique (Paris, 1991).
Latour, B., and Woolgar, S., Laboratory Life: The Social Construction of Scientific Facts (Beverly Hills, 1979).
Lengwiler, M., Risikopolitik im Sozialstaat: Die schweizerische Unfallversicherung 1870–1970 (Köln, 2006).
Lüthi, B., Invading Bodies: Medizin und Immigration in den USA 1880–1920 (Frankfurt am Main, 2009).
McKeown, A., Melancholy Order: Asian Migration and the Globalization of Borders (New York, 2008).
McLeman, R. Climate Change, Migration, and Critical International Security Considerations (Geneva, 2011).

Necochea López, R., "Demographic Knowledge and Nation-Building: The Peruvian Census of 1940," *Berichte zur Wissenschaftsgeschichte* 33, no. 3 (2010): 280–296.
Overath, P., "Bevölkerungsprognosen und das Antlitz Europas im 20. und 21. Jahrhundert," in *Die Vergangene Zukunft Europas: Bevölkerungsforschung und -prognosen im 20. und 21. Jahrhundert,* P. Overath ed. (Köln, 2011), 7–26.
Paligot, C.R., *La république raciale: Paradigme racial et idéologie républicaine (1860–1930)* (Paris, 2006).
Patel, K.K., "Überlegungen zu einer transnationalen Geschichte," *Zeitschrift für Geschichtswissenschaft* 52 (2004): 626–646.
Patriarca, S., *Numbers and Nationhood: Writing Statistics in Nineteenth Century Italy* (Cambridge, 1996).
Piguet, E., ed., *Migration and Climate Change* (Cambridge, 2011).
Porter, T.M., *Trust in Numbers: The Pursuit of Objectivity in Science and Public Life* (Princeton, 1995).
Raj, K., "Colonial Encounters and the Forging of New Knowledge and National Identities: Great Britain and India, 1760–1850," in *Nature and Empire: Science and the Colonial Enterprise*, Roy MacLeod ed., *Osiris* 15 (2001): 119–134.
Robertson, T., *The Malthusian Moment: Global Population Growth and the Birth of American Environmentalism* (New Brunswick, 2012).
Ronsin, F., *La grève des ventres: Propagande néo-malthusienne et baisse de natalité en France, 19e-20e siècles* (Paris, 1980).
Schor, P., *Compter et classer. Histoire des recensements américains* (Paris, 2009).
Schweber, L., *Disciplining Statistics: Demography and Vital Statistics in France and England, 1830–1885* (Durham, 2006).
Sharpless, J., "Population Science, Private Foundations, and Development Aid: The Transformation of Demographic Knowledge in the United States, 1945–1965," in *International Development and the Social Sciences: Essays on the History and Politics of Knowledge*, F. Cooper and R. Packard eds. (Berkeley, 1997), 176–200.
Szreter, S., "The Idea of Demographic Transition and the Study of Fertility Change: A Critical History," *Population and Development Review* 19, no. 4 (1993): 659–701.
Tooze, J.A., *Statistics and the German State: The Making of Modern Economic Knowledge, 1900–1945* (Cambridge, 2001).
Tyrrell, I., "Reflections on the transnational turn in United States history: theory and practice," *Journal of Global History* 4 (2009): 453–474.
Weingart, P., *Die Stunde der Wahrheit? Zum Verhältnis der Wissenschaft zu Politik, Wirtschaft und Medien in der Wissensgesellschaft* (Weilerswist, 2001).
Weisz, G., and Olszynko-Gryn, J., "The Theory of Epidemiologic Transition: The Origins of a Citation Classic," *Journal of the History of Medicine and Allied Sciences* 65, no. 3 (2010): 287–326.
White, G., *Climate Change and Migration: Security and Borders in a Warming World* (Oxford, 2011).
Yates, J., *Structuring the Information Age: Life Insurance and Technology in the Twentieth Century* (Baltimore, 2005).

PART I

PRODUCING DEMOGRAPHIC SUBJECTS
TRANSNATIONAL DISCOURSES

I

THE VIEW FROM BELOW AND THE VIEW FROM ABOVE

What U.S. Census-Taking Reveals about Social Representations in the Era of Jim Crow and Immigration Restriction

Paul Schor

The perceptibility of a trace of Negro or of white blood probably does not correspond uniformly to the physiological proportion of Negro and white blood in the individuals enumerated. Moreover, perceptibility is dependent upon the ability of the enumerator to perceive, and this ability varies from enumerator to enumerator.

There are undoubtedly many individuals in the United States in whom the trace of white blood has become absolutely imperceptible, and many other individuals in whom the trace, although perceptible, is not in fact perceived by the enumerator. Similarly the trace of Negro blood may have become imperceptible, or be unperceived in individual cases.

The census classification is necessarily based upon perceptibility.

—U.S. Bureau of the Census, *Negro Population, 1790–1915*

In several sections of the city, enumerators have been assigned duty on the strength that they possessed less or greater knowledge of some other language than English. In a South Side neighborhood a census-taker rapped at the door and when a corpulent lady of undoubted Teutonic extraction opened it, he bowed suavely and remarked with evident effort:

"Hast du ein Mann? [sic]"

> A surprise was in store for him. This is the reply he got:
>
> "Come right in, sir, and you needn't bother about trying to talk German. My English probably is not as bad as your German. My daughter won the English prize at the Hyde Park school and her mother has been keeping up with her most of the time. I was born in Germany, but that's no reason I'm not a good American now."
>
> And in this house the enumerator checked up 75 cents' worth of data in record time.
>
> —*Chicago Daily Tribune*, 17 April 1910

Introduction

In a social constructivist perspective, scholars have paid attention to the laws and expert debates on designing and refining census categories and their shifts over time, but have seldom focused on the discrepancies and contradictions that existed—and exist—at any given time between the various actors of a demographic and bureaucratic enquiry such as a national census. There are some anecdotes recounted by census officials or newspapers that focus on the type of "errors" or "mistakes" field agents made, but my perspective here is different: I will treat the various understandings of what the questions, answers and attitudes towards the census mean, as indicators of diverging representations of the social order. Although the views of the directors of the census have a clear normative power, I will argue that the divergent perspectives are useful in understanding the practices of census-taking, as well as the historical context in which they took place. I will look both at these variations in a synchronic perspective and at their meaning in a diachronic perspective. I will focus on the federal census of the United States as a case study, because since its beginnings the census has played a central role in constructing the statistical representation of the American population as both a policy tool and an imagined community. From the first census in 1790, it produced a representation of the population ordered by color, and the question of the borders between the races and between natives and immigrants appears to be a defining characteristic of the American census as opposed to other national censuses.[1] This chapter will focus on a few examples taken from the post-emancipation and massive immigration decades in the second half of the nineteenth century to the interwar period, which saw a sharp restriction of immigration to the United States, and a peak and decline of interest in racial and ethnic questions as far as the United States is concerned.[2] I will argue that the emphasis put by the census on demographic categories of difference along the lines of race and ethnicity produced a statistical image of the nation that is specific to the United States. In that sense, studying the interactions and negotiations that resulted in the official numbers of the American population is part of a national history. The traces left in the archives of the process through which the field survey, which in many ways resembles survey research, might also be read as interactions typical of censuses more generally. In other words national demographic enquiries combine policy objectives, scientific expertise, political motivations and interactions with the population that demand a minimal degree of cooperation on the part of the inhabitants.[3]

In that period of American history, census statistics played a key role in fueling policy and in framing a representation of a nation segmented along ethnic and racial lines. After the abolition of slavery the race question dominated demographic statistics as it did during slavery, and the question of immigration appeared to be the second great obsession of American demographers. Because the census consistently asked residents of the United States about their race and about their national origins, it reinforced certain notions and stereotypes about desirable and less desirable inhabitants. This can be observed in all aspects of census activity, from the questions asked, the categories designed and transformed, to the treatment of data, for example by cross-tabulating data about illiteracy with nationality or various social defects with origin, in keeping with the practice of the earlier period when the census was actively involved in the debates over slavery.[4] The differences that the census categories produced were embedded in a hierarchy of fit and unfit inhabitants, through various statistical indicators, which could be read as gradients on a scale of desirability (illiteracy, disease, intermarriage, length of naturalization process).

Undesirable Newcomers, Racial Anxieties, and the Fear of Mixing

In the 1870s, political debates around the demography of the nation were focusing more and more on the consequences of the changes in the origins of migrants. Census officials started to express their concerns about the assimilation of immigrants in published reports as well as in articles published in magazines, journals, or newspapers. Thus, in the report for the 1880 census, conducted under the supervision of Francis A. Walker, one of the earliest advocates of a restrictive immigration policy, one can find the following comment regretting the limits and constraints of the census law:

> In a so-called "German family," it may happen that only the father and mother are reported as born in Germany, or perhaps the parents and the eldest child, while the remaining children are reported as born in the United States, and hence to be called Americans, as distinguished from Germans. If this be not borne in mind, the census statistics will often appear inadequate to the facts of population. Thus, a visitor in Cincinnati is likely to be told that in that section of the city which is called "Over the Rhine" there are 90,000 Germans! In one sense of the word German this may be true. It is not incorrect to speak of a child of German parents, perhaps himself speaking the German language and living in a community almost

exclusively of that nationality, as a German. But this is not the point of view of the census law.[5]

The same report regretted that the census had to abide by a strict legal definition, calling "French" only those born in France and not the French-speaking populations of New England, contrasting the small numbers of those appearing in the census tables to the larger groups known by "popular repute." By providing such warnings about the statistical tables of the report, the census officials clearly wanted to alert the readers to the persistence of ethnic identities, especially in the large industrial cities, despite the fact that the law compelled the Census Office to call "Americans" inhabitants who were American citizens. While the tables were showing an important presence of foreigners concentrated in some areas, the accompanying text implied that the problem was even greater. Under the leadership of Walker, the Census Office wanted the statistics to include the second generation, which it did by creating the population of "foreign parentage" that it added to the population of the same foreign birth. This went with certain sociological and cultural assumptions about the behavior of the second generation, the census assuming that most would firmly belong to a community of descent as is clearly expressed in this passage. In the *Statistical Atlas* published after the previous census, one of the numerous innovations he brought to the census work, Walker developed a visual representation of the presence of foreigners and African Americans in the United States that he summarized in a striking formula: "Speaking broadly, where the blacks are found in the United States, the foreigners are not."[6] By comparing blacks and immigrants, Walker establishes a bold parallel between two categories that have been often treated as separate in the American context: "race" and "ethnicity." For the U.S. census since 1850, and to a certain extent since the first census in 1790, color or race is a physical attribute that all Americans posses and transmit to their offspring, whereas the foreign origin was incorporated into a socially constructed notion of foreign origin, going back to the previous generation ("foreign parentage"), but invisible in the statistics from the third generation on. "Race" or "color" is a biological attribute that is permanent, whereas ethnicity (defined as the socially constructed ascription of identity based on foreign origins) is a social attribute of the first generations.[7] The difference in practice and principle can be seen in two examples: the descendents of Japanese migrants could lose their Japanese national origin when they belonged to the third generation, but not their assignation to the "Japanese race," which explains why the Army used the criterion of race to arrest and deport Japanese Americans after Pearl Harbor, instead of Alien registration status, the majority of Japanese Americans interned being U.S. citizens born on U.S. soil.[8] The second important difference between race and ethnicity in the American context is law: race is a legal category whereas ethnicity is not; although racial minorities and ethnic minorities have both been victims of discrimination, legal segregation and discrimination only applied to colored races.

By the last decades of the nineteenth century, the written and unwritten rules for the fieldwork relied on the assumption that American cities were made of clusters of people sharing the same racial or ethnic traits, and that the canvass should be planned with this in mind. The rules of racial and ethnic assignation by household were more strictly enforced when it came to racial categories than was the case for foreign origins, with a routine practice of assuming that all members of one family belonged to the same race, and that when the color or race of a person was impossible to ascertain by direct observation or inquiry, it should be derived from the color or race of the relatives, boarders or neighbors. Obviously this reflected the reality of residential segregation in American cities and the limited occurrences of interracial marriages and mixed families. But it seems that the negative views held by the framers of the censuses (as well as by most of their contemporaries) on racial mixture led them to reduce the possibility that such families, where and when they existed, be recognized in the census statistics. Although it is difficult to prove this beyond the individual family histories that document cases of interracial families in the late nineteenth and early twentieth century, we can assume that there was more mixing taking place than what the census would show.[9] The editing that took place in the Census Office in Washington, D.C., was organized to eliminate as many cases of multiracial families as possible, as they were presumed to be errors from field agents, unless there was strong evidence that one family was really made of individuals belonging to different official racial categories. As late as 1930, the coding instructions for reporting the manuscript returns onto punch-cards insisted on the coherence of the race of children with that of their parents. It wasn't a matter of absolute identity, but strict respect of the census rules of attribution of the non-white race to the children in the unlikely case of a couple where one parent happened to be white and the other not.[10]

The United States Congress, the political body that wrote the census questions up to 1930, also wanted to make sure the census returns would confirm that thanks to the laws and customs of racial segregation, racial intermixture remained exceptional, or as Texas Representative Choice B. Randell said on the floor of the House, in December 1908:

> If there are no such marriages, then we want the satisfaction of knowing that in this great Republic, under our system of government, and under our present conditions and environments, we are moving on in the progressive march of humanity, keeping the races separate and the blood pure.[11]

The coming census of 1910 brought back to the foreground the question of racial mixture, which had been present in the census in the form of the division of the black population into *black* and *mulatto* from 1850 to 1890. In reaction to an ill-advised and impractical experiment in extreme racial categories imposed on a reluctant Census Office by Congress in 1890, the following census of 1900 dropped the measurement of degree of mixture among the African American population altogether. But the possibility of using the census to measure the racial composition of the black population, assumed to be the result of past mixing rather than current unions, kept surfacing, and Southern representatives and senators kept the issue alive. In their view, distinguishing between black and mulatto would be a way to police the color line, i.e. to make sure no light-skinned African American would be mistaken for a white person. It could also demonstrate the weight of race on social positions, as it was widely believed by self-proclaimed experts on black demography that there were important physiological, social, and moral differences between blacks and mulattoes. The crux of the matter was interracial marriages, which were by then illegal in a majority of the states, starting with all the former Confederate states, which in the wake of the segregation statutes passed since the 1890s produced legal definitions of who was black, in order to identify the individuals who would be segregated and banned from marrying white individuals. White Southerners in Congress also expected the census figures to prove that whatever mixture had taken place was a thing of the past and that their project of segregating the races by custom, law, and violence was successful.

Interestingly, another representative, from a Midwestern state, objected in these 1908 debates that requiring census field agents to enquire about interracial marriages would be most indelicate, as it would mean having male agents of the government asking women alone in their homes at the time of the census whether their absent husband was black, Asian or white. The proposal was rejected, perhaps because it was deemed impractical, perhaps because the Southern representatives who supported it did not rally a majority, and perhaps because the risk of having the government uncover embarrassing or shameful facts would compromise the cooperation of the population that was deemed essential to a "good census." As this critic of the inquiry said:

> The inquisitorial power of the enumerator ought to be limited to the things that are necessary for statistical purposes. Now, these are investigations that have in mind sociological results.

What Representative Crumpacker from Indiana meant by "sociological questions" could be reformulated as a certain vision of society based on political objectives. The history of census-taking shows that political objectives were always present, but when they were not consensual, labeling a proposal partisan was a way to diminish its merits. Crumpacker went on to talk about the humiliation that potentially 90,000 enumerators could exert upon American women during the 1910 census and deeming the inquiry very improper.

This exchange touches upon a central aspect of census-planning, namely the degree to which questions thought relevant or necessary by political authorities or statistical experts are compatible with what respondents judge useful, intelligible, or proper. In this debate in Congress we can hear divergent views of what is proper or decent, a dimension that often came up regarding racial inquiries, especially in the case of women and their conjugal situation; it reveals opposing constructions of the notions of decency that the lawmakers situated among various segments of the population. In other words, the Southern representatives supporting the intermarriage question found interracial relations absolutely improper, but they assumed that those women who were engaged in such relations would not object to this information being obtained by a male stranger in the person of a government agent, as if their standard of decency had already been shattered by the fact of the interracial union.

The interest of this question is that it involves *a priori* a different kind of interaction, verbal and not merely visual, between the census-taker and the enumerated person. In principle the race of individuals was obtained through observation and not as an answer to an explicit question, although there is evidence that as early as the 1900 census oral instructions had been given to ask the question if there was a doubt about the race of one person or of one family:

> For census purposes a negro is a person who is so classed in the community in which he resides. The enumerator is supposed to know this fact or to ascertain it by observation or inquiry.[12]

The definition of who was black or not was left up to local agents, and the survey showed discrepancies from South to North, variations understood as reflective of more or less strict enforcement of the one drop rule that defined anyone with a trace of "black blood" as black.

Asking a direct question seemed to some to be more objectionable than observing one's race or deriving it from indirect information (characteristics of the households, of other residents of the building, of the block). On the other hand, the results of the 1910 census, the very same census for which some members of Congress imagined a question about the racial identity of spouses, alerted census officials about the fluctuations of race as perceived by census agents.

The rather convoluted wording of the census report for 1910 quoted at the opening of this chapter betrays the knowledge census officials had about the socially constructed nature of the racial statistics they were churning out. In the bureaucratic idiom of census reports, the Bureau of the Census was recognizing that black and white field agents did not see race in the same way. This 1918 discussion about "perceptibility," referring to those light-skinned blacks that the census called *mulattoes*, echoes the one in Congress, as it also tried to ascertain racial admixture, yet here the problems were more practical. The census of 1920 confirmed the hypothesis expressed in this report about quantifying race in previous censuses, as the comparison of the same Southern rural enumeration districts in 1910 and 1920 will show that the proportion of *mulattoes* in the statistical *black* population varied from 10 to 20 percent when white or black field agents were used to observe and ascribe the color of the same individuals at two different censuses. The Bureau came to the rational conclusion that given the variability in the race of the agents it hired, important fluctuations in the measurement of the "degree of black blood" would occur and so decided to drop the distinction between black and mulatto altogether after the results of the 1920 census were compared to those of 1910.

Years later, in private conversations or correspondence, census directors expressed concerns about the anticipated difficulties that, according to them, would inevitably occur if black agents were used to survey white people, especially in the South.[13] The hypothesis that the perception of color (as to black or mulatto) also varied in relation to the number of whites in the locality had already been noted by two important sociologists hired by the census to write a first report on the black population in 1904: W.F. Wilcox and the black sociologist and activist W.E.B. Du Bois.[14]

Who Counts Whom?

In view of the fact that the acceptability of black enumerators by white people varied according to local contexts, as in the case of the city of Chicago during the 1930 census, for which correspondence on this topic has survived, it seems that these fears were overblown or manipulated by other agents of the census who coveted the same districts.[15] The use since the beginning of the twentieth century of black field agents, first in districts largely inhabited by African Americans, then more widely, does not seem to have caused as many difficulties as the various alarm cries would suggest.

When one looks at the internal correspondence of the census it appears that the difficulties of the fieldwork were not where they were said to be in countless newspaper articles and public declarations by census officials. Census after census, the various directors expressed worries about immigrants supposedly afraid of government agents and about women who would not disclose their age.

The archives of the census show that these fears reflected prejudice more than the reality of the interactions between the enumerators and these populations deemed difficult to enumerate. The Bureau prepared the various enumeration campaigns of the first decades of the twentieth century with special care towards immigrant communities, printing reassuring information about the coming census in foreign languages, soliciting ethnic newspapers and ethnic leaders to ensure the cooperation of immigrant families. Census officials were convinced that newcomers had a different view of "officialism," and that as immigrants often coming from countries whose regimes were not democracies, they would harbor suspicions toward government agents; the propaganda of the Census Bureau had to overcome this supposed fear if it wanted to secure information from those families as well.

This discourse about the misconceptions immigrants supposedly had about the role of a statistical agency reflected an age-old rhetoric of superiority, opposing the advanced democratic regime enjoyed by residents of the United States to almost any other form of political organization in the world. Census officials assumed that immigrants would perceive agents of the federal government as they would have considered agents of the oppressive state apparatus of their homeland. For that reason official proclamations insisted on the confidentiality of the answers, on the scientific nature of the census, and on the fact that it had nothing to do with conscription, taxes, or immigrant status.[16] What comes across from some newspaper articles, and more clearly from internal reports of the Bureau of the Census, is that these fears were largely unwarranted and that despite evidence to the contrary, they nevertheless continued to be expressed.

Repeatedly in interviews and press conferences, census officials would talk about the specific problem of securing information from immigrant neighborhoods. The first concern was about language, and the census resorted to hiring interpreters to accompany census-takers in districts where it expected to encounter large numbers of non-English speakers, but because of the extra cost, they would rather hire as enumerators people who spoke the language most spoken in the district. Normally agents were supposed to live in the district they enumerated, but when they were unable to communicate with some residents, others were hired, such as Chinese students from the University of Chicago for the Chinatown section of the city in 1920 or Polish-speaking agents originally assigned to another district but moved to the Polish neighborhood of Chicago in 1910 because their colleagues were unable to secure the answers.[17] Before the 1930 census, it was possible to hire residents who were not U.S. citizens, which made it possible for the Bureau to have a work force mirroring the composition of the local population. The main reason for hiring local residents was efficiency, as local people already knew the area, but also trust, as it was assumed that local enumerators would have easier access to residents. In practice, in large cities such as Chicago, census-takers hired locally were strangers to most of the residents, but they could make connections thanks to their local residence and it was easier for them to secure introductions from other residents to reach certain resistant households.

H.R. Campbell, supervisor of the 23rd district of Pennsylvania for the 1930 census took the initiative of asking the enumerators he had hired for the various districts under his supervision to fill a questionnaire that he designed about the fieldwork and the difficulties encountered. What clearly emerges from the many answers he sent to the Bureau in Washington is that the difficulties anticipated with the immigrant population were greatly exaggerated. He included in his questionnaire a question about the foreign population, anticipating that there would be differences. Throughout these reports, one can read the surprise of the enumerators when their prejudices and stereotypes were contradicted by their interactions with the population.

The "foreign element" is described as "superb," "splendid," "cordial." One agent reported:

> I had a cordial reception from all the people. The foreign people were more particular about giving exact data. The reason for this is that the foreign people do not want to hold anything back from the government, once they were convinced that everything was confidential. They were willing and ready to give answers to all questions asked them.[18]

Another stated:

> Probably the best thing that I can report about the 1930 census in the borough of Charleroi is the fine treatment received from all classes—white and black, American and alien. [. . .] I had no trouble with foreigners. One Hungarian woman at first hesitated, but when I spoke a few words in her language she was willing to give me the history a few generations back. I used the same plan with Germans, Italians, and Slavish.[19]

The same kind of positive remarks, tainted with surprise, came from other parts of the country, such as Ohio or California.[20] There was also criticism of the foreigners expressed, but it was rare and not so much directed at their lack of cooperation but rather at their very presence and the fact that they gave information about their jobs at a time when many American citizens were unemployed.[21]

The real surprise several enumerators across the country reported was that the people most uncooperative were the wealthiest families. One enumerator from Pennsylvania reported that she had more trouble with American citizens than with foreigners especially for questions relating to occupation, income and real estate property: "I found a few adverse in answering the questions, this is to be confined to Americans only."[22]

Other agents across the country noted the same difficulties but were more specific about class:

It is found that in the more prosperous districts of the city, people did not regard the taking of the census seriously and caused many back calls for enumerators. This could easily have been avoided had they cooperated.[23]

In the wealthy and stylish districts of the city, the homes were in some instances difficult of access for the enumerators, and the people themselves indifferent or haughty and uncivil.[24]

From the letters and reports sent by field agents, whether enumerators or local supervisors, it appears that the enumeration of foreigners went smoothly and that more problems occurred in the richer sections. But the Bureau did not publicize this impression. To the contrary, a good part of the outside communication of the Census Bureau continued to blame foreigners and the lower classes of society and anticipate that the better-educated residents would lead the cooperation and inspire the behavior of their social inferiors.

How can we account for this discrepancy between information obtained through fieldwork and the representations of the population census officials chose to develop? Does it reflect a sort of internal class conflict among census employees, or at least conflicting cultural constraints on social representations?

For one thing, it is possible that some supervisors, such as Campbell from Pennsylvania, chose to send to the Bureau in Washington a selection of reports that were mostly positive, in order to appear as a very efficient supervisor in the eyes of his superiors.[25] But it seems when reading these reports that the surprise was genuine and that the enumerators were prepared to encounter difficulties with the foreign-born population, whether because that was a commonly shared assumption or because they were specifically trained to anticipate such problems. On the other hand, the problems caused by foreigners such as language difficulties were real. But I would argue that the evidence does not show a lack of desire to cooperate on the part of the immigrants or the non-English speaking, and some of the evidence indicates that they tended to be over-zealous, the exact opposite behavior than what their reputation would lead one to expect.

Nevertheless the stereotypes were resistant and they combined class contempt, xenophobia, and a gendered vision of the population that in the press produced representations of working class women as large and ugly, as opposed to charming and hospitable middle class women. In a full double-page article of the *Seattle Sunday Times* of 11 May 1930, the text tells how in practice foreigners tended to cooperate and one enumerator interviewed in the article says:

It took less explaining to get information from aliens than from many native-born people. They were all eager to be counted and often ran down the street to meet me for fear I'd miss them.

But the large cartoon across the page shows the young visibly middle class female enumerator being chased by an angry matron armed with a knife on one side, and sipping tea with an elegant middle class woman on the opposite side. The caption, in print much larger than the article showing that this really was exceptional read:

> Invited to luncheon by a hospitable housewife and an hour later chased away by a foreign-born woman armed with a gleaming carving knife was the thrilling experience of a woman enumerator, who found census-taking in Seattle a dramatic job with lots of contrast.

The long text, which is more sober than the cartoons, also dispels another enduring myth about the census' difficulty in securing women's ages, with one census-taker saying clearly that "This age business is exaggerated." Nevertheless, the article is made largely of amusing anecdotes, with a sensational tone, and makes fun of Chinese smoking opium, African Americans unable to tell their age and described as living in "Coon Hollow" and panders to all types of prejudices and stereotypes.[26] Letters received by the Bureau, especially on the part of women enumerators, insist that, contrarily to what the newspapers say, they enjoyed the work and did not encounter major difficulties, but this picturesque account is part of the public image of census-taking.[27] From the census archives we can only guess what the fears of the immigrants might have been, through the efforts to alleviate them. It is difficult to determine the extent to which these efforts were successful. Certainly then as now, many of the uncounted inhabitants were residents fearful of government agents. By definition, they are difficult to track. We don't know about those who never replied, but it seems that whereas illegal immigrants might make themselves entirely invisible, established residents opposed to questions about taxation would not: they seemed more prone to make their refusal explicit and almost always complied when told about the penalties.

The Bureau of the Census did not indulge in the same kind of typecasting but seemed nevertheless to be reluctant to draw the lessons of the fieldwork. Both for reasons of class and racial prejudice, the public communication of the census tended to put the burden of the enumeration difficulties on groups that had the lowest social capital or prestige. Beyond prejudice, there were also objective reasons for what might be read as a distortion of the reality as it had been experienced in the field: in order to secure the largest possible cooperation of the population, the Bureau relied on a network of actors that would relay its messages, a network made of members of the local chambers of commerce, business communities, employers, and local leaders. Voicing some of the complaints of field agents about how the rich sometimes refused to see the census-taker and sent their servants instead, or displayed contempt and impatience and more generally were unwilling to answer questions about their economic situation, could have alienated some of these people who were thought to be an important tool in the way the Bureau established a connection with the general population. For these reasons, it is understandable that the Director of the Census would not publicly endorse the report sent to him by the Field Division, which seems to strike a balance between the reports of the individual agents upon which it is based and what is acceptable to say or hear from a federal agency:

> The answers of the enumerators to the question concerning what classes of people were easiest to enumerate, what classes were hardest are not very informative, owing to the fact that what was true in one district was not true in another district.
> As concerned nationalities, the reports indicated that Jewish people generally were the most cooperative; Italians, Swedes, Chinese, American Negroes, and various foreign-born peoples, the most difficult. Servants, working people, and small business families apparently were the most cooperative; the wealthier classes of people cooperated very reluctantly. As concerned marital conditions, married people seemed to be more cooperative than those unmarried. American people were reported as being both the easiest and the hardest to enumerate, as were also educated people. Of all classes of people, however, the Southern-born American Negro seemingly was the most difficult to enumerate.[28]

Conclusion

What are we to make of these various social representations that informed the census work as much as they were informed by the survey? On the one hand we can conclude that population statistics are made of several layers of social interactions and are to a certain extent artifacts. On the other hand, we can look at the complex social process of census-taking as a form of applied sociology, very much confronted with the same methodological problems that characterized survey research, although the historical actors appear to have been in denial and staying away from reflexivity as long as the numbers did not appear incoherent. Bringing back the social experiences of the past into the analysis of the production of national population statistics can contribute to the history of social sciences as much as to the social history of the sciences of government.

The specific history of census-taking exposed here also illustrates the point that as much as statistics have been an international science since the middle of the nineteenth century, the production of national population statistics is time and space specific. In the case of the United States, with the restrictive immigration laws adopted in the 1920s followed by the Great Depression, immigration and ethnic statistics became less important in the following decades, as the country saw the proportion of foreign-born steadily decline until the 1960s. Following the end of the national origins quota system in 1965 and the Civil Rights Act of 1964 and the Voting Rights Act of 1965, ethnicity and race returned to the foreground of the public role of the census. The creation of a new question about "Hispanic ethnicity" in 1970 marked a return of the immigration question. In the 2010 census, the census questionnaire had been drastically reduced to only ten questions, two being about race and Hispanic origin. The Census Bureau justified their inclusion at a time when occupational statistics disappeared from the decennial census by legal reasons, that is racial statistics were mandated to monitor nondiscrimination, and especially in compliance with the Voting Rights Act of 1965 to ensure that the vote of minorities was protected.[29] Very explicitly race and Hispanic/Latino origin are categories used by the census for policy needs, but at the same time they continue to make visible a national imagined community where race is more prominent than other criteria such as social status, language, or country of origin to classify the population into large categories.

In that sense, although the policy objectives were reversed in the 1960s, turning the census from a tool of hierarchy and differentiation that policed the color line to the official monitoring of nondiscrimination through statistics, we can observe a long-term historical continuity, beyond the fluctuations, of a national census that made and continues to make race the first category of difference. The transition was seamless and without much debate, as the policy was changed but the categories remained roughly the same, and it was only in the late twentieth century that calls for a color-blind census were made.[30] This can certainly be attributed to structural factors in American society (racial discrimination has real effects that can be measured by various indicators such as differentials in income, education or residence) but also to a specific history of public statistics, a culture of race-conscious statistics in which the census statisticians and agents played a central part. We can also suppose that the adaptation of census categories to changing local circumstances and understandings of race and ethnicity, when field agents and census officials used a rather pragmatic approach in their dealings with the answers provided by the population, enabled this apparent continuity and the remarkable longevity of U.S. racial categories in the census.

The census did not create segregation and discrimination, but it did reinforce them by naturalizing racial and ethnic categories and extended a scientific caution to prevalent practices. As we can see in hiring and personnel policies, the Census Bureau was not more racist than other agencies of the Federal bureaucracy, and perhaps less so. In fact at times it projected an image of openness and progress: the census enforced segregation in its offices in Washington, D.C., up to World War II, but in 1930 it appointed a black supervisor in the business district of Chicago, over local objections. One of its agents was during the New Deal the highest ranking black civil servant of the government, but he had only African American clerical workers under him and despite his rank had to travel in Jim Crow cars when sent on official duty in the South. Census officials, always eager to secure the benevolence of local communities, were trying to accommodate the conflicting views of various segments of the American population, not to alter them.

Notes

1. M. Nobles, "Racial Categorization and Censuses," in *Census and Identity: The Politics of Race, Ethnicity, and Language in National Censuses*, D.I. Kertzer and D. Arel eds. (Cambridge, 2002), 43–70; A. Morning, "Ethnic Classification in Global Perspective: A Cross-National Survey of the 2000 Census Round," *Population Research and Policy Review* 27, no. 2 (2008): 239–272; J. Cadiot, *Le laboratoire impérial Russie-URSS, 1860–1940* (Paris, 2007); B. Curtis, *The Politics of Population: State Formation, Statistics, and the Census of Canada, 1840–1875* (Toronto, 2001).
2. For a larger perspective on the history of the U.S. Census, see P. Schor, *Compter et classer. Histoire des recensements américains* (Paris, 2009). An English translation is forthcoming with Oxford University Press.
3. R. Necochea López, "Demographic Knowledge and Nation-Building: The Peruvian Census of 1940," *Berichte für Wissenschaftsgeschichte* 33, no. 3 (2010): 280–296.
4. In the 1840s, in the midst of the mounting crisis over slavery, the Census Office maintained, over solid demonstrations offered by outside statisticians, that freedom among blacks was positively correlated to insanity. The refusal of the Census Office to back down after the errors had been exposed show a difficulty to accept outside criticism and admit failure but also the weight of pro-slavery opinions over factual evidence. See P. Schor, "Statistiques de la population et politique des catégories aux États-Unis au XIXe siècle. Théories raciales et questions de population dans le recensement américain," *Annales de démographie historique* 1 (2003): 5–21.
5. U.S. Census Office. *Statistics of the Population of the United States at the Tenth Census (June 1, 1880)* (Washington, D.C., 1883), 460.
6. [F.A. Walker.], *Statistical Atlas of the United States, Based on the Results of the Ninth Census 1870* (Washington, D.C., 1874), 3.
7. This was true as long as the census asked questions about foreign birth (whether of the individuals or of their parents) whereas since from 1970 to 2000, the census asked an open question about "ancestry," which is more about self-perceived ethnicity with no limitation in time. The numbers were similar though. Today the U.S. Census uses an official category of "Ethnicity" to classify "Hispanics" (who can be of any "race"), but this is not the accepted standard of the term ethnicity and not the one we use when referring to the construction of ethnicity by the census in the nineteenth and twentieth centuries.
8. About the role of the Bureau of the Census in the Japanese internment, see Schor, *Compter et classer*, 328–329, and M. Anderson and W. Seltzer, "After Pearl Harbor: The Proper Role of Population Data Systems in Time of War," http://www.uwm.edu/~margo/govstat/integrity.htm.
9. For examples of interracial black and white families where all members were classified as belonging to the same race, usually black except in the case of successful "passing" ("passing" referred to blacks passing for whites, a powerful cultural obsession of that period), see M.A. Sandweiss, *Passing Strange: A Gilded Age Tale of Love and Deception Across the Color Line* (New York, 2009) or S. Taylor Haizlip, *The Sweeter the Juice: A Family Memoir in Black and White* (New York, 1994).
10. U.S. Bureau of the Census, *Fifteenth Census. Coding Instructions for the Population Schedule. Individual Card* (Washington, D.C., 1930), 4.

11. U.S. Congress, *Congressional Record*, 60th Congress, 2d Session, vol. 43, 9 December 1908, 85–86.
12. U.S. Bureau of the Census, *Negroes in the United States*, Bulletin 8 (Washington, D.C., 1904), 14.
13. This concern was voiced by the former census director in charge of the 1910 census, E. Dana Durand, in his unpublished memoirs. "Memoirs of Edward Dana Durand." 1954. Bureau of the Census Library, Suitland, MD. Papers of Census Officials. Folder number 5477, 156.
14. U.S. Bureau of the Census, *Negroes in the United States*. Prepared under the supervision of W.F. Willcox. Section on the negro farmer prepared by W.E.B. Du Bois (Washington, D.C., 1904), 17.
15. See for example the report by Frederick Kuhlman, Chicago, 29th District, Illinois. Volume 7. Supervisors' Reports and Chamber of Commerce Letters, 174–175. File UD75 (NC 3-29-81-4) Field division of the Census Bureau. Methods and Procedures of the 1930 Decennial Census. Record Group 29, National Archives of the United States, U.S. Census Files.
16. As a rule, this was true but there were cases when the U.S. government did use census data against individuals, the most extreme case being the deportation of Japanese Americans after Pearl Harbor. See Schor, *Compter et classer*, 328–329.
17. *Chicago Daily Tribune*, 17 April 1910. *Chicago Daily News*, 2 June 1920.
18. Report of J.H. Miles, Enumerator's district 63–18, Canton, PA. Reports of Enumerators to H.R. Campbell, Supervisor, Twenty-third District, Pennsylvania. Folder 3309. Fifteenth Census. Amusing Incidents. File 149, U.S. Census Files.
19. Report of William Yost, 63–37; Charleroi, ibid.
20. "Counting Uncle Sam's Children (By One of Them)." Submitted by Mrs R.J. Berry, King City, Calif. *Id*. Folder 74:16. See also other testimonies in File UD 75 (NC 3-29-81-4). Field division of the Census Bureau. Methods and Procedures of the 1930 Decennial Census. Fifteenth Census of the United States, 1930, U.S. Census Files.
21. Negative comments about immigrants are rare in the census files, see for one example Marie Kelly, 63–54, Donora, in Reports of Enumerators to H.R. Campbell, who wrote: "It was very difficult to get the information from the colored people, even harder than the foreigners. When I started out some of the foreigners even forgot how many children they had, so after I found out I went back, and I started to inquire in the house next door. That way I was able to help them to remember." Folder 3309. File 149, U.S. Census Files.
22. Cathryne E. Foley, 63–12, Canonsburg, ibid.
23. Alfred M. Mendel, Milwaukee, 10th District, Wisconsin. Volume 7. Supervisors' Reports and Chamber of Commerce Letters. File UD 75 (NC 3-29-81-4), U.S. Census Files.
24. John W. Stitt, Fort Worth, 9th District, Texas, ibid.
25. A hint at this possibility comes from the fact that the reports he sent are a selection, the originals being kept by the Chamber of Commerce of the county of Washington in southwestern Pennsylvania.
26. "Confessions of Seattle Census-Takers," *The Seattle Sunday Times*, May 11, 1930, p. 3.
27. Letters in Folder E 2, Experiences of 1930 Census. Supervisors and enumerators. File 215, Publicity file, Folder 3309. Fifteenth Census. Amusing Incidents. File 149, U.S. Census Files.
28. "Field Division Report 1930," vol. 1, p. 44, File UD 75, U.S. Census Files.
29. See the official explanation at http://2010.census.gov/2010census/text/text-form.php
30. For a recent call for profound changes in the way the census classifies Americans, see K. Prewitt, *What Is Your Race? The Census and Our Flawed Efforts to Classify Americans* (Princeton, 2013).

Bibliography

Anderson, M., and Seltzer, W., "After Pearl Harbor: The Proper Role of Population Data Systems in Time of War," http://www.uwm.edu/~margo/govstat/integrity.htm.

Cadiot, J., *Le laboratoire impérial Russie-URSS, 1860–1940* (Paris, 2007).

Curtis, B., *The Politics of Population: State Formation, Statistics, and the Census of Canada, 1840–1875* (Toronto, 2001).

Haizlip, S.T., *The Sweeter the Juice: A Family Memoir in Black and White* (New York, 1994).

Morning, A., "Ethnic Classification in Global Perspective: A Cross-National Survey of the 2000 Census Round," *Population Research and Policy Review* 27, no. 2 (2008): 239–272.

Necochea López, R., "Demographic Knowledge and Nation-Building: The Peruvian Census of 1940," *Berichte für Wissenschaftsgeschichte* 33, no. 3 (2010): 280–296.

Nobles, M., "Racial Categorization and Censuses," in *Census and Identity: The Politics of Race, Ethnicity, and Language in National Censuses*, D. I. Kertzer and D. Arel eds. (Cambridge, 2002), 43–70.

Prewitt, K., *What Is Your Race? The Census and Our Flawed Efforts to Classify Americans* (Princeton, 2013).

Sandweiss, M.A., *Passing Strange: A Gilded Age Tale of Love and Deception Across the Color Line* (New York, 2009).

Schor, P., *Compter et classer. Histoire des recensements américains* (Paris, 2009).

Schor, P., "Statistiques de la population et politique des catégories aux États-Unis au XIXe siècle. Théories raciales et questions de population dans le recensement américain," *Annales de démographie historique* 1 (2003): 5–21.

2

"Reproduction" as a New Demographic Issue in Interwar Poland

Morgane Labbé

Introduction

Since the second half of the nineteenth century the issue of population has been a central concern of nationalism in Europe. In particular, it shaped Polish territorial claims at the end of the century when the population censuses used to produce official, scientific nationality statistics enumerated the Polish population under the sovereignty of the Prussian, Russian and Austrian states. The results were strongly contested by Polish national activists who made further calculations, although based on the same sources, which were more advantageous for the Polish nation. At the end of World War I, when negotiations about the restoration of the Polish state and its spatial extension took place, the Polish experts had already prepared their own statistics. They contended that Poland was one of the most populated nations in Europe and therefore "a great nation" ready to play a political role.[1] With its eastern border not yet officially drawn, and awaiting the repatriation of its population, the new government in 1921 conducted a population census that was expected to consolidate Poland's national legitimacy and sovereignty statistically. The issue of population was still tied to the problem of nation building as the new Polish state encompassed large minorities.

Apart from serving as a discursive concept for the purpose of securing political demands, population was also a category used in theoretical models. Early on, Polish geographers worked out the relation between population density, state, and land, in a geopolitical model that assumed the geographical individuality of the Polish territory and its extension. They used scientific arguments to respond to German geographers who asserted that the area called "Mittel-Europa" was transitional and therefore could not be the space of a state.[2] During the interwar period the issue of population was developed in two additional theoretical frames:

one addressed the problem of overpopulation in Malthusian terms, and the other dealt with the issue of reproduction in reference to the theoretical proposals of Lotka and Kuczynski. While the importance of the Polish scientific work dealing with the issue of population is striking, in each of these cases the scientists and experts involved based their work on foreign scientific models. These models were not simply adopted but were transformed through their reception. This process of adaptation is remarkable, seeing as the Polish geographers who tried to defend Polish territorial claims against German geopolitical assertions did so by drawing on the German academic tradition, from Ratzel to Penck, in which they had been trained.

These findings are congruent with recent research on expertise, eugenics, and public health in Central and Southeast Europe that emphasizes the role of science in the building and administration of the newly created states, whose elites aspired to modernize the new nations' societies with the help of science.[3] The new studies underscore the process of knowledge transfer and appropriation by national elites who were mainly trained at foreign universities and supported by the scholarly programs of American foundations.[4] A distinctive feature of these science-based policies in Eastern Europe was a continuous interaction between local and international agencies during the interwar period; the same applies to the Polish population experts as well. What makes Poland an interesting case is the variety of experiences that its elites gained before World War I in three state traditions, which later had to be included in the new state structure.

The intense circulation of books, ideas, and knowledge stimulated by training, fellowship programs, or international conferences, and the outstanding ability of numerous Eastern European scholars to move and communicate in a multilingual and multicultural environment outline a transnational space for the formation of sciences that was absent in the Western countries. But while the formation of this scientific knowledge in a transnational perspective can be taken for granted, the question remains whether the sciences remained transnational in their national setting.

Against this background, the research presented in this chapter deals with the emergence of demography in interwar Poland as both a science and a practice developed in a new institute that defined "reproduction" as its primary topic of investigation. Relying on the new theoretical synthesis of Lotka and Kuczynski on the one hand, and on the program of international agencies on the other, the newly founded Polish Institute for the Scientific Investigation of Population approached the field of demography from a variety of aspects, in particular long-held geopolitical and economical views, but also new biological and eugenic approaches. The first part of this chapter is devoted to the presentation of the institutional stakes around the issue of population. In the second part, we focus on the first fertility survey undertaken by the institute and its attempts to produce new indices for reproduction amongst the Polish population. The Polish case, with its various local settings, contributes to our understanding of the dynamics of scientific knowledge produced both locally and internationally, and highlights how the national space was divided by competing projects.

Two Theses on the Polish Population in the Interwar Period: Overpopulation or Birth Decline?

During the interwar period, population was an issue dealt with in various institutional and scientific fields, whose representatives promoted different theoretical and political interests. In Poland the issue of population was discussed in the context of two conflicting theses. Two world conferences taking place in Paris in 1937 can serve as the best examples of those theses, which were equally influential in the second half of the 1930s. The first conference, entitled "Peaceful Change," was organized by the International Institute for Intellectual Cooperation, an agency of the League of Nations. It was the tenth session of a cycle named the "International Studies Conference," whose primary concern was international policy. Experts from a wide range of countries and disciplines were invited to take part, mostly as members of their national committees.[5] The conference enjoyed relative autonomy from the governmental authorities, and it received substantial financial support from two U.S. foundations, the Rockefeller Foundation and the Carnegie Endowment for International Peace, which were entitled to take part in its preparation.

One of the main topics of the Parisian conference was the "Demographic Questions," in fact the issue of overpopulation, which was of great interest to observers of the demographic situation of Eastern Europe. At the end of World War I, it was only with much difficulty that peace was restored in this part of Europe where national states had been created in territories long framed by imperial rules. Yet it was not the problem of minorities that worried the international agencies as a source of conflict, but that of overpopulation. Although the experts were constantly discussing definitions and criteria for overpopulation, they nevertheless understood the concept as rising demographic pressure on a limited amount of land and resources, which would lead to struggles over access and sharing, territorial claims, and spatial expansion. In the view of the international agencies, overpopulation was a potential threat to peace and thus a matter of international policy. Malthusian and Optimum Population theories helped the experts to model the nexus between population, growth, density, land, food, etc.

The members of the conference were population statisticians as well as economists and geographers. The scope of the conference was to formulate international recommendations to find solutions to the issue of overpopulation. For a long time migration was viewed as the peaceful solution to population pressure, but several countries such as the United States or France had recently introduced strong restrictions. The closing of their borders affected countries like Poland, whose representatives in the conference complained.[6] The director of the Polish committee, Stanisław Grabski,[7] from the University of Lwów, began his presentation on "The Problem of population in Poland and the interests of the overpopulated states" with the following words: "Poland is a country in which the population problem is particularly acute, and dominates all social and economic policy."[8] Arguing that the highest rate of population increase in Europe could be observed in Poland, he drew attention to migration as a traditional way of releasing overpopulated lands. Grabski's opinion was shared by the other Polish members as well as those in his academic environment: economists, jurists, political scientists, and geographers working mainly at the universities of Lwów or Kraków, where the doctrine of Malthus had been taught since the nineteenth century. The issue of population was considered from the point of view of international relations. This understanding was reproduced in courses developed by the Institute of Constitutional and International Law, which received substantial financial support from the Rockefeller Foundation.[9]

What is striking about these discussions is that they did not consider birth control as a solution to overpopulation. Alison Bashford has highlighted this point by arguing that the issue of birth control at the international level was too controversial (in particular for religious reasons) to achieve a necessary consensus between states.[10] Yet at the Paris conference, the issue of birth control was addressed in relation to the works of Kuczynski, who was an authority in this respect. His works showed the fertility decline that occurred in numerous populations as a consequence of the economic crisis of the 1930s. But at the conference the mention of birth control remained marginal, and in any case it was not considered as the solution to the present problem of overpopulation. That they did not even discuss it is probably due to the fact that migration had important political advantages: it was a flexible instrument for adjusting population density in the short-term that could be regulated and fixed in international conventions. In this international arena the Polish representatives complained about the new legislation imposed by Western countries that strongly limited migration flows from their country. They asked for redistribution and compensation, stressing for instance the comparative advantage of countries with colonies. This argument was also present in scholarly works. Warren Thompson in his article "Population," published in 1929, had already described the large range of world population densities in terms of inequalities, concluding: "Great Britain, France, Holland, and Australia hold enormous land areas which they cannot settle and at present will allow no one else to settle. Here we have in its crudest form the most urgent population problem of the near future. Peoples who have ceased to expand (Great Britain and Australia) are now holding great areas of unused lands, while the peoples who are just coming into their great period of expansion are confined to rather narrow territories that in some cases are also almost destitute of mineral resources."[11] Birth control would have meant a renunciation of arguments about justice, inequalities and compensation.

In the same year, also in Paris, the International Population Congress took place, gathered for the fourth time by the International Union for the Scientific Investigation of Population Problems (IUSIPS). In some respects this conference showed similarities with the first one: an international and official structure, numerous and famous participants, and support from an American foundation, this time the Milbank Memorial Fund. But it also differed from the earlier conference by focusing on the topic of reproduction. This difference is noteworthy in the case of Poland: the presentations drew attention to the issue of birth decline and developed a model of fertility transition in Poland using the results of an innovative survey conducted on this topic. The results were displayed as statistics on fertility rates. The Polish participants' apprehension regarding the population issue was thus also differential, but it referred to social, not spatial divisions. Not surprisingly, the Polish participants were not the same as those at the Peaceful Change conference, and their professional as well as institutional characteristics were also different: they were statistician-mathematicians, sociologists, physicians, coming mostly from Warsaw, and employed not at the university but in the Polish Statistical Office, where in 1931 a demographic institute was created. These participants also made up the Polish Committee of the IUSIPS.

To evaluate which of the two conferences—the Peaceful Change conference or the International Population Congress—could be regarded as being closer to "real" demography is not a relevant issue because all of the participants claimed to be specialists in population issues, and both sides underlined their arguments with theoretical and methodological references. The proceedings of the international conferences enable us to identify two distinct and contemporary Polish stances on the issue of population, and to relate them to their institutional spaces in Poland. Other features allow us to see their unequal but changing positions: the first group had a long-lasting dominant position based on a prestigious academic network with connections abroad, while the second deployed its skill more in the field of state administration and lacked international resources (most of its members had not taken part in international meetings before), but from this minor position was starting to gain international recognition.

It is therefore necessary to understand how these demographers succeeded in developing an alternative thesis focusing on the decline of fertility in an international context, while the view of an overpopulated Poland seemed unwavering, and gave solid structure to the discourses on population. If this seems to be primarily an issue for the history of scientific and expert institutions, it is as much a concern for the history of science since the condition of this success was previously a refounding of demography as a science closed to the issue of reproduction. This refounding occurred in a transnational space.

The Creation of the Polish Institute of Demography

The Polish Institute for the Scientific Investigation of Population Problems, created in 1931 within the Statistical Office, had only very few members. The most active were Stefan Szulc from the Statistical Office and Marcin Kacprzak from the Institute for Hygiene and Public Health. At its head the institute had an Honorary Director, Ludwik Krzywicki, a famous sociologist, known for his involvement in many social institutes and programs, also one of the first directors of the Statistical Office. The circumstances of the creation of the institute are poorly documented; only the official text published at this occasion described the status of the institute and defined its vocation; then in 1932, a note in the Polish Statistical Review reported on it.[12] This short, enlightening text, in which the creation of the institute is related to the impulse given by IUSIPS to gather representatives from different countries justifies its claim to be the future Polish committee (which only came into being in 1935).[13] Consequently the institute, in choosing its name and status, stayed close to the mission of IUSIPS: "The aim of the institute is the scientific study of problems of population." It added, "The institute does not entertain or seek to define any policy on population matters," and explained its position as the following: "The question of population arouses different opinions . . . The positive or negative meaning of the fast growth of the population raises so many passions that it would compromise the success of the scientific work."[14] Following another statement from IUSIPS, the institute defined its task as researching scientific methods to find the solution to population problems.

IUSIPS had defined its mission as strictly scientific under the direction of R. Pearl, who stressed the necessity of dissociating any non-scientific concerns that would undermine the validity of its activities.[15] It might be surprising to find this statement that was initially linked to the American context, being taken as such by Polish demographers. But as far as the function of the statement was to do boundary work, it also applied to the Polish situation. The text of the Polish institute also aimed to raise scientific and institutional barriers around the field of demography, criticizing other scientific claims on population as attempts at gaining acknowledgment and material resources. Its program attested to this function with its emphasis on the topic of reproduction, on statistical and mathematical formalizations, and on the collection of data.[16] It was a closing of the field, moreover: by requiring skills and competences for a statistical office rather than a university, this was a way of protecting the new science behind the walls of a pre-existing institution. The Polish opinion of the union's scientific claims allows us to observe how it unified demography in a restrictive way through its network of national committees.

In its statement the institute announced that reproduction would be the main research topic, and justified this choice by drawing attention to the decline of birth rates in Poland of around 30 to 40 percent over the last thirty years. It mentioned that it disagreed with the stances of "some economists and among the most outstanding (for instance Prof. Ad. Krzyżanowski), who consider that the disaster of Poland is the excessively fast growth of the population."[17] This refers to the famous professor of the University of Kraków who had introduced the recent Polish translation of Malthus' essay. Yet the institute considered birth statistics as too general, telling us nothing about the process of decline in various social groups. In its research program it therefore decided that its first activity would be to undertake a population survey. To inquire into the issue of reproduction was a new project, yet it was not new at the international level. The Polish demographers might have been aware of the new measurements of reproduction leading to the calculation of fertility indicators that take into account the age of women and the duration of marriage. These new indicators required detailed data, but in Poland data collection was highly imperfect. At the same time the need for new and detailed information, and for improvements in data collection outlined a new field of expertise in statistics for the demographers of the institute, and raised the barriers around the profession for economist-demographers.

To draw attention to the change occurring in the Polish population without any proof other than birth rates, the institute emphasized the long temporality of the demographic phenomenon. It asserted in this way that the population in Poland could be still increasing, but added: "In the general numbers of births, this trend is still hardly visible: we have still a high level of natality. It seems unlikely from the point of view of demography that Poland is in a situation that will lead sooner or later to what happened in the past in the western states."[18] This consideration of the new trend of Polish natality, which would announce a change in the demographic level, could be read as a forerunner of transition theory, which was conceptualized in the postwar era. It evidences what Simon Szreter identified in various precursor works of the 1930s as the birth of the theory and the early formulations of the demographic change.[19] The most comprehensive formulation was given by Warren S. Thompson in his article, "Population," in 1929.[20] Thompson classified countries into three main groups according to the level and decline of birth rates, death rates, and the rates of natural increase that represented the three steps of a transitional model. Poland was in the intermediary group including all the "Slavic People of Central Europe," Italy, and Spain. Thompson characterized them by the declines of both birth and death rates, but also by a temporal but acute growth in population caused by the faster decline of mortality. The Polish demographers did not refer to a particular publication or author, but their reasoning on the Polish population change was not here by chance; they used this frame in all their articles, including the article for the IUSIPS Journal *Population*: "Poland presents an exceptionally favorable terrain for the investigation of differential fertility as she is passing through a transitional period; although she still has high fertility on the whole, she is one of the countries having a declining birth rate."[21] The model also fitted with the traditional and stereotypical representation of the diffusion of "civilization" from the Western countries to "backward" Eastern Europe and what Polish intellectuals like Romer promoted in a new version in favor of Poland, considered as an *avant-poste* of the progress at the eastern border of Europe, while Russia still remained behind.

The Polish demographers had another ambition for their survey: to measure the natality of the different social classes, an essential distinction in their view in order to understand the decline of natality overall. Their purpose was "not only to make the survey in the intellectual profession but also in various categories of workers, craftsmen, merchants . . ."[22] The survey introduced a notion of the Polish population that was socially differentiated but that encompassed all the social classes of the national community. This perception of a social stratification consubstantial with the Polish population broke with the unifying populationist and national view, or the long prevailing elitist view of the Polish *intelligentsia*, whilst at the same time religious and ethnic differences were not considered as significant for the purposes of separating the population into relevant groups for the demographic inquiry.

The insistence of the institute on conducting a differential study on fertility must also be considered in the international context and in particular to the recent experiences of American demographers. In the 1920s, the biometrical and eugenics movements made differential natality a scientific topic and interpreted it as the result of differential biological vitalism. But in the early 1930s in the United States, in the demographic field, sociologists gained a dominant position in reaction to biological notions and undertook studies of differential fertility with the aim of explaining the difference by social causes, in particular the different practices of contraception.[23] With the support of the philanthropic foundations willing to mark out eugenics as now being associated with the rising fascist and Nazi movements, these studies multiplied and became a landmark of social demography.[24] To choose an international standard, *a fortiori* certified by the American foundations, was likely a way to gain acknowledgment and integration into international networks. It provided the Polish demographers of the institute with a frame on which to shape their assumptions on population change. Nevertheless, to carry out such a survey among the Polish population was far from being a simple matter of transferring a model, and was undoubtedly a challenge. In the specific Polish context, the demographers were required to adapt and transform it. Its reception gave rise to an innovative way of surveying, albeit imposed by material and cultural constraints, scarce financial resources, misunderstanding of new questions, and suspicion by the population.

The Survey on the "Number of Children in Families"

In contrast to other countries, the Polish institute had very limited means for undertaking a survey on the whole of, or even part of the population, whilst emphasizing the need for results on the whole-population scale. The little data collected on household composition by the population census was by no means comprehensive—the first census of 1921 was in any case too old to support the thesis of the recent change in fertility—but by 1931, the second census was in progress. The institute succeeded in receiving a grant of 3,000 złotys from the National Fund of Culture, and while the survey was in progress, was provided with substantial help for working out the results in the shorter term.[25] It was undoubtedly proof of official recognition for their project and its constant promotion by the institute. Before receiving this grant, it was only by drawing on other resources, both scientific and social, that the institute succeeded in performing the fertility survey among the Polish population.

The survey of 1932–1933, under the heading "Number of children in families," consisted of a short questionnaire in which women's biographical data was the main information collected to describe their marital and maternal life. The collection of precise information on the dates of events such as marriage, birth, and child death, necessary for measuring fertility, was a new operation with a high risk of failure. The institute was aware of these risks and had to take them into account, and these constraints explain how the institute organized the survey.

Instead of a single survey on a part of the population, the institute undertook a set of micro-surveys in local populations, each of them having been selected as being representative of a social category. As it was not possible at that time to assess statistically how representative the figures resulting from samples were,[26] their validity was secured by the assumption of the homogeneity of the surveyed groups. Assumptions also made in the foreign surveys[27] submitted to the same constraints, but the larger size of the samples made the results more reliable. The institute gave a detailed account of three of these local surveys in the Polish Statistical Review. First they chose the agrarian communities of two villages situated in Volhynia in the eastern part of Poland.[28] They were chosen because of their high social and cultural homogeneity. These protestant communities of small landowners devoted almost exclusively to agriculture displayed a very high natality, and for this reason were considered as quasi-isolated. The information that the institute collected was nevertheless considered of very good quality.

Secondly, the institute undertook a survey in Warsaw, on the population of two housing cooperatives representative of other social groups. The first one covered two buildings of social housing belonging to the Wawelberg philanthropic foundation[29] situated in the worker district of Wola.[30] This low-income housing was mainly allocated to working class and office worker families. A second area of social housing situated in Łżoliborz, another district of Warsaw, provided the institute with a further field for surveying these groups.[31] A survey was also undertaken in the industrial town of Łodz with the help of its Statistical Office, whose director was associated with the demographic institute, and the Institute of Hygiene and Public Health also conducted a survey by Polish physicians. In addition to these surveys targeting specific populations, the institute took advantage of several little individual or corporative initiatives in various places in Poland such as teachers of secondary schools, trade unions, etc.

To realize these surveys the institute relied on a range of mediators—associations, social insurance funds, local authorities, priests, and others. They brought essential resources like the material and financial help of the Wawelberg foundation, the advice and mediation of the pastor in Volhynia, and played a crucial role in defusing the population's widespread suspicion. The risk of receiving refusals and also defective replies, in particular among the working class, threatened the success of the survey. The selection of the targeted population aimed precisely to limit these risks. For instance, the Protestant communities of Volhynia were chosen because of their known high fertility, and the collection of precise information was secured by the cooperation of their pastors and probably also their good levels of literacy. Far from working like a panopticon, a metaphor often used to describe the activities of the statistical office, the institute was rather like a large social enterprise, calling for a plurality of actors and an interactive mode of exchange.

The institute gathered 15,000 full questionnaires, which was of course less than the population of all the areas covered (to give an example from of the second housing cooperative, only 250 full questionnaires were collected for an area encompassing around 700 residences), and it was indeed small-scale in comparison to foreign surveys on this topic. But this didn't prevent the institute from publishing the results in several publications. As early as 1932 they were released in Polish journals, in particular from the Statistical Office. Later they appeared in foreign reviews: in 1934 and 1935 they appeared in English in *Population*, the IUSIPS journal, as well as in the *Review of the International Statistical Institute*. Lastly, in 1937 the results appeared in French in the proceedings of the *International Population Congress*.

From the Survey to Demographic Analysis

In Poland the results were first released in 1932 in the journal of the Statistical Office in a voluminous paper of about a hundred pages with a programmatic title:

"Research on Reproduction in Poland."[32] The paper began with an introduction to demographical terminology with the aim of stressing what were considered the basic concepts of demography, whilst at the same time outlining the purpose of demography that the institute intended to achieve. This also involved emphasizing the distinction between the notions of natality, fertility, and reproduction,[33] the age dimension of the events, the importance of recording data on individuals' past lives, and so on. The article gave the results for each survey and started with the population of Volhynia, which was considered as representative of an agricultural population with a high fertility pattern. This level was stated as one "without limitation," which in the postwar period would be qualified as one of "natural fertility," which captured the attention of the demographers. The quality of the data collected encouraged the institute to work with this experimental case. In spite of the small sample size, the results were displayed in numerous cross-sectional tables. The cultural and social homogeneity of the community enabled the characterization of the whole population by its early age of marriage, which was considered to have a positive effect on fertility at all ages. The distribution of births according to the age of the mother and her age at marriage made it possible to study the marital fertility over generations. The results were stressed as the most innovative by the author, in spite of the very small figures (550 births for 100 women), because they were also a way of proving the conformity of the Polish research to the analysis of fertility promoted at an international level. A fertility table was also used by the author to explain the results given, with the various ways to read the figures in the table: the columns from top to bottom show how fertility is falling with the age of the mother; the rows from right to left show how fertility is higher the more recent the marriage; and the diagonals show how fertility varies by age, both at birth and marriage. This reading grasped the attention of the author, who asserted that the level of fertility depends less on the age of the woman than the duration of the marriage. In spite of the fluctuations explained by the very small sample size, the author highlighted trends calling for further research on larger samples with the application of mathematical statistics.

The surveys in the housing cooperatives gave rise to the same tables and calculations but this time by social groups. The respondents' occupations were divided into five categories—skilled and unskilled workers, officials, office-workers, and merchants. The large number of detailed tables (more than eighty) is striking, while the numbers of births were crossed with several variables in addition to age, social groups, level of education, religion, birth place, etc. The numbers were often small, and empty squares frequent, as though the author were willing to anticipate a further survey on a larger population and had already prepared the tables for the results. Here again the results seem to be released above all to attest to the skill of the demographers in this field.

As the survey was primarily motivated by the recent decline of the Polish natality, the article gave evidence against this by comparing the fertility rates in three periods. It concluded that the decline occurred mainly after the war but that "This fall is unequally distributed between the various groups."[34] A part is also devoted to the fertility of Poland in an international comparative frame, but the statistics used here were not detailed fertility rates, but the usual standardized natality rates, that allow comparison between the level of natality and age structure.

The Polish Survey's Reception Abroad

From 1934, the institute released articles in foreign demographic reviews. The articles were of a smaller size than in the Polish review and displayed only the main results, more cautiously preceded by a long methodological introduction. It was a common feature of statistical papers to state the rules for the production of the figures as a condition of their validity, and here this section was intended to link the Polish survey to the experiences in other countries: "The method adopted was identical with that followed in other countries for similar investigations."[35] For the international and specialized readership the article targeted the tenuous conclusions drawn from the small samples, which also had to be mitigated. It described therefore in detail how the institute had selected the sub-populations, and it stressed the assumption of their homogeneity: "It was ascertained that by examining such homogeneous groups, even when the material secured would be based on a very limited number of observations (one hundred, or even fewer, families), it was possible to formulate conclusions that it would have been impossible to justify even on the basis of a much larger number of observations on any heterogeneous groups."[36] The statement here again attested to a shared demographic knowledge, since all the statisticians in this period were facing the problem of statistical representation of results given by samples, and the censuses could not satisfy the need for precise information.[37]

The first articles were published in *Population*, the IUSIPS review,[38] with the results displayed in four tables. In contrast to the tables of the Polish review, they immediately gave the global results on fertility rates by age group for the same five social categories. The local origins of the sub-populations (villages of Volhynia, housing cooperatives of Warsaw, etc.) had been removed to make way for their social status. The rates showed high differences, which the author explained with social categories: "the fertility rate for unskilled manual workers is lower than for agriculturists, still lower for skilled manual workers, and lowest for office workers."[39] He asserted the differences in a wider pattern reducing the Polish specificity: "these proportional relations are for that matter not peculiar to Poland alone."[40] Comparisons with foreign countries were done through standardized rates of fertility, but here the level of each social category was related to the case of a particular country or place displaying the same level in a time of its demographic evolution, like for instance the Scandinavian countries and German states in 1870–80, or France in 1925–27, or even the city of Leipzig in 1924–26.[41] The diversity of the Polish rates therefore took place in this time and spatial frame of demographic change. In order to report on the decline in fertility in Poland during the preceding years, and lacking reliable figures for the oldest generations, the author again took the standardized rates at different periods between 1900 and 1930. The rates computed only for two categories—skilled workers and officials—and enabled him to measure the change: "The drop in fertility among the manual workers can be confidently termed catastrophic . . . The decreased fertility of the office workers is also considerable."[42] The figures at least gave evidence of the fertility decline, and above all its spread to the middle social groups.

The demographic claim of the institute was not seen as being limited to this empirical proof. For its leader, Szulc, the study of differential fertility by age of the mother and marital duration remained the royal way of demographic analysis and thus shaped the theoretical contribution that he wanted to make. "Perhaps the most interesting results secured when investigating differential fertility are those yielded by simultaneous considerations of the age of the women and the number of years they have been married."[43] Here again the lack of reliable figures for all the social categories led him to calculate age fertility rates by duration of marriage for only two groups, the agricultural population and the physicians. He highlights the same pattern of variation: "The values of the fertility rates are virtually unrelated to the age of the women, but almost solely vary with the duration of married life." He stressed that this variation also occurred in the different social groups: "the most striking fact is that the phenomena observed appear with equal force in the case of the rural population, with its high fertility rate, and in that of the physicians, where the rate is very low."[44] The author went from the description of empirical observations to a relation between fertility and marriage. While always cautious with the limited validity of the figures, he sketched the condition of their possibility:

> An investigation cannot be considered as concluded with this comparison: the material must also be more abundant and the methods of analysis applied must be more precise, whilst above all, the methods of mathematical statistics must be utilized. If, however we succeed in generalizing our observations then the whole method of research on marital fertility will have to be other than what has been used until now.[45]

Three years later, in 1937, the International Population Congress in Paris gave the Polish demographers another occasion to present the results of their research. Although it was the same demographic community, three of their papers discussed the topic of fertility again. The first one, "The Influence of the

Age of Women at Marriage on Fertility and Natality," by S. Szulc,[46] supported his theoretical claims. He shifted from using empirical data to reasoning based on hypotheses about the calendar and the intensity of fertility in a fictive population to demonstrate how variations in fertility depend on both variables. This way of modeling to demonstrate the validity of empirical variations, though lacking mathematical formalism, was in fact shared by the demography community in general, and in particular by those present at this conference, including Lotka.[47] After giving evidence for the influence of marriage age on the level of fertility, Szulc closed his paper with concrete suggestions for how to improve data collection to study this issue in practice. Linking empirical study, modeling, and registering was once again a strong and shared basis for developing demography as a science.[48]

In his second paper, "Differential Fertility in Poland,"[49] Szulc went back to the survey. His concern was very similar to his article in *Population*, yet the difference could be understood as a further adaptation by the Polish demographers to appeal to their international audience. It is notable through the ever cautious consideration regarding the results: "The samples of the survey cannot in any way be viewed as representative of the whole population of Poland, or even as representative of this or that main subset of the population; they could only be considered as examples of the trends in these groups."[50] The term "sample" was followed with the warning of its non-representativeness. The same reserve could explain why the author discussed only the standardized natality rates. But at the same time this global measure gave him the opportunity to assess their differential levels for a wider range of social cases: the five main occupational categories were divided into twenty-eight sub-categories named "samples." For each of them, values of natality rate were computed. These sub-categories consisted of the various small cases of the survey. For instance, the category of workers was now divided into "skilled workers in Łodz," "workers in the rural districts," or "working class families recorded in a relief program and taking advantage from its aids."[51] As he had renounced any claim on the representative value of the results, Szulc could at the same time give up the condition of homogeneity of the main categories and lead his investigation on a less generalized level to take advantage of the diversity of the cases surveyed. Moreover, he extended the calculation of the standardized rates on three periods to evince the fall in natality among workers and officials, the groups he had targeted in his assumption regarding its spread.

Measuring Reproduction in the Footsteps of Kuczynski and Lotka

In the mid-1930s, while the institute gained prominence due to the results of the fertility survey, it received an additional financial grant from a governmental agency to carry out another important project: a publication of demographic data and population indicators for the whole of Poland covering the period from 1895 to 1935. The recent achievement of the second population census and the improvement of the civil register enabled the institute to consider calculating the reproduction index on a nation-wide scale with great confidence. The Polish demographers were already familiar with the algebraic and mathematical formalisms of Kuczynski and Lotka[52] as has been attested in previous articles, but also by the mathematical training and publications of two members of the institute, Samuel Fogelson and Jerzy Neyman.[53] They were consequently eager to have the opportunity to apply them to the Polish population for the first time. The results were edited by the Statistical Office in 1936 in a voluminous publication.[54] Similar to a yearbook of vital statistics, the book consisted of 120 tables presenting statistical time series back to the nineteenth century, and demographic rates for recent dates, including graphics and maps. The book also left spaces for comments, analysis of the demographic change or presentation of technical points like a substantial chapter devoted to the long defective register system in Poland.[55] By means of this book the institute linked the publication of statistical series with the improvement of statistical recording and the calculation of indicators. In this way it tried to make explicit once again how the three stages made up the demographic knowledge that it claimed as its own.

The work performed was innovative in many respects but in particular in the chapter "The Polish Demographical Potential: Views of the Future,"[56] was a crucial issue, as it investigated following Kuczynski's formalisms and Lotka's concept of stable population. Both had given mathematical expression to population change: Lotka, using equations that linked the various demographical indicators measuring change and state of a population (birth rate, death rate, rate of increase, age distribution) came to the synthesis known as the "population stable," which is a kind of "limiting type" brought about by constant conditions of mortality and natality. In this formulation the values of the indicators are supposed to express not the values observed in the concrete population, but those resulting from constant conditions of mortality and fertility; in other words, formulated like functions or laws governing population change through the influence of any external factors. Therefore it called the rate of increase in this stable condition the "true" rate, "true" because it was not affected by age structure. Kuczynski focused on the reproduction of a population measured by means of a new indicator: the net reproduction rate, that is the number of daughters from a generation of women. He considered it the best rate because it measures the replacement that natality and fertility rates miss.

In his chapter Szulc mixed ambitious claims with reserve. By adopting the model of a stable population, he paradoxically broke with the perspectives of the methods of its components because it relied on the assumptions of evolution being taken for granted. He mentioned the ambitious recent demographic prospects made by the German Statistical Office based on this method and dealing not only with the German population but also with other European populations including Poland. Szulc's text was punctuated with warnings against an interpretation in terms of perspective, and stressed that they were only developed to characterize given levels of mortality and fertility:

> The measures obtained by this method cannot be considered as prospects, as they give precise characteristics with important implications for fertility and mortality, and allow us from the present conditions to assess how they result in the stable population, determining the demographic potential. It is possible to follow through which change in the demographic potential would lead to this or that change in the mortality or the fertility chosen.[57]

The first part of the chapter was devoted to international comparisons that typically provided the legitimate frame for introducing the new methods and at the same time assuring the professional skills of the institute. The tables displayed the new indices, the net reproduction rate and the true rate of increase, given for several countries in 1900 and 1930, with a map displaying the reproduction rates in Europe in 1933. The data came mainly from Kuczynski's works, who turned out to be a reference demographer. But the Polish institute had also completed and updated some series that led Szulc to emphasize: "it is interesting to note that the calculations made by the GUS give results similar to those of Kuczynski."[58] The second part of the chapter deals with the Polish population, described by means of the same indicators at different dates (1896/97, 1927/28, 1932, and 1934), in order to cover the whole period of demographic change. The calculations were made by the institute, which provided more detailed information about the methods, and in particular the necessity of assuming life tables and age-fertility rates to be constant to find out the value of the true rate of increase. In the mid-1930s the institute had more reliable statistical series, but not for all years and regions. There were still persisting errors in the recording of mortality, mainly for infantile deaths. Moreover, recent data were still lacking. To overcome these problems, Szulc substituted the missing table with another table considered as more reliable. For instance, for the mortality in 1932 and 1934, he selected the table of 1927/28 of the Posnania-Pomerania province, which related to a lower level of mortality that he considered as representative of the present Polish level. For 1900 he assessed the fertility rates of Poland from the rates available in that date only in Galicia, assuming that the natality in the different part of Poland was homogenous enough. To assess the level of mortality he chose the life table of Germany in 1871/80 whose mortality rates turned out to be close to the Polish one at that time. At each time the choice was based on assuming similarities. In this way Szulc introduced Polish readers to a new mode of reasoning, and the calculations were also displayed for demonstrative scope.

The values of the indicators led him to consider the natural increase (the difference between natality and mortality) in Poland in 1900 as exceptionally high, with a rate of stable population reaching 16.5 percent. Yet his aim was to characterize the increase by comparing this rate with the observed rate. Thirty years later, in 1927/28, this rate was still high, at 15.1 percent, because, he argued, the age distribution still played in favor of a high natality. But if one considers the true rate that reached 8.6 percent in 1927/28, then 3.6 percent in 1934, the decline was clear. For Szulc this "significant fall of the true rates" corresponded with a net reproduction rate reaching 1.11 at that date. It was quite a reasonable level of replacement, far from the fear of the explosive growth of the Polish population, and Szulc could oppose the grim opinion of the economists in Lwów with scientific arguments. He thus proved his mastery of demography by his reading of the various measures of population increase, successfully juggling real, true, and estimated values, whilst introducing a reasoning for modeling the evolutions. In the last part of his chapter, he focused precisely on this reasoning as he displayed new results of calculations made with an inverse hypothesis on mortality, by computing the rate in 1900 and taking the life table of Poland in 1927/28 and of Germany in 1924. He warned not to read the results as real, as "such a rate of mortality cannot exist in the circumstances to which it was applied," and explained that "it is only to show how significant the influence of mortality is on the increase of the population."[59] It is interesting to note that Szulc adopted another abstract mode of reasoning conveying new notions and meanings, that of statistical experience and simulation. This was to characterize the scientific thinking of demography modeling relations between variables, which were already widespread in theoretical works—those of Lotka in particular—but were now extending to the empirical fields. The necessity of articulating this, as Lotka stressed, would found demographic analysis as a distinct field.[60] The Warsaw institute had, if not explicitly demonstrated the issue of the "real" increase of the Polish population, at least figured out how it had to be scientifically stated to be recognized.

Conclusion

In the beginning of the 1930s there was no reason to believe that a small group of statisticians and sociologists would succeed in founding a new way of conceptualizing demography in Poland on the assumption of birth decline. The issue of population, so far mainly treated by economists and geographers with a strong academic establishment extending abroad, was addressed as a problem of overpopulation. The convergence of two events—the creation of the International Union of Population, which structured its activities with the involvement of national committees, and the founding of a Statistical Office in Warsaw assigned to the tedious duties of conducting statistical surveys and registering—connected by the interest of a few individuals, created the opportunity for their ambitious initiative. Founding and delimiting demography around reproduction and its dynamics, they succeeded in carrying out the first fertility survey in Poland with various innovative means of overcoming the huge number of difficulties in producing concrete results. Their knowledge of foreign demographic literature enabled them to shape the local issue of fertility according to the most recent international patterns, even though they gave less of a measure of fertility decline than a statistical demonstration of it. While in many countries, including in Eastern Europe, the issue of eugenics was associated with demography, here it was left aside. It is likely that on one side the links between these demographers and social scientists of the famous institute of social economics (Instytut Gospodarstwa Społecznego), and the consequences of the economic crisis in terms of the limits on the number of children in families led them to scheme differential fertility as a strictly social issue.[61]

The activities of the Polish demographical institute brings a further case study congruent with the recent research on the development of science and expertise in Eastern Europe as an interactive process between the local, national, and international levels. But the case also shows the limits of this transnational interaction, which gave rise neither to a network nor a community bearing an international project on population; it was not even a regional concern. In the world of the 1930s, "international" more often meant the coexistence of competitive nation-states than a real international cooperation around an ideal of science as a placeless and shared universal knowledge.[62] It is also congruent with another feature mentioned in this new historiography: the contribution of the state in the promotion of science and expertise. In contrast to the group of economists in Kraków and Lwów, whose activities were developed in academic or university institutions, the demographic institute in Warsaw was a state institution. The founders' claim that they were separating science and politics was more a statement of experts working for the state than the ideal of IUSIPS to conduct objective science. But the IUSIPS project was also to collect national experiences as many case studies, by contrast with the American foundations, which were willing to develop a real regional cooperation in Eastern Europe, in particular with the creation of a Danubian institute. While Kuczynski was the leading reference for the Polish demographers, there was no attempt to share a closer scientific partnership with him. Engaged in the building of their new states, these Polish experts first used the international space for technical and symbolic resources as for them, these strengthened their national concern and political struggle. This nationalization of demography should not lead us to minimize the importance of this knowledge transfer and its impulsion for scientific innovation as evidenced by the outstanding activism of the Polish institute in surveying, calculating, and formalism, as well as social concerns.

Notes

1. E. Romer, *Ilu nas jest?* (Kraków, 1917); in German translation: *Die Gesamtzahl der Polen* (Vienna, 1917).
2. D. Jędrzejczyk, "Geopolitical Essence of Central Europe in Writings of Eugeniusz Romer," *Miscellanea Geographica* 11 (2004): 199–206.
3. See M. Turda and P. Weindling, eds., *"Blood and Homeland": Eugenics and Racial Nationalism in Central and Southeast Europe: 1900–1940* (Budapest, 2007); C. Promitzer, S. Troumpeta and M. Turda eds., *Health, Hygiene, and Eugenics in Southeastern Europe to 1945* (Budapest, 2010); M. Kohlrausch, K. Steffen and S. Wiederkehr, eds., *Expert Cultures in Central Eastern Europe: The Internationalization of Knowledge and the Transformation of Nation States since World War I* (Osnabrück, 2010).
4. M. Bucur, "Remapping the Historiography of Modernization and State-Building in Southeastern Europe through Health, Hygiene and Eugenics," in *Health, Hygiene, and Eugenics in Southeastern Europe to 1945*, C. Promitzer, S. Troumpeta and M. Turda eds. (Budapest, 2010), 429–445.
5. Conférence Permanente des Hautes Etudes Internationales, *Le problème des changements pacifiques dans les relations internationales* (1938). On the importance of the economical and spatial approaches in the international policy of population issues, and in particular in this conference, see A. Bashford, "Population, Geopolitics, and International Organizations in the Mid Twentieth Century," *Journal of World History* 19, no. 3 (2008): 327–348.
6. See in particular, "Séances de la commission pour l'étude des questions démographiques," in *Le problème des changements pacifiques dans les relations internationales*, Conférence Permanente des Hautes Etudes Internationales ed. (1938), 368–424.
7. He was also a former minister and one of the main experts in the negotiations for the Treaty of Riga.
8. S. Grabski, "Le problème de la population en Pologne et les intérêts des États surpeuplés," in *Commission polonaise de coordination des Hautes Etudes Internationales, Conférence permanente des Hautes Etudes Internationales* (Lwów, 1937), 1–2.
9. The foundations were involved in this conference as far as overpopulation was considered to be an issue of international policies, but they did not cooperate with the state regarding how to deal with the issue. They did however follow and discuss the organization in the sense that the main organizers all had close relationships with the foundations, and often engaged in other programs with the foundations.
10. Bashford, "Population," 330.
11. W.S. Thompson, "Population," *American Journal of Sociology* 34, no. 6 (1929): 975.
12. S. Szulc, "Polski Instytut Badania Zagadnień Ludnościowych," *Kwartalnik Statystyczny* IX (1932), 61–63, 221–222.
13. By comparison with other Central European countries: Czechoslovakia in 1934, Hungary in 1937.
14. S. Szulc, "Polski Instytut," 61.
15. E. Ramsden, "Carving up Population Science: Eugenics, Demography and the Controversy over the 'Biological Law' of Population Growth," *Social Studies of Science* 32, no. 5–6 (2002): 857–899.
16. On the closing-up of demography, see S. Greenlagh, "The Social Construction of Population Science: An Intellectual, Institutional, and Political History of Twentieth-Century Demography," *Comparative Studies in Society and History* 38, no. 1 (1996): 26–66.
17. S. Szulc, "Polski Instytut," 62.
18. Ibid.
19. S. Szreter, "The Idea of Demographic Transition and the Study of Fertility Change: A Critical Intellectual History," *Population and Development Review* 19, no. 4 (1993): 659–701.

20. W.S. Thompson, "Population," *American Journal of Sociology* 34, no. 6 (1929): 959–975.
21. S. Szulc, "The Polish Institute for the Scientific Investigation of Population Problems. Research on Differential Fertility in Poland," *Population* 1, no. 3 (1934): 26.
22. S. Szulc, "Polski Instytut," 62.
23. For instance, see E. Sydenstricker and F. Notestein, "Differential Fertility According to Social Class," *Journal of the American Statistical Association* 25, no. 169 (1930): 9–32.
24. E. Ramsden, *Carving up Population Science*, 878. Also P. Weindling, "Modernising Eugenics: The Role of Foundations in International Population Studies," in *American Foundations in Europe. Grant-Giving Policies, Cultural Diplomacy and Trans-Atlantic Relations, 1920–1980*, G. Gemelli and R. MacLeod eds. (Brussels, 2003), 167–180.
25. "Instytucje i Zjazdy naukowe. Polski Instytut Badania Zagadnień Ludnościowych," *Kwartalnik Statystyczny* (1933): 221.
26. The theory of stratified sampling would be developed a few years later, in particular by a Polish statistician, Jerzy Neyman, who was also a member of the Polish demographic institute before emigrating to the United States in the 1930s. On the history of sampling theory: A. Desrosières, *The Politics of Large Numbers: A History of Statistical Reasoning* (Cambridge, 1998).
27. Sydenstricker and Notestein, "Differential Fertility," 10–18.
28. "Badania nad rozrodczościa w Polsce," *Kwartalnik Statystyczny* (1933), part "Evangelickie kolonje rolnicze na Wołyniu. Kolonje Janowka i Jamki powiatu łuckiego na Wołyniu," 53.
29. Built under the name "Tanie Mieszkania im. Hipolit i Ludwiki małż. Wawelbergow" in 1898 by the Polish banker H. Wawelberg, a great philanthropist who funded social and educative programs for poor families, with the aim of fostering the coexistence of Jewish and Christian families.
30. "W. Domy Fundacji Tanich Mieszkan im. Hipolita i Ludwiki małz. Wawelbergow," see Badania nad rozrodczościa w Polsce, *Kwartalnik Statystyczny* (1933), 71.
31. Warszawa Spółdzielna Mieszkaniowa na Zoliborzu, ibid., 98.
32. "Badania nad rozrodczościa w Polsce. Z polskiego Instytutu Badania Zagadnień Ludnościowych," *Kwartalnik Statystyczny* (1933): 53–141.
33. The Polish term *Rozrodczości̇a* was often used, maybe because the alternative term *Płodność* meant both "fertility" and "fecundity."
34. Badania nad rozrodczościa w Polsce. Z polskiego Instytutu Badania Zagadnień Ludnościowych, *Kwartalnik Statystyczny* (1933), 111.
35. Ibid., 16.
36. S. Szulc, "The Polish Institute for the Scientific Investigation of Population Problems: Research on Differential Fertility in Poland" *Population* 1, no. 3 (1934): 18.
37. A. Desrosières, "Three Studies on the History of Sampling Surveys: Norway, Russia-USSR, United States," *Science in Context* 15, no. 3 (2002): 377–383.
38. Szulc, "The Polish Institute," 14–35.
39. Ibid., 28.
40. Ibid.
41. Ibid., 30.
42. Ibid., 31.
43. Ibid., 32.
44. Ibid., 33–34.
45. Ibid., 33.
46. S. Szulc, "L'influence de l'âge des femmes au moment de la conclusion du mariage sur la fertilité et la natalité," in *Démographie statistique: études spéciales: nuptialité, natalité, mortalité*, Congrès international de la population ed. (Paris, 1938), 133–147.

47. J. Veron, "Alfred J. Lotka and the Mathematics of Population," *Electronic Journal for History of Probability and Statistics* 4, no. 1 (2008).
48. U. Ferdinand, "Die Kritik Robert René Kuczynskis an der englischen statistischen Registrierungspraxis," in *Zukunftswissen. Prognosen in Wirtschaft, Politik und Gesellschaft seit 1900*, H. Hartmann and J. Vogel eds. (Frankfurt, 2010), 153–174.
49. S. Szulc, "Fertilité différentielle en Pologne d'après l'enquête de l'Institut polonais d'étude scientifique des problèmes de population," in *Démographie statistique: études spéciales: nuptialité, natalité, mortalité*, Congrès international de la population (Paris, 1938), 148–161.
50. Ibid., 151.
51. Ibid., 153–158.
52. The term "formalism" means here the mathematical expression given by Lotka and Kuczynski to the population growth.
53. In particular in the article of S. Fogelson, "Matematyczna teorja ludności," *Kwartalnik Statystyczny* (1932).
54. *Zagadnienia demograficzne Polski*, Statystyka Polski, Seria C, zeszyt 41 (Warszawa, 1936).
55. S. Szulc, "Dokładnośc rejestracji urodzeń i zgonow," in *Zagadnienia demograficzne Polski*, Statystyka Polski, Seria C, zeszyt 41 (Warszawa, 1936), 133–158.
56. S. Szulc, "Potencjał demograficzny Polski. Widoki na przyszłość," in *Zagadnienia demograficzne Polski*, Statystyka Polski, Seria C, zeszyt 41 (Warszawa, 1936), 112–126.
57. Ibid., 113.
58. Ibid., 119.
59. Ibid., 125.
60. Veron, "Alfred J. Lotka," 6.
61. In this respect it is worth mentioning that in the population conference, the papers by demographers from Hungary and Czechoslovakia dealt with the impact of the economic crisis on the decline of the natality.
62. On the limits on the international cooperation in the 1930s, see the Introduction in *Shifting Boundaries of Public Health: Europe in the Twentieth Century*, S. Gross Solomon, L. Murard and P. Zylberman eds. (Rochester, 2008), 3–20.

Bibliography

"Badania nad rozrodczościa w Polsce. Z polskiego Instytutu Badania Zagadnień Ludnościowych," *Kwartalnik Statystyczny* (1933): 53–141.
Bashford, A., "Population, Geopolitics, and International Organizations in the Mid Twentieth Century," *Journal of World History* 19, no. 3 (2008): 327–348.
Bucur, M., "Remapping the Historiography of Modernization and State-Building in Southeastern Europe through Health, Hygiene and Eugenics," in *Health, Hygiene, and Eugenics in Southeastern Europe to 1945*, C. Promitzer, S. Troumpeta and M. Turda eds. (Budapest, 2010), 429–445.
Conférence Permanente des Hautes Etudes Internationales, *Le problème des changements pacifiques dans les relations internationales* (1938).
Desrosières, A., *The Politics of Large Numbers: A History of Statistical Reasoning* (Cambridge, 1998).
Desrosières, A., "Three Studies on the History of Sampling Surveys: Norway, Russia-USSR, United States," *Science in Context* 15, no. 3 (2002): 377–383.
Ferdinand, U., "Die Kritik Robert René Kuczynskis an der englischen statistischen Registrierungspraxis," in *Zukunftswissen. Prognosen in Wirtschaft, Politik und Gesellschaft seit 1900*, H. Hartmann and J. Vogel eds. (Frankfurt, 2010), 153–174.
Fogelson, S., "Matematyczna teorja ludności," *Kwartalnik Statystyczny* (1932).

Grabski, S., "Le problème de la population en Pologne et les intérêts des États surpeuplés," in *Commission polonaise de coordination des Hautes Etudes Internationales, Conférence permanente des Hautes Etudes Internationales* (Lwów, 1937), 1–2.

Greenlagh, S., "The Social Construction of Population Science: An Intellectual, Institutional, and Political History of Twentieth-Century Demography," *Comparative Studies in Society and History* 38, no. 1 (1996): 26–66.

Gross Solomon, S., Murard, L., and Zylberman, P., eds., *Shifting Boundaries of Public Health: Europe in the Twentieth Century* (Rochester, 2008).

"Instytucje i Zjazdy naukowe. Polski Instytut Badania Zagadnień Ludnościowych," *Kwartalnik Statystyczny* (1933): 221.

Jędrzejczyk, D., "Geopolitical Essence of Central Europe in Writings of Eugeniusz Romer," *Miscellanea Geographica* 11 (2004): 199–206.

Kohlrausch, M., Steffen, K., and Wiederkehr, S., eds., *Expert Cultures in Central Eastern Europe: The Internationalization of Knowledge and the Transformation of Nation States Since World War I* (Osnabrück, 2010).

Promitzer, C., Troumpeta, S., and Turda, M., eds., *Health, Hygiene, and Eugenics in Southeastern Europe to 1945* (Budapest, 2010).

Ramsden, E., "Carving up Population Science: Eugenics, Demography and the Controversy over the 'Biological Law' of Population Growth," *Social Studies of Science* 32, no. 5–6 (2002): 857–899.

Romer, E., *Ilu nas jest?* (Kraków, 1917).

"Séances de la commission pour l'étude des questions démographiques," in *Le problème des changements pacifiques dans les relations internationales*, Conférence Permanente des Hautes Etudes Internationales ed. (1938), 368–424.

Sydenstricker, E., and Notestein, F., "Differential Fertility According to Social Class," *Journal of the American Statistical Association* 25, no. 169 (1930): 9–32.

Szreter, S., "The Idea of Demographic Transition and the Study of Fertility Change: A Critical Intellectual History," *Population and Development Review* 19, no. 4 (1993): 659–701.

Szulc, S., "Dokładność rejestracji urodzeń i zgonow," in *Zagadnienia demograficzne Polski*, Statystyka Polski, Seria C, zeszyt 41 (Warsaw, 1936), 133–158.

Szulc, S., "Fertilité différentielle en Pologne d'après l'enquête de l'Institut polonais d'étude scientifique des problèmes de population," in *Démographie statistique: études spéciales: nuptialité, natalité, mortalité*, Congrès international de la population (Paris, 1938), 148–161.

Szulc, S., "L'influence de l'âge des femmes au moment de la conclusion du mariage sur la fertilité et la natalité," in *Démographie statistique: études spéciales: nuptialité, natalité, mortalité*, Congrès international de la population ed. (Paris, 1938), 133–147.

Szulc, S., "The Polish Institute for the Scientific Investigation of Population Problems. Research on Differential Fertility in Poland," *Population* 1, no. 3 (1934): 26.

Szulc, S., "Polski Instytut Badania Zagadnień Ludnościowych," *Kwartalnik Statystyczny* IX (1932).

Szulc, S., "Potencjał demograficzny Polski. Widoki na przyszłość," in *Zagadnienia demograficzne Polski*, Statystyka Polski, Seria C, zeszyt 41 (Warsaw, 1936), 112–126.

Thompson, W.S., "Population," *American Journal of Sociology* 34, no. 6 (1929): 959–975.

Turda, M., and Weindling, P., eds., *"Blood and Homeland": Eugenics and Racial Nationalism in Central and Southeast Europe: 1900–1940* (Budapest, 2007).

Veron, J., "Alfred J. Lotka and the Mathematics of Population," *Electronic Journal for History of Probability and Statistics* 4, no. 1 (2008).

Weindling, P., "Modernising Eugenics: The Role of Foundations in International Population Studies," in *American Foundations in Europe. Grant-Giving Policies, Cultural Diplomacy and Trans-Atlantic Relations, 1920–1980*, G. Gemelli and R. MacLeod eds. (Brussels, 2003), 167–180.

Zagadnienia demograficzne Polski, Statystyka Polski, Seria C, zeszyt 41 (Warsaw, 1936).

3

FAMILY PLANNING — A RATIONAL CHOICE?

The Influence of Systems Approaches, Behavioralism, and Rational Choice Thinking on Mid-Twentieth-Century Family Planning Programs

Corinna R. Unger

Introduction

"Overpopulation is a global problem. Communications, transport, and trade have made the world a unit, a single epidemiological universe. Overpopulation in one region or continent is the concern of all others . . . ."[1] What sounds much like a statement from the 1970s was made, perhaps surprisingly, in 1953. Its author was John E. Gordon, a public health specialist at Harvard University who, in the early 1950s, was working on a research project on the possibilities of "family limitation" in India, funded by the Rockefeller Foundation. Gordon and his colleagues were influential in defining the existence of "overpopulation" on the subcontinent and investigating ways and means to change the reproductive behavior of individuals and groups. Their findings appeared in 1971 in *The Khanna Study*.[2] One year later, in 1972, the report on *The Limits to Growth* appeared, causing a heated public debate in many parts of the world over the question of the availability of natural resources, population growth, and consumption.[3] *The Limits to Growth* is usually cited to illustrate the growing environmental awareness of many Western societies since the 1970s.[4] Yet the World Model described in *The Limits to Growth* was not necessarily an expression of "alternative" views on the environment and the fragility of the globe. The ideas proposed in the book were deeply anchored in Malthusian thinking about the relation between natural resources and population growth. The model advocated by the authors of the study was first and foremost a cybernetic model (based on the work of MIT scientist and computer engineer Jay W. Forrester) with a very strong technocratic undertone.[5]

What united Gordon and the authors of The Limits to Growth was their "ecological," or systems view of the world: an understanding of the globe as a closed system, whose elements were connected to, depended on, and reacted with each other.[6] In this view, "overpopulation" in one region had effects on the entire globe. Hence, in order to protect the globe from the dangers associated with demographic disequilibrium, population growth had to be controlled, "primarily through technological innovation, behavioral modification, and organizational response."[7] Most importantly, reproductive patterns had to be amended in those regions of the world that were experiencing high population growth rates. According to demographic transition theory, which dominated demographic discourse in the United States in the 1950s and 1960s, this would happen as an effect of a society's transformation from "tradition" to "modernity." Once individuals experienced the effects of urbanization and industrialization, they would automatically have fewer children, according to the theory.[8] Yet waiting for modern lifestyles to become prevalent seemed problematic in view of rapid population growth. Hence, one had to find ways of changing individual and collective reproductive behavior prior to and during the transition. Consequently, social scientists and family planning advocates had to concern themselves with how to best reach the largest possible number of individuals and persuade them to embrace family planning practices. Family planning approaches of the 1960s were based on the assumption that information, knowledge, and incentives were decisive in this regard, and that individuals would change their reproductive behavior if they had access to and were offered help with using the necessary technologies.

In this chapter, I study the reflections of rational choice theory, systems thinking, and behavioralism in mid-twentieth-century family planning policies and programs. By doing so, I do not intend to argue that all demographers and all those who were considered or considered themselves population experts embraced a systems approach. Neither do I believe that systems analysis was responsible for the prominence and sense of urgency that characterized the discourse about "overpopulation" in the postwar decades, or that all family planning programs were behavioralist in nature. However, I do argue that behavioralism, or at least popularized notions of behavioralist approaches, influenced the American view of family planning programs at home and abroad in the 1950s and 1960s, and that those programs were conceived in the larger context of systems analysis and rational choice theory. If we are to understand the history of mid-twentieth century demography and population policies, we need to be aware of those approaches, which have not received much attention in recent accounts of the history of population control and family planning.

While the concept of biopolitics may be useful to investigate contemporary attempts to control population growth, it does not say much about the specific techniques used to achieve social and physical control over individuals and populations. Also, studying the influence of social scientific approaches on demographic models and population policies is important to understand why family planning could gain such a prominent political status internationally in the second half of the twentieth century. Behavioralism and systems analysis provided family planning approaches with a scientific basis, which in turn produced political legitimacy and simultaneously affected political expectations. The strong interdependence between demography and politics cannot be understood by looking at the field of demography and family planning in isolation.[9] Demography was notably interdisciplinary in nature; thus, we need to pay attention to the academic and epistemic factors as well as to the structural and political influences that helped to shape the discipline and the translation of its theories into population policies and programs. This interplay can be studied on two levels: on the macro level in the form of discourses about global and regional demographic developments, and on the micro level concerning the required changes in individual fertility behavior.

This chapter begins with a short section on the macro level before offering an overview of the history of systems approaches, rational choice theory and behavioralism in the United States. The article then turns to the micro level, specifically to the influence of rational choice concepts, behavioralist thinking, and mass communication approaches on family planning techniques.

Carrying Capacity: The Globe as a Closed Demographic System

The postwar perception of global population growth as a growing security threat and the evolution of an "overpopulation" discourse have been treated extensively in recent years.[10] To summarize the argument of many contemporaries in the 1950s and 1960s, it may be sufficient to quote Dudley Kirk, a sociologist who had worked in the Office of Population Research at Princeton University and became Director of Demographic Research of the Population Council in New York in 1954. In a 1953 book review, Kirk stated that "many countries would be economically better off with fewer people" and that "a definitive and humane remedy for over-population must include lower human fertility."[11] When speaking of global demographic change, it is important to remember that what concerned many contemporaries was the rapid rise of population growth rates in the so-called developing world, particularly in Africa and Asia. Decolonization turned attention to what was perceived as a problem: the fact that in those areas "the dynamics of fertility and mortality patterns typically remained traditional and living standards were generally low. In these areas, an acceleration of population growth, such as generated by slowly declining mortality rates, could more readily activate Malthusian pressures, particularly when population-resource ratios were already high."[12] If development in terms of economic growth and sociopolitical improvements (education, infrastructure, public health, etc.) was to be achieved, the "population problem" had to be addressed effectively. Jawaharlal Nehru's requesting aid from the industrialized nations to help reduce India's population growth rate is the most famous example for the understanding of population growth as a hindrance to development due to scarce natural resources.[13]

The emphasis on natural resource scarcities, which had been dominating demographic discourses in the prewar era,[14] in the mid-1950s gave way to a new perspective on the relation between population size and economic performance.[15] At that time, it became clear that postwar population growth rates and economic growth rates were much higher than those witnessed in the prewar years. Under these circumstances, the role of absolute population size lost importance, while the rate of population growth, the age composition of the population, and levels of food production gained meaning. "Reflecting the then dominant view in development economics that savings and capital accumulation were the engines of economic growth, changes in demographic growth and in age distribution were seen as affecting economic performance through their effects on savings, on capital accumulation, and on the level of per capita investment needed to equip a growing labor force and to support the population in the ages of economic dependency."[16] Ansley Coale and Edgar Hoover, in their 1958 study on the role of demographic growth on economic development, came to the conclusion that "a demographic slowdown brings economic benefits, regardless of the socioeconomic characteristics and resources endowments of individual countries."[17]

Interestingly, however, the role of natural resources and the importance of space experienced a comeback in demographic debates in the late 1960s and early 1970s.[18] One of the reasons for this remarkable Malthusian comeback was the fact that the scientific optimism of the 1950s and early 1960s, specifically the belief that modern science could solve "old-fashioned" problems like resource scarcity, lost its momentum in the context of a general disillusionment with ideas of "progress" and "development." It is generally assumed that this disillusionment, which was closely tied to the rise of counterculture and "alternative" lifestyles in the second half of the 1960s, went hand in hand with a rejection of technocracy. Yet this nexus does not seem to apply to demographic debates of the time. In demography, technocratic approaches reached a climax in the late 1960s and early 1970s, precisely at the time when public criticism of the "one-dimensional man" (Marcuse) and expert-driven, top-down development concepts reached its height.[19] This was due, in part, to the fact that demography was not as established as other disciplines, and that it was "partially segregated from mainstream social science by institutional set-up."[20] Furthermore, demographers, although momentarily overshadowed by a new approach to development economics in the late 1950s and early 1960s, had never entirely forgotten the role of resources and space—which, I would argue, was partly due to demography's systems analysis background.

Understanding, Predicting, and Changing Behavior

Systems analysis experienced its breakthrough during and after World War II.[21] In many respects, the war was fought in laboratories and engineering offices. Operations research contributed essentially to the "modern" character of the war.[22] The scientists involved came from a range of disciplinary backgrounds; their interdisciplinary work helped to make the American research and development system uniquely successful (the Manhattan Project being the most famous example). For many of them, weapons and operations research offered an opportunity to develop and test new methods and technologies, and to realize projects that had not received funding before the war. Artificial intelligence and computers gained new significance because they could be employed to improve the effectiveness of bombing and intercept rockets. Once the war was over, interdisciplinary research in the fields of computing, mathematics, engineering, biology, neurology, and philosophy continued, culminating in what became known as "cybernetics."[23] The most famous example of this interdisciplinary approach were the Macy Conferences. They began in 1946 and 1948 as meetings on "Circular, Causal, and Feedback Mechanisms in Biological and Social Systems;" from 1949 on, the name was changed to "Cybernetics." Between 1946 and 1953, the Josiah Macy, Jr. Foundation funded ten meetings, giving the conferences their famous name. Among the participants were Heinz von Foerster, Margaret Mead, John von Neumann, and Norbert Wiener.[24]

While there was never a single, unified "cybernetic school," it seems safe to state that, in essence, cybernetics was concerned with regulating information systems. The goal was to identify universal laws of action and behavior in those systems and to formulate theories and develop models that applied to humans and machines alike, based on the assumption that humans were "complex functioning mechanism[s]," much like machines.[25] The underlying concept was a system of communication that worked on the basis of feedbacks and self-regulation. Computer scientists used this concept to think about artificial intelligence. Anthropologists used it to analyze cultural systems. From a cybernetic point of view, specific actions, gestures, and rites were not solely structural elements that held together a social system. They rather presented "moments in the process of the transmission of information, which provides insight into the structure of the network, the number, combinatoric and possible combination of variables, and about the possibilities of changing circuits in relation and adaptation to the environment."[26] Theoretically, such an interpretation made it possible to leave behind older notions of different levels of "civilization" and to evaluate and compare social systems solely on the basis of their "methods of transmissions and sensitivities, degrees of adaptability, distribution and redistribution of resources, transfer of knowledge" and so forth.[27] Such a "mathematical," "universalist," "non-ideological" perspective appeared particularly attractive in the Cold War context, when understanding and possibly predicting and changing the behavior of social groups and societies all over the globe gained political relevance.[28]

This concern with global developments included the phenomenon of rapid population growth in parts of the world and its effects on the globe as a system. In 1955, John von Neumann published an article on "Technological Prospects and Global Limits." In the article, Neumann, "in many respects an extreme technological optimist,"[29] argued that there was "a natural limit, that of the earth's actual size."[30] Consequently, other solutions had to be found. Hudson Hoagland, a biologist "concerned with the world population explosion," looked for possible solutions to this problem by studying "mechanisms by which nature deals with overcrowding in animal species."[31] In a 1964 essay titled "Cybernetics of Population Control," he presented studies on the behavior of rats under the conditions of acute population growth. Those studies indicated that high population density increased stress levels and resulted in physical and social pathologies. Hoagland argued that humans experienced similar problems due to increases in population density, and that their well-being and health suffered in effect. Yet should humans wait for the negative health effects to become so strong that diseases "solved" the problem of "overpopulation"? Certainly not, Hoagland stated, and argued that it was vital "that we finally decide on an optimal population for the world and, by education and social pressure, try to see to that it is not exceeded."[32] Calculating the "optimal population" and finding the technology to reach and keep this level was not the problem—human behavior was. Hence, behavioral scientists could potentially help solve the "population problem."

The study of human behavior was immensely popular in the postwar era. Whereas cybernetics was perhaps the most extravagant field of interdisciplinary research in the postwar years, behavioralism was notable because it became institutionalized so rapidly and left such a vast imprint on the general outlook of social scientific research for more than a decade. Behavioralist research and study programs were funded at numerous American universities, among them Stanford University, the University of California, Berkeley, the University of Chicago, and others. The Ford Foundation established its own behavioralist program and, between 1951 and 1957, funded it with at least $24 million.[33] To understand why the new approach generated so much excitement and received so much financial and institutional support, it is useful to emphasize the difference between behaviorism, which is usually associated with Ivan Pavlov, B. F. Skinner, and the concept of conditioning, and behavioralism, the new approach of the 1950s. Behaviorism "referred to the investigation of observable phenomena generated exclusively and linearly by external stimuli." In contrast, behavioralism "included the analysis of attitudes, beliefs, expectations, motivations, and aspirations of human action." Hence, behavioralists went beyond the traditional method of observation and included "the probing of attitudes through questionnaires," hoping to gain material that would allow them to develop models through which to predict behavior.[34] It was no coincidence that behavioralism experienced its "golden age" in the 1950s, a time when the social sciences were making every effort to prove their "scientific" character and bridge the gap between science and politics.[35] Consequently, many social scientists focused on quantitative and empirical research and emphasized the practical applicability of their findings.[36] Behavioralism overlapped with cybernetics in several ways. Most importantly, both approaches featured a highly mechanistic view of complex systems, emphasizing the role of stimuli, feedbacks, and rules, or laws, of action and behavior. Whether those systems were driven by human or artificial intelligence and decisions did not matter; instead, predictability, control, and regulation were of central importance.

The modeling counterpart to behavioralism was rational choice theory. Its origins went back to mathematical modeling and were developed, among others, by scholars interested in and related to cybernetics. The institutional basis of rational choice thinking was the RAND Corporation, a California think tank funded by the Air Force, which conducted many studies commissioned by the CIA and the State Department.[37] Although RAND, "an almost 'pure Cold War' institution,"[38] was primarily concerned with the natural and technical sciences, its work also included social scientific research. One of the tasks was to minimize the risk of nuclear war. Game theory, "the mathematical simulation of confrontational decision dilemmas," seemed to provide an answer to this challenge.[39] The first systematic account of game theory had been formulated by John von Neumann and Oskar Morgenstern in 1944.[40] Game theory and, more generally, decision theory, were taken further at RAND in the late 1940s and 1950s, eventually becoming "a point of origin for rational choice scholarship."[41]

In the 1950s and 1960s, systems analysis and rational choice concepts became popular in a variety of disciplines, above all in economics and political science, but also in sociology, psychology, and biology. As Paul Erickson argues, the rapid adoption and adaptation of rational choice approaches by those disciplines cannot solely be explained by the influence of national security issues in Cold War America. Concerns about the increasing complexity of decision-making processes in modern society loomed large in the 1950s and 1960s. In this situation, the belief that new, more "scientific" approaches were necessary to make administrative work more efficient made mathematics-based tools appear very promising.[42] Together, systems analysis, cybernetics, behavioralism, and rational choice theory formed a conglomerate of social scientific knowledge which seemed to make it possible to identify social problems (both individual and collective) and correct them ("Understanding can lead to intervention"),[43] prevent political conflicts and circumvent ideological strife, and produce a self-regulating, efficient social system.[44] Consequently, systems and rational choice concepts made their way into public administration and political decision-making processes.[45]

The American concern with political stability was not restricted to the domestic sphere; neither was the application of the new social scientific approaches to social problems. Methods and models based on or related to behavioralism, rational choice concepts, and systems analysis were transferred to societies abroad, particularly in the context of the Korean War and the Vietnam War,[46] and in connection with development aid to the Third World. As Matthew Hull has shown in a study of the transfer of social technologies of speech from the United States to India, social scientific findings and methods developed in the domestic context were considered to be easily transferable from one cultural setting to another.[47] In the postwar years, social psychologists led by German emigrant and *Gestalt* psychologist Kurt Lewin completed and professionalized work they had conducted on group and individual behavior in the 1930s and during World War II. Lewin was very much interested in the cybernetic concept of "feedback." He met Norbert Wiener at the Massachusetts Institute of Technology, where he established the Research Center for Group Dynamics in 1945, which was devoted to developing more efficient forms of social engineering. Lewin died in 1947, but his ideas lived on in the National Training Laboratory for Group Development, which was founded in the same year to study processes and methods of behavioral change. In a group setting, individuals were encouraged to critically review their behavioral patterns, change them, and learn and internalize new forms of behavior.[48]

The goal of Lewin's research on group behavior was to find ways through which to "govern people's behavior in a democratic way"—a task that gained new urgency when the United States became a superpower that based its legitimacy on the defense and promotion of democracy.[49] Since "coercion . . . could not make democratic personalities," new ways had to be found so that democratic forms of behavior could be anchored in non-democratic societies.[50] Community development and democratic patterns of communication were considered essential to provide the basis for a politically stable path to development. In the mid-1950s, then, American social psychologists, with funding from the Ford Foundation, went to India where they trained locals in conducting interviews and setting up neighborhood committees to promote participatory forms of individual and group behavior. According to the concept as formulated in the classic *Dynamics of Planned Change* (1957), the psychologists figured as "change agents" in a "client system" perceived to be in need of external intervention. In their efforts to improve the situation of the community, they would encounter "forces of resistance" produced by "tradition." To overcome this resistance, the change agents would rely on individuals they identified as "natural" or "indigenous leaders." This practice of identifying and supporting "natural leaders" was considered an important element of strengthening democratic structures on a local level, particularly in otherwise autocratic environments.[51]

Taking Hull's argument a step further, I would argue that promoting democracy was closely tied to another motive of equal importance: the goal of "modernizing" "traditional" individuals and societies. According to modernization theory, another product of interdisciplinary postwar social science research, modernization went hand in hand with democratization. Autocracy was anti-individualist, whereas democracy gave each individual a voice and guaranteed him or her freedom to make his or her own decisions. Such freedom was a requirement for economic growth. Once the rate of economic growth gained speed, the process of transformation from "traditional" to "modern" life, from autocratic exploitation to democratic liberalism, would proceed in linear fashion.[52] Against the background of this scenario, the role of defining and building up "natural leaders" gained importance beyond the local level. Western notions of the ideal social order very much influenced the search for those leaders. Most likely, they would be persons whose thinking and behavior was closer to that of the Western experts than that of the average local. The leader was to serve as model to the others, who would acknowledge the advantages of such behavior and copy it. Family planning strategies employed precisely this rationale.

Family Planning as Behavioral Modification

"It is believed that the world population crisis can largely be solved by the expansion of human knowledge, freedom, and availability of information and means so that women everywhere need reproduce only if and when they choose."[53] Statements like this one by the director of the Population Service Office of the War on Hunger Agency for International Development, R.T. Ravenholt, were numerous in the 1950s and 1960s. Most demographers and political advisors committed to slowing down population growth in Third World countries and in socioeconomically disadvantaged social groups in the United States (particularly African-Americans)[54] agreed that information and education were essential. High birth rates were both an indicator and an effect of "backwardness," which was institutionalized in "clan and tribal institutions" and other "stubborn obstacles" to "modern," self-determined ways of behavior.[55] If women learned about ways of effectively controlling and spacing the number of children they had, they would do so, it was believed, for "bearing and rearing children is hard work, and few women have unlimited enthusiasm for the task."[56] Behavioralist studies like the Family Planning Knowledge Attitudes and Practices surveys (KAP surveys)[57] conducted in the mid-1960s in several developing countries suggested that many couples could identify an ideal family size (usually between three and five children) but in reality had more children.[58] The reason for this gap between ideal and reality was believed to be the fact that "information about family planning is uneven in the underdeveloped areas, and practice is limited, primitive, and erratic."[59] Yet as urbanization progressed, more women would come into contact with information about family planning, and it would be relatively easy for them to get hold of contraceptive devices.[60] More generally, individuals would gain greater agency over their own lives in the process of socioeconomic modernization. Kurt W. Back, a social psychologist who had studied with Kurt Lewin and worked in the field of demography and family planning, argued that hegemony of "fate" would give way to "control." As traditional marriage structures receded, individuals gained a greater say in when and whom they wanted to marry, which also influenced their reproductive behavior. Similarly, fertility would no longer be "a rather uncontrolled, fateful concomitant of the expression of sexual desires" but become "dependent on a conscious decision to have children."[61]

Yet what about those women who lived in rural areas, had little or no access to information infrastructure, had no formal school education, or were illiterate? While many of them might be aware of, or want, the advantages of having fewer children, the structures shaping their lives prevented them from practicing family planning. What could be done to change the situation in such a way that they would gain the necessary knowledge about and access to contraceptives? One approach was tried out in a Pakistani pilot project. The so-called Comilla project was part of the Pakistani government's program to promote family planning launched in 1960. A year later, the Comilla project was initiated in a rural area in eastern Pakistan. It was "based on the hypothesis that family planning is a problem of modernization," and that its success depended on the extension of education.[62] To promote family planning education, the project workers developed the so-called "organizer system":

i   Villagers are encouraged to form a primary interest group;
ii   The group elects a leader who comes to the academy once a week on a specific date and discusses with the experts the problems of this group's interest and takes back information, which in turn is discussed by the group in the village;
iii   As the group identifies a new interest and sets priority on it, it selects another of its members for the new activity, who then goes to the academy to learn new skills to disseminate among the group through both discussion and demonstration.[63]

Conceptually, Comilla's set-up was very similar to the community development model propagated by the social psychologists working in Delhi.

Above all, the two concepts shared the ideal of initiating behavioral change and promoting "innovative behavior"[64] by providing the community with the relevant information through its leader. This was in line with the model advocated by the Population Council in the 1960s, which emphasized "local awareness, local interest and the emergence of a competent local leadership."[65] The basic assumption of this concept was that the reproductive behavior of social groups and societies could be changed "to some extent without fundamental changes in other components of the culture. No social system, however coercive, maintains absolute homogeneity of behavior. All systems have their dissident extremes open to innovative suggestion; all have those who conform only because of the absence of alternatives."[66] If alternatives were provided, some individuals—the "natural leaders"—would take them up, and others would follow suit. Consequently, the group members would feel that their community was changing from within, while the origin of change was situated on the outside and regulated by external observers.

Behavioral change, as much as it was considered necessary, was not supposed to take place without expert control. Hence, in practice the "choice" in "rational choice" was very limited: the Pakistani villagers were not given the opportunity to freely choose from different forms of fertility behavior according to what was most rational, or most appropriate from their point of view; instead, they were presented with pre-selected and pre-configured "options." All they could do was to accept or reject them. The report on the Comilla project confirms this finding: while the "awareness and desire among the rural people to limit family size" had grown over a period of three years and a "gradual shift in values from the large family ideal to the small family ideal" could be observed, it was also clear that "the villagers are presented with very few alternatives to develop a meaningful choice-behaviour" because they made their decisions primarily based on economic considerations.[67] Their interest in family planning was driven by the expectation that having fewer children would mean a higher income; once their income began to rise due to higher agricultural yields (which had been happening in rural Pakistan due to improved agricultural practices) they were no longer interested in limiting family size. Therefore they had to be approached as long as they were in an economic situation in which they were likely to accept the need to reduce their family sizes.[68]

Generally, one can observe a tendency among family planning advocates in the 1960s to identify situations that allowed for direct access to individual and group behavior. For example, if a peasant family were faced with a dire economic situation due to low yields, the chances to "convince" the couple to use contraceptives were much higher than in economically less challenging times. Similarly, the post-partum situation was identified as an advantageous moment to initiate behavioral change: "It seemed likely that women who undergo the obstetrical experience would be in a receptive frame of mind for assistance in family planning."[69] This would be an "acutely favorable situation with respect to motivation," according to Howard C. Taylor and Bernard Berelson, who published an influential article on the issue in 1968.[70] They argued that the post-partum approach, which the Population Council promoted through its International Postpartum Program since 1966,[71] was particularly useful because illiterate women and those they considered "indifferent or apathetic" to birth control could be reached "at the peak of a fluctuating 'motivational curve' toward family planning."[72] Furthermore, women who had just given birth in a hospital would be receiving advice from medical staff they trusted after having been cared for during delivery. "The psychological circumstances for the reception of family planning instruction at these times are thus ideal."[73] The argument was notably informed by behaviorist and behavioralist concepts like stimulus and response, motivation and reinforcement. Berelson, vice president and later president of the Population Council, was intimately familiar with those concepts: he had been the director of the Ford Foundation's behavioral sciences program from 1951 to 1957.[74] In 1970, Berelson called for an increase in post-partum programs in rural areas, where birth rates were highest.[75] If more women were to be reached through post-partum programs, more clinics had to be available and programs of "supervised maternity" had to be established. As a "demographic by-product of great importance," such programs would also "provide the means for setting up, for the first time in most developing countries, a valid system of birth registration."[76] Hence, institutionalization on a large scale was necessary to provide the required "infrastructure" for the post-partum family planning model. Together, those efforts mirrored the goal to gain control over the reproductive behavior of women, from conception to delivery, in different parts of the world.

While securing control and producing systemic stability was clearly at the heart of behavioralism-inspired family planning, one should not assume that all women in Third World countries or of "low socioeconomic status in the United States,"[77] who were included in the International Postpartum Program, helplessly or willingly gave up their sovereignty and accepted the control of health personnel, family planners and demographers over their bodies and behavior. For many women, having access to clinics, to public health resources, and to contraceptives meant a distinct improvement, one they reached out for actively.[78] Also, we should not assume that programs worked precisely the way they were planned in the New York and New Delhi offices. For one, setting up the required infrastructure was much more expensive than many developing countries could and were willing to afford. Furthermore, communicating the need for and possibilities of family planning among the non-urban populations presented a serious obstacle. Again, social science research seemed to offer a solution in the form of theories of mass-communication, as an example from India illustrates.

"An Illusion of Legitimation": Mass Communication Strategies

The Indian government opted for a mass motivation approach to promote and anchor family planning in India in the second half of the 1960s. In 1966, the Indian government's Department of Family Planning, with the support of the Ford Foundation, developed a concept to make the advantages of and need for family planning a constant in Indian public life, based on the goal set by India's Health Minister that "90 million couples ... must be brought to accept the small-family norm."[79] It was agreed that it was neither sufficient to promote the abstract notion of family planning nor to rely on the traditional media (press, radio, motion pictures and printed material); a new message and a new means to spread this message were necessary. Hence, a threefold campaign was designed, consisting of a message, a symbol, and a publicity strategy. The message was that the "appropriate" number of children for any Indian family was two or three. This message ("'Have Only Two or Three Children ... That's Plenty.'") was translated into 13 Indian languages (not into English) and combined with visual material in the form of "stylized front-view faces of a smiling mother and father, a son and a daughter."[80] "The colors are always the same, bright and attractive. The faces are drawn always in the same style. The same message is verbalized in an appealing song by a popular Indian songwriter and recorded by a singer whose voice is as familiar to Indians as Bing Crosby's once was to Americans."[81] The call to limit one's family size was combined with a newly created symbol, a red triangle. Together, the message and the symbol appeared on every available spot in Indian public life: apart from the traditional media, on "billboards, buses, matchboxes, rickshaws, pocket calendars, newspaper and magazine advertisements, carnival banners, shopping bags, official village civic registers, telephone directories, and—most importantly—the exterior walls of buildings for huge lasting paintings of the basic design. Also, permanent enameled metal signs are being distributed to the country's 100,000 post offices, and, after traditional railroad conservatism was painfully overcome, the broad sides of locomotive tenders are being used as traveling billboards."[82] The expected effect of this huge campaign was to generate discussion about family size and produce agreement among Indians that having more than two or three children was against the norm. The omnipresence of the campaign's signs and reminders would provide "an illusion of legitimation," as the campaign designers argued.[83]

Their understanding of and intent to promote visibility reflected social scientific approaches to mass communication developed since the late 1940s. During World War II, in the context of propaganda and psychological warfare, the idea had been dominant that "an active communicator manipulated the mind of a passive receiver." Contrastingly, the postwar years well into the 1960s were characterized by an understanding of mass communication according to which "the mass media served as an agent of reinforcement or a catalyst, rather than a direct stimulus."[84] Communication scholars Wilbur Schramm and John Riley, both of whom adhered to behavioralism and studied ways of influencing the behavior of individuals in authoritarian systems, were quite aware of the limits to the effects that mass media could have on individuals. For example, Riley argued that violence shown on television affected only those children "who were predisposed to violence."[85] Family planning advocates discovered those limits to the effects of mass media campaigns in their everyday efforts to inform, educate, and encourage women to embrace birth control. For example, researchers studying the adoption of specific contraceptives in a rural region of Taiwan before and after a mass information campaign in the mid-1960s found that many factors apart from the availability of technical information influenced women's willingness to use contraceptives or other means of family planning. Religious principles, fear of bodily harm, interference with sexual pleasure, and other psychological and cultural factors made acceptance difficult. If women were to overcome these obstacles, "extra individual social support must be involved," they argued.[86]

Family planning emphasized the importance of making the means of contraception available to individuals "while leaving decisions of fertility to the families concerned."[87] Yet were women really in a situation to make reproductive choices? A case study in an Indian village found that "effective husband-wife communication would seldom take place and that this could present a major obstacle to effective family planning."[88] Perhaps even more importantly, many women were not at all involved in decisions concerning their sexual and reproductive lives. For example, in one family from the Indian village a woman underwent a tubectomy without her knowledge when she was hospitalized for childbirth; her mother-in-law and her husband had taken the decision without her, and her husband's written consent had been sufficient for the sterilization to be performed.[89] As long as societies remained "traditional," cultural and individual factors presented "obstacles" to rational choice-based family planning: "illiteracy and ignorance, the ancestral need for sons, the social-security need for sons, social pressures toward parenthood, the superstitions and customs attached to menstruation, the sensitivity of sex-related behavior, peasant resistance to change," among others.[90]

Faced with these deeply anchored structural problems, many experts turned to technology. Bernard Berelson in 1970 expressed his hope to find a contraceptive that was "logistically easy, effective, simple, one-time, reversible, trouble-free, culture-free, doctor-free, coitus-free, inexpensive."[91] If such a device was available, family planning could effectively be implemented on a large scale. The chances of reaching the goal of zero population growth would be much higher if one did not have to take into account cultural and individual particularities and rely on reasoning, information, and persuasion. The "neat congruence of reasonable people with social aims was not guaranteed."[92] In this situation, technology promised to render the complexities of human behavior irrelevant.

Conclusion

It was no coincidence that Berelson emphasized the advantages of a "culture-free" solution in 1970. By that time, demographically interested anthropologists had begun to complicate the picture by emphasizing the importance of culture. They considered "culture, agency and interests ... as mutually constitutive," thereby arguing that in trying to pave the way for family planning it was not possible to treat culture as an isolated factor to be manipulated by external means.[93] Consequently, "direct techniques of 'motivating' potential family planners" had lost much of their appeal. Instead it was assumed "that significant proportions of people possess the required motivation and that continuous demand for contraceptives will probably proceed through informal person-to-person communications and a shift in community as the program takes hold."[94] Yet this meant that slowing down population growth would not be achieved through developing the "correct" family planning formula and entering it into the system. Confidence in empirically produced data about reproductive behavior was shaken when it became clear that lowered fertility rates could not be directly correlated with family planning programs (while at the same time, historical demography began to offer new insight into historical patterns and conditions of fertility decline, thereby challenging central demographic assumptions and predictions).[95] It became clear that there were many more variables to be included, most of which were intertwined and few of which could be effectively controlled. One could, of course, expand the system and make it as sophisticated as possible, as the example of the World Model developed by the authors of *The Limits to Growth* showed. Yet for good reason systems like the World Model did not focus on individual behavior. Social engineering based on the belief that individuals in developing countries could be brought to embrace family planning through information campaigns, leadership models, and positive reinforcement gave way to the macro-management of resources (land, jobs, energy, food, population), thereby effecting a perhaps unexpected revival of Malthusian thinking. Hence, after a period of about twenty years during which demographic developments had been regarded as the product of individual decisions, "population" became again considered first and foremost a "natural" resource.

In studying the history of population policies in the second half of the twentieth century, it is important to understand the dramatic effect that social scientific approaches (and fashions) had on the understanding of population growth, reproductive behavior, and the subject of "population." Only if we pay attention to the ways in which scientific theories and concepts inspired by World War II and the Cold War shaped the perception and construction of population as an entity can we understand how family planning approaches could become a reality in the lives of thousands of people across the globe. The social scientific developments of the mid-twentieth century, which were supposedly "neutral" yet in fact highly normative and contingent upon the circumstances of their evolution, left a lasting imprint on demographic practices and on the self-understanding of demographers, blurring the line "between value transformation and the transmission of technical knowledge."[96] Behavioralism and rational choice approaches greatly contributed to the optimistic understanding that the world's problems could be solved by peaceful means, and that it was indeed possible to regulate and stabilize the global system.[97] Population was considered one of the elements constituting that system, and family planning became the method of choice to balance it, with a distinct drive toward individual (particularly female) emancipation. Individuals were granted the ability to make the "right" decisions under the "right" circumstances; yet the focus on rationality and liberty was one-dimensional, leaving no room for "irrational" behavior.

Acknowledgments

This chapter has benefited from insightful comments by colleagues from the Oslo Contemporary International History Network; the Modern German History Research Seminar, University of Oxford; the German Historical Institute London; the Colloquium on Contemporary History, University of Münster; the Center for Area Studies, University of Leipzig; the Network "Population, Knowledge, Order, Transformation: Demography and Politics in the Twentieth Century in Global Perspective"; Paul-André Rosental, Universités à Sciences Po; and two anonymous reviewers.

Notes

1. John E. Gordon to James S. Simmons, Dean, Harvard School of Public Health, October 6, 1953. Rockefeller Archive Center, Rockefeller Foundation, Record Group 1.2, Series 200, Box 45, Folder 369.
2. J.E. Gordon and J.B. Wyon, *The Khanna Study: Population Problems in the Rural Punjab* (Cambridge, Mass., 1971). The Khanna Study became a famous example of demographic research and the focal point of criticism against "population control." See M. Mamdani, *The Myth of Population Control: Family, Caste, and Class in an Indian Village* (New York, 1972).
3. D.H. Meadows et al., *The Limits to Growth: A Report for the Club of Rome's Project on the Predicament of Mankind*, 3rd printing (London, 1975).
4. See J.R. McNeill, "The Environment, Environmentalism, and International Society in the Long 1970s," in *The Shock of the Global: The 1970s in Perspective*, N. Ferguson et al. eds. (Cambridge, Mass., 2010), 263–278; S. Höhler, "The Law of Growth: How Ecology Accounted for World Population in the 20th Century," *Distinktion: Scandinavian Journal of Social Theory* 14 (2007): 45–64, 51–52.
5. See E. Seefried, "Towards *The Limits to Growth*? The Book and its Reception in West Germany and Britain 1972–73," *German Historical Institute London Bulletin* 33, no. 1 (2011): 3–37; Höhler,

The Law of Growth, 54–56; N. Freytag, "'Eine Bombe im Taschenbuchformat'? Die 'Grenzen des Wachstums' und die öffentliche Resonanz," *Zeithistorische Forschungen/Studies in Contemporary History* (online edition) 3, no. 3 (2006), <http://www.zeithistorische-forschungen.de/16126041-Freytag-3-2006> (August 30, 2013); F. Hahn, *Von Unsinn bis Untergang: Rezeption des Club of Rome und der Grenzen des Wachstums in der Bundesrepublik der frühen 1970er Jahre* (PhD diss., University of Freiburg, 2006) (http://www.freidok.uni-freiburg.de/volltexte/2722/pdf/hahn_friedemann_2006_von_unsinn_bis_untergang.pdf).

6. On the production of this image through computer modeling, see P.N. Edwards, "The World in a Machine: Origins and Impact of Early Global Systems Model," in *Systems, Experts, and Computers: The Systems Approach in Management and Engineering, World War II and After*, A.C. Hughes and T.P. Hughes eds. (Cambridge, Mass., 2000), 221–253, esp. 242–248.
7. J.F. Kantner and A. Kantner, *International Discord on Population and Development* (New York, 2010), ix.
8. Of course family planning ideas and initiatives existed before demographic transition theory became popular, yet the combination of demographic observations and modernization approaches provided a particularly fruitful grounding for family planning concepts, I would argue.
9. See S. Greenhalgh, "The Social Construction of Population Science: An Intellectual, Institutional, and Political History of Twentieth Century Demography," *Comparative Studies in Society and History* 38, no. 1 (1996): 26–66; D. Hodgson, "Demography as Social Science and Policy Science," *Population and Development Review* 9, no. 1 (1983): 1–34.
10. See, among others, P. Demeny and G. McNicoll, "World Population 1950–2000: Perception and Response," *Population and Development Review* 32 (2006): 1–51; M. Connelly, *Fatal Misconception: The Struggle to Control World Population* (Cambridge, Mass., 2008); M. Frey, "Neo-Malthusianism and Development: Shifting Interpretations of a Contested Paradigm," *Journal of Global History* 6 (2011): 75–97. For a colonial perspective, see M. van Beusekom, "From Underpopulation to Overpopulation: French Perceptions of Population, Environment, and Agricultural Development in French Soudan (Mali), 1900–1960," *Environmental History* 4, no. 2 (1999): 198–219.
11. D. Kirk, Review of Robert C. Cook, *Human Fertility: The Modern Dilemma*, *Population Studies* 7, no. 1 (1953): 89–90, 90. In the same review Kirk noted that "fertility differentials in the Western world are generally dysgenic." Ibid., 90.
12. P. Demeny, "Population and the Limits to Growth," *Population and Development Review* 14 (1988): 213–244, 231.
13. Kantner and Kantner, *International Discord on Population and Development*, 20.
14. See A. Bashford, *Global Population: History, Geopolitics, and Life on Earth* (New York, 2014).
15. See, among others, M. Gottlieb, "Optimum Population, Foreign Trade and World Economy," *Population Studies* 3, no. 2 (1949): 151–169; K. Smith, "Some Observations on Modern Malthusianism," *Population Studies* 6, no. 1 (1952): 92–105; A.T. Peacock, "Theory of Population and Modern Economic Analysis I," *Population Studies* 6, no. 2 (1952): 114–122; William Petersen, "John Maynard Keynes's Theories of Population and the Concept of 'Optimum'," *Population Studies* 8, no. 3 (1955): 228–246.
16. Demeny, *Population and the Limits to Growth*, 235.
17. Ibid., 236.
18. Cf. ibid., 236–236.
19. See, for example, E.F. Schumacher, *Small Is Beautiful: Economics as if People Mattered* (London, 1973).
20. Greenhalgh, *The Social Construction of Population Science*, 47.
21. For a comprehensive history of systems approaches, see the contributions in A.C. Hughes and T.P. Hughes, eds., *Systems, Experts, and Computers*.

22. On operations research and its role in the development of cybernetics, see Wolfgang Pircher, "Im Schatten der Kybernetik: Rückkopplung im operative Einsatz: 'operational research'," in *Die Transformation des Humanen: Beiträge zur Kulturgeschichte der Kybernetik*, E. Hörl and M. Hagner eds. (Frankfurt am Main, 2008), 348–376.
23. For an excellent overview, see E. Hörl and M. Hagner, eds., *Die Transformation des Humanen*. On Soviet cybernetics, see S. Gerovitch, *From Newspeak to Cyberspeak: A History of Soviet Cybernetics* (Cambridge, Mass., 2002). On the German cybernetic "school," see C.C. Bissell, "Hermann Schmidt and German 'Proto-Cybernetics'," *Information, Communication & Society* 14, no. 1 (2011): 156–171.
24. Cf. *Cybernetics—Kybernetik: The Macy-Conferences 1946–1953. Essays & Documents*, vol. II, C. Pias ed. (Zürich, 2004). On Neumann and Wiener and their contribution to cybernetics, see Y. Rav, "Perspectives on the History of the Cybernetics Movement: The Path to Current Research through the Contributions of N. Wiener, W. McCulloch, and J.v. Neumann," *Cybernetics and Systems* 33 (2002): 779–804. Cybernetic approaches made their way into a range of academic disciplines; in applied and popularized form, they also entered into administration and politics as well as into everyday culture and life all over the globe. See C. Pias, "Zeit der Kybernetik—Eine Einstimmung," in *Cybernetics—Kybernetik*, C. Pias ed., 9–41.
25. E. Hörl and M. Hagner, "Überlegungen zur kybernetischen Transformation des Humanen," in *Die Transformation des Humanen*, 7–37, 11. My translation. Norbert Wiener and Arturo Rosenblueth stated: "'We believe that men and other animals are like machines from a scientific standpoint'." Quoted in Rav, *Perspectives on the History of the Cybernetics Movement*, 787.
26. U. Holl, "'It's (Not) an Intervention!' Kybernetik und Anthropologie," in *Cybernetics—Kybernetik*, C. Pias ed., 97–114, 108. My translation. For a nuanced overview of the very different positions and perspectives, see D. Hammond, *The Science of Synthesis: Exploring the Social Implications of General Systems Theory* (Boulder, 2003).
27. Holl, "'It's (Not) an Intervention!'," 108. My translation.
28. Cf. E. Schüttelpelz, "To Whom It May Concern Messages," in *Cybernetics—Kybernetik*, C. Pias ed., 115–130, 121. On the epistemological and methodological changes in anthropology under the conditions of the Cold War, see L. Nader, "The Phantom Factor: Impact of the Cold War on Anthropology," in *The Cold War & The University: Toward an Intellectual History of the Postwar Years*, N. Chomsky et al. eds. (New York, 1997), 107–146. Also see the contributions in C. Simpson, ed., *Universities and Empire: Money and Politics in the Social Sciences during the Cold War* (New York, 1998). One should not overstate the nexus between anthropology and Cold War national interests, however; see P. Manderl, "Deconstructing 'Cold War Anthropology'," in *Uncertain Empire: American History and the Idea of the Cold War*, J. Isaac and D. Bell eds. (Oxford, 2012), 245–266.
29. Demeny, "Population and the Limits to Growth," 227.
30. J.v. Neumann, "Technological Prospects and Global Limits [1955]," *Population and Development Review* 12, no. 1 (1986): 117–126, 118.
31. H. Hoagland, "Cybernetics of Population Control," *Bulletin of the Atomic Scientists* (Feb. 1964): 2–7, 2.
32. Ibid., 6. It seems to have been no coincidence that Hoagland was a friend and colleague of Gregory Pincus, with whom he founded the Worcester Foundation for Experimental Biology in 1944, where Pincus conducted research on hormonal contraception. In 1953, Pincus was asked by Margaret Sanger and Katherine McCormick to develop a birth control pill, which he did. In the mid-1950s, he conducted human trials first in Massachusetts, then in Puerto Rico. In 1960, the Food and Drug Administration approved the Pill for contraceptive use. http://www.pbs.org/wgbh/amex/pill/peopleevents/p_pincus.html (August 30, 2013); C. Schreiber, *Natürlich künstliche Befruchtung: Eine Geschichte der In-vitro-Fertilisation von 1878 bis 1950* (Göttingen,

2007), 129–130. Also see R. Argast, "Population under Control: Das Ciba-Symposium 'The Future of Man' von 1962 im Spannungsfeld von Reformeugnik, Molekulargenetik und Reproduktionstechnologie," in *Die vergangene Zukunft Europas: Bevölkerungsforschung und -prognosen im 20. und 21. Jahrhundert*, ed. P. Overath (Köln, 2011), 85–116, 96–100.

33. Cf. R. Robin, *The Making of the Cold War Enemy: Culture and Politics in the Military-Intellectual Complex* (Princeton, 2001), 35; E. Hauptmann, "The Constitution of Behavioralism: The Influence of the Ford Foundation's Behavioral Sciences Program on Political Science." Paper prepared for delivery at the 6th Annual Spring Workshop on History of Economics as History of Science, École Normale Supèrieure de Cachan, 19 June 2009, http://economix.fr/pdf/work shops/2009_H2S2/Hauptmann.pdf (August 30, 2013), 5.
34. Robin, *The Making of the Cold War Enemy*, 24.
35. Cf. ibid., 26–27.
36. For the case of demography, see Greenhalgh, *The Social Construction of Population Science*, 48–49.
37. On RAND, see D.A. Hounshell, "The Cold War, RAND, and the Generation of Knowledge, 1946–1962," *Historical Studies in the Physical and Biological Sciences* 27, no. 2 (1997): 237–267; Alex Abella, *Soldiers of Reason: The RAND Corporation and the Rise of the American Empire* (Orlando, 2008); S.M. Amadae, *Rationalizing Capitalist Democracy: The Cold War Origins of Rational Choice Liberalism* (Chicago, 2003), 32–47; Robin, *The Making of the Cold War Enemy*, 46–50.
38. Hounshell, "The Cold War," 261.
39. Robin, *The Making of the Cold War Enemy*, 47.
40. J.v. Neumann and O. Morgenstern, *Theory of Games and Economic Behavior* (Princeton, 1944).
41. Amadae, *Rationalizing Capitalist Democracy*, 77.
42. P. Erickson, "Mathematical Models, Rational Choice, and the Search for Cold War Culture," *Isis* 101, no. 2 (2010): 386–392, 388.
43. K.W. Back, *Family Planning and Population Control: The Challenges of a Successful Movement* (Boston, 1989), 99.
44. Noam Chomsky remembers the optimistic atmosphere of the time: "And that time, with the Macy conferences, cybernetics, communication theory, and so on, there was a feeling that the horizons were unlimited." N. Chomsky, "The Cold War and the University," in *The Cold War and the University*, N. Chomsky et al. eds., 171–194, 174.
45. Cf. Amadae, *Rationalizing Capitalist Democracy*, 72; D.R. Jardini, "Out of the Blue Yonder: The Transfer of Systems Thinking from the Pentagon to the Great Society, 1961–1965," in *Systems, Experts, and Computers*, A.C. Hughes and T.P. Hughes eds., 311–357; Eden Medina, *Cybernetic Revolutionaries: Technology and Politics in Allende's Chile* (Cambridge, Mass., 2011).
46. On the use of behavioralist and rational choice concepts in the Korean War, see Robin, *The Making of the Cold War Enemy*, 124–181. On the influence of those approaches on the American strategy in the Vietnam War, see ibid., 185–205; S. Kaufmann, "Die Wissenstransformierung der 'counterinsurgency' im Vietnamkrieg," *Zeitschrift für Geschichte* 16 (2009): 37–52.
47. M. Hull, "Democratic Technologies of Speech: From WWII America to Postcolonial Delhi," *Journal of Linguistic Anthropology* 20, no. 2 (2010): 257–282. Thanks to Susanne B. Unger for bringing this article to my attention.
48. Cf. U. Bröckling, "Über Feedback: Anatomie einer kommunikativen Schlüsseltechnologie," in *Die Transformation des Humanen*, E. Hörl and M. Hagner eds., 326–347, 329, 331–332.
49. Hull, "Democratic Technologies of Speech," 258.
50. Ibid., 259.
51. R. Lippitt, J. Watson, and B. Westley, *The Dynamics of Planned Change* (New York, 1957), cited in Hull, "Democratic Technologies of Speech," 261–262.
52. On modernization theory and its application in American foreign policy in the Cold War context, see, among others, M.E. Latham, *The Right Kind of Revolution: Modernization, Development,*

and *U.S. Foreign Policy from the Cold War to the Present* (Ithaca, 2011). On modernization theory's emphasis on individualism, see, among others, C. Klein, "Musicals and Modernization: Rodgers and Hammerstein's *The King and I*," in *Staging Growth: Modernization, Development, and the Global Cold War*, D.C. Engerman et al. eds. (Amherst, 2003), 129–162.
53. R.T. Ravenholt, "The A.I.D. Population and Family Planning Program—Goals, Scope, and Progress," *Demography* 5, no. 2 (1968): 561–573, 571.
54. On the debates about the fertility rates of African-Americans in the United States in the 1960s, on the famous report by Assistant Secretary of Labor, Daniel Patrick Moynihan, on *The Negro Family: The Case for National Action* (1965), and on the integration of family planning programs in Lyndon B. Johnson's Great Society efforts to promote racial and social equality, see Connelly, *Fatal Misconception*, 249–254; D. Geary, "Racial Liberalism, the Moynihan Report & the Daedalus Project on 'The Negro American'," *Daedalus* 140, no. 1 (2011): 53–66; D.S. Massey and R.J. Sampson, "Moynihan Redux: Legacies and Lessons," *Annals of the American Academy of Political and Social Science* 621 (2009): 6–27.
55. C. Deverell, "The International Planned Parenthood Federation—its Role in Developing Countries," *Demography* 5, no. 2 (1968): 574–577, 577.
56. Ravenholt, "The A.I.D. Population and Family Planning Program," 572.
57. On the KAP surveys in Turkey, see the contribution by H. Hartmann in this volume.
58. Cf. Ravenholt, "The A.I.D. Population and Family Planning Program," 572; T. Poffenberger, "Motivational Aspects of Resistance to Family Planning in an Indian Village," *Demography* 5, no. 2 (1968): 757–766, 758; M. Khan, "Population Control: A Two-Year Rural Action Experience," *Demography* 1, no. 1 (1964): 126–129, 129; Hodgson, *Demography as Social Science and Social Policy*, 23.
59. B. Berelson and G.A. Steiner, *Human Behavior: An Inventory of Scientific Findings* (New York, 1964), 595.
60. See, for example, J.W. Combs, Jr. and K. Davis, "Differential Fertility in Puerto Rico," *Population Studies* 5, no. 2 (1951): 104–116, 112, 115–116; Irene B. Taeuber, "Demographic Modernization: Continuities and Transitions," *Demography* 3, no. 1 (1966): 90–108. On demographic transition theory, see Szreter, "The Idea of Demographic Transition and the Study of Fertility Change."
61. K.W. Back, "New Frontiers in Demography and Social Psychology," *Demography* 4, no. 1 (1967): 90–97, 92.
62. Khan, *Population Control: A Two-Year Rural Action Experience*, 128.
63. Ibid.
64. F.W. Notestein, "The Population Council and the Demographic Crisis of the Less Developed World," *Demography* 5, no. 2 (1968): 553–560, 558.
65. Ibid., 559.
66. M.C. Balfour, R.F. Evans, F.W. Notestein, and I.B. Taeuber, *Public Health and Demography in the Far East: Report of a Survey Trip September 13–December 13, 1948* (New York, 1950), 117. Quoted in S. Szreter, "The Idea of Demographic Transition and the Study of Fertility Change: A Critical Intellectual History," *Population and Development Review* 19, no. 4 (1993): 659–701, 673.
67. Khan, "Population Control: A Two-Year Rural Action Experience," 129.
68. Cf. ibid., 129.
69. Notestein, "The Population Council and the Demographic Crisis of the Less Developed World," 559.
70. Howard C. Taylor and B. Berelson, "Maternity care and family planning as a world program," *American Journal of Obstetrics and Gynecology* 100, no. 7 (1968): 885–893, 886. Thanks to Heinrich Hartmann for bringing this article to my attention.

71. Cf. B. Winikoff and B. Mensch, "Rethinking Postpartum Family Planning," *Studies in Family Planning* 22, no. 5 (1991): 294–307, 294.
72. Taylor and Berelson, "Maternity Care and Family Planning as a World Program," 886.
73. Ibid.
74. Robin, *The Making of the Cold War Enemy*, 25.
75. B. Berelson, "The Present State of Family Planning Programs," *Studies in Family Planning* 1, no. 57 (1970): 1–11, 8.
76. Taylor and Berelson, "Maternity Care and Family Planning as a World Program," 887.
77. Winikoff and Mensch, "Rethinking Postpartum Family Planning," 294.
78. See the contribution by A. Widmer in this volume.
79. S. Chandrasekhar, "How India is Tackling her Population Problem," *Demography* 5, no. 2 (1968): 642–650, 643.
80. Frank Wilder and D.K. Tyagi, "India's New Departure in Mass Motivation for Fertility Control," *Demography* 5, no. 2 (1968): 773–779, 775.
81. Wilder and Tyagi, "India's New Departure in Mass Motivation for Fertility Control," 776.
82. Ibid., 777.
83. Ibid., 776.
84. Robin, *The Making of the Cold War Enemy*, 82.
85. Ibid., 89.
86. James A. Palmore, "Awareness Sources and Stages in the Adoption of Specific Contraceptives," *Demography* 5, no. 2 (1968): 960–972, 961.
87. Back, *Family Planning and Population Control*, 96.
88. Poffenberger, *Motivational Aspects of Resistance*, 761.
89. Cf. ibid.
90. Berelson, *The Present State of Family Planning Programs*, 1.
91. Ibid., 8.
92. Back, *Family Planning and Population Control*, 96.
93. M. Connelly, "Population Control is History: New Perspectives on the International Campaign to Limit Population Growth," *Comparative Studies in Society and History* 45, no. 1 (2003): 122–147, 129–130.
94. H.M. Raulet, "Family Planning and Population Control in Developing Countries," *Demography* 7, no. 2 (1970): 211–234, 227.
95. Cf. ibid., 229–230.
96. Back, *Family Planning and Population Control*, 5.
97. Cf. Robin, *The Making of the Cold War Enemy*, 93.

Bibliography

Abella, A., *Soldiers of Reason: The RAND Corporation and the Rise of the American Empire* (Orlando, 2008).

Amadae, S.M., *Rationalizing Capitalist Democracy: The Cold War Origins of Rational Choice Liberalism* (Chicago, 2003).

Argast, R., "Population under Control: Das Ciba-Symposium 'The Future of Man' von 1962 im Spannungsfeld von Reformeugnik, Molekulargenetik und Reproduktionstechnologie," in *Die vergangene Zukunft Europas: Bevölkerungsforschung und -prognosen im 20. und 21. Jahrhundert*, P. Overath ed. (Köln, 2011), 85–116.

Back, K.W., *Family Planning and Population Control: The Challenges of a Successful Movement* (Boston, 1989).
Back, K., "New Frontiers in Demography and Social Psychology," *Demography* 4, no. 1 (1967): 90–97.
Balfour, M.C., Evans, R.F., Notestein, F.W., and Taeuber, I.B., *Public Health and Demography in the Far East: Report of a Survey Trip September 13–December 13, 1948* (New York, 1950).
Bashford, A., *Global Population: History, Geopolitics, and Life on Earth* (New York, 2014).
Berelson, B., "The Present State of Family Planning Programs," *Studies in Family Planning* 1, no. 57 (1970): 1–11.
Berelson, B., and Steiner, G.A., *Human Behavior: An Inventory of Scientific Findings* (New York, 1964).
Bissell, C.C., "Hermann Schmidt and German 'Proto-Cybernetics'," *Information, Communication & Society* 14, no. 1 (2011): 156–171.
Bröckling, U., "Über Feedback: Anatomie einer kommunikativen Schlüsseltechnologie," in *Die Transformation des Humanen: Beiträge zur Kulturgeschichte der Kybernetik*, E. Hörl and M. Hagner eds. (Frankfurt, 2008), 326–347.
Chandrasekhar, S., "How India is Tackling her Population Problem," *Demography* 5, no. 2 (1968): 642–650.
Chomsky, N., "The Cold War and the University," in *The Cold War & The University: Toward an Intellectual History of the Postwar Years*, N. Chomsky et al. eds. (New York, 1997), 171–194.
Chomsky, N., et al., eds., *The Cold War & The University: Toward an Intellectual History of the Postwar Years* (New York, 1997).
Combs, J.W., Jr., and Davis, K., "Differential Fertility in Puerto Rico," *Population Studies* 5, no. 2 (1951): 104–116.
Connelly, M., *Fatal Misconception: The Struggle to Control World Population* (Cambridge, Mass., 2008).
Connelly, M., "Population Control is History: New Perspectives on the International Campaign to Limit Population Growth," *Comparative Studies in Society and History* 45, no. 1 (2003): 122–147.
Demeny, P., "Population and the Limits to Growth," *Population and Development Review* 14 (1988): 213–244.
Demeny, P., and McNicoll, G., "World Population 1950–2000: Perception and Response," *Population and Development Review* 32 (2006): 1–51.
Deverell, C., "The International Planned Parenthood Federation—its Role in Developing Countries," *Demography* 5, no. 2 (1968): 574–577.
Edwards, P.N., "The World in a Machine: Origins and Impact of Early Global Systems Model," in *Systems, Experts, and Computers: The Systems Approach in Management and Engineering, World War II and After*, A.C. Hughes and T.P. Hughes eds. (Cambridge, Mass., 2000), 221–253.
Engerman, D.C., et al., eds., *Staging Growth: Modernization, Development, and the Global Cold War* (Amherst, 2003).
Erickson, P., "Mathematical Models, Rational Choice, and the Search for Cold War Culture," *Isis* 101, no. 2 (2010): 386–392.
Ferguson, N., et al., eds., *The Shock of the Global: The 1970s in Perspective* (Cambridge, Mass., 2010).
Frey, M., "Neo-Malthusianism and Development: Shifting Interpretations of a Contested Paradigm," *Journal of Global History* 6 (2011): 75–97.
Freytag, N., "'Eine Bombe im Taschenbuchformat'? Die 'Grenzen des Wachstums' und die öffentliche Resonanz," *Zeithistorische Forschungen/Studies in Contemporary History* (online edition) 3, no. 3 (2006), http://www.zeithistorische-forschungen.de/16126041-Freytag-3-2006.
Geary, D., "Racial Liberalism, the Moynihan Report & the Daedalus Project on 'The Negro American'," *Daedalus* 140, no. 1 (2011): 53–66.
Gerovitch, S., *From Newspeak to Cyberspeak: A History of Soviet Cybernetics* (Cambridge, Mass., 2002).

Greenhalgh, S., "The Social Construction of Population Science: An Intellectual, Institutional, and Political History of Twentieth Century Demography," *Comparative Studies in Society and History* 38, no. 1 (1996): 26–66.

Gordon, J.E., and Wyon, J.B., *The Khanna Study: Population Problems in the Rural Punjab* (Cambridge, Mass., 1971).

Gottlieb, M., "Optimum Population, Foreign Trade and World Economy," *Population Studies* 3, no. 2 (1949): 151–169.

Hahn, F., *Von Unsinn bis Untergang: Rezeption des Club of Rome und der Grenzen des Wachstums in der Bundesrepublik der frühen 1970er Jahre* (PhD diss., University of Freiburg, 2006), http://www.freidok.uni-freiburg.de/volltexte/2722/pdf/hahn_friedemann_2006_von_unsinn_bis_untergang.pdf.

Hammond, D., *The Science of Synthesis: Exploring the Social Implications of General Systems Theory* (Boulder, 2003).

Hauptmann, E., "The Constitution of Behavioralism: The Influence of the Ford Foundation's Behavioral Sciences Program on Political Science." Paper prepared for delivery at the 6th Annual Spring Workshop on History of Economics as History of Science, École Normale Supèrieure de Cachan, 19 June 2009, http://economix.fr/pdf/workshops/2009_H2S2/Hauptmann.pdf.

Hoagland, H., "Cybernetics of Population Control," *Bulletin of the Atomic Scientists* (1964): 2–7.

Hodgson, D., "Demography as Social Science and Policy Science," in *Population and Development Review* 9, no. 1 (1983): 1–34.

Höhler, S., "The Law of Growth: How Ecology Accounted for World Population in the 20th Century," *Distinktion: Scandinavian Journal of Social Theory* 14 (2007): 45–64.

Holl, U., "'It's (Not) an Intervention!' Kybernetik und Anthropologie," in: *The Macy-Conferences 1946–1963. Essays and Documents*, C. Pias ed., vol. II (Zürich, 2004), 97–114.

Hörl, E., and Hagner, M., eds., *Die Transformation des Humanen: Beiträge zur Kulturgeschichte der Kybernetik* (Frankfurt am Main, 2008).

Hörl, E., and Hagner, M., "Überlegungen zur kybernetischen Transformation des Humanen," in *Die Transformation des Humanen: Beiträge zur Kulturgeschichte der Kybernetik*, E. Hörl and M. Hagner eds. (Frankfurt am Main, 2008), 7–37.

Hounshell, D.A., "The Cold War, RAND, and the Generation of Knowledge, 1946–1962," *Historical Studies in the Physical and Biological Sciences* 27, no. 2 (1997): 237–267.

Hughes, A.C., and Hughes, T.P., eds., *Systems, Experts, and Computers: The Systems Approach in Management and Engineering, World War II and After* (Cambridge, Mass., 2000).

Hull, M., "Democratic Technologies of Speech: From WWII America to Postcolonial Delhi," *Journal of Linguistic Anthropology* 20, no. 2 (2010): 257–282.

Isaac, J., and Bell, D., eds., *Uncertain Empire: American History and the Idea of the Cold War* (Oxford, 2012).

Jardini, D.R., "Out of the Blue Yonder: The Transfer of Systems Thinking from the Pentagon to the Great Society, 1961–1965," in *Systems, Experts, and Computers: The Systems Approach in Management and Engineering, World War II and After*, A.C. Hughes and T.P. Hughes eds. (Cambridge, Mass., 2000), 311–357.

Khan, M., "Population Control: A Two-Year Rural Action Experience," *Demography* 1, no. 1 (1964): 126–129.

Kantner, J.F., and Kantner, A., *International Discord on Population and Development* (New York, 2010).

Kaufmann, S., "Die Wissenstransformierung der 'counterinsurgency' im Vietnamkrieg," *Zeitschrift für Geschichte* 16 (2009): 37–52.

Klein, C., "Musicals and Modernization: Rodgers and Hammerstein's *The King and I*," in *Staging Growth: Modernization, Development, and the Global Cold War*, D.C. Engerman et al. eds. (Amherst, 2003), 129–162.

Kirk, D., Review of Robert C. Cook, *Human Fertility: The Modern Dilemma*, Population Studies 7, no. 1 (1953): 89–90.
Latham, M.E., *The Right Kind of Revolution: Modernization, Development, and U.S. Foreign Policy from the Cold War to the Present* (Ithaca, 2011).
Mamdani, M., *The Myth of Population Control: Family, Caste, and Class in an Indian Village* (New York, 1972).
Manderl, P., "Deconstructing 'Cold War Anthropology'," in *Uncertain Empire: American History and the Idea of the Cold War*, J. Isaac and D. Bell eds. (Oxford, 2012), 245–266.
Massey, D.S., and Sampson, R.J., "Moynihan Redux: Legacies and Lessons," Annals of the American Academy of Political and Social Science 621 (2009): 6–27.
McNeill, J.R., "The Environment, Environmentalism, and International Society in the Long 1970s," in *The Shock of the Global: The 1970s in Perspective*, N. Ferguson et al. eds. (Cambridge, Mass., 2010), 263–278.
Meadows, D.H., et al., *The Limits to Growth: A Report for the Club of Rome's Project on the Predicament of Mankind*, 3rd printing (London, 1975).
Medina, E., *Cybernetic Revolutionaries: Technology and Politics in Allende's Chile* (Cambridge, Mass., 2011).
Nader, L., "The Phantom Factor: Impact of the Cold War on Anthropology," in *The Cold War & The University: Toward an Intellectual History of the Postwar Years*, N. Chomsky et al. eds. (New York, 1997), 107–146.
Notestein, F.W., "The Population Council and the Demographic Crisis of the Less Developed World," Demography 5, no. 2 (1968): 553–560, 558.
Overath, P., ed., *Die vergangene Zukunft Europas: Bevölkerungsforschung und -prognosen im 20. und 21. Jahrhundert* (Köln, 2011).
Palmore, J.A., "Awareness Sources and Stages in the Adoption of Specific Contraceptives," Demography 5, no. 2 (1968): 960–972.
Peacock, A.T., "Theory of Population and Modern Economic Analysis I," Population Studies 6, no. 2 (1952): 114–122.
Petersen, W., "John Maynard Keynes's Theories of Population and the Concept of 'Optimum'," Population Studies 8, no. 3 (1955): 228–246.
Pias, C., ed., *Cybernetics—Kybernetik: The Macy-Conferences 1946–1953. Essays & Documents*, vol. II (Zürich, 2004).
Pias, C., "Zeit der Kybernetik—Eine Einstimmung," in *Cybernetics—Kybernetic: The Macy-Conferences 1946–1963. Essays and Documents*, C. Pias ed., vol. II (Zürich, 2004), 9–41.
Pircher, W., "Im Schatten der Kybernetik: Rückkopplung im operative Einsatz: 'operational research'," in *Die Transformation des Humanen: Beiträge zur Kulturgeschichte der Kybernetik*, E. Hörl and M. Hagner eds. (Frankfurt am Main, 2008), 348–376.
Poffenberger, T., "Motivational Aspects of Resistance to Family Planning in an Indian Village," Demography 5, no. 2 (1968): 757–766.
Raulet, H.M., "Family Planning and Population Control in Developing Countries," Demography 7, no. 2 (1970): 211–234.
Rav, Y., "Perspectives on the History of the Cybernetics Movement: The Path to Current Research through the Contributions of Norbert Wiener, Warren McCulloch, and John von Neumann," Cybernetics and Systems 33 (2002): 779–804.
Ravenholt, R.T., "The A.I.D. Population and Family Planning Program—Goals, Scope, and Progress," Demography 5, no. 2 (1968): 561–573.
Robin, R., *The Making of the Cold War Enemy: Culture and Politics in the Military-Intellectual Complex* (Princeton, 2001).
Schreiber, C., *Natürlich künstliche Befruchtung: Eine Geschichte der In-vitro-Fertilisation von 1878 bis 1950* (Göttingen, 2007).

Schüttelpelz, E., "To Whom It May Concern Messages," in *Cybernetics—Kybernetic: The Macy-Conferences 1946–1963. Essays and Documents*, C. Pias ed., vol. II (Zürich, 2004), 115–130.

Schumacher, E.F., *Small Is Beautiful: Economics as if People Mattered* (London, 1973).

Seefried, E., "Towards *The Limits to Growth*? The Book and its Reception in West Germany and Britain 1972–73," *German Historical Institute London Bulletin* 33, no. 1 (2011): 3–37.

Simpson, C., ed., *Universities and Empire: Money and Politics in the Social Sciences during the Cold War* (New York, 1998).

Smith, K., "Some Observations on Modern Malthusianism," *Population Studies* 6, no. 1 (1952): 92–105.

Szreter, S., "The Idea of Demographic Transition and the Study of Fertility Change: A Critical Intellectual History," *Population and Development Review* 19, no. 4 (1993): 659–701.

Taeuber, I.B., "Demographic Modernization: Continuities and Transitions," *Demography* 3, no. 1 (1966): 90–108.

Taylor, H.C., and Berelson, B., "Maternity Care and Family Planning as a World Program," *American Journal of Obstetrics and Gynecology* 100, no. 7 (1968): 885–893.

Van Beusekom, M.M., "From Underpopulation to Overpopulation: French Perceptions of Population, Environment, and Agricultural Development in French Soudan (Mali), 1900–1960," *Environmental History* 4, no. 2 (1999): 198–219.

Von Neumann, J., "Technological Prospects and Global Limits [1955]," *Population and Development Review* 12, no. 1 (1986): 117–126.

Von Neumann, J., and Morgenstern, O., *Theory of Games and Economic Behavior* (Princeton, 1944).

Wilder, F., and Tyagi, D.K., "India's New Departure in Mass Motivation for Fertility Control," *Demography* 5, no. 2 (1968): 773–779.

Winikoff, B., and Mensch, B., "Rethinking Postpartum Family Planning," *Studies in Family Planning* 22, no. 5 (1991): 294–307.

4

"OVERPOPULATION" AND THE POLITICS OF FAMILY PLANNING IN CHILE AND PERU

Negotiating National Interests and Global Paradigms in a Cold War World

Jadwiga E. Pieper Mooney

Demographic Discourses, New Technologies, and Population Politics after World War II

In the 1950s, when the first contraceptive pills were tested in Puerto Rico and the United States, demographers, economists, physicians, politicians, and the Catholic Church in the Americas began to discuss the unprecedented options of regulating human reproduction.[1] Some emphasized the revolutionary capability of new birth control technologies that would allow couples, and women, to regulate conception, and effectively control the number and spacing of their children. Others were quick to realize the latent potential of effective technologies that allowed new forms of population management.[2] Concerns over population dynamics, especially in the developing world, brought together representatives from private foundations, population researchers from universities, and officials from international agencies who set out to assist developing countries.[3] Individuals and institutions in the United States played a leading role in global population initiatives that took shape during the Cold War.

Some individuals, such as General William H. Draper, led key initiatives to secure funding for population activities by the United States and other countries, and by private institutions. Draper got interested in "population [questions] when President Eisenhower appointed me in 1958 as Chairman of his Committee on Foreign Aid, Military Aid and Economic Aid," and collected evidence to illustrate that population growth rates were interfering with economic development in most underdeveloped nations.[4] In the now-famous 1959 Draper Report, he asserted the need to reduce global rates of population growth and recommended U.S. government aid for the purpose of controlling population growth in the developing world. In 1965, Draper became a founding member of the Population Crisis Committee, and set out to increase public understanding of what he considered the dangers of the world population explosion.[5] He also convinced foreign governments to assist the International Planned Parenthood Federation (IPPF), and helped set up the United Nations' Population Fund.[6] In the same year, U.S. President Lyndon Johnson's public statement on population control illustrated the pervasive link many policy makers made between underdevelopment and alleged overpopulation: "less than five dollars invested in population control is worth a hundred dollars invested in economic growth."[7] Public campaigns and private foundations contributed a range of ideological incentives that helped justify growing population initiatives, all tied to the political tensions of the Cold War and to assumed threats that the poverty of developing nations might pose to their developed counterparts.

Physicians, scientists, and political leaders worldwide argued that dramatic population growth would increase underdevelopment and would become a source of political unrest and revolution. Pervasive information campaigns and advertisements in newspapers and magazines informed U.S. citizens about the threat of "hungry nations" filled with people who could ignite the "population bomb." The poor would "imperil" or "threaten the peace of the world" when their growing discontent erupted into social revolution, attacking the "civilized values" and the quality of life in the developing world.[8] Some feared a world overrun by "people dominated by Communism." Entrepreneur and sponsor of multiple population campaigns Hugh More explained that "we are not primarily interested in the sociological or humanitarian aspects of birth control," but are, instead, "interested in the use which Communists make of hungry people in their drive to conquer the earth."[9]

In the name of a "population threat," new initiatives by such groups as the Population Council, the Milbank Memorial Fund, and the Ford Foundation multiplied, all aimed at stabilizing population growth.[10] In 1964, John D. Rockefeller III, founder of the Population Council, emphasized the urgent need for political leaders in the West to address population problems that had become a key threat of the Cold War: "Until recently, I believed an even greater problem [than population growth] was the control of nuclear weapons. However, there is a justifiable hope that the use of these weapons can be prevented; but there is no hope that we can escape a tremendous growth in world population. Therefore it becomes a central task of our time to stabilize this growth soon enough to avoid its smothering consequences."[11] To protect international security and peace, Rockefeller also lobbied political leaders from around the world to support the "Statement on Population" that he presented to the UN secretary general in 1966. Heads of states should recognize the need to curb the dangers of overpopulation "as a principal element in long-range national planning," not only to advance goals of economic development, but also to help secure peace.[12]

Population initiatives, often proposed first in the United States, ranged from large-scale funding commitments for family planning programs, to the production and international distribution of information on the population threat, to research projects and individual campaigns that aimed at increasing the demographic effectiveness of family planning programs. Rockefeller maintained that couples should be able to decide the number and spacing of their children, and others, such as Kingsley Davis, supplied pioneering research results that exposed possible cultural inhibitions that might prevent poor populations from accepting family planning programs. In the end, population planners in the United States agreed that conditions conducive to fertility decline had to be created by all means necessary.[13] By 1968, the United States Agency for International Development (USAID) had become the largest single resource to support population control and family planning action in developing countries.[14] In Latin America, physicians and politicians contributed population studies and program initiatives of their own, and often adopted Neo-Malthusian demographic discourses to their specific national trajectories.

Doctors, Demographers, and Family Planning Initiatives in the 1960s

In Chile and Peru, medical doctors, frequently with close ties to the international medical establishment as grant recipients from the Rockefeller and/or Ford foundations and as practicing physicians trained in their home countries and in the United States, became pioneers in family planning program development—even if their justifications for such programs were worlds apart from each other. Among these doctors were researchers such as Jaime Zipper (Chile), who exemplified a medical elite engaged in clinical work, and those like Benjamin Viel (Chile) and José Donayre (Peru) who not only emphasized research but recognized the need to expand public health. Zipper gained fame in the international medical community for his invention of the "Zipper ring," an intrauterine device he developed and first tested on women in Chile.[15] Viel's publications on what he called a "demographic explosion" received international attention. And Latin American colleagues considered Donayre's work on population and altitude "essential . . . for understanding the relationship between socio-economic processes and demographic growth in Peru and Latin America."[16] These physicians were also closely connected to the international medical community through publications in medical journals and active participation in international conferences.

The ties among doctors from Chile, Peru, and other parts of the Americas were the result of their own initiatives, but they were also inspired through new opportunities to conduct demographic research and studies of contraceptive technology in such places as Santiago, Chile. By the mid-1960s, the Chilean capital had become a bustling center of population activities. Universities and research institutes offered seemingly endless opportunities for doctors, demographers, and global student-researcher-travelers who sought to advance their research at the Medical School and the School of Public Health of the University of Chile and, most prominently, at the Latin American Center for Demography (CELADE) under the auspices of the United Nations (UN).[17] Researchers could also work with the Latin American Center for Population and the Family (CELAP) that operated as part of the Latin American Center for Social and Economic Development (DESAL). Cooperation among the multiple institutions was manifold. Some doctors, like Mariano Requena, who focused on abortion research and worked with Viel in the field of preventive medicine, also staffed CELADE to improve the ties between doctors and demographers.[18]

The history and functioning of CELADE exemplifies the close connection between doctors and demographers in the Americas. Rising from the joint sponsorship of the UN and the Chilean government in 1957, the organization counted on ongoing international interest and support. By 1966, it was tied to the United Nations Development Program, and received financial support from the U.S. government through USAID as well as private monies from the Population Council and the Ford Foundation. Beginning in January 1968, CELADE's *Demographic Bulletin*, a journal of research results, was published semiannually and secured the global distribution of demographic information; CELADE also attracted an international body of researchers and students, who learned or perfected the principles of population studies. From its inception, an international governing board ran the organization, and members included such eminent population planners as Frank Notestein, a representative of the International Union for the Scientific Study of Population.[19] Notestein worked closely with Nelson Rockefeller, was one of the original trustees of the Population Council, and became its president in 1959.[20] These transnational relationships were often upheld by overlapping interests: Rockefeller, Notestein, and Chilean physicians like Viel, for example, agreed that the future of the region depended on policies that combined the decrease of maternal mortality with birth control and the promotion of economic development.

In Chile, the growing consensus about the need for family planning in the mid-1960s had its principal origins in two crises that doctors and policy makers sought to address: high maternal mortality rates due to self-induced abortions and uncontrolled population growth that threatened economic development.[21] In this context Chilean doctors adopted two parallel discourses and subsequent lines of action that justified a new approach to fertility regulation. They argued that effective family planning programs were needed to save the lives of those women who relied on self-induced abortions as the only method of birth control regulation available to them. Next, physicians and policy makers linked their efforts to prevent abortions and maternal mortality to global debates of "overpopulation," thereby securing the financial support of international agencies.[22]

Chilean physicians became the progenitors of new population initiatives when they began to speak about the desperate measures women took to limit the number of their children: self-induced abortion. Induced abortions and their deadly consequences were hardly a new phenomenon, but due to specific cultural and legal circumstances, physicians—and their female patients—addressed the abortion epidemic only reluctantly. Many Chileans viewed sexuality and contraception as intensely private matters, and women were reluctant to discuss topics such as unwanted pregnancies. Reproductive health specialist Bonnie Shepard explains the public silence on these issues in Chile through what she calls a "double discourse system" that maintains the status quo through repressive public policies while at the same time tolerating expanded sexual and reproductive choices behind the scenes. Rigid cultural norms perpetuate standards of a supposed proper sexual morality that needs to be upheld in the public sphere. Simultaneously, the system puts up with deviance from public norms as long as deviant acts remain private.[23] Accepting hidden violations of sexual norms, even if hypocritical, has been a useful strategy used to avoid the political costs of espousing a change in norms and traditions in Chile. But the same double-discourse system that allows secret "immoral" behaviors also prevents an honest dialogue on all matters of reproduction, including abortion.

Doctors and patients were part of a culture of silence on sexuality and reproduction that lasted well into the postwar period. Even women with access to resources and education found it difficult to learn about sex and secure access to contraceptive devices. In her memoir written for her daughter Paula, novelist Isabel Allende shared her reminiscences of the 1960s and her own coming of age. She recalled her first encounters with the need to make intimate decisions:

> I first heard the women in the office talking about a marvelous pill that would prevent pregnancy; it had revolutionized the cultures of Europe and the United States, they said, and was now available in a few local pharmacies. I investigated further and learned that one had to have a prescription to buy it. I did not dare go to the ineffable Dr. Benjamin Viel, who by then was the guru of family planning in Chile.[24]

Allende recalled how upper and middle class couples rarely talked about the details of sexual relationships: "in those days of collective hypocrisy the subject was taboo."[25] Women from wealthier families had access to private physicians and to family planning information that was unavailable to the poor, but many of them knew little about the mechanics of sex. Regardless of their class, many Chilean women learned to fear pregnancy.

In addition to the cultural constraints of addressing abortion, legal constraints contributed to the long silence on the subject. The illegal nature of induced abortion had long prevented clear documentation, as hospital statistics on abortions did not distinguish between spontaneous and provoked abortions, and provided no further information on the aborted pregnancies that could have contributed to more effective discussions of the subject early on.[26] Yet, physicians documented that self-induced abortion and maternal mortality had risen to epidemic proportions and needed to be addressed. In 1961, 4,000 interviews with women between twenty and forty-nine years of age revealed that one of every four women admitted to having had between one and thirty-five induced abortions.[27]

Doctors attempted to solve the problem by documenting not only the contexts in which women sought abortions, but also by showing that family planning programs would help reduce abortion and maternal mortality. In Santiago, medical researchers linked census data to mortality rates and to qualitative surveys on the personal histories of women in specific poor neighborhoods. They found that economic pressures, sexual abuse, anxiety about moral condemnations of children born out of wedlock, as well as the sheer inability to control pregnancies had forced many women to seek backstreet abortions, often without medical assistance.[28] Next, some doctors set up pilot projects to give lectures and distribute information on birth control. Others used the media to garner support. Popular journals, for example, published stories of female victims and the doctors who treated them. They quoted doctors who asserted that "the prevention of abortion is connected to the prevention of unwanted pregnancies via adequate education campaigns that inform women about the use of contraceptive technologies adapted to their cultural and economic realities."[29] The fieldwork studies of the 1960s, combined with women's testimonies, supplied evidence necessary to support the correlation between access to family planning devices, the prevention of unwanted pregnancies, and the decrease of self-induced abortions and their gruesome consequences. With this evidence in hand, physicians were prepared to take the steps necessary to alleviate this epidemic.

Although new and effective ways of data collection also drove Peruvian doctors' actions, population size and the "quality" of the population, rather than concerns over maternal mortality, dominated early debates.[30] In Peru, demographic discourses were long shaped by what some U.S. population planners saw as a "pervasive psychology of underpopulation." Many Peruvian doctors and demographers held that depopulation constituted not only one of the most detrimental colonial legacies, but also a major impediment to national development until well into the twentieth century.³¹ Historian Marcos Cueto shows that the physicians who founded the first medical school in the nineteenth century were driven by the desire to alleviate the alleged pressure of "underpopulation," which, in their view, prevented national development. They set out to improve public health and provide proper training for doctors whose contributions would bring down mortality rates, increase population growth and boost the progress of the nation. However, for decades, the reality of "underpopulation" remained doubtful at best, as population size was based on estimation, not on proper counting. More reliable census data could have been collected with the improved infrastructure after the turn of the century, but not everyone agreed to be counted. Many indigenous groups, for example, feared that census data would lead to increased taxation and control or abuse by the government.³²

For some Peruvians, such as urban intellectuals and physicians who sought to contribute to the nation's progress, indigenous culture represented a barrier to progress that needed to be removed.³³ Various doctors doubted that indigenous people could make positive contributions to national development, and hoped instead that European immigrants might bring about the progress they desired. Some found inspiration for this approach in countries like Argentina, where political leaders had applied the slogan "to govern is to populate," and where a massive wave of European immigrants amplified the size of the working class. Italians made up about half the population of Buenos Aires by the turn of the twentieth century, but European immigrants never came to Peru to the extent that some Peruvian leaders had hoped for. In this context, other doctors thought of a more beneficial "use" for indigenous populations by transforming them into "proper" citizens. Cueto documents that some Peruvian doctors adopted their own version of eugenics, and set out to overcome the alleged racial deficiencies of indigenous people through education, military service, and public health.³⁴

Peruvian doctors applied a eugenic dimension to population policies that was absent from debates on health and progress by Chilean doctors. Historian Nancy Stepan argues that Peruvians were not only active contributors to international debates on the subject in the nineteenth century, when the eugenics movement was widely popular in the Americas, but that they held on to their own brand of "social eugenics" longer than their counterparts in other countries in the region. This longevity can be explained by eugenicists' efforts to link proposed biological interventions to an improvement of the lives of poor people, thereby combining medical and socio-political projects. On the one hand, Peruvian doctors and eugenic advocates not only embraced the notion that the scientific engineering of marriages and reproduction would lead to racial improvement and national progress, but even went so far as to promote obligatory medical certificates for marriage.³⁵ On the other hand, they proposed to improve "racial" deficiencies and prevent such impediments to progress as criminal behavior through the education of the working classes, and by elevating their spirits through lectures, theater, and art.[36] This combination of "eugenic" interventions lasted well into the twentieth century, evident, for example, in the founding of the League of Mental Hygiene with its own eugenics department,[37] and in the connection drawn between public health and eugenics in discussions at professional conferences in 1939 and again in 1943.[38] Although Peruvian "social eugenics" was inspired by the demographics of the Peruvian population and the presence of large indigenous groups, Peruvian eugenicists often envisioned population engineering as a tool to improve living and working conditions, and not as an instrument for genetic change.[39]

In Chile, early supporters of "social hygiene," of public health, discussed pragmatic applications of eugenic concepts, focused primarily on the need to "improve" the urban poor, and occasionally addressed eugenics as pertinent to civilizing all citizens.[40] Some prominent Chileans defended the essential task of "civilizing" the poor to secure the "quality of the new generation" but government officials or social theorists did not focus on the alleged superiority of one race over another.[41] Even if most Chileans distinguished between indigenous and non-indigenous people, and even if the latter did not have the highest regard for the former, eugenicists did not emphasize the need to target indigenous populations.

One reason for the limited attention to indigenous populations as an impediment to progress may be found in the authentically Chilean discourse of *mestizaje* that originates in the heroic story of successful native (*Araucanian*) resistance to Spanish colonialism until well into the nineteenth century. In the first decades of the twentieth century, influential Chilean intellectuals such as Francisco Encina and Nicolás Palacios glorified Chile's supposed racial "primary material." Their celebration of what they presented as Chilean racial strengths was, at times, contradictory, and occasionally blamed the "racial composition" of the lower classes for the nation's economic problems. But these intellectuals nonetheless found ample praise for the alleged Araucanian contribution to what they referred to as racial stock, and as evidence of Chile's superior potential for economic progress and military strength.[42]

Another reason for the limited impact of eugenic concerns in Chile may be found in numbers. Statistics fail to reveal the complicated and changing conditions of who identifies as a member of an indigenous group, and when and why people are counted as Indian. It is hard to conclude just how many people actually claim indigenous descent in either Peru or Chile, yet the indigenous population is clearly significantly larger in the former than it is in the latter. Peru's indigenous population makes up about 35 to 40 percent of the national total.[43] In comparison, the entire indigenous population in Chile is estimated at 6.8 percent of the total population.[44]

Chile, Peru, and the United States: Agreements on the Dangers of "Overpopulation"

A close look at population initiatives by Chilean and Peruvian doctors reveals that they did not merely respond to global demographic paradigms, but actively participated in their construction. Chilean physician and pioneer of family planning Dr. Benjamin Viel published a series of much-acclaimed studies on what he called the "demographic explosion" in Latin America. He also made a case for family planning in his native Chile, where the population had more than doubled between 1920 and 1965. Santiago, the capital city, had increased five-fold in the same period as a result of a decrease in mortality rates and a concomitant increase in urban migration.[45] For Viel, the answer to women's individual—as well as familial and national—problems in Chile lay in family planning education and in ready access to a wide selection of contraceptive technologies. Peruvian doctors reacted to a dramatic population increase at just about the same time: according to census data from 1961, Peru's population increased from 6.6 million in 1940 to 10.2 million in just over twenty years.[46]

Medical doctor and demographer José Donayre, like Viel, addressed the pressures that growing populations would put on food supplies, and both shared the Neo-Malthusian vision of the post-World War II era.[47] Viel linked food shortages, urban poverty, crime, and alcoholism to the demographic explosion. Donayre combined demographic calculations with economic analysis, often negotiating the competing positions of those who saw population growth as an obstacle to development and of others who considered population increase as a force that would move the country ahead on the road to progress and economic development. He worked with the U.S.-based Population Council and the United Nations Fund for Population Activities (UNFPA) to assess population problems in the region and to identify effective family planning policies.[48] Numerous doctors and scientists from both countries also supplied additional evidence. All agreed that modernization depended on planning populations and families.[49]

In Chile, the new consensus about the need for birth control was reached when physicians linked two parallel discourses: the need to prevent maternal mortality due to self-induced abortions and the need to stimulate modernization and development by controlling family size. Medical doctors, involved in the national public health system, secured official support from the Health Ministry. As the first nationwide, official family planning programs set out to "protect the family," the Chilean Association for the Protection of the Family promoted birth control throughout the country. In Peru, the government did not sanction official national birth control programs in the 1960s, and doctors who worked on behalf of a population policy, such as José Donayre, neither found wide recognition for their efforts nor could they count on consensus at the state level.[50] Nonetheless,

Peruvian doctors adopted alternative strategies to implement wide-reaching family planning programs.

In light of the shared agreement on the many ill effects of uncontrolled population growth, Chile and Peru attracted international support and funding for both population research and action. In Santiago, CELADE expanded under the auspices of the United Nations and also trained international researchers throughout the Americas.[51] The Pan American Health Organization (PAHO) and the University of Chile also initiated a program in Research Training on Health and Population Dynamics, led by the School of Public Health of the Faculty of Medicine and funded by PAHO. Population studies undertaken at other universities and research centers confirmed just how pressing the subject of population politics had become.[52] In Peru, the government supported social scientists and medical doctors who established the Center for Population and Development Studies (CEPD), which was also sponsored by international organizations such as the Ford Foundation and the International Planned Parenthood Federation (IPPF). In 1964, Peruvian President Fernando Belaúnde supported the founding of the CEPD in the name of using population research to inform public policy. Set up to provide information, training, and research results with practical implications, the center worked in tandem with the Health Ministry's maternal and child health programs, and maintained, initially, a close relationship with the IPPF. It became a key player in the implementation of family planning programs in the nation. In short, existing relationships with individuals and institutions in the United States contributed to the growth of family planning initiatives in Chile and Peru. But physicians negotiated the implementation of programs in the context of different concepts and practices back home.[53]

The history of the CEPD and the profile of its leaders illustrate Peruvian doctors' new concern about rapid population growth in response to the 1960s census—and their successful efforts to enlist international support for program building that linked research to action.[54] Historian Raúl Necochea argues that the CEPD's early leaders were interested in research and policy design because they were of the opinion that a population problem could harm Peruvian development.[55] The center's first president was an economist by training, who had also supervised the improvement of census data collection in the nation. Dr. Donayre, the center's next director, also held the positions of consultant and later deputy chief of the Policy and Evaluation Division of the United Nations Fund for Population Activities in New York.[56] Donayre remained active at international conferences, and informed population planners about the center's approach to population and fertility issues that consisted of two parts: fertility surveys and pilot programs in family planning.[57]

CEPD staff assembled population data, led research projects on population and development, and also supported studies on the interpersonal dimensions of the communication of information about contraception. In the mid-1960s, for example, CEPD researchers conducted interviews with female patients of a private, non-profit family planning clinic in one of Lima's working class neighborhoods to help build profiles of those who were open to family planning programs. This and other studies on "opinion leadership" also sought to determine the influence family planning clinics had on people's decisions to use contraceptives, and, ultimately, sought to help increase the spread of information on and the acceptance of family planning programs.[58] Government support, as well as funds from international foundations and the U.S. Agency for International Development, also allowed the CEPD to set up family planning clinics, and to provide maternal and neonatal health care services.[59] While the CEPD also helped set up the short-lived Peruvian Association for the Protection for the Family (*Asociación Peruana de Protección Familiar*, APPF), it remained the most influential institution promoting family planning activities in the nation.[60] The CEPD, officially set up as a research institution with ties to the government and in support of child and maternal health projects, was less politically explosive than the APPF. In 1968, a military coup ousted President Belaúnde and General Juan Velasco Alvarado (1968–75), a nationalist reformer, implemented a regime of the armed forces that sought to end imperialist exploitation and to terminate U.S. involvement in Peruvian affairs.

Due to its official affiliation with the U.S.-based International Planned Parenthood Federation/Western Hemisphere Region (IPPF/WHR), the APPF became an early target of the new military government, which outlawed the institution in the name of defending national hegemony.[61] Velasco temporarily expelled the IPPF from Peru in 1974, and briefly detained the IPPF's local representative in Lima. CEPD kept a low profile, continued to operate with a focus on research projects, and remained actively involved in population questions from abroad, as its director, Donayre, accepted a position in the United States.[62]

While Peru's CEPD effectively used population data to promote a number of regional family planning programs, Chilean doctors used their understanding of specific domestic problems in conjunction with global connections to garner official government support for family planning programs. First, an advisory council of professionals from the medical schools of Santiago's major universities prepared research results to demonstrate the links between abortion, maternal mortality, and fertility regulation. Next, they transformed the council into the Comité Chileno de Protección de la Familia (the Chilean Committee for the Protection of the Family), an independent, private organization with corporate status under the chairmanship of a medical doctor. By 1965, seven family planning projects operated in Santiago, most directly connected to earlier fieldwork efforts to control abortion and decrease maternal mortality rates. Chilean doctors had secured ongoing financial and technical support from the Rockefeller and

Ford foundations as well as the U.S. Population Council.[63] The committee also negotiated an official affiliation with the IPPF/WHR.

Religion and the Protection of the Family: Planning Change in the Name of Tradition

Family planners at the highest level, meanwhile, feared that the role of the Catholic Church would undermine family planning initiatives and that religion would become one of the major impediments to family planning. For example, John D. Rockefeller III, after an audience with Pope Paul VI in July 1965, initiated a lively correspondence on population questions with the Pontiff, in which he underlined the Church's responsibility in this worldly matter. "A clear strong statement from you, from your great Church," writes Rockefeller, "would have tremendous impact in every home and every seat of government in every country where it was received. It would lift the problem of population out of politics and practical expediency and affirm it as a moral question with the welfare of the family as the principal consideration." Rockefeller went so far as to envision a solution to population problems as a result of a papal declaration in favor of family planning: "People the world over would be eternally grateful to you and the solution of the population problem would . . . be assured."[64]

The historical trajectory of family planning initiatives in Chile and Peru illustrates that the success of program implementation in both countries depended on a crucial historical juncture: programs were set in motion while the Church leadership was still debating the acceptability of artificial contraception, prior to the 1968 Papal encyclical *Humanae Vitae* that ultimately prohibited all forms of non-natural contraception. In the 1960s, priests, bishops, and laity were often influenced by the spirit of liberation theology, and by a new gospel that aimed at reconnecting the Church to its original mission of supporting the poor. The innovative spirit of the Second Vatican Council (1962–65) allowed for more flexibility in discussions regarding the topic of family planning. In 1964, Catholic clerics and laymen requested a review of the Church's traditional ban on any chemical or mechanical means of fertility regulation, an appeal they justified on the basis of modern scientific, social, and demographic evidence. Consequently, Pope Paul VI set up a commission of priests, scientists, and laymen "for the study of problems of birth."[65] The commission's decision was not quickly or easily reached. In March 1965, fifty-five members attended the fourth secret study session, and participants faithfully observed the secrecy and remained silent.

Long before Pope Paul VI's verdict appeared in 1968, priests in Chile and Peru reacted to the living conditions of poor families and justified their active support of family planning programs in the name of protecting mothers, children, and families. Priests who worked in Santiago's poor neighborhoods did not leave much written testimony on their position on birth control but often agreed to tolerate or support family planning in light of their everyday contacts. In the words of a young Chilean priest, "it is ... difficult to be too strict ... when you see how [poor people] live."[66] Bishops' comments reached the population through the popular media, confirming that "Church teaching would not replace personal awareness, which should be motivated by human moral sensibility." The journal *Ercilla* cited the bishops' conclusion: "It is therefore necessary that the individual Christian assumes, on this matter as well as on others, a mature position of personal responsibility, appropriate to human care."[67] The Chilean episcopate sanctioned individual decision making regarding a couple's use of birth control, in agreement with the options and challenges families faced.

A key 1967 document, the "Declaration of the Chilean Episcopate about Family Planning," highlights the unique juncture of Chilean national developments and the global discourse on population control.[68] The bishops introduced their position with a reference to the complexity of the "demographic problem" and conveyed the Church's willingness to find realistic solutions to the problem.[69] Referring to the Second Vatican Council, Chilean bishops acknowledged that solutions to rapid population growth should involve actions on the global level and in the family. Thereby, the declaration confirmed its tolerance for couples' personal decisions to use contraceptive devices. The Chilean episcopate expressed concern also about maternal mortality and articulated its willingness to support contraception as a lesser evil. Contraception could be justified as a possible solution to a more pressing moral and medical burden—abortion—for which contraception provided the only alternative. In circumstances in which a significant number of Chilean women were so strongly opposed to having more children that they were compelled to use a method likely to result in hospitalization or death, they argued that the prevention of abortion was not only a legitimate option but a responsibility that Catholic physicians, priests, and the majority of Chilean bishops would accept. As Cardinal Raúl Silva Henríquez of Santiago said in 1967, the position of the Church should not be considered "pro-natalist at all costs"; instead, it should advocate "responsible parenthood."[70]

Specific Chilean and Peruvian initiatives reveal that their appeal to family values and the need to protect the family augmented support for their programs. In Chile, an emblem that depicted mother, father, son, and daughter within a small triangle, became the guiding symbol of family planners.[71] In 1965, Chilean family planners renamed their first committee and inaugurated the *Asociación Chilena de Protección de la Familia* (APROFA, the Chilean Association for the Protection of the Family), which continued to operate as a private organization. In this manner, its leaders could strengthen their international ties and cooperate with the National Health Service (NHS) on the domestic level. The NHS continued to contribute material support and staff, yet APROFA's private status secured family planning programs under more independent leadership.[72] Financing from abroad, including IPPF subsidies, and ongoing funding by private institutions in the United States helped to equip clinics and expand family planning programs. APROFA became a full member of the IPPF/WHR and was granted "persona juridica" by the Chilean government in September 1966.[73]

Remarkably, doctors thereby inaugurated the first state-supported national family planning program in Chile under a government guided by Catholic social doctrine. President Eduardo Frei Montalva (1964–70), a Christian Democrat by political affiliation, endorsed the initiatives as a contribution to the well-being of women and families. Women used APROFA services, which were well connected through the network of the NHS and even advertised on radio and television programs.[74] By 1966, there were 102 family planning centers nationwide, and more than 58,000 women received contraceptives free of charge. By 1967, the government allocated funds to provide contraceptive services to an additional one hundred thousand women.[75] APROFA disseminated information on family planning and coordinated seminars and conferences with health educators, social workers, labor leaders, and volunteers. Its monthly newsletter *Boletín APROFA* was published at a circulation rate of about 4,000 and distributed in community hospitals throughout Chile. It continued to disseminate information on family planning in newspapers, radio stations, and television programs, documenting sixty-two printed articles, forty-three radio announcements, and two television programs. In Santiago, female volunteers led sixteen discussion groups composed of 450 members in poor neighborhoods.[76] APROFA became the single most active institution to promote family planning and to make birth control devices available to Chilean women.

In Peru, the programs founded by Catholic family planners preceded even the CEPD and fashioned an extraordinary alliance between doctors and the Catholic Church. Historian Raúl Necochea documents the years of cooperation between Catholics from the United States, priests of the order of the Sons of Mary and a Catholic physician, Joseph Kerrins, who first arrived in the early 1960s and helped institutionalize family planning programs under the auspices of the Church. Initially, priests with a first-hand knowledge of the misery in the poor neighborhoods of Lima distributed contraceptives to help families cope with the pressures of poverty. In this context, the protection of the family unit became central to their family planning initiatives. Too many children would pressure poor families and good parenting depended on the option to plan pregnancies and birth. Yet Kerrins and the Sons of Mary also added an educational component to the program, arguing that contraception alone would not suffice to secure healthy marriages and strong Catholic families. Necochea discusses the pragmatic and creative initiatives of priests who framed their promotion of contraception, mostly the contraceptive pill, within the language of "responsible parenting."[77] By avoiding any reference to birth control as individual right, priests supported the use of oral contraceptives as a way to ease the burdens of poor families.

The key to the success of these programs lay in the association between workshops on responsible parenthood and the distribution of information and contraceptive devices. From the perspective of program leaders, responsible parenthood was based on parents' ability to provide both material support and spiritual formation as they raised their children. In 1967, the residents of a poor Lima neighborhood, El Agustino, could attend the first free marriage workshops that put these theories into practice in a clinic set up by a doctor, a nurse, and a social worker; couples received education and free contraceptives upon request. The success of this model institutionalized effective Catholic family planning initiatives, or, in the words of Necochea, linked "Priests and Pills" to help defend the Catholic family.[78] The success of the first clinic attracted priests from other parishes, and in the same year at least four more clinics opened in poor neighborhoods of Peru's capital city. Family planning, now a "Project for Conjugal and Family Promotion in Peripheral Neighborhoods," received the support of the Cardinal and the Peruvian Christian Family Movement.[79] This endorsement was withdrawn or re-negotiated only when Kerrins, the founder and physician in charge, accepted funding from donors in the United States such as the Pathfinder Fund and the IPPF. The same resurgence of Peruvian nationalism that had already crippled other family planning programs that received foreign funding also impaired Catholic initiatives. Nonetheless, couples' participation in the project did not end with such nationalist attacks or with the *Humanae Vitae* as many people had accepted family planning as a part of their lives.

Studies of women's contraceptive practice in Chile and Peru only confirmed the conclusions drawn by demographers at the time; namely, that "the behavior of Catholic women toward [birth control] does not seem to be different from that of other women."[80] In Peru, researchers found that "of the women who reported their religion as Catholic and who were using contraceptives, 78 percent were using a method not approved of by their Church—that is, a method other than rhythm or various degrees of abstinence."[81] And in Chile, medical doctors found that "the behavior of Roman Catholics with respect to birth control was not different from that of non-Catholic women."[82] Indeed, religion was not a significant factor either in the decision to practice birth control or in the choice of method. Catholic and non-Catholic women alike had relied on methods ranging from the contraceptive pill and IUDs, to diaphragms and condoms, to sterilization.[83] When, in 1968, the papal Encyclical *Humanae Vitae* emphasized "that each and every marriage act (*'quilibet matrimonii usus'*) must remain open to the transmission of life," many Church officials and practicing Catholics were surprised about the rigid conservative position it claimed to defend, but couples, more often than not, held on to their reliance on family planning methods.[84]

Revisiting the Politics of Fertility Regulation: Old Realities and New Questions

In 1978, Jerry Weaver, social science analyst for the U.S. Department of State, noted that the political aspects of family planning became visible after the 1974 International Conference on Population in Bucharest, where some developing countries took an outspoken position in opposition to demographic visions of a Neo-Malthusian bent that promised to bring development through population control.[85] At the Bucharest conference, a coalition of developing nations rejected the official document that summarized the conference resolutions, the United Nations' Population Draft Plan of Action. Members of the coalition insisted that their countries' problems were caused not by "overpopulation," but by an unequal distribution of wealth among nations, caused in part by international terms of trade in favor of "First World" nations.[86] The Peruvian delegation that had travelled to Bucharest sided with the coalition and supported this position, an unsurprising move given the political priorities of the incumbent military regime. Clearly, the tensions in Bucharest prove what the history of the trajectory of family planning programs in Chile and Peru had shown early on: demographic discourses are shaped by global and national political competitions, and an apolitical history of family planning, or demographic discourses in a political vacuum, are simply non-existent.

These international connections promoted initiatives that helped some couples, or women, to plan and regulate pregnancies and birth. Yet international links could also bring new obstacles to family planning, when political leaders condemned the programs as "weapons of imperialism" and as a way to limit population size in developing countries.[87] In Peru, the nationalist-leftist regime of General Velasco Alvarado chose to condemn family planning programs in the name of exploitation and promoted pro-natalism as a new national policy. In Chile, later attacks of family planning programs were influenced by a different political trajectory: the government of President Salvador Allende (1970–73) condemned APROFA's international ties, and suspended IPPF funding of family planning. In 1973, when a military coup ousted Allende's leftist coalition government, family planning programs were cut not by the political left, but by a right-wing military that briefly emphasized pro-natalism and adopted a short-lived population policy in 1978.

The case studies of Chile and Peru establish the importance global demographic discourses have on policies within the nation state. As we compare and contrast Chilean and Peruvian family planning policies, we see processes of selective adoption by policy makers who negotiate international support for contraception in different political settings. Chilean physicians fashioned alliances with scientists, policy makers, and social engineers at home and abroad, and succeeded in institutionalizing fertility regulation as family planning and in spreading the civic respectability of birth control in the name of protecting the family. Many women did profit from gaining access to contraceptives, as made evident by the decline in abortion and maternal mortality rates. Peruvian doctors and demographers could not count on early institutionalized program development, but found ways to overcome political obstacles at the time. The Center of Population and Development Studies was supported by the government and maintained links to the Ministry of Health. It remained an autonomous institution, and thereby survived the attacks by pronatalist political leaders.[88]

Evidence from case studies in Peru and Chile illustrates that the notion of a regionally defined history of a "Latin American experience" with birth control and demography is misleading at best. Doctors and population specialists in Chile and Peru (and other Latin American countries) often had connections to the same international institutions, such as the Population Council, the Rockefeller Foundation, and universities in the United States. Yet, evidence of two distinct histories of family planning presented in this study illustrates that their reception and appropriation of demographic concepts and family planning practices depended on specific historical trajectories and on political negotiations situated in the contexts of nation states.

Acknowledgments

Excerpts are reprinted from *The Politics of Motherhood: Maternity and Women's Rights in Twentieth-Century Chile*, by Jadwiga E. Pieper Mooney, © 2009, by permission of the University of Pittsburgh Press.

Notes

1. See L. Marks, *Sexual Chemistry: A History of the Contraceptive Pill* (New Haven, 2001).
2. The new availability of the contraceptive pill fueled the controversy about the supposed meaning and purpose of fertility regulation, informed by references to women's obligations (to limit population size) as well as by references to rights (of women and couples to plan children). This tension is also expressed in differing choices of terminology. See, for example, D.T. Critchlow, "Birth Control, Population Control, and Family Planning: An Overview," *Journal of Policy History* 7, no. 1 (1995): 1–21.
3. For discussions of this subject, see Pan American Health Organization, *Meeting of the Advisory Committee on Medical Research, 4, Washington, D.C., 14–18 Jun. 1965: Report of the PAHO/WHO Conference on Population Dynamics* (Washington, D.C., 1965). For reference to specific research programs that also involved Chile and Peru, see Pan American Health Organization, *Meeting of the Advisory Committee on Medical Research, 5, Washington, D.C., 13–17 Jun. 1966: PAHO/WHO Research and Training Activities in Population Dynamics in Latin America* (Washington, D.C., 1966). For a specific example on such cooperation see J.O. Alers'

discussion of the Cornell Peru Project. J.O. Alers, "Population and Development in a Peruvian Community," *Journal of Inter-American Studies* 7, no. 4 (1965): 423–448.
4. http://www.trumanlibrary.org/oralhist/draperw.htm#transcript.
5. W.H. Draper, Jr., et al., "The Population Question," in *Composite Report of The President's Committee To Study the United States Military Assistance Program* (Washington, D.C., 1959), 94–96, 120.
6. P.T. Piotrow, *World Population Crisis: The United States Response* (New York, 1973). Piotrow was also Draper's secretary. See the insightful section on "the general" in M. Hvistendahl, *Unnatural Selection: Choosing Boys Over Girls, and the Consequences of a World Full of Men* (New York, 2011), 123–138.
7. President Lyndon B. Johnson, Speech to the United Nations, June 25, 1965.
8. See ads by the Campaign to Check the Population Explosion: "Hungry Nations Imperil the Peace of the World," *New York Times*, February 23, 1969, sec. IV, 5; and "The Population Bomb Threatens the Peace of the World," *New York Times*, February 9, 1969, sec. IV, 5.
9. As cited by M. Connelly, "The Cold War in the *longue durée*: Global Migration, Public Health, and Population Control," in *The Cambridge History of the Cold War*, vol. 3, M.P. Leffler and O.A. Westad eds. (Cambridge, 2010), 478. For references to the "communist threat" and its frequent link to the "threat" of overpopulation, see also the open letter to President Johnson, sponsored by the Hugh Moore Fund, in *New York Times*, December 13, 1964, sec. IV, 5.
10. F. Notestein, "The Population Council and the Demographic Crisis of the Less Developed World," *Demography* 5, no. 2 (1968): 553–560.
11. S.J. Segal, "Introductory Remarks," in *Intra-Uterine Contraception, Proceedings of the Second International Conference, October 2–3, 1964, New York City*, Population Council and S.J. Segal eds. (Amsterdam, 1965), 1.
12. See copy of the *United Nations World Leaders' Statement on Population*, John D. Rockefeller 3rd Papers, Sub-series 4, Population Interests, 1965–(1970–1978), Folder 513, RFA, Rockefeller Archive Center (RAC).
13. K. Davis, "Population Policy: Will Current Programs Succeed?" *Science* 158, no. 3802 (1967): 730–739.
14. According to some sources, A.I.D. donations increased from $2.1 million in 1965 to $34.7 million in 1968. R.T. Ravenholt, "The A.I.D. Population and Family Planning Program—Goals, Scope, and Progress," *Demography* 5, no. 2 (1968): 561–573.
15. J. Zipper, M.L. Garcia, and L.L. Pastene, "Intra-Uterine Contraception with the Use of a Flexible Nylon Ring: Experience in Santiago de Chile," *Intra-Uterine Contraception; Proceedings of the Second International Conference, October 2–3, 1964, New York City*, Population Council and S.J. Segal eds. (Amsterdam, 1965), 88.
16. These comments referred to the work of Donayre and others on population and altitude; see L.A. Sobrevilla, J. Donayre Valle, F. Moncloa, R. Guerra Garcia, *Población y Altitud* (Lima, 1965), as cited in Instituto Latinoamericano de Relaciones Internacionales, *Aportes* (Paris, 1970), 72.
17. CELADE continued to attract international researchers from the Americas; three-fourths of the demographic studies were led by international organizations present in Chile. For details, see M. Errázuriz, *El tratamiento del problema de población en la producción de los científicos sociales en Chile, 1958–1972* (Santiago de Chile, 1974).
18. For a list of Chilean institutions and references to funding see Lubin to Lamontagne, Background submitted to John D. Rockefeller III, October 5, 1966; Folder 821, IPPF Communication; John D. Rockefeller 3rd Papers, RG5, Series 3, Box 100, Rockefeller Foundation Archives, RAC. Excerpts on Chile are reprinted from *The Politics of Motherhood: Maternity and Women's Rights in Twentieth-Century Chile*, by Jadwiga E. Pieper Mooney, © 2009, by permission of the University of Pittsburgh Press.

19. Elizaga to Remiche, "Report on CELADE Activities," August 9, 1968. Folder: FC-Chile 67–68 CELADE; Population Council, Accession II, unprocessed material, Box 6. Rockefeller Foundation Archives, RAC. The International Union for the Scientific Study of Population was originally founded in 1928 and set up again in 1947 to promote research on demography and population-related issues by international professionals and scientists. For more information on the history of the Union, also see M. Labbé's chapter in this volume.
20. See "Frank W. Notestein," in A.J. Coale, *Ansley J. Coale: An Autobiography* (Philadelphia, 2000), 14–20.
21. For a general introduction to the history of fertility regulation in Chile, see X. Jiles Moreno and C. Rojas Mira, *De la miel a los implantes: historia de las políticas de regulación de la fecundidad en Chile* (Santiago de Chile, 1992).
22. For a detailed analysis of this process, and for an analysis of the politics of family planning in Chile, see J.E. Pieper Mooney, *The Politics of Motherhood: Maternity and Women's Rights in Twentieth-Century Chile* (Pittsburgh, 2009).
23. B. Shepard, "The 'Double Discourse' on Sexuality and Reproductive Rights in Latin America: The Chasm between Public Policy and Private Actions," in *Perspectives on Health and Human Rights*, S. Gruskin et al. eds. (New York, 2005), 247–271.
24. I. Allende and M.S. Peden, *Paula* (New York, 1995), 100.
25. Allende and Peden, *Paula*, 102.
26. Due to the illegal nature of abortion and due to some difficulty with identifying self-induced abortion, data on abortions in public hospitals provided few details about the circumstances under which abortions took place. Abortion remained a criminal offense under the Chilean Penal Code of 1874, and even as therapeutic abortion remained legal in Chile between 1931 and 1989, only a small number of health officials considered the economic hardships or personal misery of individual women faced with unwanted pregnancy. See F. Klimpel, "El aborto en la legislación chilena," in F. Klimpel, *La mujer, el delito y la sociedad* (Buenos Aires, 1946), 232. Therapeutic abortion was legalized under the Health Code of 1931; physicians could provide abortions without criminal penalties to save the woman's life, to prevent the birth of an infant with birth defects, and if pregnancies had been the outcome of rape or incest.
27. Rolando Armijo referred to up to thirty-five abortions at the IPPF Conference in Santiago. See International Planned Parenthood Federation, and R.K.B. Hankinson, *Proceedings of the Eighth International Conference of the International Planned Parenthood Federation, Santiago, Chile, 9–15 April, 1967* (London, 1967), 143. For more data provided by the first influential epidemiological studies on abortion, see R. Armijo and T. Monreal, "Epidemiology of Provoked Abortion in Santiago, Chile," in *Population Dynamics: International Action and Training Programmes*, M. Muramatsu and P.A. Harper eds. (Baltimore, 1965), 137–160; M. Requena, "Condiciones determinantes del aborto inducido," *Revista Médica de Chile* 94 (1966), 714–722.
28. H. Romero, E. Medina, and J. Vildósola, "Aportes al conocimiento de la procreación," *Revista chilena de higiene y medicina preventiva* 15, no 3–4, (1953): 73–90. For women's explanations of why they had abortions, see ibid., 77.
29. March 27, 1963. *Ercilla* (1453), 17.
30. Chilean studies of abortion also inspired a new treatment of the problem in Peru—and, indeed, self-induced abortion was studied in the 1960s. But the topic did not receive the same degree of attention in Peru as it did in Chile. See M.-F. Hall, "Birth Control in Lima, Peru: Attitudes and Practices," *The Milbank Memorial Fund Quarterly* 43, no. 4 (1965): 409–438; and M.-F. Hall, "Planning in Lima, Peru," *The Milbank Memorial Fund Quarterly* 43, no. 4 (1965): 100–116.
31. R. Clinton, "Opposition to Population Limitation in Latin America," in *Research in the Politics of Population*, R. Clinton, and R.K. Godwin eds. (Lexington, Mass., 1972), 99–100.

32. M. Cueto, "La vocación por volver a empezar: las políticas de población en el Perú," *Revista Peruana de Medicina Experimental y Salud Publica* 23, no. 2 (2006): 123–131. For information about the complexities of racial classification and the impact ideological commitments had on scientific practice in Peru, see R. Necochea López, "Demographic Knowledge and Nation-Building: The Peruvian Census of 1940," *Berichte zur Wissenschaftsgeschichte* 33, no. 3 (2010): 280–296.
33. For references to the efforts of white urban intellectuals who sought to civilize indigenous populations through education, see F. Wilson, "Indians and Mestizos: Identity and Urban Popular Culture in Andean Peru," *Journal of Southern African Studies* 26, no. 2 (2000), 244; Wilson also discusses the complex and shifting racial categories that marked Peruvian society.
34. W. Mendoza and O. Martinez, "Las ideas eugenésicas en la creación del Instituto de Medicina Social," *An Fac Med* 60, no. 1 (1999): 55–60, as cited in Cueto, *La vocación*, 130.
35. Such certificates were supposedly required in Peru in the 1930s, but given that certificates could easily be falsified, many considered this legal requirement a farce. N. Stepan, *The Hour of Eugenics: Race, Gender, and Nation in Latin America* (Ithaca, 1991), 125, note 54.
36. Carlos Aguirre makes this link to the prevention of criminal behavior in C. Aguirre, *The Criminals of Lima and Their Worlds: The Prison Experience, 1850–1935* (Durham, 2005), 58. For an outstanding discussion of the complex politics of race in Peru, see the histories of the ideologies of *mestizaje* and *indigenismo* in M. de la Cadena, *Indigenous Mestizos: The Politics of Race and Culture in Cuzco, Peru, 1919–1991* (Durham, 2000).
37. Stepan, *The Hour of Eugenics*, 50, note 33.
38. Ibid., 61.
39. A. Lavrin, *Women, Feminism, and Social Change in Argentina, Chile, and Uruguay, 1890–1940* (Lincoln, 1995), 165.
40. Ibid., 165.
41. L. Fiol-Matta, *A Queer Mother for the Nation: The State and Gabriela Mistral* (Minneapolis, 2002), 12–19.
42. For details, see the discussion by T. Miller Klubock, "Nationalism, Race and the Politics of Imperialism: Workers and North American Capital in the Chilean Copper Industry," in *Reclaiming the Political in Latin American History: Essays from the North*, G.M. Joseph ed. (Durham, 2001), 236–238. See also N. Palacios, *Raza chilena: Libro escrito por un chileno y para los chilenos* (Santiago de Chile, 1918); and F.A. Encina, *Nuestra inferioridad económica, sus causas, sus consecuencias* (Santiago de Chile, 1955).
43. D.J. Yashar, *Contesting Citizenship in Latin America: The Rise of Indigenous Movements and the Postliberal Challenge* (Cambridge, 2005), 225–226.
44. M. Sznajder, "Ethnodevelopment and Democratic Consolidation in Chile: The Mapuche Question," in *Contemporary Indigenous Movements in Latin America*, E.D. Langer and Elena Muñoz eds. (Wilmington, 2003), 17–34.
45. See, for example, B. Viel, "Family Planning in Chile," *The Journal of Sex Research* 3, no. 4 (1967): 284–291; B. Viel, "The Population Explosion in Latin America," *Proceedings of the Academy of Political Science* 30, no. 4 (1972): 42–49; and B. Viel, *La explosión demográfica. Cuantos son demasiados?* (Santiago, 1966).
46. See M. Cueto, *La vocación*, 123–133, for detailed references to the data and the impact it had on population planners in Peru. Starting in the post World War II period, Peruvians documented population pressures that were allegedly hard to handle. Cueto documents that census data was believed to be more reliable than ever, and that population growth was reflected not only in an increase of birth, but evident also in problems as a result of migration. Between 1940 and 1961, for example, the population increased from 7.1 million to 10.3 million, and between 1961 and 1971, it reached the peak of just over 14.1 million inhabitants. Migration from the

countryside to the city exposed the shortcomings of services and the lacking infrastructure evident, for example, in housing and health services.
47. J. Donayre, *Demografía, planificación y desarrollo* (Lima, 1970).
48. J. Donayre, *Peru* (New York, 1973).
49. For Viel, the main health problem in Chile remained accelerated population growth. See Viel to Weir, December 20, 1966, Folder: International Planned Parenthood Federation, 1971, Family Planning; RF, 100A, RFA, RAC.
50. R.L. Clinton, "The Policy Climate for Population Policy in Peru," *Paper Prepared for delivery at the 2000 meeting of the Latin American Studies Association, March 16–18, 2000, Hyatt Regency Miami*, 2000, 11.
51. For a detailed list of Chilean institutions and for references to funding, see Lubin to Lamontagne, Background submitted to John D. Rockefeller III, October 5, 1966; Folder 821, IPPF Communication; John D. Rockefeller 3rd Papers, RG5, Series 3, Box 100, RFA, RAC.
52. Pan American Health Organization. 1966. *Advisory Committee on Medical Research. Fifth Meeting. Washington. D.C. 13–17 June 1966* (Washington, D.C., 1966). Also available at http://hist.library.paho.org/English/ACHR/RES5_14.pdf.
53. For discussion of the CEPD, see R. Necochea, "La Asociación Peruana De Protección Familiar Y Los Inicios De La Anticoncepción En El Perú (1967–1975)," *Histórica* 33, no. 1 (2009): 102–123; and R. Necochea, "Priests and Pills: Catholic Family Planning in Peru, 1967–1976," *Latin American Research Review* 43, no. 2 (2008): 41–48.
54. B.S. Bradshaw, "Fertility Differences in Peru: A Reconsideration," *Population Studies* 23, no. 1 (1969): 5–19.
55. See Necochea, *La Asociación Peruana*, 102–123; and Necochea, *Priests and Pills*, 41–48.
56. J. Saunders, J.M. Davis and D.M. Monsees, "Opinion Leadership in Family Planning," *Journal of Health and Social Behavior* 15, no. 3 (1974), 217.
57. For insights on the Center's mission and activities, see J. Donayre and C.F. Westoff, "Research Planned by the Center of Studies of Population and Development in Peru," *The Milbank Memorial Fund Quarterly* 46, no. 3 (1968), Part 2, Proceedings of the Forty-Second Conference of the Milbank Memorial Fund. New York City, October 17–19, 1967, 155–166.
58. J. Saunders, J.M. Davis and D.M. Monsees, "Opinion Leadership in Family Planning," *Journal of Health and Social Behavior* 15 (1974): 217–227.
59. J. Donayre, "Población y Revolución," *Acta Herediana* 6, no. 1–2 (1970), 5–7, as cited in Necochea, *Priests and Pills*, 41.
60. Bradshaw, "Fertility Differences."
61. Ministry of Health Resolution 000293-73-SA/DS, *Diario Oficial El Peruano*, December 20, 1973, as referenced in R. Necochea, *Priests and Pills*, 41.
62. Cueto, "La vocación," 126.
63. According to documentation by the Rockefeller Foundation, these projects included the "Viel-Requena show in the Western Health Region, the Faúndes operation in the Southern Region, the Avendaño-Zipper group at the Barros Luco, two units at the Hospital Aguirre under the obstetrician Professor Puga and the gynecologist Professor Wood; and two further units in the Central Region, one under Professor García, and one at the School of Public Health under Dr. Plaza and Professor Adriasola." See JZM (John Maier) Trip Diary, March 16–19, 1965; RF A76 309A Folder: University of Chile Family Planning 1965 (excerpt, no page number). Unprocessed. RFA, RAC. The Rockefeller and Ford Foundations, as well as the Population Council, provided significant technical and financial support for these initiatives.
64. John D. Rockefeller 3rd to His Holiness Pope Paul VI, July 16, 1965, John D. Rockefeller 3rd Papers, Folder 511, Box 74, RG 5, Series 3, RFA, RAC.
65. "Pope Asks Ruling on Birth Control," *New York Times*, March 30, 1965, 1, 6.

66. As cited in L. Gross, *The Last, Best Hope: Eduardo Frei & Chilean Democracy* (New York, 1967), 169. In various Santiago neighborhoods, priests had encouraged birth control in response to the problem of abortion and maternal mortality. See Dr. Benjamín Viel, interview with the author, December 1996.
67. "Para Católicos: Un problema de conciencia," *Ercilla*, April 12, 1967, no. 1662, 8.
68. "Declaración del Episcopado Chileno sobre la Planificación de la Familia," *Mensaje* 16, June 1967, no. 159, 256–262.
69. Previous studies concerned with excessive population growth encouraged the Church to address the population problem. See, for example, L. Leñero Otero, *Población, iglesia y cultura: Sistemas en conflicto* (Mexico, 1970).
70. Cardinal Raúl Silva Henríquez, "La Iglesia y la Regulación de la Natalidad: Palabras del Exmo. Sr. Cardenal Raúl Silva H. en la Academia de San Lucas de Santiago, Junio de 1967," *Mensaje* 16, August 1967, no. 161, 362.
71. "La Planificación familiar en los dibujos animados," *Boletín APROFA* 4, August 1968, no. 8, 1.
72. The NHS provided support without managing the family planning programs. See J. Rosselot, "Regulación de la Natalidad en el Servicio Nacional de Salud de Chile," *Cuadernos Médico-Sociales* 7, no. 2 (1966): 16–22.
73. APROFA became a "full member" of the IPPF/WHR in and was granted *persona jurídica* by the government by Decree No. 2194, on September 5, 1966. See O. Avendaño, *Desarrollo Histórico de la Planificación de la Familia en Chile y en el Mundo* (Santiago, 1975), 13–14.
74. "Control de la natalidad: Tema del día," *Boletín APROFA* 2, no. 3 (March 1966): 1.
75. International Planned Parenthood Federation and Hankinson, *Proceedings of the Eighth International Conference of the International Planned Parenthood Federation, Santiago, Chile, 9–15 April, 1967*, 181.
76. "Chile: Chilean Association for Family Welfare," Folder: International Planned Parenthood Federation, Family Planning 1969–70, RF, A76, 100A, 8–9, RFA, RAC.
77. Necochea, *Priests and Pills*, 1.
78. Ibid., 34–56.
79. Ibid., 34–56.
80. C. Miró, "Some Misconceptions Disproved," in: *Family Planning and Population Programs: A Review of World Developments*, International Conference on Family Planning Programs and Bernard Berelson eds. (Chicago, 1966), 33–34.
81. M.-F. Hall, "Birth Control in Lima, Peru," Part 1: 427.
82. This has also been observed in research studies of induced abortion. See M. Requena, "Epidemiology of Induced Abortion in Santiago, Chile," *Demography* 2 (1965): 33–49.
83. In 1968, Josefina Losada de Masjuan's fieldwork study on women's contraceptive practice in poor Santiago neighborhoods affirmed that "religion is not a decision-making factor in reference to contraceptive use." J. Losada de Masjuan, *Comportamientos anticonceptivos en la familia marginal* (Santiago de Chile, 1968), 42.
84. G. Jones and D. Nortman, "Roman Catholic Fertility and Family Planning: A Comparative Review of the Research Literature," *Studies in Family Planning* 1, no. 34 (1968): 2.
85. J.L. Weaver, "The Politics of Latin American Family-Planning Policy," *The Journal of Developing Areas* 12, no. 4 (1978): 415–437.
86. J.L. Finkle and B.B. Crane, "The Politics of Bucharest: Population, Development, and the New International Economic Order," *Population and Development Review* 1, no. 1 (1975): 87–114.
87. J. Consuegra, "Birth Control as a Weapon of Imperialism," in *The Dynamics of Population Policy in Latin America*, T.L. McCoy ed. (Cambridge, Mass., 1975), 163–181.
88. For evidence of absence of early state-led family planning program in Peru, see also G. Angeles, D.K. Guilkey and T.A. Mroz, "The Determinants of Fertility in Rural Peru: Program Effects in

the Early Years of the National Family Planning Program," *Journal of Population Economics* 18, no. 2 (2005): 367–389; and J.N. Gribble, S. Sharma and E.P. Menotti, "Family Planning Policies and Their Impacts on the Poor: Peru's Experience," *International Family Planning Perspectives* 33, no. 4 (2007): 176–181.

Bibliography

Aguirre, C., *The Criminals of Lima and Their Worlds: The Prison Experience, 1850–1935* (Durham, 2005).
Alers, J.O., "Population and Development in a Peruvian Community," *Journal of Inter-American Studies* 7, no. 4 (1965): 423–448.
Allende, I., and Peden, M.S., *Paula* (New York, 1995).
Angeles, G., Guilkey, D.K., and Mroz, T.A., "The Determinants of Fertility in Rural Peru: Program Effects in the Early Years of the National Family Planning Program," *Journal of Population Economics* 18, no. 2 (2005): 367–389.
Armijo, R., and Monreal, T., "Epidemiology of Provoked Abortion in Santiago, Chile," in *Population Dynamics: International Action and Training Programmes*, M. Muramatsu and P.A. Harper eds. (Baltimore, 1965), 137–160.
Avendaño, O., *Desarrollo Histórico de la Planificación de la Familia en Chile y en el Mundo* (Santiago, 1975).
Bradshaw, B.S., "Fertility Differences in Peru: A Reconsideration," *Population Studies* 23, no. 1 (1969): 5–19.
Clinton, C.L., "The Policy Climate for Population Policy in Peru," *Paper Prepared for delivery at the 2000 meeting of the Latin American Studies Association, March 16–18, 2000, Hyatt Regency Miami*, 2000.
Clinton, R., "Opposition to Population Limitation in Latin America," in *Research in the Politics of Population*, R. Clinton and R.K. Godwin eds. (Lexington, Mass., 1972).
Cole, A.J., *Ansley J. Coale: An Autobiography* (Philadelphia, 2000).
Connelly, M., "The Cold War in the *longue durée*: Global Migration, Public health, and Population Control," in *The Cambridge History of the Cold War*, vol. 3, M.P. Leffler and O.A. Westad eds. (Cambridge, 2010).
Consuegra, J., *"Birth Control as a Weapon of Imperialism,"* in *The Dynamics of Population Policy in Latin America*, T.L. McCoy ed. (Cambridge, Mass., 1975), 163–181.
Critchlow, D.T., "Birth Control, Population Control, and Family Planning: An Overview," *Journal of Policy History* 7, no. 1 (1995): 1–21.
Cueto, M., "La vocación por volver a empezar: las políticas de población en el Perú," *Revista Peruana de Medicina Experimental y Salud Publica* 23, no. 2 (2006): 123–131.
Davis, K., "Population Policy: Will Current Programs Succeed?" *Science* 158, no. 3802 (1967): 730–739.
De la Cadena, M., *Indigenous Mestizos: The Politics of Race and Culture in Cuzco, Peru, 1919–1991* (Durham, NC, 2000).
Donayre, J., *Demografía, planificación y desarrollo* (Lima, 1970).
Donayre, J., *Peru* (New York, 1973).
Donayre, J., "Población y Revolución," *Acta Herediana* 6, no. 1-2 (1970): 5–7.
Donayre, J., and Westoff, C.F., "Research Planned by the Center of Studies of Population and Development in Peru," *The Milbank Memorial Fund Quarterly* 46, no. 3 (1968), Part 2, Proceedings of the Forty-Second Conference of the Milbank Memorial Fund, New York City, October 17–19, 1967, 155–166.

Draper, W.H. Jr., et al., "The Population Question," in *Composite Report of The President's Committee To Study the United States Military Assistance Program* (Washington, D.C., 1959).

Encina, F.A., *Nuestra inferioridad económica, sus causas, sus consecuencias* (Santiago de Chile, 1955).

Errázuriz, M., *El tratamiento del problema de población en la producción de los científicos sociales en Chile, 1958–1972* (Santiago de Chile, 1974).

Finkle, J.L., and Crane, B.B., "The Politics of Bucharest: Population, Development, and the New International Economic Order," *Population and Development Review* 1, no. 1 (1975): 87–114.

Fiol-Matta, L., *A Queer Mother for the Nation: The State and Gabriela Mistral* (Minneapolis, 2002).

Gribble, N., Sharma, S., and Menotti, E.P., "Family Planning Policies and Their Impacts on the Poor: Peru's Experience," *International Family Planning Perspectives* 33, no. 4 (2007): 176–181.

Gross, L., *The Last, Best Hope: Eduardo Frei & Chilean Democracy* (New York, 1967).

Hall, M.-F., "Birth Control in Lima, Peru: Attitudes and Practices," *The Milbank Memorial Fund Quarterly* 43, no. 4 (1965): 409–438.

Hall, M.-F., "Planning in Lima, Peru," *The Milbank Memorial Fund Quarterly* 43, no. 4 (1965): 100–116.

Hvistendahl, M., *Unnatural Selection: Choosing Boys Over Girls, and the Consequences of a World Full of Men* (New York, 2011).

International Planned Parenthood Federation, and R.K.B. Hankinson, *Proceedings of the Eighth International Conference of the International Planned Parenthood Federation, Santiago, Chile, 9–15 April, 1967* (London, 1967).

Jiles Moreno, X., and Rojas Mira, C., *De la miel a los implantes: historia de las políticas de regulación de la fecundidad en Chile* (Santiago de Chile, 1992).

Jones, G., and Nortman, D., "Roman Catholic Fertility and Family Planning: A Comparative Review of the Research Literature," *Studies in Family Planning* 1, no. 34 (1968): 2.

Klimpel, F., "El aborto en la legislación chilena," in F. Klimpel, *La mujer, el delito y la sociedad* (Buenos Aires, 1946).

Klubock, T.M., "Nationalism, Race and the Politics of Imperialism: Workers and North American Capital in the Chilean Copper Industry," in *Reclaiming the Political in Latin American History: Essays from the North*, G.M. Joseph ed. (Durham, 2001), 236–238.

Lavrin, A., *Women, Feminism, and Social Change in Argentina, Chile, and Uruguay, 1890–1940* (Lincoln, 1995).

Leñero Otero, L., *Poblacíon, iglesia y cultura: Sistemas en conflicto* (Mexico, 1970).

Losada de Masjuan, J., *Comportamientos anticonceptivos en la familia marginal* (Santiago de Chile, 1968).

Marks, L., *Sexual Chemistry: A History of the Contraceptive Pill* (New Haven, 2001).

Mendoza, W., and Martinez, O., "Las ideas eugenésicas en la creación del Instituto de Medicina Social," *An Fac Med* 60, no. 1 (1999): 55–60.

Miró, C., "Some Misconceptions Disproved," in: *Family Planning and Population Programs: A Review of World Developments*, International Conference on Family Planning Programs and Bernard Berelson eds. (Chicago, 1966), 33–34.

Necochea, R., "Demographic Knowledge and Nation-Building: The Peruvian Census of 1940," *Berichte zur Wissenschaftsgeschichte* 33, no. 3 (2010): 280–296.

Necochea, R., "La Asociación Peruana De Protección Familiar Y Los Inicios De La Anticoncepción En El Perú (1967-1975)," *Histórica* 33, no. 1 (2009): 102–123.

Necochea, R., "Priests and Pills: Catholic Family Planning in Peru, 1967–1976," *Latin American Research Review* 43, no. 2 (2008): 41–48.

Notestein, F., "The Population Council and the Demographic Crisis of the Less Developed World," *Demography* 5, no. 2 (1968): 553–560.

Palacios, N., *Raza chilena: Libro escrito por un chileno y para los chilenos* (Santiago de Chile, 1918).
Pan American Health Organization, *Advisory Committee on Medical Research. Fifth Meeting. Washington. D.C. 13–17 June 1966* (Washington, D.C., 1966).
Pan American Health Organization, *Meeting of the Advisory Committee on Medical Research, 4, Washington, D.C, 14–18 Jun. 1965: Report of the PAHO/WHO Conference on Population Dynamics* (Washington, D.C, 1965).
Pan American Health Organization, *Meeting of the Advisory Committee on Medical Research, 5, Washington, D.C, 13–17 Jun. 1966: PAHO/WHO Research and Training Activities in Population Dynamics in Latin America* (Washington, D.C., 1966).
Pieper Mooney, J.E., *The Politics of Motherhood: Maternity and Women's Rights in Twentieth-Century Chile* (Pittsburgh, 2009).
Piotrow, P.T., *World Population Crisis: The United States Response* (New York, 1973).
Ravenholt, R.T., "The A.I.D. Population and Family Planning Program—Goals, Scope, and Progress," *Demography* 5, no. 2 (1968): 561–573.
Requena, M., "Condiciones determinantes del aborto inducido," *Revista Médica de Chile* 94 (1966), 714–722.
Requena, M., "Epidemiology of Induced Abortion in Santiago, Chile," *Demography* 2 (1965): 33–49.
Romero, H., Medina, E., and Vildósola, J., "Aportes al conocimiento de la procreación," *Revista chilena de higiene y medicina preventiva* 15, no. 3–4, (1953): 73–90.
Rosselot, J., "Regulación de la Natalidad en el Servicio Nacional de Salud de Chile," *Cuadernos Médico-Sociales* 7, no. 2 (1966): 16–22.
Saunders, J., Davis, J.M., and Monsees, D.M., "Opinion Leadership in Family Planning," *Journal of Health and Social Behavior* 15, no. 3 (1974): 217–227.
Segal, S.J., "Introductory Remarks," in *Intra-Uterine Contraception, Proceedings of the Second International Conference, October 2–3, 1964, New York City*, Population Council and S.J. Segal eds. (Amsterdam, 1965).
Shepard, B., "The 'Double Discourse' on Sexuality and Reproductive Rights in Latin America: The Chasm between Public Policy and Private Actions," in *Perspectives on Health and Human Rights*, S. Gruskin et al. eds. (New York, 2005), 247–271.
Sobrevilla, L.A., Donayre Valle, J., Moncloa, F., and Guerra Garcia, R., *Población y Altitud* (Lima, 1965).
Sznajder, M., "Ethnodevelopment and Democratic Consolidation in Chile: The Mapuche Question," in *Contemporary Indigenous Movements in Latin America*, E.D. Langer and Elena Muñoz eds. (Wilmington, 2003), 17–34.
Stepan, N., *The Hour of Eugenics: Race, Gender, and Nation in Latin America* (Ithaca, 1991).
Viel, B., "Family Planning in Chile," *The Journal of Sex Research* 3, no. 4 (1967): 284–291.
Viel, B., *La explosión demográfica. Cuantos son demasiados?* (Santiago, 1966).
Viel, B., "The Population Explosion in Latin America," *Proceedings of the Academy of Political Science* 30, no. 4 (1972): 42–49.
Weaver, J.L., "The Politics of Latin American Family-Planning Policy," *The Journal of Developing Areas* 12, no. 4 (1978): 415–437.
Wilson, F., "Indians and Mestizos: Identity and Urban Popular Culture in Andean Peru," *Journal of Southern African Studies* 26, no. 2 (2000).
Yashar, D.J., *Contesting Citizenship in Latin America: The Rise of Indigenous Movements and the Postliberal Challenge* (Cambridge, 2005).
Zipper, J., Garcia, M.L., and Pastene, L.L., "Intra-Uterine Contraception with the Use of a Flexible Nylon Ring: Experience in Santiago de Chile," *Intra-Uterine Contraception; Proceedings of the Second International Conference, October 2–3, 1964, New York City*, Population Council and S.J. Segal eds. (Amsterdam, 1965), 88.

5

REVISITING THE EARLY 1970S COMMONER-EHRLICH DEBATE ABOUT POPULATION AND ENVIRONMENT

Dueling Critiques of Production and Consumption in a Global Age

Thomas Robertson

Introduction

Many Americans saw the first Earth Day rallies in 1970 as a celebration of what the United States had in common—its natural heritage—at a time when the nation was bitterly divided about the Vietnam War, race relations, and so much else. If unity did indeed exist on environmental matters at this time (a big assumption), it wouldn't last for much longer. The 1970s saw debates rage about environmental ideas, as critics on both the left and the right began to think through environmental issues. Indeed, on many issues, even environmentalists themselves disagreed bitterly. One of the key areas of disagreement was population growth.[1]

Conservationists had long been concerned with population growth. Indeed, it was two "proto-environmental" conservationists—Fairfield Osborn and William Vogt—who had helped ignite American concern with environmental degradation and population growth after World War II with separate 1948 Malthusian bestsellers, Osborn's *Our Plundered Planet* and Vogt's *Road to Survival*. Since then Malthusian concerns had played a driving role within environmental politics, just as ecological thinking had added a scientific basis to the American population control movement.[2] Thus it came as a shock when in late 1970, just months after the first Earth Day, a dispute broke out between two of America's most prominent environmentalists about how much blame to place on human population growth for the world's environmental woes. Neither the environmental movement nor the population movement would be the same afterwards.

Both Barry Commoner and Paul Ehrlich were what historian Donald Fleming called "politico-scientists"—scientists who felt an obligation not only to publicize the lessons of their science, but to lobby public officials to incorporate these lessons into public policy.[3] Commoner was, according to *Time* magazine, the "Paul Revere of Ecology:" the biologist who had sounded the alarm about nuclear fallout in the early 1960s and about detergents and other technologies a few years later. Ehrlich was also a biologist who preached the importance of ecology, but with a different vision. He had gained fame because of his 1968 book *The Population Bomb*, which defined environmental problems with regard to population growth. Ehrlich's views earned particular attention because they contradicted Pope Paul VI's 1968 encyclical reaffirming the Catholic Church's stance against birth control, *Humanae Vitae ("Of Human Life")*, and because of his repeated appearances on Johnny Carson's "Tonight Show" starting in 1970.

The Commoner-Ehrlich debate, as it has come to be known, played out in dramatic fashion in a number of public, acrimonious disputes beginning in 1970, including a legendary face-to-face encounter at the U.N. Conference on the Environment in Stockholm in 1972. In these debates about the future path of environmentalism, intellectual struggle walked hand in hand with personal rancor.[4]

Although those who followed environmental events in the early 1970s know about this showdown, many of the subsequent generations do not, and not much has been written about it (or indeed, the environmental movement more generally).[5] The point of this chapter is not to rehearse the Commoner-Ehrlich debates, but to better contextualize the ideas and dynamics that drove their disagreements, especially since these dynamics continue to shape our lives. Ultimately, Commoner and Ehrlich had different views of the history of environmental problems, and the role of population growth within it. Each blamed different factors for causing environmental problems and identified different turning points in environmental history. The Ehrlich-Commoner debates have a lot to teach us about the early environmental movement, but also about population and environment dynamics in general.

Historians have often suggested that Ehrlich and Commoner represent two fundamentally different ways of approaching population and environment problems, with Ehrlich emphasizing scientific models drawn supposedly from nature, and Commoner placing his view of nature and the environment within a larger social and often socialist analysis. This characterization is accurate and useful, but only to an extent. Commoner did call for restructuring the economy to make corporate producers more accountable, and Ehrlich did stress the inevitable crash predicted by population biology. But by the time of their debates

Ehrlich's Malthusian vision contained within it a strong political-economic critique—one that, although flawed in important ways, was itself strongly critical of capitalism, just differently so. Whereas Commoner, the man who had taken on the nation's nuclear testing program and its detergent companies, believed that the environmental problems owed to "changes in productive technologies," Ehrlich focused on consumption, the "superconsumers" he worried about in *The Population Bomb*.

The Paul Revere of Ecology

Barry Commoner's working class background, socialist leanings, and early environmental career set the course for the dispute with Ehrlich. Commoner was born in Brooklyn in 1917 to a Russian immigrant tailor and his wife. He came to know and love science through the city, where as a youth he used to examine specimens from Brooklyn's Prospect Park under a microscope. Paying for his schooling with a series of odd jobs, he studied zoology at Columbia, graduating in 1937, and received a Ph.D. in biology from Harvard in 1941. He was born at just the right time to see the changes that World War II brought to American life, especially to the nation's environment. In the words of one early chronicler of his career, Commoner launched his career "in the shadow of the Bomb."[6]

Commoner's wartime service gave him an early understanding of the dangers of new technologies, in this case DDT. Working for the Navy reserves in 1942, Commoner helped design methods for quick mass spraying of DDT, for use on the beaches of the Pacific prior to American amphibian invasions. Malaria had become as big an obstacle to American troops as fighting the enemy, and so DDT was seen as a miracle chemical. But when he tested his methods on the Jersey shore, Commoner noticed that the chemicals killed thousands of fish. Society, he would find out, would only learn of the dangerous side effects of DDT and similar "miracle" chemicals only well after the new technology had already been adopted.

Just after the war, Commoner learned a lesson about the public accountability of science that would later fuel his dispute with Ehrlich. At the end of the war, Commoner worked for the Senate subcommittee charged with an extraordinarily delicate task: deciding the best way for a democracy in a time of great military uncertainty to oversee an atomic weapons program. During the war, the Manhattan Project had mobilized new forms of scientific-governmental cooperation to create previously unimaginable forms of warfare—as well as new forms of secrecy. Only a few scientists truly understood the technology involved, and no one in 1945 and 1946 knew for sure what its military and civilian applications would be, much less its medical and moral implications. At the time, the nation's military needs were also uncertain: no one knew whether new forms of international cooperation would bring a stable peace, or whether the already deteriorating relationship with the Russians would bring renewed war. During the war, scientists, top military officials, and only a handful of civilian officials had run the nation's atomic program. The program was so secret that Vice President Truman learned of it only after he had become president. The American public learned of it only with the attacks on Hiroshima in August, 1945. Not long after the end of the war, the May-Johnson Bill, which proposed maintaining military control, brought the issue of who would control the nation's atomic program to a head. Critics felt that in a democracy civilians had to control such terrifying and unpredictable weapons. Surveying scientists, Commoner found they were overwhelmingly against the idea of military control. His work helped kill the bill. In its stead came the McMahon Act of 1946, which mandated civilian control. Historians generally regard this decision as a rare moment of clearheadedness in the history of American atomic policy.[7]

During the 1950s and 1960s, Commoner continued to pioneer efforts to make modern science more accountable to the general public. In the late 1950s and early 1960s, Commoner's St. Louis Committee for Nuclear Information, a group he founded in 1958 to supply ordinary citizens with knowledge about the dangers of nuclear fallout, played a major role in pressuring the American government to end above-ground nuclear testing, which it did with the Nuclear Test Ban in 1963. It did this with campaigns, including the innovative baby tooth survey, to raise awareness about the problems of Strontium-90 and Iodine-131. Historians have probably not done enough to show how the wave of liberal reform that swept through American society in the 1960s in part grew out of environmental activism, particularly the anti-fallout and anti-pesticide campaigns of the early 1960s. If they did, they would surely highlight Rachel Carson's *Silent Spring* (1962), and also the work of Barry Commoner.

During the mid-1960s, Commoner's renamed St. Louis Committee for Environmental Information began researching other damaging technologies that had emerged during the previous few decades, including detergents, insecticides, and plastics. Among many achievements, his group was one of the first to expose how detergents were polluting America's waters. Commoner's 1965 book *Science and Survival* brought these problems to the attention of a wide readership. When *Time* anointed Commoner the "Paul Revere of Ecology" in 1970, the title suited him well: Commoner was a man of the people, not of the elite, who used ecology to warn citizens of a danger they could not yet see.[8]

Commoner's crusade against pollution coincided with a pivotal debate among biologists about the future of their field, as Fleming stresses. Ever since the discovery of DNA in the early 1950s increasing numbers of biologists had come to see molecular biology as the wave of the future. Like many others, Commoner, on the other hand, favored the kind of biology that focused on the primacy of living organisms. He thought that broad biological approaches such as ecology could help in the fight against those who, in his words, "exaggerate our power to control the potent agents which we have let loose in the environment." In many ways, the fight against pesticides and pollution gave Commoner and the kind of biology he favored a powerful *raison d'être*.[9]

In *Barry Commoner and the Science of Survival*, Michael Egan identifies three principles that drove Commoner's science-information movement: that scientists needed to better explain the complexities of the technologies they developed; that their first duty was to the public, not corporations or the government; and that despite these first two imperatives, they should never dictate how nonscientists should interpret the moral or political elements of scientific findings. For example, stressing the limits of scientific expertise on moral matters such as the dangers of nuclear weapons, Commoner pointed out, "There is ... no scientific way to balance the possibility that a thousand people will die from leukemia against the political advantages of developing more efficient retaliatory weapons." These ideas about the proper role of science and scientists in a democracy would fuel the dispute with Ehrlich on population matters.[10]

The Bombthrower

Compared to Commoner, Paul Ehrlich was more suburban than urban, more West Coast than East Coast, and more grounded in a different type of biological tradition: population ecology. This background led him to understand the environmental crisis facing Americans in the late 1960s in a very different way.

Ehrlich was fascinated by biology from a young age. Born in 1929 to liberal Jewish parents, he grew up in Maplewood, New Jersey, a suburb outside Newark, "chasing butterflies and dissecting frogs." As a high school student, he liked to visit the biologists at the American Museum of Natural History in New York. He studied biology at the University of Pennsylvania, and then pursued a Ph.D. in entomology and population studies at the University of Kansas, graduating in 1957.

While an undergrad, Ehrlich read William Vogt's *Road to Survival* and Fairfield Osborn's *Our Plundered Planet*. Published within a few months of each other in 1948, *Road to Survival* and *Our Plundered Planet* applied the lessons of 1930s wildlife ecology, which increasingly focused on the links between consumption patterns and environmental quality, to World War II, which they blamed on competition for scarce resources and the environmental problems that resulted. Both warned of recurring war if the industrial world spread its environmental destructive consumption patterns around the world. The American landscape once rested in balance, Vogt wrote, but then came "the rise of cities with millions of inhabitants needing to be fed" and "the concept of the American standard of living." He cautioned against spreading American consumer patterns around the planet. To anyone who "thinks in terms of the carrying capacities of the world's lands," the American wartime promise of a higher standard of living embodied in President Roosevelt's idea of "freedom from want" was "a monstrous deception."[11]

To this strand of conservation informed by animal ecology, Ehrlich added the insights of the Darwinian Synthesis, the mid-century combination of genetics and field biology that produced a new consensus among biologists about the power of Darwin's theory of natural selection. As a newly minted Ph.D. in the late 1950s, Ehrlich helped with one of the earliest investigations of natural selection at work in the wild, a study of Lake Erie's water snakes. Examining the changing proportion of snakes with bands and snakes without bands in different environments, Ehrlich believed he was seeing evolution at work before his very eyes. Within the natural world, natural selection highlighted the importance of environmental scarcities, population growth, and reproduction. Not coincidentally, this was the part of Darwinian thinking that owed most to Thomas Malthus, whose ideas formed an important framework for Darwin to reach his revolutionary conclusions. The new emphasis on natural selection also shaped how Ehrlich and many other biologists thought about human society. It reinforced a sense that human beings, like all animals, had strong sexual drives; rejected the idea that human beings stood apart from—over and above—nature; and challenged the idea of social progress because it emphasized that evolution came about by chance variation and adaptation, not by divine design.[12]

In 1959, not long after his research on natural selection among Lake Erie snakes, Ehrlich and his wife, Anne, moved to Stanford University in Palo Alto, California. At the time California and especially the San Francisco Bay area were becoming fertile territory for environmental Malthusians, including Berkeley demographer Kingsley Davis, Humboldt State University biologist Raymond Dasmann, University of California-Santa Barbara biologist Garrett Hardin, and many future stalwarts of Zero Population Growth, an organization Ehrlich would help found a decade later.[13] Many of the symptoms of the population problem were on display not far from Ehrlich's home in Palo Alto: tremendous economic and suburban growth, threatened national parks and wilderness areas, and troubled inner cities. Oakland and San Francisco were close by, and Watts, Los Angeles, the site of the decade's first urban riots, not too far to the south. At the same time, the Golden State was also home to many of the technological innovations, especially in agriculture, that gave modernizers hope. As the nation's largest and most modern agricultural producer, California epitomized the agricultural revolution that President Lyndon Johnson hoped to export to around the world.

Studying the population dynamics of checkerspot butterflies at Stanford's Jasper Ridge biological research station in the early 1960s, Ehrlich made a discovery that would make his reputation as a scientist and transform his thinking about humans and their food supply. The breakthrough came after Ehrlich and his colleague Peter Raven noticed a peculiar pattern. Certain plants at Jasper Ridge contained chemicals that, like a potent insecticide, discouraged all insects except one: the checkerspot butterfly. Ehrlich and Raven concluded that the butterflies and these plants had evolved in relationship with each other. "Coevolution" became an important branch of evolutionary and ecological theory, and for Ehrlich, reinforced the central tenet of ecology: that organisms are bound to each other in surprising ways.[14]

Ehrlich was also profoundly affected by the mid-1960s food crisis in India. Having visited India in mid-1966, right in the middle of the food crisis, Ehrlich used examples from the subcontinent throughout *The Population Bomb* to illustrate every major aspect of the population problem: the extent of the Third World "population explosion," how this explosion threatened political unrest and even war, how the "green revolution" and other solutions actually made the situation worse, and why the United States needed to go beyond voluntary birth control programs. Elsewhere, he called India "the ultimate convincer."[15] India's food problem also alarmed a number of prominent environmentalists, such as Lester Brown, future founder of Worldwatch; Garrett Hardin, author of "The Tragedy of the Commons" and "Lifeboat Ethics;" and future Zero Population Growth (ZPG) and Sierra Club director Carl Pope. The overriding goal of many population-minded environmentalists, historian Donald Fleming noted in 1972, was "no more Indias."[16]

Ehrlich's understanding of India differed markedly from the approach taken by the "modernizers" within the Johnson administration: whereas they saw poverty as essentially a cultural condition that could be overcome with technological solutions such as "green revolution," hybrid seeds, and birth control programs, Ehrlich saw places such as India as beyond hope because of biological realities. India had outbred its carrying capacity, and disaster loomed. "As zoologists know well," he said in 1972, "animal populations often considerably overshoot the carrying capacity of their environment—a phenomenon invariably followed by a population crash." Green revolution programs, he insisted, would only make matters worse by degrading environments.[17]

In the mid-1960s, arguing against highly-touted green revolution technologies put Ehrlich up against two formidable forces. Many believed that new hybrid seeds would solve not just the problem of world hunger but also the Cold War in the developing world. Ehrlich countered with his own hard-to-argue-with approach: a preventative strategy. Why not prevent hungry populations from coming into existence in the first place? If that was possible, then no environmentally destructive green revolution was needed.[18]

With this strategy, Ehrlich helped reconceptualize how to protect nature. In addition to targeting new technologies of production—such as DDT or the green revolution—he also zeroed in on demand. If population growth could be curtailed, then the demand for destructive technologies could be reduced. Even though his logic was flawed and reductive—it did not eliminate faulty technologies and often overlooked vast disparities in consumption—Ehrlich, like Osborn and Vogt before him, refocused attention on the consumption side of environmental problems, a real breakthrough. This logic had important political consequences. Without necessarily losing sight of systemic drivers such as capitalism, it made environmental problems into something that not only governments could control, but also individual Americans. The personal was political. Envisioning imminent collapse, Ehrlich called for much stronger measures than the Johnson administration. At home, Ehrlich sought "drastic" programs in population planning. He considered the idea of placing chemical contraceptives in the water supply but decided it was infeasible. More likely, he wrote, were less drastic measures, such as reversing the government's system of encouraging reproduction, and creating financial disincentives with taxes on children, cribs and diapers. He called for a Department of Population and Environment, with duties such as writing a federal law "guaranteeing the right of any woman to have an abortion" and providing sex education "at the earliest age recommended by those with professional competence in this area—certainly before junior high school." Ehrlich remained vague about coercive measures in the United States.[19]

Ehrlich also wanted broad social change in the United States. He wanted "extremely fundamental changes" in American approaches to sex, religion, and the economy.[20] In particular, Ehrlich also wanted the nation to rethink its obsession with economic growth. The "whole economy," he said, "is geared to growing population and monumental waste." Drawing from Robert and Leona Rienow, he singled out new babies. "Each new baby is viewed as a consumer to stimulate an ever-growing economy." He listed the vast supplies that each baby would require in a lifetime: 26,000,000 gallons of water, 21,000 gallons of gasoline, 10,000 pounds of meat, 28,000 pounds of milk and cream, over $5,000 in school building materials, $6,300 worth of clothing, and $7,000 worth of furniture (in 1967 dollars). "It's not a baby," Ehrlich concluded, "it's a Superconsumer."[21]

If Ehrlich had limited his recommendations to the United States, he might have received less criticism. Internationally, he was far more authoritarian. He advocated a system of "triage" to govern American foreign aid in which the United States should distribute food aid only to those nations not beyond hope. Nations too far out of balance, such as India, would only waste resources needed elsewhere. To Ehrlich, there was no other "rational choice." If this wasn't chilling enough, Ehrlich also wanted to see the U.S. support forced sterilization programs, such as a plan by the Indian minister Sripati Chandrasekhar that had been rejected by Indian authorities. "When he [Chandrasekar] suggested sterilizing all Indian males with three or more children, we should have applied pressure on the Indian government to go ahead with the plan. We should have volunteered logistic support in the form of helicopters, vehicles, and surgical instruments. We should have sent doctors to aid in the program by setting up centers for training para-medical personnel to do vasectomies. Coercion? Perhaps, but coercion in a good cause . . . . We must be relentless." As it turned out, the political tides would turn, and forced sterilization would become Indian state policy during in the mid-1970s.[22]

By early 1970, though, Ehrlich had shifted his focus away from the Third World and toward overconsumption by middle class Americans. A talk he gave in Wisconsin in mid-March 1970, just a month before Earth Day, gives a sense of Ehrlich's new emphasis on the dangers of American consumption and imperialism. "I would like to point out that the population problem first of all," Ehrlich opened the address,

> is primarily a problem of the affluent whites of the world . . . In our country for instance, our minority groups—the Blacks, the Chicanos and so on—are generally sufferers from white pollution, not creators of it. I would like to point out that the Vietnam War . . . is part and parcel of the whole thing. Our legions are marching over there and elsewhere in the world because we—a very small portion of the world's population—consume what is now estimated to be thirty three and a third percent of the natural resources . . . Fundamentally the rich of the world are still stealing from the poor.

Americans, Ehrlich pointed out in *National Wildlife* in April 1970, "are really looting the world to maintain our level of affluence." In *Mademoiselle* that same month, he called Americans the "champion looters and polluters of the globe."[23]

Ehrlich v. Commoner

As Malthusian arguments about overpopulation gained sway among environmentalists during the 1960s and early 1970s, Commoner grew increasingly vocal in opposition. After several clashes with Ehrlich during late 1970, Commoner made a full-scale public attack in 1971 in a book that would become an environmentalist classic, *The Closing Circle: Nature, Man, and Technology*. On the surface, *The Closing Circle* appeared to be another in the growing series of books on the nation's environmental problems. In clear and eloquent terms, Commoner detailed how pollution destroyed the intricate natural cycles that life on Earth depended upon. He pulled no punches in his criticism of societies that ignored ecological patterns. But he also pulled few punches in attacking Malthusian environmentalism, which he equated with "political repression." Commoner devoted many words to criticizing environmentalists—here meaning Malthusians—who, he said, paid too much attention to "a single facet of what in nature is a complex whole." If nothing else, Commoner's attack is an indication that, by 1971, it appeared that Ehrlich, Garrett Hardin, Gaylord Nelson and others had turned population into a chief—if not the chief—concern of environmentalists.[24]

So many rumors exist about the "Ehrlich-Commoner debate" that it is perhaps useful to detail what Commoner did not say in the book. Commoner never argued that population growth and affluence played no role in the creation of pollution and environmental problems. He also never said that population growth in the Third World was not a problem. And he never said that he favored all-out economic growth. Nonetheless, Commoner missed few opportunities to attack Malthusian approaches. Blaming population growth for causing only 10 to 20 percent of environmental damage, far less than he ascribed to other factors, he rejected increased population growth as a core problem.

To support this claim, Commoner offered his own theory of environmental history, one that focused on the technological changes that accompanied postwar capitalism. In particular, Commoner zeroed in on the "huge array of new substances" resulting from a "sweeping revolution in science" as the main culprit behind America's environmental woes during the postwar years. "While production for most basic needs—food, clothing, housing—has just about kept up with the 40 to 50 percent or so increase in population . . . " he noted, "the kinds of goods produced to meet these needs have changed drastically." In particular, he attacked the use of synthetic detergents, synthetic fabrics, aluminum, plastics, concrete, truck freight, non-returnable bottles, and synthetic fertilizers. With this argument Commoner implied that, as long as technological problems were eliminated, the increased economic growth that Malthusian environmentalists had been railing against since the late 1940s was acceptable.[25]

Ehrlich countered with his own version of history. In a prominent article in the *Bulletin of the Atomic Scientists* called "One Dimensional Ecology," he and co-author Richard Holdren described *The Closing Circle* as "inexplicably inconsistent and dangerously misleading." Commoner, they contended, misunderstood two crucial points: that severe environmental degradation long predated World War II, and that population growth and affluence had contributed profoundly to environmental problems after World War II.[26]

Much of this was an argument about origins and turning points. Whereas Commoner saw the key juncture in humankind's relationship with nature to be World War II and the development of modern industrial capitalism, Ehrlich and Holdren believed that it occurred millennia ago, when nomadic hunter-gatherers first switched to sedentary agriculturalism. As proof, they pointed to earlier eco-catastrophes: the desertification of the Tigris and Euphrates Valleys, the expansion of the Sahara, and the Irish potato famine, as well as to the overfishing of the oceans, the destruction of the world's salt marshes and estuaries, and the pollution of the atmosphere through agricultural burning and through the removal of plant cover.[27]

Regarding the postwar period, Ehrlich and Holdren contended that Commoner did not really grasp how population-driven consumption worked. Population growth, they argued, was not just additive, as Commoner claimed, but multiplicative. If both population rates and affluence rates grew, Ehrlich and Holdren wrote, the impact was greater than the mere sum of their growth rates. For example, they argued, if population grew by 20 percent and consumption by 20 percent, the cumulative effect would far exceed 40 percent. Indeed, it would be the product—a much higher amount. Ehrlich and Holdren clarified this multiplicative relationship by introducing their "IPAT" formula, which would shape environmental thinking for years. According to this formula, environmental impact (I) could be determined by multiplying population (P) with affluence (A) and technology (T). They would deploy this formula many times during the decade.

Ehrlich and Commoner clashed on three main points. First, they differed over the role of scientific experts in society. By 1971, Commoner had been working tirelessly for over two decades to make governmental decisions about nuclear weapons and other environmental risks more open and accountable to the public. This background made him nervous about the Malthusians' call to put decisions about sex, families, and consumption in the hands of authorities. Commoner's most damning criticism of the Malthusians was that they were "repressive."

In retrospect, it seems that Ehrlich mainly lost this point. He was never able to convince people why granting vast power to authorities was necessary. In a democracy, it was simply too hard to argue against individual freedom and public accountability. But Ehrlich's logic for making this particular argument has often been forgotten. Ehrlich and the other Malthusians were not just power-mongers looking for any basis to increase their authority, and it was not just that they believed that "crisis" called for extreme measures. They argued that public accountability with population decisions differed dramatically from public accountability with nuclear issues. This was because, just as it would be imprudent to have the scientific and military foxes looking after the nuclear henhouse, it wouldn't be a good idea to rely on individual people to make responsible decisions about their own sexual and consumptive habits. They argued that people couldn't be trusted with reproduction—there were simply too many built-in incentives, including powerful biological forces, pushing toward irresponsibility. Ehrlich and the Malthusians wanted people to have as much autonomy as possible over their reproductive lives, except in cases where their decisions could undermine the safety of the entire group. They believed this view akin to public health decisions about inoculations or disease outbreaks.

Ehrlich and Holdren believed that Commoner pandered to unsustainable personal desires. Scientists must not "delude" the American public: "the truth is that we must grapple simultaneously with overpopulation, excessive affluence, and faulty technology." Commoner, they believed, took the easy way out by suggesting that Americans could solve environmental problems by simply reforming technology, without limiting population behavior or reducing consumption. But real change meant tough medicine. "Facing honestly the need for population control and de-development exposes one to the painful criticism of being both anti-people and anti-poor . . . " Someone had to be the hardheaded doctor willing to dispense unpleasant truths. "In fixing the blame for environmental deterioration on faulty technology alone," Ehrlich and Holdren concluded, "Commoner's position is uncomplicated, socially comfortable and, hence, seductive. Apparently, people want desperately to believe that questions as knotty as how to control population and how to redistribute wealth need not be confronted."[28] Although calling Commoner's views "uncomplicated" and "socially comfortable" is an unfair exaggeration, Ehrlich and Holdren's call to "redistribute wealth" illustrates that their environmental critique, although flawed in many ways, did include a substantial social vision after all.

The second big issue dividing Commoner and Ehrlich: Ehrlich's critique of capitalism focused on consumption, while Commoner's focused on production. Drawing from Fairfield Osborn and William Vogt and several decades of population biology that stressed consumption as key to ecological cycles, Ehrlich generally attacked the stress on increased consumption within the U.S. economy, which the Kennedy and Johnson administrations had self-consciously accelerated. On the other hand, Commoner, the man who had taken on the nation's nuclear testing program and its detergent companies, believed that the real problem still lay on the production side. The problem, he repeatedly said, boiled down to "changes in productive technologies."[29]

Part of this was a decision about feasibility. What pillar of modern society would be easier to move? This argument could play out in a very abstract level: was capitalist production easier to change or capitalist consumption? But both positions could be reduced, although not without losing important components, to a more concrete level: was changing technology more realistic or getting people to use birth control? For Ehrlich's part, he saw the moral difficulty of denying people material goods once they were born, whether they needed them for survival or merely to be equal with others who had much, much more. He thought the best way to avoid this choice was to avoid their births in the first place, especially through birth control. If spreading and expanding birth control could, at the same time, help with other social causes—such as liberating women, or uplifting blacks, or winning the Cold War—then all the better.

Commoner's followers could also make a strong practical argument. If the main problem was productive technologies such as new plastics and detergents, couldn't we eliminate many of our pollution problems by simply eliminating those technologies? Doing so would be relatively simple—hadn't they made a lot of progress with their campaign against soaps and detergents? Doing so also wouldn't require undoing the growth that had lifted so many working class Americans into the middle class in the previous three decades. Moreover, these changes could also be accompanied by measures to expand birth control technologies and access, but without risking harsh control measures.

The issue of economic growth became crucial. Ehrlich's argument had developed from an anti-growth perspective, which he had sharpened during the early 1970s, often targeting white middle class consumption. Commoner's position on growth was more ambiguous. Although he belonged to a larger environmental movement very skeptical of materialism and economic growth, his argument in reduced form focused on eliminating certain forms of technology, which to a large extent could be reconciled with economic growth.

As the 1970s unfolded, this difference would have huge political implications. Commoner's views appeared much easier to align with old left politics of Keynesian growth, a policy dear to the heart of many Americans, especially liberals and working class advocates. On the other hand, Ehrlich's views, which he originally presented as above politics, ended up in a political dead end. By trying to become more aware of race and class concerns with his critiques of middle class consumption, Ehrlich began to attack a dream of material comfort to which many people around the U.S.—and the world—aspired. Ironically, with his attacks on middle class growth, in the end Ehrlich may have raised more doubts about Malthusian environmentalists among the poor and the non-white, both at home and abroad.

Third, Ehrlich and Commoner also disagreed about the "Third World." In *The Closing Circle*, Commoner offered a left-leaning interpretation. European powers had encouraged population growth in their colonies for assistance with material extraction, he said, then abandoned colonies when they found synthetic substitutes. Now Europeans were saying the Third World was overpopulated. Economic growth in these areas was not the problem, he suggested, but part of the solution. Third World population growth would level off by the improvement of living standards, reduced infant mortality, old age insurance, and voluntary contraceptive practice. Believe in the demographic transition model, Commoner appeared to be saying.[30]

Ehrlich countered that Commoner had unfounded faith in "the self-regulation of human populations." Even in the unlikely event that a demographic transition began overnight, it would be a century before Third World growth rates decreased to current First World rates. Ehrlich also attacked Commoner's "misplaced faith on man's ability to industrialize instantly without environmental damage." But he agreed that people of the underdeveloped world deserved better. Whereas Commoner imagined an expanding economic pie, Ehrlich focused on redistributing the existing pie. "Mankind's only chance for improving the lot of the poor significantly," he and Richard Holdren wrote, "lies in diverting energy and other resources from extravagant affluence in the DCs to necessity-orientated uses in the UDCs."[31]

Environmentalists were asked to align with either Ehrlich or Commoner, although many refused to pick sides. Performer and environmental activist Pete Seeger, for instance, decided that both population and technology deserved urgent attention. "Commoner has convinced me," he wrote,

> that technology and our private profit politics and society must be radically changed and quickly. But I'm still working hard for Zero Population Growth (ZPG), because even if population growth is only 5 percent or 10 percent of the U.S. environmental crisis, it's a big world problem, and one can't expect others to work on it if we don't. The world is the concern of everyone.

Seeger agreed with Commoner about coercion, though, adding, "I'm in favor of ZPG as soon as it can be achieved by persuasion, not force."[32]

Conclusion

Revisiting the famous debates between Barry Commoner and Paul Ehrlich in their larger context helps remind us of the complexities of population and environment dynamics in the postwar period. It also reminds us of the complexities of the overlapping environmental and population control movements of these decades. Especially after 1970s, there was no single way of understanding human population growth, even among ecologists. This was not just because Commoner combined his ecological view with a socioeconomic critique and Ehrlich did not; it was because Commoner's critique of capitalism varied from a different, but equally powerful critique of capitalism offered by Ehrlich. Whereas Commoner focused his critique on the faulty technologies and lack of accountability within modern capitalism's production systems, Ehrlich's critique focused on the problems of unbridled consumption increasingly apparent within postwar capitalist systems.

What has subsequent history shown us about the two positions? In my view, not that one was right and the other wrong, but rather the wisdom of Pete Seeger's call to focus on both the problems of production and the problems of consumption. This bears out when we look at the greatest environmental challenge of the next half century, the industrialization of developing world countries like China and India. Clearly, the development of faulty industrial technologies such as coal-fired power plants within an environment where ordinary citizens have neither the knowledge nor political mechanisms through which to demand accountability, especially in China, is a tremendous problem. But just as clear is the problem of growing populations in these places in tandem with the spread of a level of consumption that rivals the unsustainable standards set by the West.

Notes

1. For environmentalism, see S.P. Hays, *Beauty, Health, and Permanence: Environmental Politics in the United States, 1955–1985* (New York, 1987); R. Gottlieb, *Forcing the Spring: The Transformation of the American Environmental Movement* (Washington, D.C., 1993); A. Rome, "'Give Earth a Chance': The Environmental Movement and the Sixties" *Journal of American History* 90, no. 2 (2003); and F. Dunaway, "Gas Masks, Pogo, and the Ecological Indian: Earth Day and the Visual Politics of American Environmentalism," *American Quarterly* 60 (2008): 67–99.
2. For more on Osborn and Vogt and the overlap of the U.S. environmental and population control movements, see T. Robertson, "Total War and the Total Environment: Fairfield Osborn, William Vogt, and the Birth of Global Ecology," *Environmental History* (2012); T. Robertson, *The Malthusian Moment: Global Population Growth and the Birth of American Environmentalism* (New Brunswick, 2012); F. Pearce, *The Coming Population Crash and Our Planet's Surprising Future* (Boston 2010); B.-O. Linner, *The Return of Malthus: Environmentalism and Post-war Population-Resource Crises* (Isle of Harris, 2003).
3. D. Fleming, "Roots of the New Conservation Movement," *Perspectives in American History* 6, no. 40 (1972).
4. The first Commoner-Ehrlich clash came as part of testimony at the National Commission on Population Growth and the American Future in November, 1970. "Summary of the Commission Meetings," November 17–18, 1970, EP, Series 1, Box 44, "President's Commission on Population Growth and The American Future" folder. A second round of dispute broke out at the December, 1970 American Association for the Advancement of Science annual meeting in Chicago. An excellent overview is in M. Egan, *Barry Commoner and the Science of Survival: The Remaking of American Environmentalism* (Cambridge, 2007), chapter 4.
5. Indeed, surprisingly little has been written about the environmental movement and the scientist-activists who were so central to it. As Michael Egan points out in his wonderful recent book on Barry Commoner, *Barry Commoner and the Science of Survival: The Remaking of American Environmentalism*, historians have devoted much more time to grassroots environmental organizations than to the politically oriented scientists—other than Rachel Carson—who placed a spotlight on the nation's growing environmental problems. Egan's book has added a great deal to our understanding about Commoner, his background and ideas, and the historical moment. This chapter draws heavily on Egan's deep research and adds to it new research on Ehrlich.
6. For background on Commoner, see A. Becher, *American Environmental Leaders: From Colonial Times to the Present*, vol. 1 (Santa Barbara, 2000); and Egan, *Commoner*. Quotation from Fleming, *Roots*, 41.
7. For more, see Becher, *American Environmental Leaders*. Also see Fleming, *Roots*, 41. B. Balogh, *Chain Reaction: Expert Debate and Public Participation in American Commercial Nuclear Power, 1945–1975* (Cambridge, 1991).
8. Ibid., 42.
9. B. Commoner, *Science and Survival* (New York, 1966), 12. See also Fleming, *Roots*.
10. See Egan, *Commoner*, 79. Quotation from ibid., 103.
11. F. Osborn, *Our Plundered Planet* (Boston, 1948); W. Vogt, *Road to Survival* (New York, 1948), 41, 44, 165.

12. G.A. Mitman and R.L. Numbers, "Evolutionary Theory," in *Encyclopedia of the United States in the Twentieth Century*, Stanley I. Kutler ed., vol. 2 (New York, 1996), 868–871. For Ehrlich's Lake Erie work, see J.H. Camin and P.R. Ehrlich, "Natural Selection in Water Snakes (*Natrix sipedon* L.) on Islands in Lake Erie," *Evolution* XII (1958), 504–511; P.R. Ehrlich, and J.H. Camin, "Natural Selection in Middle Island Water Snakes (*Natrix sipedon* L.)," *Evolution* XIV (1960), 136; Ehrlich and Holm, *Evolution*, 137–139. This study paralleled and slightly postdates Kettlewell's famous moth experiments in England.
13. Donald Critchlow noticed this pattern, too. D.T. Critchlow, *Intended Consequences: Birth Control, Abortion, and the Federal Government in Modern America* (New York, 1999), 156–157.
14. For coevolution, see P. Ehrlich and P. Raven, "Butterflies and Plants: A Study in Coevolution," *Evolution* 18 (1964): 586–608; and P. Ehrlich, *The Machinery of Nature* (New York, 1986), 145–146.
15. Ehrlich to Susan K. Ingraham, November 12, 1968, EP, Box 22, Correspondence, Outgoing, November 1968, Ehrlich papers, Stanford University Archives.
16. Brown watched India closely as a USDA analyst of international agricultural trends. L. Brown, *Man, Land & Food: Looking Ahead at World Food Needs* (Washington, D.C., 1963); L. Brown, *World without Borders* (New York, 1972); L.R. Brown and E.P. Eckholm, *By Bread Alone* (New York, 1974). *U.S. News and World Report* even featured Brown in a cover story on the India's agricultural problems in early 1964. Carl Pope was a Peace Corps volunteer in north India in the late 1960s. Carl Pope, *Sahib: An American Misadventure in India* (New York, 1972). G. Hardin, "Tragedy of the Commons," *Science* 162 (1968): 1243–1248; and "Living on a Lifeboat," *Bioscience* 24 (1974): 10. Hardin visited South Asia in 1970. For "no more Indias" see D. Fleming, *Roots of the New Conservation Movement*, 52.
17. Paul Ehrlich, "One-Dimensional Ecology," *The Ecologist* 2, no. 8 (1972): 11–21, 13.
18. For background on the Green Revolution, see N. Cullather, *The Hungry World: America's Cold War Battle Against Poverty in Asia* (Cambridge, Mass., 2010) and D. Kinkela, *DDT and the American Century: Global Health, Environmental Politics, and the Pesticide that Changed the World* (Chapel Hill, 2011).
19. Paul R. Ehrlich, *The Population Bomb* (New York, 1968), 135, 140.
20. Ibid., 172.
21. Ibid., 149.
22. Ibid., 161, 166.
23. Paul Ehrlich Address, Madison, Wisconsin, March 13, 1970, University of Wisconsin-Madison Archives; "MAN is the Endangered Species," *National Wildlife* (1970), 39; Peter Collier, "An Interview with Ecologist Paul Ehrlich," *Mademoiselle*, April 1970. For more on Ehrlich, see T. Robertson, *The Malthusian Moment*.
24. B. Commoner, *The Closing Circle: Nature, Man, and Technology* (New York, 1971). Much of *The Closing Circle* was serialized in *The New Yorker*. Quotations from *The Closing Circle*, 214, 183.
25. Commoner, *The Closing Circle*, 131, 129, and 144.
26. P. Ehrlich and R. Holden, "One-Dimensional Ecology," *The Ecologist* 2 (1972): 8, 11 [first appeared in *Bulletin of the Atomic Scientists*].
27. Commoner's idea contradicted one of Ehrlich's most longstanding and deeply-held beliefs—that man's deleterious impact on the environment dated back thousands of years. Indeed, Ehrlich made just this point in his first public statement on environmental problems, "The Biological Revolution," in 1965. He liked to start speeches and articles with this history. In 1970, for instance, he wrote in the newsletter of the Center for the Study of Democratic Institutions that man's adoption of agriculturalism "may have been the most important single happening in the history of the earth ... It ... marked the beginning of the potentially lethal disturbance by man of the ecological systems upon which his life depends." Paul Ehrlich, "The

Biological Revolution," Presented at Stanford Conference "A New Look at 1984—Forces and Ideas Shaping the Future," Riverside, California, January 31, 1965, EP, ACCN 2000-296, Box 1, Folder 11, 4. Also printed in the *Stanford Review* (September-October 1965): EP, Series 8, Box 1, "Press Clippings 1965–1968, Folder 3 of 6." Quote from Paul Ehrlich, "The Biological Revolution," *The Center for Study of Democratic Institutions [Newsletter name unknown]*, 1970, EP, Series 6, Box 26, Folder 28, 28–29.

28. All quotes in this paragraph are from *One-Dimensional Ecology*, 20.
29. Ibid., 177.
30. Commoner, *The Closing Circle*, 235–246.
31. Ehrlich, *One-Dimensional Ecology*, 11, 19–20.
32. P. Seeger, "Letter to the Editor," *Environment* 14, no. 5 (June 1972): 40.

Bibliography

Balogh, B., *Chain Reaction: Expert Debate and Public Participation in American Commercial Nuclear Power, 1945–1975* (Cambridge, 1991).
Becher, A., *American Environmental Leaders: From Colonial Times to the Present*, vol. 1 (Santa Barbara, 2000).
Brown, L., *Man, Land & Food: Looking Ahead at World Food Needs* (Washington, D.C., 1963).
Brown, L., *World without Borders* (New York, 1972).
Brown, L., and Eckholm, E.P., *By Bread Alone* (New York, 1974).
Collier, P., "An Interview with Ecologist Paul Ehrlich," *Mademoiselle*, April 1970.
Commoner, B., *Science and Survival* (New York, 1966).
Commoner, B., *The Closing Circle: Nature, Man, and Technology* (New York, 1971).
Critchlow, D.T., *Intended Consequences: Birth Control, Abortion, and the Federal Government in Modern America* (New York, 1999).
Cullather, N., *The Hungry World: America's Cold War Battle Against Poverty in Asia* (Cambridge, Mass., 2010).
Dunaway, F., "Gas Masks, Pogo, and the Ecological Indian: Earth Day and the Visual Politics of American Environmentalism," *American Quarterly* 60 (March 2008): 67–99.
Egan, M., *Barry Commoner and the Science of Survival: The Remaking of American Environmentalism* (Cambridge, 2007).
Ehrlich, P., "One-Dimensional Ecology," *The Ecologist* 2, no. 8 (1972), 11–21.
Ehrlich, P., *The Machinery of Nature* (New York, 1986).
Ehrlich, P., *The Population Bomb* (New York, 1968).
Ehrlich, P., and Camin, J.H., "Natural Selection in Water Snakes (*Natrix sipedon* L.) on Islands in Lake Erie," *Evolution* 12 (1958): 504–511.
Ehrlich, P., and Camin, J.H., "Natural Selection in Middle Island Water Snakes (*Natrix sipedon* L.)," *Evolution* 14 (1960).
Ehrlich, P., and Raven, P., "Butterflies and Plants: A Study in Coevolution," *Evolution* 18 (1964): 586–608.
Ehrlich, P., and Holm, R., *The Process of Evolution* (New York, 1963).
Fleming, D., "Roots of the New Conservation Movement." *Perspectives in American History* 6 (1972).
Hardin, G., "Living on a Lifeboat," *Bioscience* 24, no. 10 (1974).
Hardin, G., "Tragedy of the Commons," *Science* 162 (1968): 1243–1248.
Hays, S.P., *Beauty, Health, and Permanence: Environmental Politics in the United States, 1955–1985* (New York, 1987).

Gottlieb, R., *Forcing the Spring: The Transformation of the American Environmental Movement* (Washington, D.C., 1993).

Kinkela, D., *DDT and the American Century: Global Health, Environmental Politics, and the Pesticide that Changed the World* (Chapel Hill, 2011).

Linner, Bjorn-Ola. *The Return of Malthus: Environmentalism and Post-war Population-Resource Crises* (Isle of Harris, 2003).

Pearce, F., *The Coming Population Crash and Our Planet's Surprising Future* (Boston, 2010).

Mitman, G.A., and Numbers, R.L., "Evolutionary Theory," *Encyclopedia of the United States in the Twentieth Century*, Stanley I. Kutler ed., vol. 2 (New York, 1996), 868–871.

Osborn, F., *Our Plundered Planet* (Boston, 1948).

Pope, C., *Sahib: An American Misadventure in India* (New York, 1972).

Robertson, T., *The Malthusian Moment: Global Population Growth and the Birth of American Environmentalism* (New Brunswick, 2012).

Robertson, T., "Total War and the Total Environment: Fairfield Osborn, William Vogt, and the Birth of Global Ecology," *Environmental History* (2012).

Rome, A., "'Give Earth a Chance': The Environmental Movement and the Sixties," *Journal of American History* 90, no. 2 (2003).

Seeger, P., "Letter to the Editor," *Environment* 14, no. 5 (June 1972): 40.

Vogt, W., *Road to Survival* (New York, 1948).

PART II

DEMOGRAPHIC KNOWLEDGE IN PRACTICE

TRANSFERS AND TRANSFORMATIONS

6

COUNTING PEOPLE

The Emerging Field of Demography and the Mobilization of the Social Sciences in the Formation of State Policy in South Korea since 1948

John P. DiMoia

Introduction

In September 1948, the Rockefeller Foundation sent a team of its leading demographers and population experts to tour large sections of Asia—then still commonly labeled "the Far East" in American parlance—evaluating the region in the aftermath of war.[1] Among the figures present on behalf of the foundation were the team of Marshall Balfour and Roger Evans, along with a second pair of researchers, social scientists Drs. Frank Notestein and Irene Taeuber of Princeton University's Office of Population Research (OPR). In a preliminary fashion, the foundation was in the midst of considering whether to make major changes to its approach to the provision of medical care in the international context, and this series of site visits would provide considerable insight into the possibility of taking future action. At the same time, the extent of any such program, as well as the appropriate language through which to mobilize, was itself very much in question. The term "population" might hold problematic associations if tied to any explicit effort to curb or limit fertility.[2] The language of the mission was therefore carefully coded in the broader vocabulary of health, with population issues remaining implicit, rather than a stated goal of the visits.

With this cluster of issues at hand, the team members reported back on the receptiveness towards the prospect of change, and the pressing demographic concerns of the period began to make themselves felt in a number of different ways. With poor material circumstances stemming from the aftermath of war—a lack of infrastructure, neglect of record keeping during the later stages of combat—the challenge of fertility would not be easily addressed; moreover, it carried with it tensions associated with previous efforts at public health conducted in the region. In the case of South Korea specifically, the main object of focus here, Dr. Taeuber's visit coincided neatly with the nation's formation, with independence coming on August 15th, barely a month earlier. This intersection does not figure critically in Taeuber's observations, although she does dwell briefly on the legacy of the Japanese colonial public health system (1910–1945) in her remarks, singling it out for praise for the accomplishment of successfully limiting and reducing mortality on its watch, thereby setting up conditions for the present problem of a rapid population increase.[3] During its rule, Japan had placed the majority of its public health officers under the auspices of the police bureau, making for an effective, if enormously controversial legacy.

Taeuber, who later published a major work on Japan and its population within the next decade (1958), was not a Korea specialist, and like many of the American scholars working in East Asia, had come as a result of her overlapping interest with Japan and the possibility of reforming its civil institutions in the postwar period.[4] These remarks do not mean that Taeuber's interest was uninformed; however, her papers—held at the Western Historical Manuscripts Collection (WHMC) at the University of Missouri-Columbia—are filled with her extensive notes, taken in both English and (apparently) in Japanese, highlighting the difficulty of translating methods of counting across linguistic and cultural lines.[5] With its extensive population data records and its exceptionalist appeal to Western-based scholars as a model for an alternative modernity, postwar Japan held enormous interest for American social scientists as a case study. In particular, the New Deal and its adherents represented the apex of American faith in the transformative potential of a progressive social science as an egalitarian means for understanding and remediating an entire range of social ills, in this case, applying the knowledge to bear upon an entirely new geographical and cultural context.[6]

Although Dr. Taeuber could not have known it, her brief remarks on Korea, captured in the foundation's subsequent report, would prove extremely telling in terms of many of the measures adopted by the new state. For example, the Republic of Korea (ROK) would adopt an extremely aggressive approach towards family planning within less than two decades (1964), seeking to curb fertility, especially among the nation's rural population.[7] On this point, Taeuber emphasized precisely the need for such a program, but could not imagine a means to accomplish it, given the county's relative lack of infrastructure and, more importantly, the lack of a trained bureaucratic class to carry out the work. Aware of the legacy of Japanese colonialism, although cautiously positive about its effects for public health, Taeuber hinted at a need, and specifically a South Korean need, for a new category of trained experts to design and implement a broad range of social programs to bring about an effective and thorough transformation on behalf of the nation.

Continuity and Rupture with Colonial History (1910–1945): Using the Past to Mobilize

In making this tentative suggestion, Taeuber was aware of the diverse precedents in the region, both Japanese and Korean, and for the purposes of simplification, she reduced this complex history to a set of three intersecting layers. First, she considered the preceding Japanese context, both in terms of the system of household or family registry (*koseki*) and in the conduct of population censuses taken at regular intervals, as the most important precedent.[8] Next, she acknowledged the role of the American occupation or United States Military Government in Korea (USAMGIK, 1945–1948), which despite its brief tenure, had made some attempt at instituting reforms, citing perceived problems with Japanese models as a major justification for implementing change. Finally, Taeuber turned to the new nation, the Republic of Korea (1948–), recognizing the opportunity to begin on fresh terms. This last stage was perhaps the most intriguing, as Taeuber's suggestion here implies a conscious break or contrast with past tradition, rather than maintaining a pattern of continuity with a much longer Korean history, such as the Chosŏn period (1392–1910) immediately preceding colonial rule.

In 1948, no one could have known that the division of the Korean peninsula would take on long-term implications, and each of the two Koreas saw the temporary arrangement as an opportunity to claim legitimacy for itself amidst a heated ideological clash. This meant that in symbolic and material terms, South Korea would benefit from its ability to lay claim to the traditions of Chosŏn Korea, to say nothing of the lengthy history of the peninsula prior to the fourteenth century. Taeuber's gesture, therefore, clearly does not reflect the ideals of her South Korean counterparts, many of whom would be invested precisely in establishing links with the past. Her project, one of establishing a new statistical program that would bring South Korea much closer in line with American and international demographic models, emphasized the past only as a form of justification, a means to understand the need for change within the present set of circumstances. In this context, she also spent time investigating the statistics of North Korea (1948–), anticipating that the Soviet legacy of occupation, however brief, might produce differences worthy of notice.

This chapter, therefore, in offering its brief account of the impact of demography in the South Korean context, has to offer some qualifying remarks at the outset. By "demography," I mean specifically the influx of newer statistical and social science approaches towards population introduced into the ROK as of the late 1940s, with a perceived need for social reform and an entire range of issues surrounding fertility providing much of the impetus. These newer approaches would include both new means of using data, as well as more systemic methodological issues introduced by international partners. At the same time, the previous introduction of Japanese models in the early twentieth century constituted a similar effort at "reform" (1910), and I will refer to this history as well, both in terms of its efforts at bringing change, and in terms of its use as a negative example after 1945 by American, Korean, and a range of international actors.[9] Prior to the twentieth century, I recognize a much longer history to the Korean peninsula and the practice of a variety of methods of counting or census-taking for taxation purposes, but I will restrict my discussion primarily to the late nineteenth and early to mid-twentieth centuries in the interest of maintaining a tight focus on what might be best characterized as the introduction of a "Cold War demography," a conflux or intersection of ideological interests and their related statistical practices.

In making this choice, I also recognize the relevance of imperial and postwar Japan for this discussion as a formative context for at least part of what would take place in South Korea. Not only as an imperial power, but also as a close postwar partner, Japan would send its development and demographic experts to Korea as part of the family planning effort in the mid-1960s (JOICP, the Japan Organization for International Cooperation in Family Planning), even as the conjoined issues of Japanese language and practice remained enormously sensitive. With the official normalization of relations between the two countries taking place in 1965, past antagonisms were (nominally) set aside, although numerous echoes of colonial practice made for slow progress.[10] The introduction of Taiwan as a third partner in a regional relationship adds another layer to this story: Taiwan, much like the ROK, saw itself as a new nation needing to gain control over its population and social issues in the post-1945 period, especially as Taiwan continued to harbor ambitions of returning to the Chinese mainland.[11]

For these East Asian state actors, cumulatively, the arrival of a new style of demography accomplished at least two tasks simultaneously. First, it allowed them to do things, meaning that a wide range of social ambitions and projects could be carried out more effectively: in this context, statistics would take on material implications far beyond their meaning, as an abstract means to generate an approximation of the number of residents in a given area. Along with this nation-building activity, the refurbished postwar nations of Japan, Taiwan, and South Korea would gain access to international networks of partner nations, and perhaps most critically, related sources of funding to carry out their ambitions. For South Korea, demography served as a conduit to channel funding from sources as diverse as the Rockefeller Foundation, the Ford Foundation, the China Medical Board (CMB), SIDA (Sweden International Development Agency), and even Japan and its development branch, OTCA (Overseas Technical Cooperation Agency), following the restoration of diplomatic relations.[12] In other words, if demographic reform brought funding to transform the nation's statistics, it also legitimated the ROK in the eyes of its partners.

This vast influx of funding resources, ideas, and practices (1945–early 1980s) does not mean that South Korea would adopt wholesale everything that arrived at its doorstep, nor does this imply that its international partners gave freely without expecting some type of supervisory role in the form of increased financial and regulatory oversight. Rather, the relationship created by demography meant a new form of mediation; more specifically, mediation between the state and its citizens, many of whom had reason to be suspicious of its claims, given prior history. With much of the nation continuing to reside in "rural areas"—and this category, too, could and would be redefined in demographic terms—the ROK state needed a means to communicate with and gain a better sense of its population and their diverse needs.[13] The data gathered through such work would be critical in reporting back to its international partners, no small task given the critical role of the United States in terms of funding and providing economic planning assistance throughout the period, and especially in dispensing guidance concerning the set-up of five-year economic plans.

Vital Statistics and the USAMGIK Occupation (1945–1948): A "Government of Interpreters"

This last remark offers a convenient point at which to intervene, as Dr. Taeuber actually arrived fairly late on the scene, with the American occupation having commenced in late 1945, barely three weeks after the surrender of Japanese forces. In the haste to get bodies on the ground quickly to establish a semblance of control, the American 10th Army relocated from its base on Okinawa, assuming responsibility for the southern half of the Korean peninsula in the first week of September.[14] With virtually no language or area-specific skills at its disposal, the USAMGIK (United States Army Government in Korea) would be looking for appropriate models of conduct, operating on the baseline assumption that Japanese precedents were problematic, given the palpable tensions associated with colonialism. At the same time, the majority of the individuals in skilled positions—whether Japanese or ethnic Korean—had worked and trained under this system, meaning that the United States had to rely on a range of interpreters and intermediaries during the initial stages.

For statistics specifically, the initial concern lay primarily in the massive operations associated with repatriation, a process that would stretch from the islands of the South Pacific to include Northeast Asia and Hokkaido. Tessa Morris-Suzuki of Australia National University has emphasized in her recent work the centrality of this period for contributing to the formation of a postwar Japanese immigration policy, and equally, the period has much to say about both

North and South Korea with respect to their attitudes about maintaining their respective national borders, referring to both land and sea.[15] In conjunction with the occupation conducted by SCAP GHQ (Supreme Command Allied Powers, General Headquarters) based in Tokyo, USAMGIK began its task of escorting Japanese civilian and military personnel to the home islands, while asking many ethnic Koreans to return "home" in corresponding fashion.

This vast program of enforced migration required that the Americans examine past records to have some idea of the populations with which they would be dealing, with the outward-bound Japanese being processed for return home, and Koreans, likewise, departing from the Japanese home islands to reside on the peninsula. Four major port cities in the southern half of Korea—Inchon, Kunsan, Mokpo, and Pusan—were designated as vast quarantine stations, where this activity of processing migrants would be handled simultaneously in parallel columns of refugees.[16] Along with the expected logistical difficulties, USAMGIK authorities began to complain about Japanese record keeping almost immediately, focusing specifically on the practice of maintaining a *koseki*, or household registry, as the object of their indignation. Typically held at the family home, the *koseki* stood as a standard means of establishing their and their family members' lineage. According to American actors in 1945 however, it failed in at least one fundamental way. By tying the individual to the site of the family home for the purposes of registration, the method failed to account for the vast series of labor migrations that had brought large numbers of Koreans to work in Japan during the most recent two to three decades (late 1920s–1945).

Mobilizing Migration as a Problem

In other words, many of the Koreans cited in these registries continued to be listed for a residence at which they had last lived, in some cases, as long ago as the mid to late 1920s. The failure to account for patterns of movement made it extremely difficult for USAMGIK to track and process incoming Koreans, as well as to determine an appropriate place to send them. Of course, it did not help matters when a number of these returning Koreans also indicated their displeasure at being forced to return to sites which they did not necessarily regard as "home," especially in the case of younger individuals, born and raised in Japan. Illegal migration soon became a problem throughout the occupation, with small boats ferrying Koreans and Taiwanese to and from the Japanese home islands, and this activity has more recently generated a good deal of scholarly interest.[17]

If this activity held implications for legal practice, especially with respect to creating and enforcing new forms of immigration law, it had even greater consequences for the enforcement of public health throughout the greater Northeast Asia region, a major concern with the amount of movement going on, both documented and undocumented. As early as 1942, the United States had begun its preparations for a series of anticipated postwar occupations by setting up the School for Military Government, based at the University of Virginia, and by setting up a series of Civil Affairs Training Schools (CATS) at a cluster of leading universities.[18] Specific to our story here, Dr. William R. Willard, who assumed a leading position in the USAMGIK Bureau of Public Health and Welfare, did his training as part of the Army Specialized Training Division (ASTP) program at Yale University, taking an accelerated series of lectures and seminars concerning the creation of a public health program, with the expected outcome that he and others in his cohort would end up in Japan.[19]

The reality that the majority of these trainees would later end up in Korea, not Japan, is a well-documented story, and this development created an even greater need to rely on the skills and experience of local personnel, whether we define these in terms of Koreans or Japanese, those who had worked in positions of responsibility. For his part, Willard was not concerned about the possibility of illegal migration, which lay outside of his purview, but rather, the possibility of a major disease outbreak. Included in his previous work were studies related to vaccination, and a doctoral thesis concerning a trial effort at developing a pneumonia control program using New Haven as a case study; but taking control over the medical program of a new culture was a different venture, both in terms of its scale and in what could be assumed.[20] In other words, Willard wanted vital statistics because he needed to know about the typical Korean life cycle and what might be regarded as a baseline set of norms, especially if any problems occurred. With the confidence of a mid-century American, Willard assumed to a great extent that "culture" could be read and understood in terms of its broad patterns, given enough effort.

When outbreaks of disease soon occurred (1946–1948), as might be expected, the need for these new types of statistics underwent a transformation from a minor bureaucratic worry to a major concern, one requiring a mixture of ideology and pedagogy. In particular, the cholera outbreak of 1946 (May–September) has begun to receive a good deal of attention in the literature, recalled as a time of heavy rains (*changma*), with the spread of disease corresponding to the movement patterns of refugees from the southeast ports of entry (likely Pusan) to the northwest (Seoul and Incheon). At least from the USAMGIK standpoint, the ability to address this situation lay in the newer models of public health and practice associated with the occupation. In other words, the occupation tended to credit many of its own interventions with the waning of the crisis, with the terminal point coming sometime in early fall of that same year.

A more recent literature has begun to question the effectiveness of the occupation and its measures, arguing that in fact there was a good deal of continuity between American models and the existing public health system, one based largely on Japanese precedents.[21] Regardless, the critical factor to note here is that the occupation was able to mobilize perception on its behalf, and a good deal of this energy would carry over to the emerging institutions of an independent South Korea. For practices such as medicine and public policy, this observation would become even more relevant with the outbreak of the Korean War (1950–1953), which rapidly made the nation an international priority as a recipient of aid. Again, to be clear, South Korea retained a significant portion of its cultural heritage, value systems, and institutions dating to the Chosŏn period, but the overlay of first Japanese models of practice, and now increasingly American and international models of practice, would lead to the creation of a complex, hybrid culture. Most critically, the ROK knew that it needed to embrace these newer models in the post-Korean War era, at least nominally, to assure the continuing flow of international aid and material relief.

The exigencies of the Korean War thus became one of the critical factors in providing an impetus for the widespread adoption of biomedicine: the sheer number of injuries and casualties on a mass scale required a system that could handle and process bodies at a rapid rate, and traditional forms of Korean medical practice (hanuihak) were not optimally designed for this type of approach. Moreover, America and its international partners used the Korean context as a learning opportunity for military medicine and public health, sending mobile surgical units to the rear areas.[22] In particular, vascular surgery would witness a great deal of innovation due to the chance to work with multiple cases, and the field of infectious disease also came into play, especially with the hanta virus (or hemorrhagic fever, HFRS), which affected the kidneys.[23] The wartime period and the subsequent period of reconstruction (1950–1953, 1954–1960) brought enormous amounts of funding, equipment, and a corresponding drive to incorporate new forms of practice. Within this setting, earlier calls for statistical reform now found a great deal of space in which to develop.

Family Planning and the ROK State (1954–1960, 1961–1968)

Surprisingly, though, there was a good deal of reluctance to develop initiatives at the state level, at least in terms of adopting measures that would address the entire population. In the immediate aftermath of the war, the government of President Syngman Rhee allowed a number of grass roots organizations to conduct their activities without interference, but expressed reluctance at offering any kind of official endorsement. Much of this activity involved the intersection of interests between Protestant churches, a variety of social reformers, and elements carrying over from the colonial period.[24] It is probably also safe to argue that calls for social reform were tempered by the material realities of the period, which left behind enormous deprivation and destruction from the war. In any case, the appeal of demography in this context was not obvious, even as fertility continued to remain a problem.

The next major change that would come corresponded roughly to the political changes of early 1961, with a military coup placing a junta, and ultimately, the figure of Park Chung-hee, in power. In contrast to his predecessor, Park and his small group of military leaders needed to consolidate their power and to create the impression of responsiveness, even as their hold over the state's resources would remain tentative during the initial period of adjustment (1961–1963). Among the elements placed on the agenda almost immediately as part of the new state's program of reforms was family planning, now considered a top priority. During the initial stages, this strategy meant forming a domestic community of family planning representatives, and linking to international partners willing to provide assistance. The PPFK (Planned Parenthood Federation of Korea) quickly took the lead, gathering from elements already in play, and linked up with the International Planned Parenthood program to create a nexus of interests.

In this context, demography stood as a central part of what would take the form of individual national family planning programs in each of the three major Northeast Asian partners: Japan, Taiwan, and South Korea.[25] The colonial context meant that there was considerable overlap with prewar Japanese activities, and certainly, many of the actors were aware of this factor, especially in the case of Taiwan.[26] When the University of Michigan mobilized its Population Studies Center (PSC) to set up its program in Taichung in the early 1960s, the university specifically recruited Dr. John Y. Takeshita, a Japanese-American sociologist from UCLA, bringing him into the program.[27] Takeshita and others like him, scholars and family planning program representatives, would use Japanese language extensively in their interactions with Taiwanese villagers, aware that many in the population possessed these skills as part of the recent colonial legacy. In Taiwan, this issue was treated as a pragmatic concern, while in South Korea it held far more sensitive overtones.

The Japanese language issue is worth considering here as it provides concrete evidence of a point made previously: although it would be mobilized as "new," family planning as a form of practice in much of Northeast Asia was clearly drawing on a number of precedents dating to the prewar period, especially with respect to Japanese attempts to introduce reforms in its colonies.[28] Certainly in the related areas of medical practice, newer approaches to mothering, and even early forms of birth control technologies, Meiji and Taisho Japanese doctors were aggressive in working with and mobilizing a wide range of interventions. At the same time, given the colonial setting, these technocratic forms of expertise have to be read with caution, placed in the context of the types of control they might afford. For our interest here in the immediate postwar, the remarkable development is the extent to which all three national family planning programs used these resources without a great deal of controversy, successfully constructing a "progressive" image for birth control and related means of reducing fertility.

In the South Korean case specifically, the decision to proceed with a national family planning program coincided with the new government, as noted previously, and the transition meant a sudden availability of resources for interested parties. If migration, morbidity, and mortality represented major demographic concerns during the occupation (1945–1948) and Korean War periods (1950–1953), the focus shifted now to fertility and the means to measure, evaluate, and curb or limit its growth, an obsession that would dominate much of South Korean social science over the next two to three decades. In terms of expertise, this meant two things: first, new opportunities to study abroad for those young and ambitious enough to form a new group of elites, with many of this first generation of individuals possessing prior Japanese training. To cite a prominent example, Dr. Kwon E. Hyock of Seoul National University would attend the University of Minnesota for a master's degree, adding to his existing training in the Korean context, before assuming leadership over the Seungdong-gu project, an urban-based effort to study population and housing conditions in southeastern Seoul.[29] Dr. Kwon earned this opportunity through a program of exchange known as the "Minnesota Project" (1954–1962), set up between the two universities, and sponsored by the ICA (International Cooperation Administration), the American body responsible for coordinating technical aid.

Along with his counterpart at Yonsei University, Dr. Yang Jae-mo, Dr. Kwon would form part of an elite group of younger scholars and bureaucrats, those in the South Korean academy mobilized on behalf of the incoming government and its ambitious projects. This should not be taken to mean, however, that all of the incoming models represented something "new" per se. As already noted, Dr. Kwon, like many of his generation, possessed extensive training under the Japanese system, and in fact, strong traces of Japanese biomedicine would continue to inform South Korean practice well into the 1970s, with many of these individuals continuing to hold powerful positions. That is, the version of biomedicine taught by the Japanese at the imperial university (1910–1945), itself an approximation of earlier German forms, continued to shape Korean practice. For his part, Dr. Yang began publishing studies of local sites and their specific health needs in the immediate aftermath of the Korean War, so that he was well-informed of the problems specific to Korea by the time of the new decade. Together, these two individuals oversaw a great deal of the collective activity mobilized under the broad rubric of family planning.

If Dr. Kwon's Seungdong-gu project covered a large section of southeast Seoul ("urban") along the banks of the Han River, Dr. Yang's Koyang study, administered by his graduate students at Yonsei University and Severance Hospital ("rural"), began the task of addressing the problems of rural populations and their needs. Again, Dr. Yang had already published several studies in the previous decade, so in many ways this new work represented a continuation of his interests. What was new, though, was the state's interest in encountering and documenting these individuals as thoroughly as possible, placing the Korean family unit on the agenda as a national problem. To offer a summary of the issues, the typical Korean woman in the early 1960s experienced an average of six live births during her reproductive years (defined as the years from sixteen to the early forties), with this figure offering the prospect of a population growing without limitation. Moreover, the government was just beginning to recognize that many in this population—composing an estimated 70 percent of South Koreans—did not necessarily respond to campaigns conducted through means such as print, television, or radio.

It was precisely in this context that demography began to gain increasing importance as an emerging field of study, here referring not only to the earlier interest in morbidity and mortality dating to the late 1940s, but now developing an increasing interest in fertility and the possibility of documenting the life cycle in the nation's rural communities. In the social science of the time, limiting fertility would bring corresponding "demographic dividends," a succession of smaller birth cohorts that would allow a nation to invest its savings in new infrastructure and access to education. In the early 1960s, South Korean family planning representatives would visit Taichung, the base for the Taiwan program, and thus we know that there was communication between the respective national programs, just as there was certainly exchange with Japan, despite the lingering tensions from colonial times.[30] For the ROK, the critical issue centered on the question of how to convey its message to these communities, to the small villages nestled in the mountains, to a population that might or might not have interest, and typically lacked access to the forms of media that could be most easily sponsored by the state. The famous KAP (Knowledge Attitude Practice) surveys taken at this time assumed that potential recipients of birth control technologies wanted to use these methods, if only they were made aware of their availability.

While working on this problem of mass communication, an issue that evolved over the course of at least the next two decades, the South Korean academy also began to tackle a related issue, that of building a system for demography, an infrastructure that could sustain the growth of the field. As already indicated, the initial leaders of the family planning movement, scholars like Dr. Kwon and Dr. Yang, sometimes went abroad for further education, but these individuals did not have the freedom to take several years of leave. This is not to ignore the critical contributions made by at least two other groups, the various interest groups carrying over from the postwar period (1954–1960), and the valuable contributions of women, especially at the level of care—midwives, trainees, and still later, Mothers' Club members.[31] But for our purposes here, the demographic impulse would require a core group of younger scholars who would train abroad and return to establish South Korea's demographic centers at its major universities and also within key governmental bodies.

A Demographic Infrastructure and its Legacy (Late 1960s–1987)

Of these individuals, many would study at leading American centers for demography, among these, the University of Michigan (PSC), Princeton University (OPR), Johns Hopkins University, and the University of North Carolina (Carolina Population Center). To note a prominent example, Dr. Sook Bang, who received his doctoral degree from Michigan in 1968, served with the Yonsei-Koyang program in the field throughout much of his doctoral study. Collaborating with Dr. Yang Jae-mo, Dr. Bang produced a number of publications prior to defending his dissertation, and would be ready to step right in and assume a role as a major collaborator alongside his senior and mentor. This style of relationship, combining the pursuit of academic work with socially valuable "labor," made for an extremely appealing field, one in which the two pursuits—academic research as a supplement to bureaucracy—served to mutually reinforce one another. From the perspective of international partners, moreover, this ensured that aid programs continued to develop, and that they would be in good hands, with responsibility falling to junior scholars.

By the mid-1960s, family planning, while still a major state priority, was hardly the only use for the sources of new data, as South Korea was then undergoing a massive social transformation that would require social statistics of all kinds. In the course of its economic planning, frequently done in conjunction with international partners, the ROK needed information both as an input and as a form of justification to set reasonable goals, satisfactory both to domestic interests as well as foreign partners. In terms of managing local concerns, the ROK state began to pay increasing attention to the category of manpower (*illyok*), now defined in terms of the availability of highly skilled labor in select areas. This category appeared most often in publications assessing the prospects for industrial growth, but scientific and technical capacity was also very much a part of the dialogue, and this was also a time when the nation began to successfully recruit returnees to take positions at new GRIs (government research institutes), especially KIST (Korea Institute of Science and Technology).[32] Although much of this activity was driven by American funding, the assumptions and vocabulary tend to reflect earlier Japanese models.

If the recruitment of high level scientists with foreign doctoral degrees met the criteria for the establishment of new scientific or technical institutes, the state's agenda at a more basic level consisted of an upgrade to entirely new categories of workers, those who would take positions as highly skilled workers in a more sophisticated economy. The motivations informing the early 1970s push towards

Heavy and Chemical Industry (HCI) has generated a great deal of scholarship in recent years, but less attention has been paid to how this strategy would affect more basic issues such as pedagogy: the system of technical education, and the approach towards recruiting and training engineers.[33] Here again, the collection of statistics would prove enormously valuable in terms of helping to set the state's planning agenda, and indeed, it is easy to find numerous publications from this period (1965–1979) covering the problem of "scientific manpower," addressing the category briefly, before turning to its significance within the newer style of industrial economy envisioned for South Korea. In this respect, the collection of social statistics served as both a performance and the abstract instantiation of what would later take a material form.

If this last point stretches the boundaries of a more traditional definition of demography, recognizing that the pace of social change was extremely rapid, it may help to conceive of "demography" not just in terms of a social or national basis, but also in terms of understanding the activities of groups taking place on a much smaller scale, that is, as niche demographics or categories. Technical workers and scientists represented two such categories, and given their placement within a new vision of the economy, the amount of attention they received should not be surprising. At quite a different placement within the social spectrum, rural farmers and villagers also began to receive a great deal of attention from the state during the decade of the 1960s, first at the level of family planning, but then even more critically at the level of public health and rural revitalization campaigns as well, carrying into the next decade. Demography in this respect served as a contact zone between the individual and the state, providing the latter access into the activities and whereabouts of the former, making it absolutely essential as a new form of knowledge.

In both of these areas, family planning and rural mobilization—with the latter growing particularly strong, especially with the *Saemaul Undong* ("New Village") movement of the 1970s—the uses of demography as a form of state intervention has to be conceived of as more than a bureaucratic exercise, and equally as an intervention by the Park Chung-hee security state. If the *Saemaul Undong* has often been portrayed as a comprehensive rural revitalization program, it might also be read in terms of the state seeking to create a new type of citizen. Demography, broadly defined here as a new field in terms of the return of new degree holders from abroad, became critical to the functioning of the new state and the accomplishment of its slate of social ambitions. Previous scholarship has wonderfully demonstrated the related role played by other major bureaucratic institutions in recent South Korean history, with Greg Brazinsky's *Nation-Building in South Korea* (2007) and Seungsook Moon's *Militarized Modernity and Gendered Citizenship* (2005) both doing an admirable job of outlining the role of the ROK military as a vast nexus of personal relationships, providing training and skills that later transferred over to the South Korean corporate world.

In the case of demography, even while not seeking to impart a malign image, we need to recognize that along with the more conspicuous features of the *Yushin* ("Restoration") state (1972–1979)—the suspension of the constitution, along with personal freedoms—would come a vast bureaucratic organization designed to give the state a higher degree of knowledge about its citizens and their personal activities. From the early 1970s onwards, demography would work along with the family planning campaigns to encourage ROK soldiers in the reserve "Home Army" to submit to "voluntary" vasectomies, with many taking this option as a means to curtail their period of reserve service.[34] For rural campaigns, the state grew increasingly interested in the physical facilities and material conditions of individual villages, recognizing that its ability to communicate with these residents was critical in any national effort, whether geared towards education, public health, or military service. Again, one does not have to read the demographic impulse as a dark one necessarily, but one should recognize that it gave the South Korean state access into the lives and homes of its citizens.

Post-Democratization Demography? (Post-1987)

If the growth of demography both as a formal academic field and as a bureaucratic institution corresponded roughly to the development of a state bureaucracy, what role would the field play in the creation of a "new" South Korea after 1987? Certainly the state would no longer need to exert its will in quite the same fashion as it had under military rule, but still, this does not mean that the need for statistics would diminish. In fact, many of the developments expected with the opening of the society might suggest the opposite trend, with President Kim Young-sam's (1993–1998) stated goal of "globalization" (*saegaewha*) implying a need for even greater transparency when searching for reliable metrics. This trend would be augmented a decade later with the Asian financial crisis of 1997, and a call for greater transparency in dealing with economic and fiscal matters. In other words, the emergence of demography after 1945 enabled the state to perform any number of vital tasks and social enterprises, and the circumstances post-1987 would further this trend, while also allowing for oversight and the possible participation of non-state actors.

That is to say, the story of South Korean demographics in the last twenty to twenty-five years has been one of capturing and representing the needs of an increasingly complex plural society, with the data-gathering process itself coming into question by various civil society parties, as these numbers have the power to shape and determine the allocation of resources. First and foremost, demographics or even more commonly the "demographic problem" took on a very different meaning in South Korea—and indeed in much of East Asia—by the mid-1980s, with declining fertility rates. While scholars continue to debate the possible link between this trend and previous family planning efforts, others attribute the development to a natural outcome of the goals of the developmental state, with wider opportunities for employment and higher education for women, and with a marked transition of movement away from the rural to the urban. Still, whatever the motivations, the falling fertility rates have brought into focus the issue of a rapidly ageing society, with accompanying higher costs for health care, along with a stable or slightly declining population, given that the replacement rate is no longer being met.

South Korea has also experienced demographic transformation through international migration, in this case, not so much the rural-to-urban pattern of domestic movement which characterized much of the second half of the twentieth century, but rather, the nation's emergence as a desirable site for foreigners, a place in which to live and work. As the economy began to grow in the 1970s and 1980s, South Korea had to begin importing much of its labor for construction and similar types of "dirty" industries, jobs that Koreans no longer found desirable. With the arrival of these short-term economic migrants, the ROK constructed the bureaucratic apparatus necessary to process and track these groups, operating on the assumption that their presence was a temporary one, and that they would return home following the completion of a job. This practice has changed significantly in the past two decades, as increasingly foreigners have begun to settle in large urban clusters like Seoul, underscoring the country's genuine emergence as a cultural and economic site.

As a conjoined cluster—the problem of declining fertility, along with the increasing appeal of migration over the long term to South Korea, especially among Southeast Asian populations, such as Vietnamese and Filipinos—these developments constitute what we can characterize as the present focus of demography. Of course, meeting the needs of an ageing society is also emerging as a concern, but the situation does not appear quite as acute as compared with that of Japan. Still, South Korea recognizes that it needs to devote larger amounts of its social capital to counting, tracking, and supporting the integration of foreigners into its population, while at the same time meeting the needs of its own citizens. Certainly major cities are generally much better at offering foreign-language assistance in the form of documents and signs, although the extreme countryside can be forbidding for those who do not speak or communicate with at least some elementary level of Korean. Again, these trends should serve as a reminder of how rapidly the country has transformed itself in the last forty to fifty years, especially post-Korean War.

And if demography no longer carries with it the explicit stamp of governmental authority, especially that of state scrutiny, it represents a form of contention in a state where civil society still lacks transparency and has only existed for about two to three decades. Rather than a largely top-down model, with demographic information carrying absolute authority, a diverse set of interests is able to participate in the process of gathering and compiling this type of information, with the actors using it for their own purposes. Within the last several years, the dissolution of the authority of the household registry has finally made inroads into what was seen as the patriarchal hold over the family, with family and inheritance ties dominated by this form of practice. Still, these recent changes do not mean that South Korea has in any way reached a point at which the process of transformation will stop, nor are all parties satisfied with the current state of the implied social contract.

Notes

1. M.C. Balfour et al., *Public Health and Demography in the Far East: Report of a Survey Trip, September 13, 1948–December 13, 1948* (New York, 1950).
2. The report makes this point in the context of postwar sensitivities about the legacy of Nazi science, as well as that of imperial Japan, although it is not clear how much was known about the latter case at the time of publication.
3. Dr. Taeuber's remarks are framed carefully, but she and other Rockefeller experts make such remarks. William R. Willard, head of the USAMGIK Bureau of Public Health and Welfare in Korea (1945) would make similar observations in his own publications. See William E. Willard, "Some Problems in Public Health Administration in the United States Army Military Government in Korea," *Yale Journal of Biology and Medicine* 19, no. 4 (1947): 661–670.
4. I. Taeuber, *The Population of Japan*, (Princeton, 1958). Dr. Taeuber's papers are housed at the University of Missouri-Columbia, Western Historical Manuscripts Collections (WHMC). I have not been able to verify her level of Japanese language proficiency, although the collection contains numerous examples of notes (apparently in her handwriting) both in English and Japanese.
5. Ibid.
6. John Dower has made this point for Japan, and although it might be different for Korea, there is certainly evidence of optimism in social science, with many recent graduates of the Army's CATS (Civil Affairs Training Schools) turning up in Korea.
7. J.P. DiMoia, "Let's Have the Appropriate Number of Children and Raise Them Well!": Family Planning and Nation-Building in South Korea, 1961–1968," *EASTS* (East Asian Science Technology and Society) 2, no. 3 (2008): 361–379.
8. Irene Taeuber Papers, WHMC, University of Missouri-Columbia.
9. A. Lankov, "Busy Bodies," in *The Dawn of Modern Korea* (Seoul, 2007), 118–120. Lankov implies that the 1911 census, coinciding with the start of colonialism, is the first "modern" census to be taken, as opposed to a census taken for taxation purposes. Again, I recognize that Koreanists would most likely favor an origins date much earlier than this.
10. Aya Homei of Manchester University works on the Japanese postwar programs.
11. Taiwan would become especially important by the early 1960s with its family planning program assisted by Dr. Ronald Freedman of the University of Michigan's Population Studies Center (PSC). See R. Freedman, *Observing Taiwan's Demographic Transition: A Memoir* (Taichung, 2007). For more on the larger prewar context of Japanese interests in the areas of population, eugenics, and demography, see the work of Sumiko Otsuba, Metropolitan State University.

For prewar China and the KMT context, see Y.J. Chung, *Struggle for National Survival: Chinese Eugenics in a Transnational Context, 1896–1945* (New York, 2002). Yuling Huang of SUNY-Binghamton is presently working on a dissertation on the post-World War II Taiwanese anti-natalist transition.

12. The OTCA annual volumes for Japan are available through the National Diet Library, and are highly relevant for Korea for the late 1960s, when Japan was helping South Korea with its Anti-Parasite campaigns.
13. South Korean family planning materials by the late 1960s would explicitly mobilize the category of 농촌 (rural) residents as the target audience.
14. T.B. Turner, "Chapter XVIII Japan and Korea," in *Preventive Medicine in World War II, Volume VIII*, J. Lada ed. (Washington, D.C., 1976).
15. T. Morris-Suzuki, *Borderline Japan: Frontier Controls, Foreigners and the Nation in the Postwar Era* (New York, 2010).
16. History of Evacuation and Repatriation through the Port of Pusan, Korea, September 28, 1945–November 15, 1945. Available on CDR through the U.S. Institute for Military History, Carlisle Barracks.
17. C. Aldous and A. Suzuki, *Reforming Public Health in Occupied Japan, 1945–52: Alien Prescriptions?* (New York and London, 2011). Tessa Morris-Suzuki has also written on this.
18. I have not looked at all of the CATS (Civil Affairs Training Schools) materials for various universities, but I have had the chance to look at Yale CATS specifically, which is where Dr. Willard trained. Other materials at Yale are stored in the Charles E.A. Winslow papers at Yale.
19. W.E. Willard, "Some Problems in Public Health Administration in the United States Army Military Government in Korea," *Yale Journal of Biology and Medicine* 19, no. 4, (1947): 661–670.
20. This is taken from Dr. Willard's graduate work at Yale. See W.E. Willard, *An Attempt to Develop a Pneumonia Control Program in New Haven, 1936–1937* (Ph.D. diss., Yale University).
21. Chris Aldous has argued this in several different places.
22. I refer here not just to American mobile surgical units, but also those of NORMASH (Norway) and other allied partners.
23. Re. vascular surgery: personal communication, Justin Barr, Yale University. Re. the hanta virus: personal communication, Dr. Kim Geun-bae, Chongbuk National University.
24. Dr. Sonja Kim of SUNY-Binghamton works on this, although covering an earlier period prior to 1945. See S. Kim, *Contesting Bodies: Managing Population, Birthing, and Medicine in Korea, 1876–1945* (Ph.D. diss., UCLA, 2008).
25. Although I focus here primarily on Northeast Asia, Southeast Asia remains rich with possibilities for comparative demographic and family planning work for this period. See *Two is Enough: Family Planning in Indonesia under the New Order, 1968–1998*, A. Niehof and F. Lubis eds. (Leiden, 2003).
26. Freedman does not talk about this per se in his memoirs, but there are memos in the PSC papers indicating that this was a concern. Also, the Rockefeller (RAC) materials for Korea contain many mentions of the Japanese language issue.
27. John Y. Takeshita, Faculty File, University of Michigan, Bentley Historical Library.
28. Sonja Kim addresses this, as does Sabine Fruhstuck in *Colonizing Sex: Sexology and Social Control in Modern Japan* (Berkeley, 2003).
29. There are numerous publications stemming from this project available at the Seoul National University Library.
30. In Seoul, materials to establish this relationship can be found via the KAHP (Korean Association for Health Promotion) museum, and in Tokyo, at the National Diet Library.
31. There remains ample room here for oral history research, as many of these individuals are still active.

32. See the Seoul National University doctoral dissertation of Dr. Moon Manyoung on the formation of KIST. In Korean: KIST의 설립과 변천 1966-1980 : 계약연구기관에서 국책연구기관 으로 = Early history of KIST, 1966–1980: from contract research to national project research / 문만용 (Ph.D. diss., Seoul National University).
33. Kim Hyung-A, *Korea's Development under Park Chung Hee: Rapid Industrialization, 1961–1979* (London, 2005).
34. This program of offering incentives to home reserve members began in 1973 and would continue through the 1980s.

Bibliography

Aldous, Ch., and Suzuki, Akihito, *Reforming Public Health in Occupied Japan, 1945–52: Alien Prescriptions?* (New York and London, 2011).

Balfour, M.C. et al., *Public Health and Demography in the Far East: Report of a Survey Trip, September 13, 1948–December 13, 1948* (New York, 1950).

Chung, Y.J., *Struggle for National Survival: Chinese Eugenics in a Transnational Context, 1896–1945* (New York, 2002).

DiMoia, J.P., "'Let's Have the Appropriate Number of Children and Raise Them Well!': Family Planning and Nation-Building in South Korea, 1961–1968," *EASTS* (East Asian Science Technology and Society) 2, no. 3 (2008): 361–379.

Freedman, R., *Observing Taiwan's Demographic Transition: A Memoir* (Taichung, 2007).

Fruhstuck, S., *Colonizing Sex: Sexology and Social Control in Modern Japan* (Berkeley, 2003).

History of Evacuation and Repatriation through the Port of Pusan, Korea, September 28, 1945–November 15, 1945.

Lankov, A., *The Dawn of Modern Korea* (Seoul, 2007).

Hyung-A, K., *Korea's Development under Park Chung Hee: Rapid Industrialization, 1961–1979* (London, 2005).

Kim, S.M., *Contesting Bodies: Managing Population, Birthing, and Medicine in Korea, 1876–1945* (Ph.D. diss., UCLA, 2008).

Manyoung, M., *KIST 의 설립과 변천 1966–1980 : 계약 연구 기관에서 국책 연구 기관 으로 = Early History of KIST, 1966–1980: From Contract Research to National Project Research* / 문만용 (Ph.D. diss., Seoul National University).

Morris-Suzuki, T., *Borderline Japan: Frontier Controls, Foreigners and the Nation in the Postwar Era* (New York, 2010).

Niehof, A., and Lubis, F., eds., *Two is Enough: Family Planning in Indonesia under the New Order, 1968–1998* (Leiden, 2003).

Taeuber, I., *The Population of Japan* (Princeton, 1958).

Takeshita, J.Y., Faculty File, University of Michigan, Bentley Historical Library.

Turner, T.B., "Japan and Korea," in *Preventive Medicine in World War II*, vol. VIII, J. Lada ed. (Washington, DC, 1976).

Willard, W.E., *An Attempt to Develop a Pneumonia Control Program in New Haven, 1936–1937* (Ph.D. diss., Yale University).

Willard, W.E., "Some Problems in Public Health Administration in the United States Army Military Government in Korea," *Yale Journal of Biology and Medicine* 19, no. 4 (1947): 661–670.

7

Laparoscopy as a Technology of Population Control
A Use-Centered History of Surgical Sterilization

Jesse Olszynko-Gryn

Introduction

Bombay gynecologist Pravin Mehta "peered through" the laparoscope, a "stainless-steel probe with a pistol grip and a light source." He located and grasped a fallopian tube "in the instrument's crab-like claw and, squeezing a trigger, snapped a plastic ring over the captured tube, making a tight ligature, rather in the manner of a stapler."[1] When the second tube was similarly ligated, Mehta invited *Times* correspondent Trevor Fishlock to "look through the laparoscope at his handiwork, at the tube tied neater than a sailor's reef knot."[2] It was May 1981 and the tubes belonged to Manbhar, a thirty-year-old mother of two sons and one girl who had "walked six miles across the desert to have herself sterilized" at a makeshift clinic or "camp" set up in a school sixty miles south of Jaipur, Rajasthan. She had heard about a new operation performed by a "magic telescope" that was "so quick and efficient that she would be back in time to cook the evening meal and could be working next day in the fields."[3] Since the heyday of population control in the 1970s,[4] millions of women like Manbhar have been sterilized by the scope, making tubal ligation (or tubectomy) the most prevalent form of contraception worldwide.[5] In India and other countries, tubal ligation is often known simply as "the operation."[6]

Population control advocates viewed surgical sterilization as a "technological fix"[7] that could be done to the poor and uneducated masses, with or without their consent. Tales of forced sterilization continue to hold "a kind of gory appeal,"[8] and there are too many studies to cite here.[9] We have histories of the second most popular contraceptive in the world today: the IUD (intrauterine device), which can be inserted into women's bodies immediately after childbirth.[10] Other technologies including contraceptive pills, vacuum aspirators, chemical spermicides and even failures such as "anti-fertility vaccines" and the "male pill" have all found their historians.[11] But despite its significance, the technology of sterilization has not received much historical analysis. Laparoscopy is a special kind of endoscopy, or minimally invasive (keyhole) surgery, performed through a small incision in the abdomen. The scope separates the surgeon's eye and hand, allowing the patient's interior body to be explored and manipulated without the trauma of open abdominal surgery (laparotomy).[12] Although more invasive and traumatic than vasectomy,[13] the application of laparoscopy to gynecology made tubal ligation more acceptable to women by removing the need for general anesthesia and lengthy hospitalization.[14] The major insider's account attributes the take-off of laparoscopy in the 1960s to the sexual revolution and legal reforms in the United States,[15] where it was affectionately dubbed "belly-button" or "Band-Aid" surgery. But this is the first study to examine the design and use of the scope in the context of global population control from the perspective of surgeons, their social networks and material practices.

This chapter is about how surgical sterilization became the world's most widely used (and most controversial) contraceptive technology at the expense of other options, radically circumscribing women's contraceptive choice.[16] More generally, it is about what happens when tools and techniques are transferred from place to place and how studies of "things in use" can supplement our policy-centered histories of population control and our innovation-centered histories of technology.[17] It analyzes the role of surgeons as "intermediary actors" in a network of governmental organizations, private companies, feminist activists, and the women or "lay end users" who were sterilized.[18] Sizable financial investments played a major role in scaling-up and stabilizing the use of the scope, so I will also follow the money to investigate links between the technology and business of sterilization.[19] But my main aim is to show how the materiality of surgical interventions into women's bodies matters to our historical accounts of the policies and practices of contraception. Following technologies instead of projects, institutions and social movements can be a useful methodology for analyzing transnational processes,[20] so I will follow the scope to India to examine the adoption and implementation of laparoscopy by a gendered family planning service that has consistently drawn criticism for its reckless and inhumane treatment of India's poorest women.[21]

Places of Innovation:
Making Laparoscopy Affordable, Efficient, and Portable

Radically new surgical techniques of visualization and manipulation were introduced into gynecological practice in Europe by entrepreneurial surgeons and private companies in the 1950s and 1960s. Notably, medical instrument manufacturers Karl Storz and Richard Wolf made "cold light" fiber-optic systems available for testing to Hans Frangenheim, the leading West German laparoscopist.[22] In Europe, scopes were used mainly as a diagnostic tool in gynecologic oncology and infertility treatment, but rarely for sterilization. Perhaps because of the legacy of eugenics, tubal ligation was a relatively uncommon procedure in Germany, accounting for only about 5 percent of laparoscopies in the 1970s.[23] But in the early 1970s a small group of American gynecologists began to experiment with sterilization, some regarding it as "the only indication for laparoscopy."[24] Laparoscopic sterilization used electrically induced heat (diathermy) to cauterize the fallopian tubes. A major drawback of this method was the significant risk of internal injuries to the patient. For this reason, and also because they were protective of their time-honored skills, mainstream gynecologists widely perceived laparoscopy as the unnecessarily risky and unproved domain of a small group of enthusiastic dilettantes or "cowboys of the operating room."[25] Undeterred, laparoscopists resourcefully built a network for themselves by supplying the growing and lucrative market for technologies of population control.[26]

"Population control" was the watchword of an environmental movement that had gathered considerable momentum by 1968, the year Stanford ecologist Paul Ehrlich predicted inevitable mass starvation in his sensational bestseller, *The Population Bomb*, and founded the organization, Zero Population Growth.[27] Based at Johns Hopkins Hospital in Baltimore, Maryland, a world leader in medical innovation, gynecologist Clifford Wheeless was America's leading champion of laparoscopic sterilization for domestic and international population control.[28] In 1970 he estimated it would cost $30 million to sterilize every woman in Maryland who was over the age of thirty with at least three children.[29] At $500 per operation (around $2,960 in 2012), he argued that state governments and private insurance companies could not afford to finance mass sterilization on the scale required for population control in the United States.[30] As Wheeless put it in the *Journal of Reproductive Medicine*:

> Recent trends in family planning and population control demand thorough evaluation of methods of surgical sterilization as to mortality, morbidity, effectiveness, simplicity and hospital cost. For local and state governments to support surgical sterilization in indigent populations, a method must be available that will allow large numbers of patients to be sterilized without the usual extended hospital stay and its associated cost.[31]

Wheeless promoted laparoscopy as a money saver that would reduce the average cost per operation to less than $100 ($591) and hospitalization from one week to 24 hours. Crucially, he promised a technique that could be performed not only by a skilled surgeon such as himself, but also by the average nonspecialist in 30 minutes or less.[32] Laparoscopy, he claimed, was easy to learn and could be taught to paramedics in "underdeveloped countries," where the low operating time would permit "many sterilizations per day."[33]

The results of a pilot study involving twenty-five local women were encouraging, so Wheeless expanded his trial to include women from further afield. They were charged a "package price" of $125 ($739) for the entire procedure, including an overnight stay at a boarding house and a follow-up examination one month later.[34] From 1968 to 1972 around 3,600 women were sterilized at Johns Hopkins. Most came from Maryland, but a few were referrals from other states where local hospitals required a husband's signature, proof of marital status or committee approval. At Johns Hopkins, however, as long as the patient was a consenting adult (21 years or older), the only requirement was her desire to be sterilized. A younger woman could be sterilized only if she was assessed by the hospital review authority as "mentally retarded" or if she had already given birth to three or more children.[35]

Feminist journalists frequently interviewed and quoted Wheeless on the liberating promise of laparoscopy, which received highly favorable coverage in newspapers and women's magazines.[36] The *New York Times* anticipated a "second contraceptive revolution" based on the dream of a perfectly reversible method, which would grant surgeons even greater control over human reproduction and make postoperative regret a thing of the past.[37] On the other hand, the same paper acknowledged that some poor countries like India offered "assembly-line sterilization camps complete with door prizes," a reference to cheap incentives including plastic radios.[38] Despite the potential hazard of internal electrical injury, Wheeless recommended laparoscopy for immediate overseas use in population control programs, "without waiting for a better technique to be developed."[39]

Exporting the scope, however, was not a straightforward or unproblematic process. On the contrary, a concerted effort was needed to overcome major obstacles associated with redesigning a high-precision instrument for use in makeshift clinics. Laparoscopic equipment was expensive and difficult to transport. American Cytoscope Makers, Karl Stortz, and Richard Wolf manufactured a single unit for $3,000–5,000 ($12,800–21,300) and the equipment required to inflate the abdomen with gas for greater maneuverability was bulky.[40] Wheeless solved these problems by scaling down the scope and by substituting its highly specialized components for cheaper generic ones. He used miniature valves from the aerospace industry to reduce the size of the standard Simm pneumoperitoneum machine (for gas), and by using an everyday $90 ($363) pediatric scope with an ordinary penlight, he brought the cost down by a factor of ten to around $400 ($1,610).⁴¹ A bespoke "suitcase-size sterilization kit" manufactured in Pennsylvania by Medical Technologies International was first field tested in San José, Costa Rica, and then proposed for use in rural parts of the United States and in overcrowded city hospitals.⁴² Although Wheeless argued that inexpensive instruments would someday liberate physicians from dependence on "third-party institutions,"⁴³ he would begin to work closely with the various organizations involved in population control, especially the United States Agency for International Development (USAID).

Building Networks:
Training Surgeons, Distributing Scopes, and Scaling Up

The 1970s saw various national and international organizations, agencies, and institutions including the Ford Foundation, Population Council (financed by the Rockefeller Foundation), United Nations Fund for Population Activities (UNFPA) and the World Health Organization (WHO), financing research in contraceptive technologies and overseas family planning services, on which development aid to poor countries was increasingly being made contingent.⁴⁴ Under the leadership of Reimert T. Ravenholt, the influential director of USAID's Office of Population, the federal agency became by far the biggest spender on population control programs, with a budget that increased from $75 million in 1970 to $200 million in 1978 ($443 million to $704 million).⁴⁵ In the early 1970s Ravenholt agreed to support laparoscopy over competing alternatives primarily as a result of an excursion Wheeless made to Nepal in 1971.

His Majesty's Government of Nepal's Family Planning Project relied mainly on condoms, contraceptive pills and around 4,000 vasectomies every year, including in remote hilly areas where paramedical teams were flown by helicopter.⁴⁶ Female sterilization was negligible when Wheeless first introduced laparoscopy to the Maternity Hospital of Kathmandu. Together, Wheeless and his protégé Kanti Giri, a Nepalese gynecologist who had previously trained at Johns Hopkins, sterilized over 200 women in one month. Next, Giri travelled on her own to "primitive settings" including the Pokhara Valley, where she performed dozens of operations in a single day. She claimed that the introduction of laparoscopy to Nepal marked a new era in family planning and recommended it for neighboring countries (China and India) with even more "acute" population problems.⁴⁷ By 1977, she had personally sterilized over 1,500 women and was training future laparoscopists.⁴⁸ Upon returning to the United States, Wheeless presented his experience in Nepal as a test run for more ambitious projects at a Virginia conference set up by Ravenholt to determine how to allocate the millions earmarked for population control.⁴⁹

So far the agency had spent a negligible portion of its budget in support of surgical sterilization.[50] Vasectomy was practical, safe and already played a major role in population control programs in India, Pakistan, Taiwan, and South Korea. Women, on the other hand, were considered under-enrolled for the level needed for population control. Tubal ligation was an attractively one-off and provider-controlled alternative to pills and condoms, but current methods would have to be simplified and made practical before they could be implemented on a mass scale. Ravenholt, whose "myopic ethnocentrism" could be shocking,[51] kicked off the Virginia conference with an overview of USAID's position:

> The primeval strength of the sexual drive and the associated hyper-fecundity of the world's women are contributors to one of the world's problems. Technology is a very important determinant on how rapidly we can move to curb the excessive population growth which occurs as a result.[52]

It is not surprising that surgery, a "technology of control" that enables the surgeon to intervene into and manipulate the living structures of a (female) patient's body,[53] was highly compatible with Ravenholt's gendered view of the global threat posed by Third World women's uncontrollable sexuality.[54] Many population control advocates endorsed a technological fix that promised to render cultural resistance and irrational (female) behavior irrelevant.[55] Even so, laparoscopy was not the only technology of female sterilization showcased in Virginia and USAID was faced with a choice of competing alternatives.

Researchers at the Battelle Population Study Center in Seattle, Washington, were developing a different method based on blocking the junction of the fallopian tubes and uterus (tubal occlusion). A ballooning silicone rubber cap was being developed at the Western Pennsylvania Hospital, Pittsburgh, to provide reversible sterilization. Progress with outpatient culdoscopy (the vaginal route to visualizing and operating on the uterus), and non-surgical methods including quinacrine injections were also presented. Ravenholt did not share Wheeless's confidence that laparoscopy was easy to learn, so it was not a foregone conclusion that USAID would back him. In Ravenholt's words, it would take "500,000 Bob Wheelesses" or comparably talented surgeons to implement laparoscopy on the scale needed for population control.[56] But Wheeless was, as Ravenholt put it, already "charging ahead" with laparoscopy. His positive experience in Nepal had given him an edge over competitors, making it easier for Ravenholt to decide in favor of a technique that had already been field-tested.

At first Wheeless received $50,000 ($283,000) from USAID to travel to El Salvador, Ecuador, India, Malaysia, Panama, and Thailand, where he trained physicians to use scopes paid for by the agency. Next, USAID joined forces with private companies to make simplified and more robust scopes for hard travelling. In 1972 USAID ordered a handful of prototype kits from American Cystoscope

Makers Inc., and from Medical Technology International for field testing at home and abroad. A 1973 conference in Geneva debated various proposals for technical modifications and in 1974, the agency agreed to purchase 150 scopes from the lowest bidder. By the end of the initial contract period, USAID had purchased 250 scopes for around $3,000 ($14,000) per kit.[57]

The agency established the Program for International Education in Gynecology and Obstetrics (PIEGO), which extended Wheeless's program at Johns Hopkins to include the University of Pittsburgh in Pittsburgh, Pennsylvania, Washington University in St. Louis, Missouri, and the American University in Beirut, Lebanon. Gynecologists visiting from overseas received four to six weeks of didactic and clinical instruction in contraceptive technologies, including laparoscopy. Before operating on a woman for the first time, a trainee could practice on "Gynny," the pet name given to the popular plastic pelvic simulator made by Ortho, which resembled a woman's body from the waist down with stumps for legs (figure 7.1).[58] Scopes were delivered and assembled by a trainer on a follow-up visit to the graduate's home institution. By 1975 PIEGO had donated 175 scopes to 315 physicians in over fifty countries to the tune of $5 million ($21 million). Smaller organizations including the Association for Voluntary Sterilization and the Pathfinder Fund collectively distributed a further 100 scopes. By 1977 these numbers had increased to more than 1,400

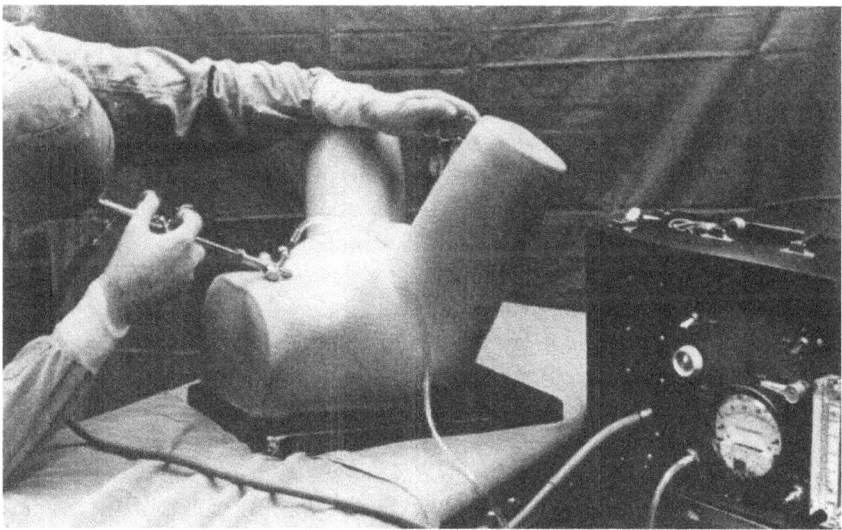

Figure 7.1. A promotional image of Ortho's pelvic teaching model "Gynny." Reprinted from J.F. Hulka, J.I. Fishburne, J.P. Mercer and K.F. Omran, "Laparoscopic Sterilization with a Spring Clip: A Report of the First Fifty Cases," *American Journal of Obstetrics and Gynecology* 116 (1973): 715–718, 716, Copyright 1973, with kind permission from Elsevier.

physicians from sixty-eight countries. An estimated 500,000 sterilizations had been performed using 809 scopes.[59] Beyond USAID and PIEGO, the American Association of Gynecological Laparoscopists (AAGL) dispatched teams of "flying doctors" to teach laparoscopy abroad, including in China soon after the government's notorious one-child policy was introduced in 1978.[60] Business was booming and an expanding and dynamic network of individual surgeons, academic institutes, private companies, and development organizations was scaling up and globalizing laparoscopy as never before.[61]

Globalizing Laparoscopy: Overcoming Controversy with Clips, Rings, and Bands

In the case of surgical sterilization it was, paradoxically, the high level of skill required to safely handle the complex, high precision and expensive equipment that attracted a minority of ambitious surgeons to laparoscopy, at the expense of proven but less flashy alternatives such as laparotomy, culdoscopy, and vasectomy.[62] Even under conditions perceived as ideal in the United States, paramedics were not generally expected to be able to master the technique.[63] The footswitch could be accidentally activated in a moment of distraction, so a high degree of skill and concentration was required to safely operate the spark-gap equipment.[64] In 1973 the AAGL's Complications Committee found that the incidence of severe electrical burns was disturbingly on the rise.[65] Eleven Johns Hopkins patients had sustained severe gastrointestinal injuries in 36,000 operations in four years. A puzzled Wheeless speculated that a bit of ileum (the terminal section of the small intestine) resting against the scope could be electrically burned if the operative instrument inadvertently made contact between the metal grasping forceps and the metal scope. In five instances, the surgeon had seen the forceps touch the intestine as the current was being passed through the fallopian tube and six women had endured laparotomy to repair the damage.

To minimize the risk of bowel injury, which seemed associated with operative speed, a proposed sterilization clinic in the United States would limit the maximum number of operations to ten per day. As Frangenheim put it, however, leading European laparoscopists worried that gynecologists in "underdeveloped" countries could end up standing "day and night" by their operating tables performing nothing but sterilizations.[66] This was generally expected to have undesirable consequences. The leading British laparoscopist Patrick Steptoe warned his American colleagues that he "wouldn't be happy about going into underdeveloped areas and showing them [local gynecologists] a few cases. They'll have accidents."[67] So, the American project of exporting laparoscopy had some very prominent critics, especially in the UK and Western Europe. American devotees of laparoscopy were undeterred, but even as they trained doctors and distributed scopes worldwide, they actively researched safer alternatives at home.

At Johns Hopkins, metal surgical clips normally used to ligate small blood vessels during delicate surgery were repurposed for sterilization.[68] But six of the fifty-two volunteers who were sent home without additional contraception fell pregnant, cutting short a preliminary study of the mostly harmless but unreliable "hemoclips."[69] Wheeless's colleague at Johns Hopkins, In Bae Yoon, had greater success with silicone plastic rings, which also raised (once again) the tantalizing prospect of controlled reversibility. By 1975 the Yoon band (or Falope ring) had been field tested in around 2,000 operations in the United States, Philippines, and South Korea with no reports of pregnancies or major complications. Yoon had taken out a U.S. patent and more than sixty physicians from Egypt, India, Iran, Mexico, and Thailand had received training in the new technique. The USAID-funded project to speed simplified methods of female sterilization from innovation to use was the "cornerstone" of gynecology at Johns Hopkins in the 1970s,[70] but Wheeless and Yoon were not the be-all and end-all of laparoscopy in this decade.

A popular spring-loaded plastic clip with teeth to firmly grip and partly destroy the fallopian tube was developed by gynecologist Jaroslav Hulka at the University of North Carolina (UNC) at Chapel Hill (figure 7.2).[71] Hulka's research was financed by the Carolina Population Center, which by the mid 1970s had channeled $34 million ($145 million) from organizations including USAID and the Ford Foundation into various university departments.[72] The center was perceived as strategically located for field testing new contraceptive technologies destined for the global South under realistically "backward" conditions in America's impoverished rural South.[73] A prototype applicator and clips were first tested in rhesus monkeys in Puerto Rico, quickly approved for clinical trial in human subjects and then tested on fifty women at North Carolina Memorial Hospital.[74] Applicators were made and distributed to international research centers and in two years the clips had been used to sterilize over 1,000 women in ten cities including Los Angeles, Fort Worth, London, Bombay, Bangkok, and Singapore. Richard Wolf redesigned the applicator based on field experience and randomized trials were set up to compare clips versus cauterization. On the grounds that the evaluation of surgical equipment was not regulated by any U.S. legislation, that conducting a long-term study in a mobile society was impractical and that he had presented his results at a medical conference, Hulka declared his "experiment" over and began inserting clips routinely without asking his patients for special consent to participate in a clinical trial.[75] The university relinquished the clips to Richard Wolf and they became the most important source of patent royalties to UNC in the 1980s.[76]

As the "panorama" of accessories expanded beyond Yoon bands and Hulka clips,[77] the techniques rapidly spread from America's southern states to the global South (figure 7.3). By the mid 1970s USAID had spent $1.4 million on

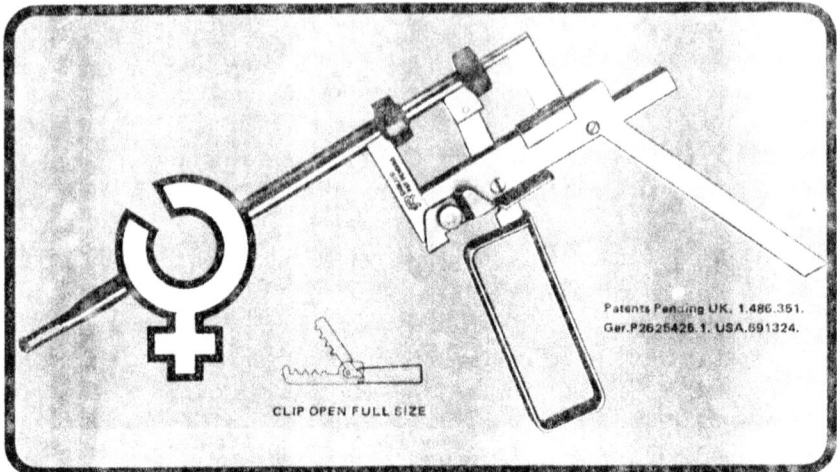

Figure 7.2. A promotional flyer from the late 1970s for Rocket's gun-like clip applicator dramatically evokes female sterilization by the broken gender symbol for woman. Reprinted with kind permission from Rocket Medical PLC and the Jaroslav Hulka Papers, David M. Rubenstein Rare Book & Manuscript Library, Duke University.

sterilization research and $6 million on surgical equipment in comparison to $25 million on condoms and $62 million on oral contraceptives.[78] In contrast to the costlier project of perpetually replenishing the supply of pills and condoms,[79] the process of training surgeons and distributing scopes was intended to be self-perpetuating. Local authorities were expected to gradually assume responsibility for training and certifying second and third generation surgeons, disburdening the American taxpayer. This process was referred to as the "seeding" or "rebound" effect by Louis Keith, the first treasurer of the AAGL, who took pride as "a citizen and taxpayer" that federal money had spread laparoscopy around the world. It was "staggering to look at the sums invested" in scopes and kits, the core of projects "designed to multiply themselves at local expense."[80] With pills and condoms, there was simply no exit strategy for USAID, but sterilization could potentially continue if and when international family planning fell out of favor with taxpayers.

Commercial technologies intended for overseas countries were incrementally simplified and made more efficient in international clinical trials. A logical end point of this process was reached in 1977 with gun-like devices designed to apply clips, bands or rings. One such device, the Laprocator™, was made in Newtown, Pennsylvania by KLI Inc., a private company with two manufacturing plants and a school for training foreign nationals in the repair and maintenance of surgical equipment. In 1973 members of the first AAGL teaching excursion had lugged an eighty-pound suitcase around Beirut.[81] A few years on, KLI's kit weighed only ten pounds for easy transport, cost half as much as a standard scope, and dispensed with bottled gas and electrical current altogether (figure 7.4).

Commissioned by USAID to meet the increasing international demand for female sterilization, the Laprocator could be manufactured in industrial quantities rather than in small batches. Within a year, the U.S. Food and Drug Administration (FDA) had approved and registered the Laprocator for sale. KLI manufactured different kits for different socioeconomic segments of the "medical market." The Tri-Control System (with optical, electrosurgical, and pneumatic components) was their "most sophisticated" product, but thanks to global demand, their low-cost Falope Ring System "was rapidly becoming the new standard for female sterilization." Ravenholt expected that USAID would purchase thousands of Laprocators and would finally be able to supply every interested "medical school and teaching hospital in the developing world" with an affordable and easy-to-use sterilization kit.[82] Although millions of middle-class American women chose to have their "tubes tied" in the 1970s, the extreme disparity between "contraceptive consumers" in the United States,[83] and the "clients" of international programs was exacerbated by the ruthless implementation in the field of technologies and techniques designed to maximize efficiency.

Figure 7.3. A world map showing the distribution of the 509 scopes purchased and distributed by USAID by 1976. Reprinted from R.T. Ravenholt, Willard H. Boynton, Dorothy N. Glenn, J. Joseph Speidel, Gerold van der Vlugt, Andrew T. Wiley and Gerald F. Winfield, "Worldwide program

experiences of the Agency for International Development," in *Laparoscopy*, edited by Jordan M. Phillips, 281–292, 291 (Baltimore: Williams & Wilkins Company, 1977), Copyright 1977 with kind permission from Wolters Kluwer.

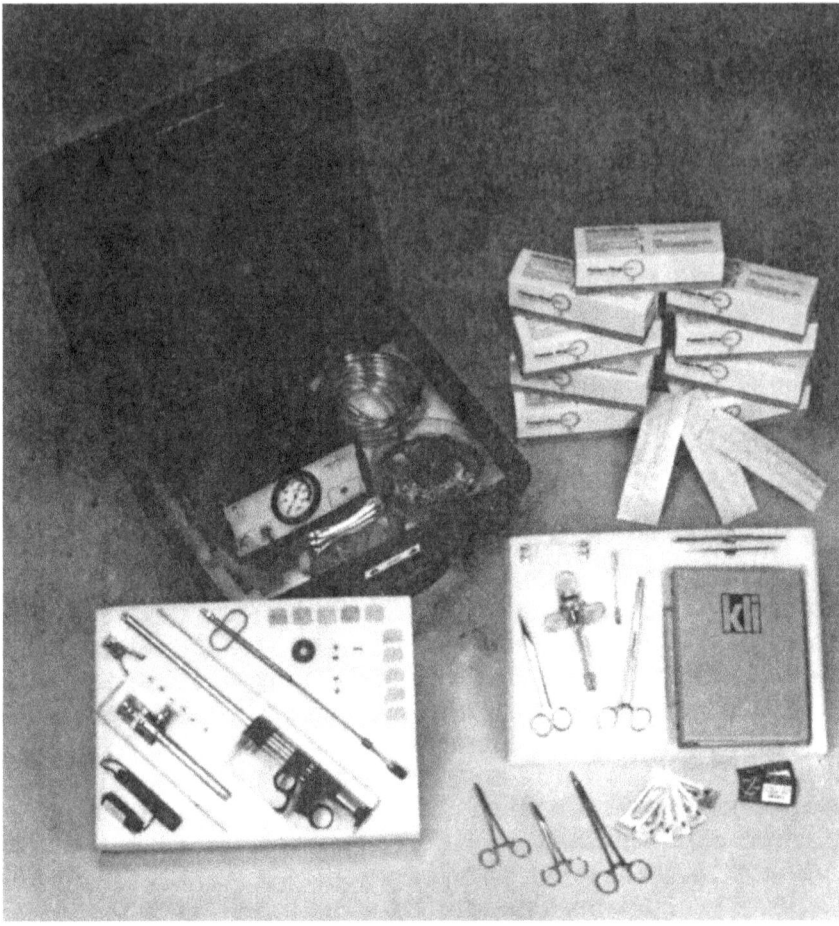

Figure 7.4. A promotional display of the compact KLI Laprocator system with instructional manual and reserve boxes of Falope rings. Reprinted from Ronald T. Burkman, "Evaluation of the Laprocator System," in *Surgical Equipment and Training in Reproductive Health*, edited by Ronald T. Burkman, Ronald H. Magarick and Ronald S. Waife, 50–55, 51 (Baltimore: JHPIEGO, 1980), Copyright 1980 with kind permission from JHPIEGO.

Localizing Laparoscopy: Fast, Cheap, and Out of Control

Rivaled only by China's one-child policy in terms of scale and notoriety, India has one of the oldest and most ambitious family planning programs in the world.[84] In the mid-1960s the Indian Ministry of Health launched a massive media campaign with a red triangle symbolizing family planning and set ambitious targets to insert Population Council-supplied IUDs into women.[85] By 1972, however, women had revolted against the painful "Lippes loops" and Indian family planners were shifting their attention to men. Massive vasectomy "festivals" were put on with USAID support first in Kerala, where 80,000 were sterilized in two months, and then in other states to meet rising government targets.[86] The Emergency period (June 1975–March 1977), when elections and civil liberties were controversially suspended in response to crop failures and economic crisis, resulted in more forceful drives. Most of the 8.26 million sterilizations performed in rural camps in 1976 were vasectomies of poor men. The notorious excesses of family planning during the Emergency were generally credited with Indira Gandhi's electoral defeat in 1977,[87] dramatized in post-Emergency critiques of family planning, and immortalized in world-famous historical fiction.[88] Women became the primary target of mass sterilization drives only after the Emergency, when the reputation of vasectomy was ruined and it had come to be regarded as a form of castration.[89]

Although it is more complicated, riskier, costlier, and has a longer recovery time than vasectomy, by the late 1980s, over 90 percent of surgical sterilizations in India were performed on women.[90] In terms of sheer numbers, laparoscopy was a global success. But it was also "localized" by its encounters with new actors in different cultural settings.[91] This final section returns to Pravin Mehta, the gynecologist from Calcutta who trained at Johns Hopkins and implemented laparoscopic sterilization on an unprecedented scale in India. Soon after he was recognized in the *Guinness Book of Records 1999* for having sterilized nearly 400,000 women,[92] Mehta bragged in the *Times of India* that he had taken the scope to "remote corners of the country" lacking electricity and running water. He had "streamlined things so much that patients [did] not even have to change their clothes during the procedure."[93]

Mehta first used the scope in a municipal hospital in the upscale Prabhadevi district of Bombay at the start of the Emergency period, when it seemed that compulsory sterilization for women with three or more children was on the cards.[94] Compulsion was officially abandoned as a policy, but in 1979 the neighboring state of Gujarat endorsed "voluntary" laparoscopic sterilization to "revitalize" a flagging family planning program.[95] As part of the program, Mehta sterilized over ten thousand women in one year using the Laprocator, which he raved about in the American journal, *Obstetrics and Gynecology*:

> The general belief that the laparoscope, an expensive, sophisticated, fragile instrument, is unsuitable for mass sterilization programs is in error . . . laparoscopic sterilization with the Falope ring is much safer, speedier, and cheaper than other techniques, and can be used in the patient's own rural setting.[96]

Mehta developed a "no exposure" technique to encourage "orthodox rural Indian women" who resented undressing in his presence to "volunteer" for sterilization (figure 7.5). He also developed and started using a "single puncture" technique, which saved time but increased the risk of internal injury to women. It was

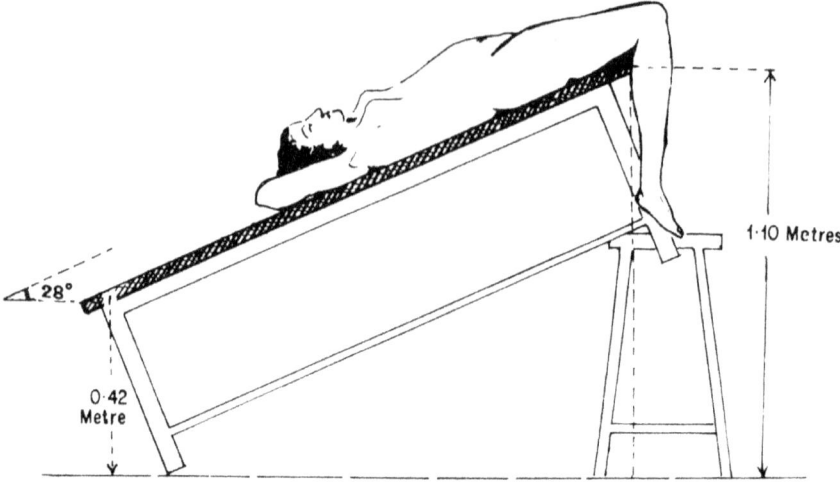

Figure 7.5. Mehta's preferred operating position: though apparently sketched nude, patients remained dressed in their everyday clothing with their midriffs conventionally exposed. Reprinted from Pravin V. Mehta, "Laparoscopic Sterilizations (16,803) without Vaginal Manipulation," *International Journal of Gynaecology and Obstetrics* 20 (1982): 323–325, 324, Copyright 1982 with kind permission from Elsevier.

standard practice to sterilize the surgical equipment between operations but asepsis was "cumbersome," so Mehta developed a quicker method of cleaning the scope in hot water and swabbing it with alcohol.[97] His performance increased from just over 10,000 operations in 1979 to almost 60,000 in 1981.[98] In 1989 he claimed in the *British Journal of Obstetrics and Gynecology* to have sterilized 250,136 women,[99] a number that seemed implausibly high to John Guillebaud, the medical director of the Margaret Pyke Centre, a leading family planning clinic in London.

Guillebaud was particularly incredulous of Mehta's "record" of 156 sterilizations in just under two hours. So to verify these extraordinary claims, he journeyed to a rural school near Calcutta to observe Mehta in action, videotaping him with elapsed time display to verify his speed. Astonishingly, Mehta spent less than one minute with each woman. Guillebaud also contacted a government secretary responsible for sterilization camps in West Bengal who independently confirmed Mehta's track record and informed him that most medical associations and individual gynecologists in India disapproved of Mehta's careless and high-speed methods.[100] Guillebaud too was critical of Mehta for lack of counseling and humaneness. He suggested that female nurses should provide preliminary pelvic exams and water should be boiled and changed more frequently to reduce the risk of hepatitis B and HIV infection.[101] He also argued that it would be "more humane" for the woman to be carried by stretcher to the recovery area, rather than "the present system of walking between two helpers."[102]

Despite the urgency to defuse what Mehta echoed Paul Ehrlich in calling "the population time bomb in developing countries,"[103] Guillebaud argued that he could have taken the time "to greet each woman by name and give her reassuring commentary, so that she is treated with gentleness and dignity."[104] Instead, women were numbered with stickers on their foreheads and arranged in two lines of even and odd in front of makeshift operating tables. In his hands, laparoscopy was a faster, cheaper, and riskier operation. Mehta crisscrossed India "on a war footing,"[105] working tirelessly in the country's poorest states including Rajasthan, Madhya Pradesh, Bihar and Orissa. His performance, recently described by one feminist film critic as "chilling and revolting," was captured in Deepa Dhanraj's classic feminist documentary *Something Like a War* (1991).[106] Mehta, who bragged to the film crew about his national service even as he walked from woman to woman, "snipping tubes,"[107] was clearly an extreme case, an exceptionally zealous maverick and a flashpoint for controversy and criticism. But since the 1980s feminist activists and social scientists have revealed that he was not alone in riding roughshod over women's basic rights.[108]

In 1982 the *Times of India* ran the upbeat headline, "With the scope there's hope," which described laparoscopic sterilization as "an outpatient procedure like visiting a dentist to have your teeth extracted."[109] In 1989, however, a headline in the same newspaper condemned the "High sterilisation death toll," emphasizing the unquantifiable trauma caused by the death of an individual mother with a family to take care of.[110] In the early 1990s the government responded to postoperative deaths caused by septicemia, peritonitis, tetanus and meningitis as well as to concerns regarding hepatitis and HIV transmission, by establishing regulations to cap the number of operations performed by a single team using two scopes at three per hour.[111] However a scathing 2000 review by Johns Hopkins based researchers found that these regulations were rarely followed in practice.[112] Recent fieldwork has shown that, in contradiction of official policy, women are still poorly informed about their choices, vasectomy is rarely proposed as an option, and a figure of authority such as a social worker, husband, or mother-in-law typically chooses sterilization on behalf of the woman who is to go under the knife.[113] Despite long-term government efforts to promote alternatives, family planning in India has become stabilized as female sterilization, a woman's burden.

Discussion: Beyond Choice and Coercion?

Some years before he would win the 1998 Nobel Prize in Economics, the Indian economist Amartya Sen weighed in on population control, eloquently arguing that pressuring poor women into sterilization camps with incentives and threats was, even by the standards of a country as poor as India, "a practice of remarkable barbarity and injustice."[114] Sen singled out "the unacceptability of coercion" and cited the "remarkable success in fertility reduction based on . . . women's empowerment and agency" in the state of Kerala.[115] Yet a study published in the same year revealed that a surgical team working under "appalling" conditions in Kerala had performed forty-eight operations in just over two hours in clear violation of official regulations.[116] Citing Sen, these findings were presented as particularly worrisome insofar as Keralan women were perceived as being more empowered than their counterparts in other states.[117]

As with many modern technologies, the story of laparoscopy is about progress towards faster speed, smaller size, lighter weight, and lower cost. But along the way, disturbing trade-offs have moved various commentators to condemn the most efficient form of female sterilization as chilling, revolting, barbarous, and unjust. Obviously, this story of technical change cannot be understood adequately outside the politics of international development and population control in the 1970s, a decade when U.S. foreign policy and gynecological surgery became strongly intertwined. In this period, purposes far beyond the immediate surgical control of an individual woman's body were materialized in scopes and clips. These things were imbued with the pressure to meet quotas, the obsession with efficiency, and the urgency to defuse India's population bomb. Laparoscopy was not merely symbolic or symptomatic of a particular social order. In the field, it perpetuated and reinforced gender and class inequalities, lack of choice, and a basic disregard for human dignity.

On a more general level, this chapter has examined where our choices to use a particular technology are located. It has shown how decisions made in the United States in the 1970s were modified and stabilized in India, where they still endure today. For better or for worse, the ways we decide to use a new technology tend to become "strongly fixed" in the material equipment, infrastructure and expertise our societies have invested in, losing much of the flexibility that existed at the outset.[118] In time, they may also acquire cultural legitimacy and even approval. In rural Andhra Pradesh, for example, tubal ligation has become a valuable symbolic resource exploited by young mothers to rapidly acquire the prestigious status of "senior woman."[119] Like legislative acts, policies, or regulations, technologies also constitute social habits that can endure for generations. Laparoscopy in India (and Puerto Rico) is a case in point. As such it deserves the same level of analysis that scholars have accorded to the discourses, organizations and social movements of population control. Gender and class inequalities are not only embodied in discriminatory policies and projects, but also in tangible things like stainless steel probes and spring-loaded plastic clips.

Since the 1980s, a central aim of feminist studies of technology has been to cast women as agents and not merely as passive victims of technology.[120] Of course, relatively affluent women have often enjoyed a certain degree of autonomy and control over their own bodies as patients and consumers.[121] KamaSutra condoms, for example, have been successfully marketed to Indian "yuppies" since the early 1990s and many educated urban women ironically prefer "traditional" methods like withdrawal and rhythm.[122] But when it comes to less well-off women, contraceptive choices are often severely constrained.[123] Despite the alleged decline of the one-size-fits-all paradigm and rise of the "cafeteria" approach to contraception,[124] poor, uneducated women remain India's "most avid consumers" of sterilization.[125] Manbhar may have chosen to walk miles across the desert to have her tubes tied, but did she have any other options?[126] I want to conclude this chapter by suggesting that we need to move beyond our obsession with agency, choice and coercion to start asking questions of a more tangible sort. We need to investigate how material technologies of population control worked (and often perpetuated inequalities) in practice, what the field conditions were like, and how bodily interventions, regardless of whether they were forced, voluntary, or something in between, were viscerally experienced by the women who encountered them in the most personal and intimate ways.

Acknowledgments

This chapter began as a term paper for Thomas Schlich, whose Canada Research Chair in History of Medicine at McGill University supported the fieldwork. Frank Suerich-Gulick was there at the start and I received generous feedback from participants at workshops in Basel, Berlin, Cambridge, Paris and Sherbrooke between 2009 and 2013. Rohan Deb Roy, Colin A.M. Duncan, Heinrich Hartmann, Sarah Hodges, Nick Hopwood, Ilana Löwy, Véronique Mottier, Dmitriy Myelnikov, Thomas Robertson, Thomas Schlich, Corinna Unger and Patrick Wagner are just some of those who commented on drafts. Research was supported by the Wellcome Trust (grant no. 088708), the Fonds québécois de la recherche sur la société et la culture (FQRSC), the Cambridge Commonwealth Trust, and Robinson College.

Notes

1. T. Fishlock, "Women walk across desert to be sterilized," *Times*, 29 May 1981, 6.
2. T. Fishlock, *Gandhi's Children: India in the Eighties* (New York, 1983), 41.
3. Fishlock, "Women walk across desert."
4. M. Connelly, "Population Control is History: New Perspectives on the International Campaign to Limit Population Growth," *Comparative Studies in Society and History* 45 (2003): 122–147.
5. J.A. Ross, D.H. Huber and S. Hong, "Worldwide Trends in Voluntary Sterilization," *International Family Planning Perspectives* 12 (1986): 34–39; J.E. Rioux and M. Daris, "Female Sterilization: an Update," *Current Opinion in Obstetrics & Gynecology* 13 (2001): 377–381.
6. For example, on "la operación" in Puerto Rico, see L. Briggs, *Reproducing Empire: Race, Sex, Science, and U.S. Imperialism in Puerto Rico* (Berkeley, 2002), 145.

7. T. Schlich, "The Technological Fix and the Modern Body: Surgery as a Paradigmatic Case," in *A Cultural History of the Human Body in the Modern Age*, L. Kalof and W. Bynum eds., (London, 2010), 71–92.
8. J. Schoen, *Choice and Coercion: Birth Control, Sterilization, and Abortion in Public Health and Welfare* (Chapel Hill, 2005).
9. See, for example, S. Trombley, *The Right to Reproduce: a History of Coercive Sterilization* (London, 1988); P.R. Reilly, *The Surgical Solution: a History of Involuntary Sterilization in the United States* (Baltimore, 1991); H. Bruinius, *Better For All the World: The Secret History of Forced Sterilization and America's Quest for Racial Purity* (New York, 2006); M.A. Largent, *Breeding Contempt: The History of Coerced Sterilization in the United States* (New Brunswick, 2008).
10. A. Dugdale, "Inserting Grafenberg's IUD into the Sex Reform Movement," in *The Social Shaping of Technology*, D. MacKenzie and J. Wajcman eds. (Buckingham, 1999), 318–324; "Devices and Desires: Constructing the Intrauterine Device, 1908–1988" (Ph.D. dissertation, University of Wollongong, 1995); C. Takeshita, *The Global Biopolitics of the IUD: How Science Constructs Users and Women's Bodies* (Cambridge, 2012).
11. See, for example, J. van Kammen, "Representing Users' Bodies: The Gendered Development of Anti-fertility Vaccines," *Science, Technology & Human Values* 24 (1999): 307–336; N. Oudshoorn, *The Male Pill: a Biography of a Technology in the Making* (Durham, 2003); T. E. Tunç, "Designs of Devices: The Vacuum Aspirator and American Abortion Technology," *Dynamis* 28 (2008): 353–376; L. Marks, *Sexual Chemistry: a History of the Contraceptive Pill* (New Haven, 2010); I. Löwy, "'Sexual Chemistry' Before the Pill: Science, Industry and Chemical Contraceptives, 1920–1960," *British Journal for the History of Science* 44 (2011): 245–274.
12. S. Hirschauer, "The Manufacture of Bodies in Surgery," *Social Studies of Science* 21 (1991): 279–319, 301; E. Shohat, "'Lasers for Ladies': Endo Discourses and the Inscriptions of Science," in *The Visible Woman: Imaging Technologies, Gender, and Science*, P.A. Treichler, L. Cartright, and C. Penley eds. (New York, 1998), 57–89; James R. Zetka, *Surgeons and the Scope* (Ithaca, 2003).
13. M. Guttmann, *Fixing Men: Sex, Birth Control, and AIDS in Mexico* (Berkeley, 2007), 134.
14. I. Dowbiggin, *The Sterilization Movement and Global Fertility in the Twentieth Century* (Oxford, 2008), 171.
15. G.S. Litynski, *Highlights in the History of Laparoscopy* (Frankfurt, 1996), 115–122.
16. On the limits of contraceptive choice: B. Hartmann, "Contraceptive Choice: a Multitude of Meanings," in *Issues in Reproductive Technology*, H. Bequaert Holmes ed. (New York, 1994), 3–9.
17. On use-centered history of technology: D. Edgerton, "Ten Eclectic Theses on the Historiography of Technology," *History and Technology* 16 (1999): 111–136; *The Shock of the Old: Technology and Global History Since 1900* (London, 2006), 211–212; "Innovation, Technology, or History: What is the Historiography of Technology About?" *Technology and Culture* 51 (2010): 680–697. The latest policy-centered history of population control is D.S. Hoff, *The Population Debate and Policy Making in US History* (Chicago, 2012).
18. On users: J. Bruce, "Users' Perspectives on Contraceptive Technology and Delivery Systems," *Technology in Society* 9 (1987): 359–383; A. Rudinow Saetnan, "Women's Involvement With Reproductive Medicine: Introducing Shared Concepts," in *Bodies of Technology: Women's Involvement With Reproductive Medicine*, Ann Rudinow Saetnan, Nelly Oudshoorn and Marta Kirejczyk eds. (Columbus, 2000), 1–30; N. Oudshoorn and T. Pinch, "How Users and Non-users Matter," in *How Users Matter: The Co-construction of Users and Technology*, N. Oudshoorn and T. Pinch eds. (Cambridge, 2003), 1–25.

19. J.-P. Gaudillière, "The Pharmaceutical Industry in the Biotech Century: Toward a History of Science, Technology and Business?" *Studies in History and Philosophy of Science* 32 (2001): 191–201.
20. M. Murphy, "Technology, Governmentality, and Population Control," *History and Technology* 26 (2010): 69–76.
21. For the latest outcry: G. Chamberlain, "UK Aid Helps to Fund Forced Sterilisation of India's Poor," *The Observer*, Sunday 15 April 2012, 24.
22. G.S. Litynski, "Hans Frangenheim: Culdoscopy vs. Laparoscopy, The First Book on Gynecological Endoscopy, and 'Cold Light,'" *Journal of the Society of Laparoendoscopic Surgeons* 1 (1997): 357–361. See also J. Hecht, *City of Light: The Story of Fiber Optics* (Oxford, 2004).
23. R. Israel e.a. "Overview of Laparoscopy," *Contemporary Ob/Gyn* 4 (1974): 111–160.
24. H. Frangenheim, "On the Development of Gynecologic Laparoscopy: a Recording of Human Ovulation," *Journal of Reproductive Medicine* 10 (1973): 227–229.
25. L. Keith, "Putting Laparoscopy on the Academic Map: Early and Continuing Scholarship by the AAGL," *Journal of Minimally Invasive Gynecology* 14 (2007): 549–552.
26. Compare with the case of modern fracture care: T. Schlich, *Science, Surgery and Industry: a Revolution in Fracture Care, 1950s–1990s* (New York, 2002), 2.
27. T. Robertson, *The Malthusian Moment: Global Population Growth and the Birth of American Environmentalism* (New Brunswick, 2012).
28. R.M. Kluchin, *Fit to be Tied: Sterilization and Reproductive Rights in America, 1950–1980* (New Brunswick, 2009), 70.
29. In 2012, the relative value of $30 million from 1970 ranges from $138 million to $453 million. A purchasing power calculator would multiply $30 million by the Consumer Price Index (CPI) to obtain $177 million. All conversions to 2012 dollars in this chapter are made using the CPI calculator at MeasuringWorth.com <http://www.measuringworth.com/index.php> (13 September 2013).
30. C.R. Wheeless, "Outpatient Tubal Sterilization," *Obstetrics and Gynecology* 36 (1970): 208–211, 208.
31. C.R. Wheeless, "A Rapid, Inexpensive, and Effective Method of Surgical Sterilization by Laparoscopy," *The Journal of Reproductive Medicine* 2 (1969): 65–69, 65.
32. Wheeless, "A Rapid, Inexpensive, and Effective Method," 65.
33. Ibid., 68.
34. Wheeless, "Outpatient Tubal Sterilization," 209.
35. C.R. Wheeless and B.H. Thompson, "Laparoscopic Sterilization: Review of 3600 Cases," *Obstetrics and Gynecology* 42(1973): 751–758, 758.
36. Kluchin, *Fit to be Tied*, 71–72.
37. J.E. Brody, "Gynecologist describes quick method of sterilization," *New York Times*, 7 April 1972, 16. See also A.M. Siegler, J. Hulka and A. Peretz, "Reversibility of Female Sterilization," *Fertility and Sterility* 43 (1985): 499–510.
38. L.A. Westoff, "Sterilization," *New York Times*, 29 September 1974, 259.
39. C.R. Wheeless, "Outpatient Sterilization by Laparoscopy Under Local Anesthesia in Less Developed Countries," in *Female Sterilization: Prognosis for Simplified Outpatient Procedures*, Gordon W. Duncan, R.D. Falb and J.J. Speidel eds. (New York, 1972), 125–129, 128.
40. C.R. Wheeless, "An Inexpensive Laparoscopy System for Female Sterilization," *American Journal of Obstetrics and Gynecology* 123 (1975): 727–733.
41. C.R. Wheeless, "Laparoscopy," *Clinical Obstetrics and Gynecology* 19 (1976): 277-298.
42. C.R. Wheeless, "Laparoscopic Sterilization Kit," *Obstetrics and Gynecology* 42 (1973): 303–306, 304.
43. Wheeless, "An Inexpensive Laparoscopy System," 732–733.

44. J. Sharpless, "World Population Growth, Family Planning, and American Foreign Policy," *Journal of Policy History* 7 (1995): 72–102; N. Oudshoorn, "From Population Control Politics to Chemicals: The WHO as an Intermediary Organization in Contraceptive Development," *Social Studies of Science* 27(1997): 41–72; M. Frey, "Neo-Malthusianism and Development: Shifting Interpretations of a Contested Paradigm," *Journal of Global History* 6 (2011): 75–97.
45. M. Connelly, *Fatal Misconception: The Struggle to Control World Population* (Cambridge, Mass., 2008), 289.
46. A.S. David, "Nepal: National Development, Population, and Family Population," *Studies in Family Planning* 1 (1969): 6–16.
47. K. Giri, "Experience of Outpatient Laparoscopic Sterilization in Nepal," in *Advances in Voluntary Sterilization*, M.E. Schima et al. eds. (Amsterdam, 1974), 36–41.
48. R.T. Ravenholt, W.H. Boynton, D.N. Glenn, J.J. Speidel, G. Van der Vlugt, A.T. Wiley, G.F. Winfield, "Worldwide Program Experiences of the Agency for International Development," in *Laparoscopy*, J.M. Phillips ed. (Baltimore, 1977), 281–292, 285.
49. *Female Sterilization: Prognosis for Simplified Outpatient Procedures*, G.W. Duncan, R.D. Falb and J.J. Speidel eds. (New York, 1972); D. Schneider Johnson, "Female Sterilization: Prognosis for Simplified Outpatient Procedures," *Contraception* 5 (1972): 155–163.
50. J.J. Speidel, "The Role of Female Sterilization in Family Planning Programs," in *Female Sterilization*, G.W. Duncan, R.D. Falb and J.J. Speidel eds. (New York, 1972), 89–105, 99.
51. D.G. Gillespie, "Reimert T. Ravenholt, USAID's Population Stalwart," *Population Today*, 28 (2000): 5.
52. R.T. Ravenholt, "Overview of the Offices of Population, A.I.D., on Sterilization," in *Female Sterilization*, 1–3, 1.
53. Schlich, *Science, Surgery and Industry*, 240.
54. See F. Eldhom, O. Harris and K. Young, "Conceptualising Women," *Critique of Anthropology* 3 (1977): 101–103; *Third World Women and the Politics of Feminism*, C. Talpade Mohanty, A. Russo and L. Torres eds. (Bloomington, 1991); N. Singh, "Of Victim Women and Surplus Peoples: Reproductive Technologies and the Representation of 'Third World' Women," *Studies in Political Economy* 52 (1997): 155–173; C. Talpade Mohanty, "'Under Western Eyes' Revisited: Feminist Solidarity Through Anticapitalist Struggles," *Signs* 28 (2003): 499–535.
55. See C. Unger's chapter in this volume.
56. Ravenholt, *Overview of the Offices of Population*, 1–2.
57. Ravenholt et al., *Worldwide Program Experiences*, 285–286.
58. On Ortho's "Gynny," see W. Kline, *Bodies of Knowledge: Sexuality, Reproduction, and Women's Health in the Second Wave* (Chicago, 2010), 47–48. On simulators more generally, see E. Johnson, "The Ghost of Anatomies Past: Simulating the One-sex Body in Modern Medical Training," *Feminist Theory* 6 (2005): 141–159; "Simulating Medical Patients and Practices: Bodies and the Construction of Valid Medical Simulators," *Body & Society* 14 (2008): 105–128.
59. Ravenholt et al., *Worldwide Program Experiences*, 287.
60. R.M. Soderstrom, "Report of 'Flying Doctors Teaching Team': Teaching Laparoscopy in Foreign Countries," *Gynecological Laparoscopy, Principles and Techniques*, J.M. Phillips, L.G. Keith eds. (New York, 1974), 403–405; G. Range, "Laparoscopists Exchange Medical Information with Chinese Gyns," *Ob.Gyn. News*, 15 April 1980, 1 and 44.
61. Compare with the lucrative global joint-replacement industry: J. Anderson, F. Neary, J.V. Pickstone, eds., *Surgeons, Manufacturers and Patients: a Transatlantic History of Total Hip Replacement* (New York, 2007).

62. R.T. Ravenholt et al., "The Use of Surgical Laparoscopy for Fertility Management Overseas," in *Endoscopy in Gynecology*, J.M. Phillips ed. (Downey, 1978), 213–225, 216.
63. Speidel, *The Role of Female Sterilization*, 105.
64. C.R. Wheeless and B.H. Thompson, "Laparoscopic Sterilization: Review of 3600 Cases," *Obstetrics and Gynecology* 42 (1973): 751–758.
65. J.F. Hulka et al., "Complications Committee of the American Association of Gynecological Laparoscopists. First Annual Report," *Journal of Reproductive Medicine* 10 (1973): 301–306, 305.
66. H. Frangenheim, "On the Development of Gynecologic Laparoscopy: a Recording of Human Ovulation," *Journal of Reproductive Medicine* 10 (1973): 227–229, 227.
67. Israel et al., "Overview of Laparoscopy," 154.
68. B.H. Thompson and C.R. Wheeless, "Failures of Laparoscopy Sterilization," *Obstetrics and Gynecology* 45 (1975): 659–664.
69. C.R. Wheeless, "Laparoscopically Applied Hemoclips for Tubal Sterilization," *Obstetrics and Gynecology* 44 (1974): 752–756, 754.
70. J.A. Rock, T.R.B. Johnson and J. Donald Woodruff, *Department of Gynecology and Obstetrics, the Johns Hopkins University School of Medicine, the Johns Hopkins Hospital: the First 100 Years* (Baltimore, 1991), 247.
71. Compare with a barbed IUD designed to pierce the uterus: A. Tone, "Violence by Design: Contraceptive Technology and the Invasion of the Female Body," *Lethal Imagination: Violence and Brutality in American History*, M.A. Bellesiles ed. (New York, 1999), 373–392.
72. G. Weisz and J. Olszynko-Gryn, "The Theory of Epidemiologic Transition: The Origins of a Citation Classic," *Journal of the History of Medicine and Allied Sciences* 65 (2010): 287–326, 300.
73. On the perception of southern states as "underdeveloped": W. Rushing, "Cold War Racial Politics and Global Impression Management: North Carolina Economic Development as a Case Study," *Current Sociology* 48 (2000): 51–69.
74. Hulka et al., "Laparoscopic Sterilization."
75. J.F. Hulka, et al., "Spring Clip Sterilization: One-year Follow-up of 1,079 Cases," *American Journal of Obstetrics and Gynecology* 125 (1976): 1039–1043.
76. J.F. Hulka, "History of the Spring Clip Development," in *Obstetrics and Gynecology at the University of North Carolina. The First Half Century*, C.H. Hendricks, R.C. Cefalo and W.E. Easterling eds. (Chapel Hill), 73–75.
77. T.H. Lean, "The Panorama of Laparoscopic Technology in Female Sterilization," *Australian and New Zealand Journal of Obstetrics and Gynaecology* 16 (1976): 100–105.
78. Weisz and Olszynko-Gryn, "The Theory of Epidemiologic Transition," 282–285. In 2012, this would be roughly equivalent to $5.9 million for sterilization, $25.6 million for surgical equipment, $107 million for condoms, and $264 million for pills.
79. On the population discourse and the contraceptive pill: E.-M. Silies, "Verhütung als Mittel gegen Bevölkerungswachstum. Expertendiskussion und öffentliche Debatten in Westdeutschland in den 1960er Jahren," *Berichte zur Wissenschaftsgeschichte* 33 (2010): 246–262.
80. Keith, "Putting Laparoscopy on the Academic Map," 225.
81. Soderstrom, "Report of 'Flying Doctors Teaching Team.'"
82. J.R. Jenk to R.T. Ravenholt, 4 November 1977, "Development of the KLI Laprocator System, 1976–1977," <http://www.ravenholt.com/> (15 December 1998).
83. See A. Tone, "Contraceptive Consumers: Gender and the Political Economy of Birth Control in the 1930s," *Journal of Social History* 29 (1996): 485–506.
84. For the earlier history: M. Vicziany, "Coercion in a Soft State: The Family Planning Program of India," *Pacific Affairs* 55 (1982–1983): 373–402 and 557–592; B.N. Ramusack, "Embattled Advocates: The Debate over Birth Control in India, 1920–1940," *Journal of Women's History* 1 (1989): 34–64; Emma Tarlo, *Unsettling Memories: Narratives of the Emergency in Delhi*

(London, 2003); M. Connelly, "Population Control in India: Prologue to the Emergency Period," *Population and Development Review* 32 (2006): 629–667; S. Hodges, ed., *Reproductive Health in India: History, Politic, and Controversies* (Hyderabad, 2006); S. Hodges, *Contraception, Colonialism and Commerce: Birth Control in South India, 1920–1940* (Aldershot, 2008); S. Ahluwalia, "Demographic Rhetoric and Sexual Surveillance: Indian Middle-class Advocates of Birth Control, 1902–1940s," in *Confronting the Body: The Politics of Physicality in Colonial and Post-colonial India* J.H. Mills and S. Sen, eds. (London, 2004), 183–202; *Reproductive Restraints: Birth Control in India, 1877–1947* (Champaign: University of Illinois Press, 2008); R. Nair, "The Construction of a 'Population Problem' in Colonial India, 1919–1947," *Journal of Imperial and Commonwealth History* 39 (2011): 227–247; I. Löwy, "Defusing the Population Bomb in the 1950s: Foam Tablets in India," *Studies in History and Philosophy of Biological and Biomedical Sciences* 43 (2012): 583–593.

85. C. Unger in this volume; Takeshita, *The Global Biopolitics of the IUD*, 66.
86. J. Palmer, "Festivals with a Purpose," *War on Hunger* 1 (1972): 6; S. Krishnakumar, "Kerala's Pioneering Experiment in Massive Vasectomy Camps," *Studies in Family Planning* 3 (1972): 177–185; Frey, *Neo-Malthusianism and Development*, 93.
87. Tarlo, *Unsettling Memories*, 145.
88. See S. Rushdie, *Midnight's Children* (London, 1981) and "The Free Radio" in *East, West* (London, 1994); R. Mistry, *A Fine Balance* (London, 1996).
89. Fishlock, *Gandhi's Children*, 43.
90. B. Hartmann, *Reproductive Rights and Wrongs: Global Politics of Population Control and Contraceptive Choice* (Boston, 1995), 253.
91. Saetnan, "Women's Involvement," 12. David Edgerton refers to this process as "creolisation": *The Shock of the Old*, 43–47.
92. N.D. Motashaw, "Endoscopy in India," *News Scope* 5(2000): 4.
93. Times Team, "11 feted for commitment to social work," *Times of India*, 8 January 2000, 3.
94. P.V. Mehta and K.B. Pathak, "Some Problems of Compulsion in Family Planning," *Journal of Biosocial Science* 9 (1977): 273–277.
95. P.V. Mehta, "Laparoscopic Sterilization with the Falope Ring: Experience with 10,100 Women in Rural Camps," *Obstetrics and Gynecology* 57 (1981): 345–350, 345.
96. Ibid., 349.
97. On the history of asepsis (versus antisepsis), see T. Schlich, "Asepsis and Bacteriology: a Realignment of Surgery and Laboratory Science," *Medical History* 56 (2012): 308–334.
98. P.V. Mehta, "Laparoscopic Sterilization Camps: a Retrospective," *Journal of Obstetrics and Gynaecology of India* 32 (1984): 191–193.
99. P.V. Mehta, "A Total of 250,136 Laparoscopic Sterilizations by a Single Operator." *British Journal of Obstetrics and Gynaecology* 9 (1989): 1024–1034.
100. J. Guillebaud, "Mass Laparoscopic Sterilizations," *British Journal of Obstetrics and Gynaecology* 96 (1989): 1019–1021, 1020.
101. See M. Vicziany, "HIV and AIDS in India: Love, Disease and Technology Transfer to the Kamasutra Condom," *Contemporary South Asia* 10 (2001): 95–129," and "HIV and AIDS in India: Blood, Money, Blood Banks and Technology Transfer," *Contemporary South Asia* 10 (2001): 381–414.
102. Guillebaud, *Mass Laparoscopic Sterilizations*, 1020.
103. Mehta, *Laparoscopic Sterilization*, 345.
104. Guillebaud, *Mass Laparoscopic Sterilizations*, 1020.
105. P.V. Mehta, J.G. Kulkarni and A. Mehta, "A Quick Method of Sterilizing a Laparoscope Used in 127,726 Falope Ring Tubal Ligations," *Journal of Obstetrics and Gynaecology of India* 33 (1983): 438–441.

106. M. Sinha, "Witness to Violence: Documentary Cinema and the Women's Movement in India," *Indian Journal of Gender Studies* 17 (2010): 365–373, 369.
107. Ibid.
108. See A. Maharatna, "India's Family Planning Programme: an Unpleasant Essay," *Economic and Political Weekly* 37 (2002): 971–981, 975.
109. R.H. Dastur, "With the scope there's hope," *Times of India*, 28 November 1982, 4.
110. U. Rai, "High sterilisation death toll," *Times of India*, 31 August 1989, 10.
111. M. Ramanathan, T.R. Dilip, and S.S. Padmadas, "Quality of Care in Laparoscopic Sterilisation Camps: Observations from Kerala, India," *Reproductive Health Matters* 6 (1995): 84–93, 84.
112. M.A. Koening, G.H.C. Foo and K. Joshi, "Quality of Care Within the Indian Family Welfare Programme: a Review of Recent Evidence," *Studies in Family Planning* 31 (2000): 1–18, 1.
113. A. Char, M. Saavala, T. Kulmala, "Male Perceptions on Female Sterilization: a Community-based Study in Rural Central India," *International Perspectives on Sexual and Reproductive Health* 35 (2009): 131–138, 135; A. Char, M. Saavala and T. Kulmala, "Influence of Mother-in-law on Young Couples' Family Planning Decisions in Rural India," *Reproductive Health Matters* 18 (2010): 154–162.
114. A. Sen, "Population Policy: Authoritarianism Versus Cooperation," *International Lecture Series on Population Issues, John D. and Catherine T. MacArthur Foundation*, 1995, 28.
115. Ibid., 21.
116. Ramanathan et al., "Quality of Care in Laparoscopic Sterilisation Camps," 84.
117. Ibid., 92.
118. L. Winner, "Do Artefacts Have Politics?" *Daedalus* 109 (1980): 121–136, 127.
119. M. Säävälä, "Understanding the Prevalence of Female Sterilization in Rural South India," *Studies in Family Planning* 20 (1999): 288–301, 289.
120. Oudshoorn and Pinch, "How Users and Non-users Matter," 5.
121. On patient-consumers in Britain: A. Mold, "Patient Groups and the Construction of the Patient-consumer in Britain: an Historical Overview," *Journal of Social Policy* 39 (2010): 505–521; "Making the Patient-consumer in Margaret Thatcher's Britain," *Historical Journal*, 54 (2011): 509–528.
122. W. Mazzarella, *Shoveling Smoke: Advertising and Globalization in Contemporary India* (Durham, 2003); A. Malwade Basu, "Ultramodern Contraception: Social Class and Family Planning in India," *Asian Population Studies* 1 (2005): 303–323.
123. See I. López, "Agency and Constraint: Sterilization and Reproductive Freedom Among Puerto Rican Women in New York City," *Urban Anthropology* 22 (1993): 299–323; L. Briggs, "Discourses of 'Forced Sterilization' in Puerto Rico: The Problem with Speaking Subaltern," *Differences* 10 (1998): 30–66; J. Schoen, "Between Choice and Coercion: Women and the Politics of Sterilization in North Carolina, 1929–1975," *Journal of Women's History* 13 (2001): 132–156.
124. N. Oudshoorn, "The Decline of the One-size-fits-all Paradigm, or, How Reproductive Scientists Try to Cope with Postmodernity," in *The Social Shaping of Technology*, D. MacKenzie and J. Wajcman eds. (Buckingham, 1999), 325–340.
125. S. Gosh, "Tying Tubes, Titrating Populations: The Politics of Female Sterilization in India," unpublished paper presented at the Irmgard Coninx Foundation on Population Politics and Human Rights. Berlin, Germany (14–20 February 2007).
126. On how women's reproductive choices can be radically circumscribed and dominated by oppressive structures of gender and class: R.S. Hegde, "Sons and M(others): Framing the Maternal Body and the Politics of Reproduction in a South Indian Context," *Women's Studies in Communication* 22 (1999): 25–44; J. Agnihotri Gupta, "Riddled with Secrecy and Unethical Practices: Assisted Reproduction in India," in *Bodies of Technology*, 239–253.

Bibliography

Ahluwalia, S., "Demographic Rhetoric and Sexual Surveillance: Indian Middle-Class Advocates of Birth Control, 1902–1940s," in *Confronting the Body: The Politics of Physicality in Colonial and Post-Colonial India*, J.H. Mills and S. Sen (London, 2004), 183–202.

Ahluwalia, S., *Reproductive Restraints: Birth Control in India, 1877–1947* (Champaign, 2008).

Anderson, J., Neary, F., Pickstone, J.V., eds., *Surgeons, Manufacturers and Patients: A Transatlantic History of Total Hip Replacement* (New York, 2007).

Basu, A.M., "Ultramodern Contraception: Social Class and Family Planning in India," *Asian Population Studies* 1 (2005): 303–323.

Briggs, L., "Discourses of 'Forced Sterilization' in Puerto Rico: The Problem with Speaking Subaltern," *Differences* 10 (1998): 30–66.

Briggs, L., *Reproducing Empire: Race, Sex, Science, and U.S. Imperialism in Puerto Rico* (Berkeley, 2002).

Bruce, J., "Users' Perspectives on Contraceptive Technology and Delivery Systems," *Technology in Society* 9 (1987): 359–383.

Bruinius, H., *Better for All the World: The Secret History of Forced Sterilization and America's Quest for Racial Purity* (New York, 2006).

Burkman, R.T., "Evaluation of the Laprocator System," in *Surgical Equipment and Training in Reproductive Health*, RT. Burkman, R.H. Magarick and R.S. Waife eds. (Baltimore, 1980), 50–55.

Char, A., Saavala, M., and Kulmala, T., "Influence of Mother-in-law on Young Couples' Family Planning Decisions in Rural India," *Reproductive Health Matters* 18 (2010): 154–162.

Char, A., Saavala, M., and Kulmala, T., "Male Perceptions on Female Sterilization: a Community-based Study in Rural Central India," *International Perspectives on Sexual and Reproductive Health* 35 (2009): 131–138.

Connelly, M., "Population Control in India: Prologue to the Emergency Period," *Population and Development Review* 32 (2006): 629–667.

Connelly, M., "Population Control is History: New Perspectives on the International Campaign to Limit Population Growth," *Comparative Studies in Society and History* 45 (2003): 122–147.

Connelly, M., *Fatal Misconception: The Struggle to Control World Population* (Cambridge, Mass., 2008).

David, A.S., "Nepal: National Development, Population, and Family Population," *Studies in Family Planning* 1 (1969): 6–16.

Dowbiggin, I., *The Sterilization Movement and Global Fertility in the Twentieth Century* (Oxford, 2008).

Dugdale, A., "Devices and Desires: Constructing the Intrauterine Device, 1908–1988." Ph.D. diss., University of Wollongong, 1995.

Dugdale, A., "Inserting Grafenberg's IUD Into the Sex Reform Movement," in *The Social Shaping of Technology*, D. MacKenzie and J. Wajcman eds. (Buckingham, 1999), 318–324.

Duncan, G.W., Falb, R.D., and Speidel, J.J., eds., *Female Sterilization: Prognosis for Simplified Outpatient Procedures* (New York, 1972).

Edgerton, D., "Innovation, Technology, or History: What is the Historiography of Technology About?" *Technology and Culture* 51 (2010): 680–697.

Edgerton, D., "Ten Eclectic Theses on the Historiography of Technology," *History and Technology* 16 (1999): 111–136.

Edgerton, D., *The Shock of the Old: Technology and Global History Since 1900* (London, 2006).

Eldhom, F., Harris, O., and Young, K., "Conceptualising Women," *Critique of Anthropology* 3 (1977): 101–103.

Fishlock, T., *Gandhi's Children: India in the Eighties* (New York, 1983).

Frangenheim, H., "On the Development of Gynecologic Laparoscopy: a Recording of Human Ovulation," *Journal of Reproductive Medicine* 10 (1973): 227–229.
Frey, M., "Neo-Malthusianism and Development: Shifting Interpretations of a Contested Paradigm," *Journal of Global History* 6 (2011): 75–97.
Gaudillière, J.-P., "The Pharmaceutical Industry in the Biotech Century: Toward a History of Science, Technology and Business?" *Studies in History and Philosophy of Science* 32 (2001): 191–201.
Gillespie, D.G., "Reimert T. Ravenholt, USAID's Population Stalwart," *Population Today* 28 (2000): 5.
Giri, K., "Experience of Outpatient Laparoscopic Sterilization in Nepal," in *Advances in Voluntary Sterilization*, M.E. Schima et al. eds. (Amsterdam, 1974), 36–41.
Guillebaud, J., "Mass Laparoscopic Sterilizations," *British Journal of Obstetrics and Gynaecology* 96 (1989): 1019–1021.
Gupta, J.A., "Riddled With Secrecy and Unethical Practices: Assisted Reproduction in India," in *Bodies of Technology: Women's Involvement with Reproductive Medicine*, A.R. Saetnan, N. Oudshoorn and M. Kirejczyk eds. (Columbus, 2000), 239–253.
Guttmann, M., *Fixing Men: Sex, Birth Control, and AIDS in Mexico* (Berkeley, 2007).
Hartmann, B., "Contraceptive Choice: a Multitude of Meanings," in *Issues in Reproductive Technology*, H.B. Holmes ed. (New York, 1994), 3–9.
Hartmann, B., *Reproductive Rights and Wrongs: Global Politics of Population Control and Contraceptive Choice* (Boston, 1995).
Hecht, J., *City of Light: The Story of Fiber Optics* (Oxford, 2004).
Hegde, R.S., "Sons and M(others): Framing the Maternal Body and the Politics of Reproduction in a South Indian Context," *Women's Studies in Communication* 22 (1999): 25–44.
Hirschauer, S., "The Manufacture of Bodies in Surgery," *Social Studies of Science* 21 (1991): 279–319.
Hodges, S., ed., *Reproductive Health in India: History, Politic, and Controversies* (Hyderabad, 2006).
Hodges, S., *Contraception, Colonialism and Commerce: Birth Control in South India, 1920–1940* (Aldershot, 2008).
Hoff, D.S., *The Population Debate and Policy Making in US History* (Chicago, 2012).
Hulka, J.F., et al., "Laparoscopic Sterilization with a Spring Clip: A Report of the First Fifty Cases," *American Journal of Obstetrics and Gynecology* 116 (1973): 715–718.
Hulka, J.F., et al., "Spring Clip Sterilization: One-year Follow-up of 1,079 Cases," *American Journal of Obstetrics and Gynecology* 125 (1976): 1039–1043.
Hulka, J.F. "History of the Spring Clip Development," in *Obstetrics and gynecology at the University of North Carolina. The First Half Century*, C.H. Hendricks, R.C. Cefalo and W.E. Easterling eds. (Chapel Hill), 73–75.
Hulka, J.F., et al., "Complications Committee of the American Association of Gynecological Laparoscopists. First Annual Report," *Journal of Reproductive Medicine* 10 (1973): 301–306.
Israel, R., et al., "Overview of Laparoscopy," *Contemporary Ob/Gyn* 4 (1974): 111–160.
Johnson, D.S., "Female Sterilization: Prognosis for Simplified Outpatient Procedures," *Contraception* 5 (1972): 155–163.
Johnson, E., "Simulating Medical Patients and Practices: Bodies and the Construction of Valid Medical Simulators," *Body & Society* 14 (2008): 105–128.
Johnson, E., "The Ghost of Anatomies Past: Simulating the One-sex Body in Modern Medical Training," *Feminist Theory* 6 (2005): 141–159.
Keith, L., "Putting Laparoscopy on the Academic Map: Early and Continuing Scholarship by the AAGL," *Journal of Minimally Invasive Gynecology* 14 (2007): 549–552.
Kline, W., *Bodies of Knowledge: Sexuality, Reproduction, and Women's Health in the Second Wave* (Chicago, 2010).

Kluchin, R.M. *Fit to be Tied: Sterilization and Reproductive Rights in America, 1950–1980* (New Brunswick, 2009).
Koening, M.A., Foo, G.H.C., and Joshi, K.,, "Quality of Care Within the Indian Family Welfare Programme: a Review of Recent Evidence," *Studies in Family Planning* 31 (2000): 1–18.
Krishnakumar, S., "Kerala's Pioneering Experiment in Massive Vasectomy Camps," *Studies in Family Planning* 3 (1972): 177–185.
Largent, Mark A. *Breeding Contempt: The History of Coerced Sterilization in the United States* (New Brunswick, 2008).
Lean, T.H., "The Panorama of Laparoscopic Technology in Female Sterilization," *Australian and New Zealand Journal of Obstetrics and Gynaecology* 16 (1976): 100–105.
Litynski, G.S., "Hans Frangenheim: Culdoscopy vs. Laparoscopy, the First Book on Gynecological Endoscopy, and 'Cold Light,'" *Journal of the Society of Laparoendoscopic Surgeons* 1 (1997): 357–361.
Litynski, G.S., *Highlights in the History of Laparoscopy* (Frankfurt, 1996).
López, I., "Agency and Constraint: Sterilization and Reproductive Freedom Among Puerto Rican Women in New York City," *Urban Anthropology* 22 (1993): 299–323.
Löwy, I., "'Sexual Chemistry' Before the Pill: Science, Industry and Chemical Contraceptives, 1920–1960," *British Journal for the History of Science* 44 (2011): 245–274.
Löwy, I., "Defusing the Population Bomb in the 1950s: Foam Tablets in India," *Studies in History and Philosophy of Biological and Biomedical Sciences* 43 (2012): 583–593.
Maharatna, A., "India's Family Planning Programme: an Unpleasant Essay," *Economic and Political Weekly* 37 (2002): 971–981.
Marks, L., *Sexual Chemistry: a History of the Contraceptive Pill* (New Haven, 2010).
Mazzarella, W., *Shoveling Smoke: Advertising and Globalization in Contemporary India* (Durham, 2003).
Mehta, P.V., "A Total of 250,136 Laparoscopic Sterilizations by a Single Operator," *British Journal of Obstetrics and Gynaecology* 9 (1989): 1024–1034.
Mehta, P.V., "Laparoscopic Sterilization Camps: a Retrospective," *Journal of Obstetrics and Gynaecology of India* 32 (1984): 191–193.
Mehta, P.V., "Laparoscopic Sterilization with the Falope Ring: Experience with 10,100 Women in Rural Camps," *Obstetrics and Gynaecology* 57 (1981): 345–350.
Mehta, P.V., "Laparoscopic Sterilizations (16,803) Without Vaginal Manipulation," *International Journal of Gynaecology and Obstetrics* 20(1982): 323–325.
Mehta, P.V., and Pathak, K.B., "Some Problems of Compulsion in Family Planning," *Journal of Biosocial Science* 9 (1977): 273–277.
Mehta, P.V., Kulkarni, J.G., and Mehta, A., "A Quick Method of Sterilizing a Laparoscope used in 127,726 Falope Ring Tubal Ligations," *Journal of Obstetrics and Gynaecology of India* 33 (1983): 438–441.
Mistry, R., *A Fine Balance* (London, 1996).
Mohanty, C.T., "'Under Western Eyes' Revisited: Feminist Solidarity Through Anticapitalist Struggles," *Signs* 28 (2003): 499–535.
Mohanty, C.T., Russo, A., and Torres, L., eds., *Third World Women and the Politics of Feminism* (Bloomington, 1991).
Mold, A., "Making the Patient-consumer in Margaret Thatcher's Britain," *Historical Journal* 54 (2011): 509–528.
Mold, A., "Patient Groups and the Construction of the Patient-consumer in Britain: an Historical overview," *Journal of Social Policy* 39 (2010): 505–521.
Motashaw, N.D. "Endoscopy in India," *News Scope* 5 (2000): 4.
Murphy, M., "Technology, Governmentality, and Population Control," *History and Technology* 26 (2010): 69–76.

Nair, R., "The Construction of a 'Population Problem' in Colonial India, 1919–1947," *Journal of Imperial and Commonwealth History* 39 (2011): 227–247.

Oudshoorn, N., and Pinch, T., "How Users and Non-users Matter," in *How Users Matter: The Co-construction of Users and Technology*, N. Oudshoorn and T. Pinch eds. (Cambridge, Mass., 2003), 1–25.

Oudshoorn, N., "From Population Control Politics to Chemicals: The WHO as an Intermediary Organization in Contraceptive Development," *Social Studies of Science* 27 (1997): 41–72.

Oudshoorn, N., "The Decline of the One-size-fits-all Paradigm, or, How Reproductive Scientists Try to Cope with Postmodernity," in *The Social Shaping of Technology*, D. MacKenzie and J. Wajcman eds. (Buckingham, 1999), 325–340.

Oudshoorn, N., *The Male Pill: a Biography of a Technology in the Making* (Durham, 2003).

Palmer, J., "Festivals with a Purpose," *War on Hunger* 1 (1972): 6.

Ramanathan, M., Dilip, T.R., and Padmadas, S.S., "Quality of Care in Laparoscopic Sterilisation Camps: Observations from Kerala, India," *Reproductive Health Matters* 6 (1995): 84–93.

Ramusack, B.N. "Embattled Advocates: The Debate over Birth Control in India, 1920–1940," *Journal of Women's History* 1 (1989): 34–64.

Range, G., "Laparoscopists Exchange Medical Information with Chinese Gyns," *Ob.Gyn. News*, 15 April 1980, 1 and 44.

Ravenholt, R.T. et al., "Worldwide Program Experiences of the Agency for International Development," in *Laparoscopy*, J.M. Phillips ed. (Baltimore, 1977), 281–292.

Ravenholt, R.T., "Overview of the Offices of Population, A.I.D., on Sterilization," in *Female Sterilization: Prognosis for Simplified Outpatient Procedures*, G.W. Duncan, R.D. Falb and J.J.Speidel eds. (New York, 1972), 1–3.

Ravenholt, R.T. et al, "The Use of Surgical Laparoscopy for Fertility Management Overseas," in *Endoscopy in Gynecology*, J.M. Phillips ed. (Downey, 1978), 213–325.

Reilly, P.R., *The Surgical Solution: a History of Involuntary Sterilization in the United States* (Baltimore, 1991).

Rioux, E., Daris, J., and Daris, M., "Female Sterilization: an Update," *Current Opinion in Obstetrics & Gynecology* 13 (2001): 377–381.

Robertson, T., *The Malthusian Moment: Global Population Growth and the Birth of American Environmentalism* (New Brunswick, 2012).

Rock, J.A., Johnson, T.R.B., and Woodruff, J.D., *Department of Gynecology and Obstetrics, the Johns Hopkins University School of Medicine, the Johns Hopkins Hospital: the First 100 Years* (Baltimore, 1991).

Ross, J.A., Huber, D.H., and Hong, S., "Worldwide Trends in Voluntary Sterilization," *International Family Planning Perspectives* 12 (1986): 34–39.

Rushdie, S., *East, West* (London, 1994).

Rushdie, S., *Midnight's Children* (London, 1981).

Rushing, W., "Cold War Racial Politics and Global Impression Management: North Carolina Economic Development as a Case Study," *Current Sociology* 48 (2000): 51–69.

Säävälä, M., "Understanding the Prevalence of Female Sterilization in Rural South India," *Studies in Family Planning* 20 (1999): 288–301.

Saetnan, A.R., "Women's Involvement with Reproductive Medicine: Introducing Shared Concepts," in *Bodies of Technology: Women's Involvement with Reproductive Medicine*, A.R. Saetnan, N. Oudshoorn and M. Kirejczyk eds. (Columbus, 2000), 1–30.

Schlich, T., "Asepsis and Bacteriology: a Realignment of Surgery and Laboratory Science," *Medical History* 56 (2012), 308–334.

Schlich, T., "The Technological Fix and the Modern Body: Surgery as a Paradigmatic Case," in *A Cultural History of the Human Body in the Modern Age*, L. Kalof and W. Bynum eds. (London, 2010), 71–92.

Schlich, T., *Science, Surgery and Industry: a Revolution in Fracture Care, 1950s–1990s* (New York, 2002).
Schoen, J., "Between Choice and Coercion: Women and the Politics of Sterilization in North Carolina, 1929–1975," *Journal of Women's History* 13 (2001): 132–156.
Schoen, J., *Choice and Coercion: Birth Control, Sterilization, and Abortion in Public Health and Welfare* (Chapel Hill, 2005).
Sen, A., "Population Policy: Authoritarianism Versus Cooperation," *Journal of Population Economics* 10 (1997): 3–22.
Sharpless, J., "World Population Growth, Family Planning, and American Foreign Policy," *Journal of Policy History* 7 (1995): 72–102.
Shohat, E., "'Lasers for Ladies': Endo Discourses and the Inscriptions of Science," in *The Visible Woman: Imaging Technologies, Gender, and Science*, P.A. Treichler, L. Cartright and C. Penley eds. (New York, 1998), 57–89.
Siegler, A.M., Hulka, J., and Peretz, A., "Reversibility of Female Sterilization," *Fertility and Sterility* 43 (1985): 499–510.
Silies, E.-M., "Verhütung als Mittel gegen Bevölkerungswachstum. Expertendiskussion und öfentliche Debatten in Westdeutschland in den 1960er Jahren," *Berichte zur Wissenschaftsgeschichte* 33 (2010): 246–262.
Singh, N., "Of Victim Women and Surplus Peoples: Reproductive Technologies and the Representation of 'Third World' Women," *Studies in Political Economy* 52 (1997): 155–173.
Sinha, M., "Witness to Violence: Documentary Cinema and the Women's Movement in India," *Indian Journal of Gender Studies* 17 (2010): 365–373.
Soderstrom, R.M. "Report of 'Flying Doctors Teaching Team': Teaching Laparoscopy in Foreign Countries," in *Gynecological Laparoscopy, Principles and Techniques*, J.M. Phillips and L.G. Keith eds. (New York, 1974), 403–405.
Speidel, J.J., "The Role of Female Sterilization in Family Planning Programs," in *Female Sterilization*, G.W. Duncan, R.D. Falb and J.J. Speidel eds. (New York, 1972), 89–105.
Takeshita, C., *The Global Biopolitics of the IUD: How Science Constructs Users and Women's Bodies* (Cambridge, Mass., 2012).
Tarlo, E., *Unsettling Memories: Narratives of the Emergency in Delhi* (London, 2003).
Thompson, B.H., and Wheeless, C.R., "Failures of Laparoscopy Sterilization," *Obstetrics and Gynecology* 45 (1975): 659–664.
Tone, A., "Contraceptive Consumers: Gender and the Political Economy of Birth Control in the 1930s," *Journal of Social History* 29 (1996): 485–506.
Tone, A., "Violence by Design: Contraceptive Technology and the Invasion of the Female Body," in *Lethal Imagination: Violence and Brutality in American History*, M.A. Bellesiles ed. (New York, 1999), 373–392.
Trombley, S., *The Right to Reproduce: a History of Coercive Sterilization* (London, 1988).
Tunç, T.E., "Designs of Devices: The Vacuum Aspirator and American Abortion Technology," *Dynamis* 28 (2008): 353–376.
Van Kammen, J., "Representing Users' Bodies: The Gendered Development of Anti-fertility Vaccines," *Science, Technology & Human Values* 24 (1999): 307–336.
Vicziany, M., "Coercion in a Soft State: The Family Planning Program of India," *Pacific Affairs* 55 (1982–1983): 373–402 and 557–592.
Vicziany, M., "HIV and AIDS in India: Blood, Money, Blood Banks and Technology Transfer," *Contemporary South Asia* 10 (2001): 381–414.
Vicziany, M., "HIV and AIDS in India: Love, Disease and Technology Transfer to the Kamasutra Condom," *Contemporary South Asia* 10 (2001): 95–129.
Weisz, G., and Olszynko-Gryn, J., "The Theory of Epidemiologic Transition: The Origins of a Citation Classic," *Journal of the History of Medicine and Allied Sciences* 65 (2010): 287–326.

Wheeless, C.R. "A Rapid, Inexpensive, and Effective Method of Surgical Sterilization by Laparoscopy," *The Journal of Reproductive Medicine* 2 (1969): 65–69.

Wheeless, C.R. "An Inexpensive Laparoscopy System for Female Sterilization," *American Journal of Obstetrics and Gynecology* 123 (1975): 727–733.

Wheeless, C.R. "Laparoscopically Applied Hemoclips for Tubal Sterilization," *Obstetrics and Gynecology* 44 (1974): 752–756.

Wheeless, C.R. "Laparoscopic Sterilization Kit," *Obstetrics and Gynecology* 42 (1973): 303–306.

Wheeless, C.R. "Laparoscopy," *Clinical Obstetrics and Gynecology* 19 (1976): 277–298.

Wheeless, C.R. "Outpatient Sterilization by Laparoscopy Under Local Anesthesia in Less Developed Countries," in *Female Sterilization: Prognosis for Simplified Outpatient Procedures*, G.W. Duncan, R.D. Falb and J.J. Speidel eds. (New York, 1972), 125–129.

Wheeless, C.R., "Outpatient Tubal Sterilization," *Obstetrics and Gynecology* 36 (1970): 208–211.

Wheeless, C.R., and Thompson, B.H., "Laparoscopic Sterilization: Review of 3600 Cases," *Obstetrics and Gynecology* 42 (1973): 751–758.

Winner, L., "Do Artefacts Have Politics?" *Daedalus* 109 (1980): 121–136.

Zetka, J.R., *Surgeons and the Scope* (Ithaca, 2003).

8

A TWOFOLD DISCOVERY OF POPULATION

Assessing the Turkish Population by its "Knowledge, Attitudes, and Practices," 1962–1980

Heinrich Hartmann

> The couples of Turkey approve of family planning. On the national front, they know that the Turkish population is growing rapidly and a substantial number think it should grow more slowly ... A smaller family norm seems already to be established in many Turkish minds. ... The Turkish people have very few ideological objections to contraception and they would like to learn how to practice it effectively. They very strongly wish that the government would organize a program to inform them about family planning.
>
> —B. Berelson, "Turkey: National Survey on Population," in: *Studies in Family Planning*

Introduction

Bernard Berelson's description of Turkey's situation in 1964 was the result of the first international expertise assessing the prospects of a family planning program in Turkey in the early 1960s. Turkey's doors were open to international experts and to local Turkish teams. A general state planning policy euphoria ruled the country and as part of it, a concerted population policy seemed to be within reach. In 1978, four years after retiring from the presidency of New York's Population Council, "Barney" Berelson still classified Turkey as being one of the countries that would probably have a national program in the future, and that showed an "administrative potential" to build up a national program.[1] Astonishingly, little had been achieved in terms of a national program to reduce birth rates in the period between 1963 and 1978. By the end of the 1970s, the country was no longer seen as being at the forefront of population policy, as the optimistic statements of the early 1960s suggested. The interests of international experts moved away from Anatolia, and other regions of the world became more important.

This chapter seeks to look at the population dynamics and structural changes in Turkish population programs between 1963 and 1978. It inquires into the interest of international experts in Turkish family planning programs and it relates these dynamics to the arrival of transnational agents and institutions in family planning as well as to shifts in their baseline assumptions. I will also take a look inside the epistemic negotiations between different cultures and systems of knowledge. In doing so, the chapter will tend to place Turkey into the rationales of international development discourses and practices that experienced an important new impulse with the conjuncture of global overpopulation discourses in the late 1950s and 1960s.[2]

Turkey was neither the first nor the most prominent place for family planning programs around the globe. However, this chapter argues that it played an important role in the minds of the international family planning movement for a certain period of time. The relative openness of state officials in terms of their willingness to modernize their country along the lines of Western modernization theory was particularly strong after the political turning point of 1960. The new emphasis on state planning was a tool of a new Keynesian development policy. This not only implied new and heavy investment by the state, but also a new approach to public health and population issues. They were now addressed in the framework of a coherent development policy, and the economic dimension of this "overpopulation" issue became part of the political debate about the future of Turkey. After the *coup d'état* of 1960, the Turkish Ministry of Health thus took on new activities, and the early introduction of a Department for Family Planning was one of them. The relative openness of national agents as well as the already existing grid of health care institutions in rural areas made Turkey appear full of opportunities for international experts.[3] In addition to this, the country seemed to be a convenient entrance gate to the wider Middle East and to Muslim countries in general.[4] Turkey's laic state policy combined with its important role in the Islamic world seemed to hasten its formation as a new role model to inquire about the relatedness of fate and reproductive behavior. Furthermore, it played a prominent role in the reflections on the implementation of new programs in Islamic countries.[5]

Thus, the history of Turkish family planning not only opens up questions about new forms of development aid in the Cold War context, it also forces us to reflect on the role of international expertise in the construction of national social policies. Contemporaries and involved agents saw social knowledge as a viable part of modernity, one that could be easily transferred in space and time.

However, the diverging experiences of these agents raised questions about the motives of scientists as well as about the different backgrounds and contexts of social policies. Historical research analyzed elements of a European "culture of intervention" that slowly shifted away from state-interventionism towards the "self" as the regulatory concept of prevention.[6] If this is the case, discourses and practices of public health and reproductive behavior could then be a key to understand whether this general pattern also applies to other regions of the world. It might thus differentiate our understanding of a homogenous European model. Or—in the case of Turkey—it might also show us to what extent scientific discourses contributed to substantiate geographical and cultural borders. In the minds of postwar experts in applied social sciences, such as the New York family planning experts, a behavioralist approach allowed precisely a generalized pattern that abstracted from cultural particularities.[7] All that counted was individual behavior and motives. Implicitly, the action of many international experts in Turkey was based on the assumption that the country was different from the "modern world," and that it was part of the "targeted Third World" as well as a predominantly "Muslim space." This chapter is thus also about the differences between a "neutral" behavioralist approach and these basic assumptions.

In this respect, the construction of population as a "social problem" was everything but self-evident and deserves our attention from a history of knowledge perspective. In his almost classical paper on the construction of expert knowledge, Michel Callon demonstrates how deeply the definition of a problem is a process of exclusion. It excludes alternative forms of knowledge, it excludes alternative objects, and it excludes alternative expertise. It can thus be understood as cutting a chosen object out of a web of competing relations and isolating it.[8] Experts' defining of population as a problem also means defining their own peer group as the right group of experts to act on this problem.[9]

But looking to historical settings often tends to make arguments look a lot more complicated. Family planning was not exclusively the reserve of a monopoly of international experts; on the contrary, it was subject to international expertise as much as to national social policy and local knowledge. It thus points to the different layers of knowledge, where a transnational dimension could coexist with other scales of expertise.[10] Population as an object of regulation was subject to a variety of epistemic interests that were not all directly linked to global discourses. Various ways of thinking can coexist, not only within one country, but also within one institution, within one political movement, or even within one individual's mind. A multilayered understanding of this specific construction of social knowledge in the case of population control and family planning may therefore also open a different understanding of the ways in which agents interacted in this field.

Turkish population policy thus presents a fitting object with which to reflect on this aspect of a transnational history of demographic discourses and practices.

Through the strong context of a national modernization policy and the local settings of reproduction knowledge, it offers insights into a multidimensional construction of social knowledge.

Unique Backgrounds and Isolated Factors

Concepts in population control embraced new methods and assumptions in the 1960s. Above all the human was a living being, and its features were therefore results of behavior that could be scientifically analyzed, explained, and modified.[11] Circles of experts, at least of the New York-based international organizations and foundations, were concerned with new forms of human development through public health measures, and widely shared certain behavioralist assumptions. The field of family planning and birth control was one of the best and foremost examples of bringing these new approaches into practice.[12] Already in the 1940s and early 1950s, eminent scholars like Frank Notestein acknowledged that the increasing world population was most probably not the result of lacking knowledge on contraception itself, because in virtually all parts of the world contraceptive techniques were part of the traditional knowledge of societies.[13] Instead, social structures were to be blamed for the gap between an existing contraceptive knowledge and effective reproductive behavior. This made it necessary to integrate new socio-structural arguments into the rationale of population policy and the family planning experts.[14] It necessarily also implied a rather extensive set of new schemes and techniques for inquiring into this gap. The social scientists involved wanted widespread and transposable schemes to evaluate the knowledge of local populations and to likewise improve their own programs. In every stage of a new program, from the first surveys to the follow-up studies, the adaption of a behavioralist model was the central hypothesis that was only thinkable through new cybernetic methods, and thus heavily reliant on technological innovations like interview coding and card punching. But it was not only a question of the right techniques; the new approach also relied on the selection of significant case studies. Political contexts and the "attitudes of the intellectuals"[15] seemed to present important factors for the successful implementation of family planning programs.

In this respect, Turkey looked like a "promised land" for population policy experts. After the *coup d'état* in 1960, notions of Turkish development underwent a radical change. General Cemal Gürzel's insurrection against president Adnan Menderes was partly an emergency break against the fact that Turkey depended more and more on foreign financial aid. Possible solutions to this situation adopted much the same logic of the postwar planning euphoria. Together with the OECD's economic experts, the new government under Atatürk's former companion, president İsmet İnönü, issued a five-year plan that was meant to free the Turkish economy from international economic dependency. However, within this state-driven program, new forms of interventionism took shape and the new plan not only targeted an increase in productivity but also issued new forms of social policy. Defining population policy as an issue of the welfare state's policy was also anchored in these new "European" conceptions of regulating the social.[16] The first Turkish five-year plan in the postwar period covered the years from 1963 to 1967. It led to a restructuring of Turkish governmental institutions, and particularly the Ministry of Health. Such new forms of interventionism were now accompanied by the work and support of international experts.

The introduction of a new culture of social intervention and a new health policy in Turkey coincided with the question of defining development in an era of "new global needs." These policies also shifted away from supporting governments' financial policies and big infrastructural schemes, yet they embraced new project design, acting much more directly on the "social."[17] One urgent field of policy making was the regulation of a growing "world population." In late 1962, freshly appointed undersecretary Nusret H. Fişek, sent an official request to New York's Population Council, requesting assistance in the construction of new plans for birth control. In order to design its own plan for population control, Fişek asked for financial and technical help. To encourage an interest in Turkey's problems, he pointed out that 43 percent of the population was under fourteen years of age and that the average rate of the population's yearly increase approached three percent.[18] Frank Notestein was the right person to contact. With the letter of January 10th 1963, Notestein proposed to send a mission to Turkey that could prepare a report and make recommendations for the establishment of such a program. A similar undertaking in the preceding years in India, Pakistan, and South Korea had already been established by the Population Council. The matter was immediately taken up during a personal meeting between Notestein and Turkish representatives on February 22nd and 23rd in Ankara; six weeks later the official mission arrived in Turkey.

This mission was clearly not the only one of its kind. As mentioned above, similar missions were sent to countries in Central and East Asia among others.[19] The council thus forged a kind of "best practice" in the implementation of population policy, yet in certain respects, the Turkish mission was special. The Population Council's experts developed a new way of making sense of the collected data. The mission was led by the head of the council's scientific unit C. Parker Mauldin, and Leslie Corsa Jr. Other members included Marshall C. Balfour, former medical expert of the Rockefeller foundation, and Howard C. Taylor, gynecologist at Columbia University. The most important member was the council's vice-president, Bernard Berelson. Both Mauldin and Berelson stressed the importance of accurate and proper statistical preparations for any population policy whatsoever,[20] and recommended even in their preliminary observations the inclusion of a "survey of knowledge of, attitudes towards, and practice of contraceptives, plus fertility histories"[21] into the catalogue of population policies in Turkey:

> Such information is important in order to establish success or failure of the program more quickly than can be done with the vital statistics.... In addition, it is our impression that the villagers are much readier for family planning information and supplies than is generally supposed; hence such data on this topic could contribute substantially to decisions regarding the promotion of education efforts. Furthermore, this information would guide other policy decisions by showing what groups are more and less ready for family planning, and thus help to build an economic as well as an effective program.[22]

The Turkish government agreed to this so-called KAP approach (Knowledge, Attitudes, and Practice), and suggested that interview samples be taken from 1,000 people from rural, semi-urban, urban, and metropolitan areas.[23] When the Population Council's expert team came to Turkey to carry out the interviews in the summer of the same year, they discovered that they were not the first in the field.[24] Earlier during the summer of 1962, the Turkish Ministry had already asked USAID for help on the back of a UN mission enhancing community development in Turkey.[25] The steering committee had been formed together with scholars from MIT and Columbia University, to inquire about the health conditions and attitudes towards development in Turkish villages in general, already emphasizing the role of local elites.[26] It hereby embraced the behavioralist assumption of modernization theorists that socioeconomic structures in the villages deserved closer attention, if individual behavior was to be changed.[27] In this sense, the Turkish projects were of crucial importance for international experts in family planning.

The new enterprise of Turkey's first KAP study adopted parts of the infrastructure of this preceding project as well as some of the interviewing teams, which were mainly formed from school teachers during their summer holidays. The Population Council's expert George W. Angell was sent to Turkey to advise the interviewers, and reported back optimistically on the attitudes of interviewees: "in most cases, hesitancy is overcome before the hot questions are reached."[28]

As early as October 1963, the Turkish government was able to transmit the first results of the survey to the Population Council in New York. In doing so it met its own deadline to coincide with the meeting of the Gynecological Association, taking place in Ankara at around the same time.[29] The zealousness of this concerted action also resulted from the fact that the results would be used to convince the Population Council to approve a much bigger grant in mid-October enabling further activities in Turkey. But the results themselves were flawed and lacked comparability. Questions were not properly adapted to local situations and the coded data did not meet the Population Council's expectations to shed light on personal behavior. George Angell opined: "we have tried to do too many things for too many people."[30]

The demographic division of the Population Council pushed strongly towards new shores in the early 1960s. New forms of statistical reflectiveness should support planning programs and actions where impact surveys, local knowledge, and the new methods of KAP studies played a crucial role.[31] Together with USAID, the council issued "sample questions" to be included into national surveys. After initial experiences in Taiwan, the method was applied elsewhere, namely South Korea. The first Turkish demands came at the very moment of increasing interest in these new modes of demographic expertise. Political change within the country coincided with a new step in scientific thinking on population. Demand for new research and offers of new expertise in the field seemed to coincide, and Turkey thus became one of the precursors for this method.

Optimism and Backlashes

The fact that from the very beginning of the program Turkey had a proper statistical "back-up" already pointed to the important new dimension of social assessments that gained increasing importance in the 1960s and 1970s. In retrospect, the most astonishing fact is not so much this integration into more general contexts, but rather how quickly scientists tried to make sense of these statistical surveys.[32] Bernard Berelson came to Turkey in April 1964 to present the results at a seminar on population organized by the Turkish government.[33] Despite all his rhetorical emphasis, his statements about the real statistical results were modest. Above all he highlighted the gap between the consciousness of a need for contraception and the corresponding reproductive behavior of individuals. On the same occasion, Howard C. Taylor presented a paper on the requirements of statistical surveys for any kind of future birth control program.[34] As their colleague Nusret Fişek summarized one year later at the "epicenter" of family planning, the Geneva International Conference on Family Planning Programs, everything now had to focus on the "difference between wishing and acting" of local agents.[35] From the international point of view, Turkey was now an integral part of a new approach to reproductive behavior. Together with South Korea and Taiwan, it presented one of the most prominent cases for the execution of new family planning program projects.[36]

This was not quite how things seemed when seen from a national point of view. At Berelson's and Taylor's presentations, the conference rooms at the Ankara conference of 1964 had been only half-full and the key officials were not present.[37] The Population Council still failed to convince Turkish government representatives to commit to the Council's recommendations, given that it had just succeeded getting "population in the air again." Experts in New York were waiting in vain to get Turkish programs started. Dudley Kirk described the mood in New York as a general "Let's get going,"[38] but the government showed caution. The first initiative for a Turkish program went up in smoke and the first KAP survey suffered a similar fate.

The idea of a proper Turkish population program however, was not completely abandoned. Family planning disappeared from the ministry's top priority list, which instead adopted a focus on a "maternal and child health care" approach. But things began to change through new project designs and the idea of model regions made the whole difference, bringing together the rationales of national programs and international experts. In 1965, the Ministry of Health established a "Rural Health District" at Etimesgut, not far from Ankara. This new project was closely linked to the ambitions of integrating social welfare into new concepts of state planning. The ministry's aims were twofold from the very beginning: firstly, to provide health care to rural populations as well as educating specialized staff for rural health stations; and secondly, to assess the impact of healthcare operations and research on practices of rural health administration.[39] The idea of healthcare through a grid of rural health posts and centers went back to the times of Kemal Atatürk, but was now systematically realized in Etimesgut. Programs of Maternal and Child Health Care were quickly integrated into the district's health plan as well as a new program in family planning,[40] allowing village midwives to distribute contraceptives and promote their use.[41] New KAP studies were carried out in 1967 for this comparably small district and for a sample of just over 50,000 inhabitants.

The Population Council's experts quickly adopted this idea of model regions to show the impact of family planning programs through concise follow-up studies. They were, however, not intent on following the ministry's official program in Etimesgut, and instead looked for an alternative region in which to install a more explicit family planning program. The council's experts quickly scanned the rest of the world for comparable experiences, only to find examples in Barbados' Koyang Studies, which proved too limited to be adapted to Turkey.[42] In 1966, Dr. Necedet Erenus from Hacettepe University in Ankara came up with a proposal for a program in south-east Anatolian Diyabakır,[43] the only project region in the country's Kurdish dominated periphery. The council's special envoy Robert Gillespie managed to produce new educational material, especially audiovisual material, from his experiences. Fieldworkers were supposed to visit individual homes and try to get answers to open questions in order to measure the gap between individual knowledge and behavior following the Council's KAP principles. But Gillespie quickly encountered difficulties: Turkish officials intervened if the interview questions concerned ethnic dimensions, which for the American experts seemed to be an important point for a program in southeast Anatolia. Local populations proved to be very reluctant to collaborate with foreigners, and some newspapers even accused experts of working for the American secret service.[44] The Diyabakır program was the first program to be abandoned after only a short duration.

Instead the council's experts now focused on Tarsus in Southern Anatolia as the place for the Turkish impact study and for finally "getting tough in Turkey."[45] It seemed to be the only way to convince officials to follow the council in its implementation logic and to "get them to see FP [Family Planning] as a crusade."[46] Nevertheless, the council's agents still underestimated the differences between the Turkish ways of thinking about these programs and their own project designs. When Turkish officials visited the council's headquarters in New York early in 1967, the lines of conflict were laid bare. Despite all interest in joining worldwide programs, the Turkish government was very reluctant to hand over all activities to international organizations. A nationwide program, led by foreign experts, based on the principle of quick moving-in and moving-out was not what the Turkish government supported. The Turkish representatives even called into question the new Tarsus project, which was meant to move forward international efforts that had been stymied up until now.[47] Despite all heavy investments from international officials, the advancement of any separate family planning program was in danger. Nusret Fişek, probably the most important contact person for the international health organizations within Turkey, later explained the Turkish rationale: it was all about keeping the new efforts inside the old structure of rural health services. Family planning should be added to the competences of village midwives and doctors in local health centers.[48] Much of this might be explained by the divergence between experts and government officials, the latter intending to keep all efforts of population control in the sovereignty of the state. Family planning remained an important goal, but it should be kept inside the official institutions of the Turkish state. Beside this general reflection, new scientific research underpinned the importance of local midwives in ensuring a proper acceptance and follow-up of the measures taken.

Taylor-Berelson in Turkey

Berelson's reaction to the "disaster of the Turks' visit," as field officer John Ross put it, revealed that Tarsus and Turkey in general were far too important to be abandoned by the council. Instead, he admitted "that my own expectations for Turkey were exaggerated—not on any substantive or technical ground but on political grounds,"[49] thus he showed eagerness "to do better in the future," in other words, trying harder to convince the Turks to follow the project designs of the New York experts, but also to make new concessions.

The enterprise of establishing the KAP studies globally as a new instrument of implementation and political action in the field of demography and family planning was probably the most important project for the council's vice-president Bernard Berelson in the mid-1960s. In 1966, the council started the big post-partum project, which was part of a new methodology of family planning.[50] In 150 mostly urban hospitals around the globe, gynecological experts targeted women in the post-partum phase to promote further use of contraceptives. Ankara Maternity Hospital at Hacettepe University was the Turkish participant.[51] The test period of this global program reached a relatively high level of acceptance that brought the council's experts to consider it for global use. Thus, a new method was defined, but what remained unknown was the required infrastructure for its propagation and acceptance among rural populations without access to hospitals. Over the next years, it was the council's most important concern to determine the needs for spreading the program, allowing an applicable "administrative guidance to policy."[52] Berelson, who became president of the Population Council in 1968, insisted on relating this question to the KAP studies and their excessive interviewing techniques. Every project step was to be accompanied by the collection of corresponding "service statistics" that would allow the social contexts related to it to be traced back.[53] Together with Howard C. Taylor, he started in 1969 to glue together this methodology into the Taylor-Berelson method,[54] which involved a six-step implementation of post-partum projects in developing countries, emphasizing an "urban model" and a "rural model."

An important part of this new agenda was the statistical information on the existing infrastructure and the socioeconomic status of the countries. Taylor and Berelson argued on the background of eight case studies. As Turkish records went back to 1963, it was a particularly important keystone for their arguments because it allowed a relatively long-run experience. Despite all problems, Turkey remained a crucial country for the Population Council to demonstrate the need for and effectiveness of family planning in developing countries.

In light of these dynamics in the field of transnational demographical research, Turkey was not the only country targeted by the Population Council. Bringing family planning back to the Turkish agenda was crucial for the Population Council's experts, but it now had to be achieved in the frame of Turkish national institutions. Neither a separate program nor the open guidance of Turkish officials by international experts seemed possible. Instead, it was necessary to negotiate the terms with official Turkish institutions, the Ministry of Health and Social Assistance, the State Planning Organization, and the newly founded Hacettepe Institute of Population Studies, responsible for the Turkish demographical survey. John Ross was now well aware that things could only advance if a joint program that included KAP questions in the survey "would offer . . . a political umbrella."[55] Ross was conscious that this probably meant waiting for the Turkish programs to "mature," but still thought it the best solution.

Things started to look better for the programs in late 1967, when the State Planning Organization decided to prepare a new and extended demographic survey within the second Five-Year Plan (1968–1972), which would also include more regions in its sample. The organization therefore approached the Population Council again, and announced that this time a separate village survey would be carried out, asking for "village attitudes."[56] The idea of hopping onto the SPO bandwagon revived enthusiasm among the New York experts, above all Bernard Berelson, who thought that "this would let us have our cake and eat it. We might even consider paying for this part of the survey."[57] It would allow them to get a more precise idea of the situation in Turkey through new and more concise results than the outdated data sheets from 1963. By revising this material, several of the scholars involved had to acknowledge that the poor data quality was also due to technical incompatibilities. A lot of "inconsistencies . . . crept in on the way from the villages to Columbia University,"[58] where Howard C. Taylor was in charge of evaluating the material. In order to cope with these material problems, new village surveys would also embrace technological innovation in statistical evaluation, such as new card-punching systems.[59]

After all, it was neither the SPO nor the Population Council's agents who made the most intensive use of the data; rather, it was the Ford Foundation's field officer in Turkey, Frederick Shorter, together with Ferhunde Özbay, who presented a first, relatively rough analysis of the data.[60] As more and more activities were carried out on the village level, Ford's involvement in rural development became increasingly important for the general activities in family planning. Still, complaints about the reliability of data were exchanged between New York and Ankara. The SPO suspected interviewers in east and south-east Anatolia were not sufficiently precise about interviewing, coding, and punching, interpreting the official handbooks and guidelines in their own way.[61] In order to make further and more intensive use of the data, regional and local case studies seemed indispensable, but pointed to the universal distrust of New York and Ankara's experts regarding the situation on the ground, the qualification of local personnel and insecure data transmission.

The Era of "Social Experiments"

Coding systems, card punching, and statistical evaluation of medical programs all required precision in the assessment of impact factors and the ability to plan and foresee social behavior. State planning euphoria in the context of development programs thus favored these new behavioralist scientific approaches, inspired by modernization theory. It was only a matter of time before the new Turkish institutions like the SPO, and the freshly founded Turkish Development Foundation (TDF), would join the American experts in this vision of things, promoting a more experimental model. It thus revived the Tarsus program in 1969 to carry out what program director Aykut Toros later called a "social experiment."[62]

TDF's president, Altan Ünver invested heavily in the Tarsus project. A new hospital was established and a grid of eighteen rural maternal health centers were set up in the relatively small district of Tarsus. Additionally, the program arranged for a particularly "strong evaluation component."[63] Toros also received support from Nusret Fişek, still head of population studies at Hacettepe, and from the private IPPF-related Pathfinder Fund. Turkish officials now adopted the idea of an integrated but specialized program that would promote "maternal and child health care" outside the rural health institutions, and thus embraced a global trend towards maternal and child health care, strongly backed by the initiatives of the World Health Organization and others.[64] A collaboration with the existing Ankara post-partum project was at hand through Fişek, and the president of Hacettepe Medical School, İhsan Doğramacı. As a member of the executive board of both UNICEF and the WHO, the latter was also a guarantor for international attention on Turkey's new ways of family planning.[65]

In retrospect, the ambition of the study was described as follows:

> To investigate, in Turkey, the impact of socioeconomic change on fertility, to understand the broader implications of different fertility paths, and thus to enhance our understanding of the issues surrounding Turkey's rapid population growth phenomenon and to contribute to the knowledge with which more realistic decision making and planning is possible. At the same time, the study may have considerable relevance to other countries in the developing world.[66]

The TDF addressed the Population Council relatively late with a request for support. Only in 1971 did Altan Ünver send a letter to New York, asking for financial backing and expert advice.[67] Seemingly, Turkish officials this time preferred to keep the initiative in-house and to involve the international experts only at a second stage.[68] Despite the initial reluctance in steering this project, it was modeled on what was now called the "Taylor-Berelson-Method." Council assistant Roy Treadway described it as follows:

> We have essentially six different types of treatment, and in that sense you could call it a field experiment. One area is receiving no program, another area only commercial distribution of contraceptives, a third area only distribution of contraceptives and education, and three areas various combinations of medical services and varying price structure as well as variations in the sex of doctor.[69]

Treadway also pointed out that the price structure variations and the investigations on the relevance of doctors' sex were categories imposed by the Population Council, but they seemed acceptable to Turkish government officials. This time, the efforts of bringing together integrated national public health programs with KAP and follow-up studies succeeded early in 1972.[70]

Generally speaking, the negotiations around 1970 convinced international and national agents that family planning had to move away from the idea of a national and systematically applied program towards a more case-by-case approach, where not only the "targeted" population groups shifted, but also the funding and steering committees of these projects should be more heterogeneous. When Roy Treadway reported one year later on the character and progress of Tarsus, this became very visible:

> The interest [of the TDF] in the project has shifted somewhat to developing it for use by a private agency in family planning work, such as DFT [Development Foundation of Turkey],[71] rather than doing it as a program management project for the national government in some way. This seems to be much more realistic, given their current situation.[72]

In either case, by the mid-seventies the foundation was convinced that family planning was one of the three pillars of Turkish development in the future, as well as the support for agricultural expertise and rural development. Based on the Tarsus experiments, it set up a permanent research project on the "broader [economic] implications of different fertility paths."[73]

A more focused way of setting up programs also met the basic assumption of the council's experts. These were not about acting directly on the entire population, but much more about constructing models and giving policy makers clear-cut and technocratic advice on how to reduce fertility. In other words, it was all about a new scientific approach to politics, enabling decision makers to feed computers with data to garner well-defined results. One of the short-term successes of the Tarsus program was to gain experience to improve the use of computers:

> An ameliorated computer program for family planning program input estimates could not only indicate what would be necessary to get the family planning program started ... , but would provide a basic tool for administrators by indicating alternative paths possible for reaching the targets (showing the parameters within which the program could operate), and by providing a mechanism for prompt evaluation of the program results achieved in terms of implications for the future.[74]

Population and its development had to be calculated and integrated into new planning paradigms in the age of modernization through system management. This was in the air at the time as the new staff arriving at the Turkish institute for population studies were trained on these technical standards, many earning their master or Ph.D. degrees in European and U.S. universities, and often financed with grants from the Population Council or other eminent institutions.

In many respects, Turkey was not an isolated case. Most obviously, the Population Council remained keen on the idea of a possible international comparison through a homogenous methodology. It is remarkable to see how much the construction of this methodology was related to its later outcomes: Taylor and Berelson had argued on the basis of case studies. These cases also happened to be the regions where further steps of the Taylor-Berelson method were applied. This was typically the case in Tarsus province, where in a second step, the project deliberately moved away from the emphasis on contraception towards responsible behavior through education.[75] The follow-up project "Tarsus II" was designed to determine the impact of "mobile medical teams," which did not primarily perform medical treatment or distribute contraceptives, but informed on the availabilities of institutions and offered fundamental awareness training.[76]

But more than Tarsus itself, two other projects took up this idea and developed it further. The first of them was the Seyhan project, that claimed that it:

> is not a research program but a service program to be used as a laboratory for the implementation of the national program. This argument is based on the fact that the Ministry of Health needs a field program that could service a progressive area, an area with an ethnically heterogeneous population which is growing relatively fast....[77]

This quotation from the project plan summarizes particularly well the scientific ambitions behind a new series of programs in Turkey, but also behind a new generation of program support at the Population Council.

It became manifest to a further extent in a subsequent program carried out with the support of the Population Council. This program was located in Yozgat district, east of Ankara, prepared in 1974. The guiding idea of the Yozgat projects was to define lines of comparisons, but this time not for comparison with other Turkish regions, but with foreign regions. In particular, Yozgat was placed in a matrix of three comparable projects, the others being located at the Island of Bohol (Philippines) and in the district of Mojokerto (Indonesia). This special "experimental" setting was steered by the Population Council, even if the official responsibility for each of these programs remained in the hands of the respective national governments.

In 1974, Howard Taylor and Robert Lapham officially reported on this "Program for Family Planning based on Maternal/Child Health Services" to a wider public.[78] To make the lines of comparison as homogenous as possible, the projects relied on the post-partum approach, providing information on contraception to women after childbirth. This information was to be transmitted by trained midwives at a very local level, allowing a supervision of individual cases over a relatively long time period. They now openly stated that such programs under the guidance of the Population Council were not set up for the direct purpose of birth control itself, but for the "acquisition of knowledge"[79] that would allow governments in developing countries to make precise estimates of the costs and impacts of such programs. In other words, it was designed as an observatory for state planning policies. This was made possible through the relatively strong "evaluation component" of this program. Two of five steps were concerned with statistical monitoring and improvements in project administration. Here, the influence of Turkish experiences was particularly strong: for the follow-up and KAP studies, as well as for the collection of vital statistics, the "target population" was broadly interviewed. Among these interviewees were members of local authorities, school teachers, religious leaders, etc.[80] Taylor and Lapham clearly followed the practice used in Turkey's first KAP study eleven years earlier. It now served as an example for studies in other "developing countries." Since the early 1960s and the massive financial aid by the OECD, the country had become accustomed to pronouncing itself as being part of this community of developing countries.

This new generation of projects was no longer the unilateral action of the Population Council. Despite the fact that most of the experts related in one way or another to the council, programs now were financed by the United Nations Population Fund (UNFPA), by USAID, or by national health ministries. Even though the underlying paradigms of the council's experts had succeeded in reaching international attention, the programs had also considerably altered its shape and the original "laboratory approach" subsisted in part. Using districts and regions as "field laboratories," as the council originally planned to do, lacked a sense of the reality of the political situation and social realities in the participating countries. The later evaluation advisor of Yozgat project, Belgin Tekce, resumed some years later as follows:

> It would have been far too expensive, and unattainable in practice, to establish all the experimental controls needed to identify and quantify cause and effect. It was possible, however, to plan observations that would yield reasonably good measurements of certain key conditions at the beginning of the project and at its conclusion, which would be helpful in judging the amount of change.[81]

Tarsus and Yozgat were the most ambitious projects in the history of Turkish family planning, although their mission was simply to serve as a "laboratory" for experiences to identify opportunities, and no longer as programs for the direct control of population size. In a more political way, the diverging paths of both projects revealed fundamental differences between visions of modernity. Tarsus was in a way the result of the attempts to improve Turkish political institutions in that it identified and highlighted pitfalls in modernization and the lack of infrastructure. New ways of family planning should be carried out by the representatives of the Turkish government inside the institutions of the Turkish ministries and local administrations. In Yozgat, population was the object of potential intervention and planning, and reproductive attitudes and behavior were modeled through intensive use of new cybernetic methods. Card-punching was one of the major activities of the project staff. Turkey thus stood for a wide range of new possibilities.

The differences in the program design also revealed the fundamental hopes and interests that all sides invested into such a project. In the Tarsus project, the population was mainly stratified on a topographic basis, and the origin of different groups were identified as "plane, slope and mountains." The project of UNFPA and the Population Council in Yozgat had a much more social approach to the stratification of population. The former emphasized the role of existing institutions, whereas the latter followed much more the idea of a social experiment, where Turkey was reduced more or less to a favorable political and economic context.

Understanding the differences between both approaches has a broad relevance, away from the single context of birth control programs. It also points to the contentions of the seemingly homogenous conceptions of modernity in the 1960s and 1970s. What appeared as similarities in many of the project descriptions was based on widely differing assumptions, the most important of which was the awareness of the population itself. For remote Anatolia, attempts at rural modernization, either by foreign missions or by their own government were not new. In the 1920s, the Kemalist party built up institutions like the people's houses that were meant to bring national politics together with modern life in many villages.[82] In the 1930s and 1940s, many villages had a proper village institute whose mission was to spread education and the means of agricultural modernization into the rural Turkish countryside.[83] Not only had people in these regions of Turkey experienced these attempts at modernization, they also had developed particular, and often critical attitudes towards them. As Zürcher points out, important parts of the Anatolian population were already reluctant to accept international expertise and support, well before the Marshall plan's rural mechanization projects came to the country.[84] This is even more the case for the public health offensives of the 1960s and 1970s. It was common among non-Turkish staff members to complain about the reluctance of the local population. Anti-Americanism seemed to play a certain role in the problems the international programs encountered, but was probably not the only reason for the population's negative attitude towards new projects.

The evolution of these projects certainly reveals more than just a dialectical process between international expertise and national institutional traditions, indeed, Turkish experts significantly contributed to the construction of scientific models at the Population Council. Turkish agents were themselves divided between the rationales of the Turkish Ministry of Health and of international foundations. In the Turkish case, those ambiguities of knowledge were extremely difficult to overcome. A national family planning program that seemed within reach in the mid-1960s was not realized and Turkey was stuck in the halting mode of diverging model experiments.

Conclusion

To implement a family planning movement and program in Turkey was a complex process that involved the Turkish national government as well as the local population, individual academic scholars, and experts from international organizations. It was partly due to this conglomerate of interests that the reproductive knowledge, attitudes and practices of the Turkish population became a highly politicized epistemic object.

Despite the rather disillusioning dynamics for the ambitious Turkish projects of family planners, the different projects revealed a shift in the rationales of the Turkish state and the culture of governance. The State Planning Organization of Turkey became an important factor of Turkish policy making in the 1960s. National elites after Mustafa Kemal's death were primarily involved in securing the maintenance of national unity and the leadership of their secular understanding of politics.[85] It was used to perceive development as a process steered "from above," geared towards big infrastructure projects.[86] It now saw itself confronted by new challenges for international experts as well as state planners, a new culture of social governance that made important data about the socioeconomic structure of the population available. Family planning experts, for instance, needed the data from the national census as baseline information for their own data collection, or as Aykut Toros pointed out: national initiatives, such as a national demographic survey, "should be capable of providing demographic (and other socioeconomic) information to the policy makers of the country without too much delay."[87]

Despite the high hopes of experts in the early 1960s to make Turkey a vanguard in the implementation of family planning, the history of these projects points much more to the importance of political negotiations than to the significance of technocratic expertise. The development of a somewhat scientocratic regime of social interventions by a new expert culture was in the Turkish case just one vision that did not come to fruition as opposed to other cases of development policy. Even though the political climate and some prominent agents were particularly open to it after the Turkish *coup d'état*, the country did not become a role model or a *primus inter pares* of the "developing world." The relative failure of these attempts was due both to an institutional disequilibrium between international experts and national institutions on the one hand, and an increasing reluctance of local populations towards these international programs of experts on the other.[88]

Acknowledgments

Important evidence for this chapter comes from the Rockefeller Foundation and the Population Council Archives at the Rockefeller Archives Center. I want to thank all the staff and especially Tom Rosenberg for their valuable support of my research.

Notes

1. B. Berelson, "Prospects and Programs for Fertility Reduction: What? Where?," *Population and Development Review* 4, no. 4 (1978): 579–616.
2. M. Connelly, *Fatal Misconception: The Struggle to Control World Population* (Cambridge, Mass., 2008); J. Sharpless, "Population Science, Private Foundations, and Development Aid: The Transformation of Demographic Knowledge in the United States, 1945–1965," in *International Development and the Social Sciences*, F. Cooper and R. Packard eds. (Los Angeles, 1997), 181–182.
3. E.J. Zürcher, *Turkey: A Modern History* (London and New York, 2004), 264–275.
4. J. Rettie, "Turkey," *News of Population and Birth Control* no. 120 (1963), International Planned Parenthood Federation ed.
5. Turkey's religious authorities issued a fatwa in 1960, underpinning the fundamental compatibility of religion and family planning. In doing this, they quickly became pioneers on this matter, as is reflected by their prominent role in a small volume edited by Olivia Schiefflein by the Population Council in 1967; *Muslim Attitudes Toward Family Planning*, O. Schiefflein ed. (New York, 1967).
6. M. Lengwiler and S. Beck, "Historizität, Materialität und Hybridität von Wissenspraxen. Die Entwicklung europäischer Präventionsregime im 20. Jahrhundert," *Geschichte und Gesellschaft* 34, no. 1 (2008): 521.
7. J.A. Mills, *Control: A History of Behavioral Psychology* (New York, 2000), 153–155. Also see C. Unger's chapter in this volume.
8. M. Callon, "Elements of a Sociology of Translation: Domestication of the Scallops and the Fishermen of St Brieuc Bay," in *Power, Action and Belief. A New Sociology of Knowledge?* J. Law ed. (London, 1986).
9. In the field of development studies, this perspective is taken up by post-development studies, and most prominently by A. Escobar, *Encountering Development: The Making and Unmaking of the Third World* (Princeton, 1995), 21–53.
10. S. Jovchelovitch, *Knowledge in Context: Representations, Community and Culture* (London, 2007).
11. Mills, *History*, 153–155.
12. See C. Unger's chapter in this volume; Connelly, *Fatal Misconception*, 203.
13. F. Notestein, "Population, the Long View," in *Food for the World*, T. Schultz ed. (Chicago, 1945), 66.
14. D. Hodgson, "Demography as Social Science and Policy Science," *Population and Development Review* 9, no. 1 (1983), 11–12.
15. This is how Nusret Fişek put it with regard to the Turkish case: N.H. Fişek, "Problems in Starting a Program," in *Family Planning and Population Programs: A Review of World Developments*, B. Berelson et al. eds. (Geneva 1965), 300–301.

16. L. Raphael, "Die Verwissenschaftlichung des Sozialen als methodische und konzeptionelle Herausforderung für eine Sozialgeschichte des 20. Jahrhunderts," *Geschichte und Gesellschaft* 22, no. 2 (1996): 168–172. Reestablishing "population" as an issue of the "welfare state" was an important postwar issue in several European countries. For the German and the French case see P.A. Rosental, *L'intelligence démographique. Sciences et politiques des populations en France (1930–1960)* (Paris, 2003); C. Kuller, *Familienpolitik im föderativen Sozialstaat. Die Formierung eines Politikfeldes in der Bundesrepublik 1949–1975* (München, 2004).
17. A.L.S. Staples, *The Birth of Development: How the World Bank, Food and Agriculture Organization, and World Health Organization Changed the World, 1945–1965 (Kent 2006)*, 137–160.
18. Nusret Fişek to Frank Notestein, 26 December 1962; Rockefeller Archive Center (RAC) Population Council, Accession II Correspondence, Box 59, Folder "Population Council Advisory Mission," FC-O Turkey 63.
19. See M. Dörnemann's chapter on Kenya for another example.
20. W. Parker Mauldin Diary Notes 1 April 1963; RAC Population Council, Accession II Correspondence, Box 59, Folder "Population Council Advisory Mission," FC-O Turkey 63.
21. Preliminary Observations, 18 April; RAC Population Council, Accession II Correspondence, Box 59, Folder "Population Council Advisory Mission," FC-O Turkey 63.
22. Ibid.
23. Under-Secretary Turan Gönen to Bernard Berelson, 25 May 1963; RAC Population Council, Accession I General Files, Box 53, Folder 818.
24. Resolution, 10 June 1963; RAC Population Council, Accession I General Files, Box 53, Folder 818.
25. United Nations Technical Mission to Turkey. Community Organization and Development, The Community Development Programme in Turkey. Its Evolution and Strategy of Operation, prepared for the State Planning Organization of Turkey by Abid Hussain, by the United Nations Technical Assistance Administration, 27 May 1964; United Nations Archives, Series 175, Box 2047, Folder 5.
26. Ibid., 41.
27. See C. Unger's chapter in this volume. On the history of these new approaches to rural and community development, see N. Sackley, "The Village as Cold War Site: Experts, Development, and the History of Rural Reconstruction," in: *Journal of Global History* 6, no. 3 (2011): 481–504; N. Cullather, *The Hungry World: America's Cold War Battle against Poverty in Asia* (Cambridge, 2010).
28. George W. Angell to Joseph Stycos 22 August 1963; RAC – Population Council, Accession II, Correspondence, Box 59, Folder "Min. of Health-Angell, George; FC-O Turkey 63–66."
29. W. Parker Mauldin to Nusret Fişek, 8 October 1963; RAC Population Council, Accession I General Files, Box 53, Folder 818.
30. George W. Angell to Joseph Stycos 22 August 1963; RAC – Population Council, Accession II, Correspondence, Box 59, Folder "Min. of Health-Angell, George; FC-O Turkey 63–66."
31. *The Population Council. A Chronicle of the First Twenty-Five Years, 1952–1977*, Population Council Inc. ed. (New York 1977), 65–68.
32. On the importance of the Turkish case in this context, see Dodgson, *Demography*, 23–24.
33. Berelson published his presentation afterwards in a volume on Muslim attitudes towards family planning, issued by the Population Council; *Attitudes de l'islam face à la régulation des naissances*, O. Schieffelein, ed. (New York 1974 [1967]), 44–60.
34. Program of the Nüfus Semineri, 27–30 April 1964; RAC Population Council, Accession II Correspondence, Box 59, Folder "Ec & Soc. Studies Conf Seminar 1964; FC-O Turkey 63–65."
35. Fişek, *Problems*, 298.
36. *The Population Council*, 53–54.

37. Bernard Berelson to W. Parker Mauldin, 4 May 1964; RAC Population Council, Accession II Correspondence, Box 59, Folder "Ec & Soc. Studies Conf Seminar 1964; FC-O Turkey 63–65."
38. Dudley Kirk to John A. Ross, 28 September 1966; RAC Population Council, Accession II Correspondence, Box 59, Folder "Turkey Min of Health-Ross, John; FC-Turkey 66."
39. Hacettepe University School of Medicine, Institute of Community Medicine: An Account of the Activities of the Etimesgut Rural Health District, 1967, 1968 and 1969; RAC, Rockefeller Foundation, Record Group 2 – Correspondence, Series 805 – Turkey, 1970, Reel 45.
40. N.H. Fişek, "An Integrated Health / Family Planning Program in Etimesgut District/Turkey," *Studies in Family Planning* 5, no. 7 (1974): 210–220.
41. The use of contraceptives was prohibited in Turkey until 1965 – inherited almost unconsciously from the French social code law, adapted in 1924; see congratulations from the Population Council to Nusret Fişek; RAC Population Council, Accession II Correspondence, Box 58, Folder "Turkey Min of Health-Ross, John; FC-Turkey 66."
42. Letter 14 October 1966 Richmond K. Anderson to John A. Ross; RAC Population Council, Accession II Correspondence, Box 59, Folder "Turkey Min of Health-Ross, John; FC-Turkey 66."
43. Memo John Ross to Lewis Anderson and others, 20 August 1966; RAC Population Council, Accession II Correspondence, Box 59, Folder "Turkey Min of Health-Ross, John; FC-Turkey 66."
44. Memo Robert Gillespie to Lewis Anderson, 3 June 1966; RAC Population Council, Accession II Correspondence, Box 59 "Folder Min of Health-Gillespie, Robert; FC-O Turkey 66."
45. John Ross to Bernard Berelson, 29 December 1966; RAC Population Council, Accession II Correspondence, Box 59, Folder "Turkey Min of Health-Ross, John; FC-Turkey 66."
46. Ibid.
47. John Ross to Bernard Berelson, 25 April 1967, and response from B. Berelson, 5 May 1967; Ibid.
48. Fişek, *An Integrated Health / Family Planning Program*, 212–213.
49. Bernard Berelson to John Ross, 5 May 1967; RAC Population Council, Accession II Correspondence, Box 59, Folder "Turkey Min of Health-Ross, John; FC-Turkey 66."
50. G.I. Zatuchni, "International Post-Partum Family Planning Program: Report on the First Year," *Studies in Family Planning* 1, no. 22 (1967): 1–23.
51. RAC Population Council, Accession I Correspondence, Box 70, Folder 1301.
52. H.C. Taylor and B. Berelson, "Comprehensive Family Planning Based on Maternal/Child Health Services. A Feasibility Study for a World Program," *Studies in Family Planning* 2 (1971), 23.
53. Best documented in J.A. Ross, F.F. Stephan and W.B. Watson, *A Handbook of Service Statistics in Family Planning Programs*, Population Council ed. (New York, 1968).
54. H.C. Taylor and B. Berelson, "Maternity Care and Family Planning as a World Program," *American Journal of Obstetrics and Gynecology* 100, no. 7 (1968): 885–893; B. Berelson, "Beyond Family Planning," *Science* 163, no. 3867 (1969), 539.
55. John Ross to Dudley Kirk, 10 April 1967; RAC Population Council, Accession II Correspondence, Box 59, Folder "KAP; FC-O Turkey."
56. Ahmet Tuğac to Bernard Berelson, 23 November 1967; RAC Population Council, Accession II Correspondence, Box 59, Folder "KAP; FC-O Turkey."
57. Note from Bernard Berelson to REF, 4 December 1967, ibid.
58. Lewis Anderson to John Ross, 28 December 1967; ibid.
59. W. Parker Mauldin to Ahmet Tuğac, 8 December 1967; ibid.
60. F. Özbay and F.C. Shorter, "Turkey. Changes in Birth Control Practices 1963 to 1968," *Studies in Family Planning* 1, no. 51 (1970): 1–7.

61. Yaşar Heperkan to Parker Mauldin, 27 September 1968; RAC Population Council, Accession II Correspondence, Box 59, Folder Folder "KAP; FC-O Turkey."
62. A. Toros, *Tarsus II – A Social Experiment in Fertility Control. A Report Prepared for the Development Foundation of Turkey* (New York, November 1972), Population Council Collection, HB 903. F4T8.
63. John Ross to Bernard Berelson, 22 January 1971; RAC Population Council, Accession II Correspondence, Box 58, Folder "Development Foundation of Turkey FC-Turkey 72."
64. Staples, *Birth*.
65. Ibid.
66. Altan Ünver to John Ross 13 May 1974; RAC Population Council, Accession II Correspondence, Box 58, Folder "Development Foundation of Turkey. Demographic Goals & Family Planning Project 1972–1974."
67. Joel Montague to Altan Ünver, 24 September 1971; ibid.
68. On the "nationalization" of American development programs, see C.R. Unger, "Toward Global Equilibrium: American Foundations and Indian Modernization, 1950s to 1970s," *Journal of Global History* 6, no. 1 (2011): 121–142. K. McCarthy, "From Government to Grassroots Reform: The Ford Foundation's Population Programs in South Asia, 1959–1981," in *Philanthropy and Cultural Context: Western Philanthropy in South, East, and Southeast Asia in the 20th Century*, S. Hewa and P. Hove eds. (Lanham, 1997), 129–156. Also see Kathleen D. McCarthy, "U.S. Foundations and International Concerns," in *Philanthropy and Culture: The International Foundation Perspective*, Kathleen D. McCarthy ed. (Philadelphia, 1984), 3–24, 11–13.
69. Roy Treadway to Everett M. Rogers, 2 November 1971; ibid.
70. Roy Treadway to Altan Ünver, 31 March 1972; ibid.
71. Both TDF and DFT refer to the same organization, Türkiye Kalkınma Vakfı, and are used arbitrarily in the sources.
72. Roy Treadway to Curtis McLaughlin, 26 February 1973; RAC Population Council, Accession II Correspondence, Box 58, Folder "Development Foundation of Turkey. Demographic Goals & Family Planning Project 1972–1974."
73. Newsletter of Altan Ünver (TDF), 2 January 1976; in: RAC, Rockefeller Foundation, Record Group 2, Correspondence, Series 805, Reel 1976.
74. Estimates of Family Planning Inputs, without date (probably June 1974); ibid.
75. This was the main emphasis of the so-called Tarsus II project. Toros, *Tarsus II*.
76. Toros, *Tarsus II*, 14.
77. Service Program Plan Seyhan Province 1972, RAC Population Council, Accession II Administrative Files, Box 2.
78. H.C. Taylor and R.J. Lapham, "A Program for Family Planning Based on Maternal/Child Health Services," *Studies in Family Planning* 5, no. 3 (1974): 71–82.
79. Ibid., 71.
80. Ibid., 77.
81. B. Tekce, *The Yozgat Maternal and Child Health and Family Planning Project: Baseline Information on Socioeconomic and Demographic Conditions*, Population Council ed. (Cairo, 1979).
82. E. J. Zürcher, *The Young Turk Legacy and Nation Building: From Ottoman Empire to Atatürk's Turkey* (New York, 2010), 246–254; H. L. Kieser, *Der verpasste Friede. Mission, Ethnie und Staat in den Ostprovinzen der Türkei 1839–1938* (Zürich, 2000).
83. A. Karaömerlioğlu, "The Village Institutes Experience in Turkey," *British Journal of Middle Eastern Studies* 25 (1998), 49.
84. Zürcher, *Young Turk Legacy*, 254–255. On the broader context of "induced modernity" in the Mediterranean in the postwar era, G. Sapelli, *Southern Europe Since 1945: Tradition and Modernity in Portugal, Spain, Italy, Greece and Turkey* (London, 1995), 104–107.

85. K. Karpat, *Turkey's Politics: The Transition to a Multi-Party System* (Princeton, 1959); F. Ahmad, "Politics and Political Parties in Republican Turkey," in *The Cambridge History of Turkey, vol. IV: Turkey in the Modern World*, R. Kasaba ed. (Cambridge, 2008).
86. S. Pamuk, "Economic Change in Twentieth-Century Turkey: Is the Glass More Than Half-full?," in *The Cambridge History of Turkey, vol. IV: Turkey in the Modern World*, R. Kasaba ed. (Cambridge 2008), 292–293; B. Park, *Modern Turkey: People State and Foreign Policy in a Globalized World* (London, 2012), 11–14.
87. Toros, *Tarsus*, 8.
88. Ahmad, *Politics*, 245–246.

Bibliography

Ahmad, F., "Politics and Political Parties in Republican Turkey," in *The Cambridge History of Turkey, vol. IV: Turkey in the Modern World*, R. Kasaba, ed. (Cambridge, 2008).
Berelson, B., "Beyond Family Planning," *Science* 163, no. 3867 (1969).
Berelson, B., "Prospects and Programs for Fertility Reduction: What? Where?," *Population and Development Review* 4, no. 4 (1978): 579–616.
Berelson, B., "Turkey: National Survey on Population," *Studies in Family Planning* 5 (1964).
Callon, M., "Elements of a Sociology of Translation: Domestication of the Scallops and the Fishermen of St Brieuc Bay," in *Power, Action and Belief: A New Sociology of Knowledge?*, J. Law ed. (London, 1986).
Connelly, M., *Fatal Misconception: The Struggle to Control World Population* (Cambridge, Mass., and London, 2008).
Cullather, N., *The Hungry World: America's Cold War Battle Against Poverty in Asia*, (Cambridge, 2010).
Escobar, A., *Encountering Development: The Making and Unmaking of the Third World* (Princeton, 1995), 21–53.
Fişek, N.H., "Problems in Starting a Program," in: *Family Planning and Population Programs. A Review of World Developments*, B. Berelson et al. eds. (Geneva, 1965), 300–301.
Hodgson, D., "Demography as Social Science and Policy Science," *Population and Development Review* 9, no. 1 (1983).
Jovchelovitch, S., *Knowledge in Context: Representations, Community and Culture* (London, 2007).
Karaömerlioğlu, A., "The Village Institute's Experience in Turkey," *British Journal of Middle Eastern Studies* 25 (1998).
Karpat, K., *Turkey's Politics: The Transition to a Multi-Party System* (Princeton, 1959).
Kieser, H.L., *Der verpasste Friede. Mission, Ethnie und Staat in den Ostprovinzen der Türkei 1839–1938* (Zürich, 2000).
Kuller, C. *Familienpolitik im föderativen Sozialstaat. Die Formierung eines Politikfeldes in der Bundesrepublik 1949–1975* (München, 2004).
Lengwiler, M., and Beck, S., "Historizität, Materialität und Hybridität von Wissenspraxen. Die Entwicklung europäischer Präventionsregime im 20. Jahrhundert," *Geschichte und Gesellschaft* 34, no. 1 (2008).
McCarthy, K.D., "From Government to Grassroots Reform: The Ford Foundation's Population Programs in South Asia, 1959–1981," in *Philanthropy and Cultural Context: Western Philanthropy in South, East, and Southeast Asia in the 20th Century*, Soma Hewa and Philo Hove eds. (Lanham, 1997), 129–156.
McCarthy, K.D., "U.S. Foundations and International Concerns," in *Philanthropy and Culture: The International Foundation Perspective*, K.D. McCarthy ed. (Philadelphia, 1984), 3–24.

Mills, J.A., *Control: A History of Behavioral Psychology* (New York and London, 2000).
Notestein, F., "Population, the Long View," in: *Food for the World*, T. Schultz ed. (Chicago, 1945).
Pamuk, S., "Economic Change in Twentieth-Century Turkey: Is the Glass More Than Half-full?" in *The Cambridge History of Turkey, vol. IV: Turkey in the Modern World*, R. Kasaba ed. (Cambridge, 2008).
Özbay, F., and Shorter, F.C., "Turkey: Changes in Birth Control Practices 1963 to 1968," *Studies in Family Planning* 1, no. 51 (1970): 1–7.
Park, B., *Modern Turkey: People State and Foreign Policy in a Globalized World*, (London and New York, 2012).
Population Council Inc., ed., *The Population Council: A Chronicle of the First Twenty-Five Years, 1952–1977* (New York, 1977).
Raphael, L., "Die Verwissenschaftlichung des Sozialen als methodische und konzeptionelle Herausforderung für eine Sozialgeschichte des 20. Jahrhunderts," *Geschichte und Gesellschaft* 22, no. 2 (1996).
Rosental, P.A., *L'intelligence démographique. Sciences et politiques des populations en France (193–1960)* (Paris 2003).
Ross, J.A., Stephan, F.F., and Watson, W.B., *A Handbook of Service Statistics in Family Planning Programs*, Population Council ed. (New York, 1968).
Sackley, N., "The Village as Cold War Site: Experts, Development, and the History of Rural Reconstruction," *Journal of Global History* 6, no. 3 (2011): 481–504.
Sapelli, G., *Southern Europe Since 1945: Tradition and Modernity in Portugal, Spain, Italy, Greece and Turkey* (London, 1995).
Schiefflein, O., *Muslim Attitudes Toward Family Planning* (New York, 1967).
Sharpless, J., "Population Science, Private Foundations, and Development Aid: The Transformation of Demographic Knowledge in the United States, 1945–1965," in *International Development and the Social Sciences*, F. Cooper and R. Packard eds. (Los Angeles, 1997).
Staples, A.L.S., *The Birth of Development: How the World Bank, Food and Agriculture Organization, and World Health Organization Changed the World, 1945–1965* (Kent, 2006).
Taylor, H.C., and Berelson, B., "Comprehensive Family Planning Based on Maternal/Child Health Services: A Feasibility Study for a World Program," *Studies in Family Planning*, 2 (1971).
Taylor, H.C., and Berelson, B., "Maternity Care and Family Planning as a World Program," *American Journal of Obstetrics and Gynecology* 100, no. 7 (1968): 885–893.
Taylor, H.C., and Lapham, R.J., "A Program for Family Planning Based on Maternal/Child Health Services," *Studies in Family Planning* 5, no. 3 (1974): 71–82.
Tekce, B., *The Yozgat Maternal and Child Health and Family Planning Project: Baseline Information on Socioeconomic and Demographic Conditions*, Population Council ed. (Cairo, 1979).
Unger, C.R., "Toward Global Equilibrium: American Foundations and Indian Modernization, 1950s to 1970s," *Journal of Global History* 6.1 (2011): 121–142.
Zatuchni, G.I., "International Post-Partum Family Planning Program: Report on the First Year," *Studies in Family Planning* 1, no. 22 (1967): 1–23.
Zürcher, E.J., *The Young Turk Legacy and Nation Building: From Ottoman Empire to Atatürk's Turkey* (New York, 2010).
Zürcher, E.J., *Turkey: A Modern History* (London and New York, 2004), 264–275.

9

SEEING POPULATION AS A PROBLEM

Influences of the Construction of Population Knowledge on Kenyan Politics (1940s to 1980s)

Maria Dörnemann

Introduction

In 1976, a Population Studies and Research Institute (PSRI) was founded at the University of Nairobi. However, unlike what its name suggests, research on population was only one of its tasks and occupations, and the main aim that singles the institution out as unique was defined as "providing [Kenya] with the necessary atmosphere to formulate and implement a comprehensive population policy."[1] This aim is surprising, because in Kenya, official and government-supported population policies were introduced with a national family planning program in 1967, nine years before the establishment of the PSRI. Therefore, it might be useful to focus on the authors of the above aim and what they intended in formulating it. Population policy in the form of family planning programs was, since its inception and shortly after Kenyan independence in 1963, largely inspired, funded, and equipped by foreign aid agencies. One of the most active organizations in those years was the private U.S.-based Population Council, a circle of experts founded in 1952 and committed to the diagnosed problem of rapid population growth in the newly emerging Third World.[2] Organizations like the Population Council began to export recipes to developing countries in order to regulate the problematized population growth. Kenya is thus one of many examples where population policy was a transnational affair. But many of the foreign experts advising the Kenyan government on population policy measures coming from the Population Council or other organizations were not always satisfied with the results, as they expected the implemented measures to have far greater effects on population structure in the target countries. In Kenya, they lacked sufficient infrastructure to be able to produce population knowledge and data on population evolution, as well as a countrywide acceptance of population policy measures. Situated at the interface between the production of population knowledge and its application, the Population Studies and Research Institute was intended to cover for these missing aspects. If one follows the expectations of the Population Council, which provided technical assistance to the building up of the PSRI and wrote the report from which the above-cited task description originated, this act of institution building can be read as the signature of a shifting population policy approach performed by expatriates: population policy should no longer only be about transferring solutions, but should also address the emergence of the "problem." If the institute should—in the words of the Population Council—provide the country with a specific "atmosphere," this meant nothing other than creating a countrywide awareness for population as a problem.

The problematization of population growth in the developing world has received much attention by historians throughout recent years. We have stories describing the emergence of an international "population control movement" destined to solve the problem on a global scale.[3] Since they are largely told from the perspective of this idea's advocates, we are less informed about how different countries in the developing world shared the consequences of this belief.

This chapter is about how the construction of population knowledge influenced and structured politics in Kenya. At the center of this analysis stands the construction of a population problem and its transfer between different contexts. The main aim is to historicize the perception of the Kenyan population through analyzing acts of its problematization in three dimensions: firstly, in models or concepts to which population was related; secondly, in population knowledge in the form of numbers and data; and thirdly, in political realities or contexts. The concept of population implied a specific conception of societal organization, expectations of living conditions, and projections on future development.[4] Experts conceived of population in the context of social engineering, planning, and development thinking.[5]

The process of population construction is thus conceived as one of "co-production."[6] Kenyan population was construed from different angles and perspectives. While members of foreign aid agencies understood Kenya's population as one piece of a global puzzle, Kenyan experts embedded population knowledge and policies mainly into nation-building agendas. If the notions "global" or "national" are not understood as levels indicating hierarchically ordered or encompassing entities, but—as James Ferguson suggested—as "modes of operation,"[7] it becomes clear that the construction of population knowledge and its political implications were circumscribed to specific "contact zones"[8] in which those perspectives and agendas were debated. This analytical tool describes a sphere in which actors with different perspectives and backgrounds met in order to transfer knowledge, concepts, practices, and money.[9]

The main characters of this chapter are actors in the political sphere, which means that they fall back on models and data created, gathered, and interpreted by demographers, without creating, gathering, or interpreting them by themselves. Kenya is taken as a platform in order to construe a network of actors who cared about population and stem from different contexts, such as British colonial officers, international organizations committed to population control, experts, and Kenyan functional elites.

The chapter is structured in three parts. The first part focuses on the transfer of tools, examining modes of perception and construction of the African population in Kenya since the 1940s. The second part addresses the transfer of models, concentrating on the nexus between population and economy. Finally, the third part enlightens the changing approach from a transfer of solutions to a transfer of the problem.

Transferring Tools: Modes of Perception and Construction of the African Population in Kenya since the 1940s

Until 1963, the settler colony of Kenya was part of the British Empire. The colonial discourse through which British settlers or colonial officers perceived the African population took shape in two modes of problematization: firstly as a narrative of decline, and secondly as one of growth. The first perspective dominated the discourse until the 1940s and was not fully replaced afterwards by the incipient assumption of rapid African population growth. Rather, both narratives coexisted. The purpose of the following section is to examine the possibility and conditions of this improbable coexistence of two contradicting narratives. Of central concern here is the relationship between the construction of population knowledge, ideological presuppositions, and political consequences as a conglomerate that informed both narratives.

The narrative of decline structured the perception of the African population in Kenya from the outset of its colonization and the influx of settlers since 1900.[10] Yet, the impression of a declining or stagnating population was hardly based on specific demographic data. Apart from some small-scale observations by medical officers or governors,[11] population estimates were interwoven with the tax system[12] and there was no colony-wide systematic counting of the African population. Instead, the narrative obtained its plausibility within the context of the Kenyan settler economy. Labor was the concept to which population was related. For what Lynn Thomas has described as "one of the most coercive labor systems in British colonial Africa,"[13] settlers were in constant and urgent need of African workers to dispose of. While this system had disastrous effects for

African populations, the shortage of a healthy workforce found its expression in settler complaints about the population decline.[14]

An alternative to the perspective of a declining or stagnating African population announced itself slowly but surely, beginning in the 1930s. It was not by chance that the emergent narrative of African surplus population coincided with a more fundamental shift in colonial policy. This coincidence becomes manifest in the land question. It can be considered as one of the first cases in which the tools of the described shift in colonial policy were applied. Land has been a sensitive and important issue from the beginning of the colonial undertaking, because the relations between the colonial administrative apparatus, the settlers, and large parts of the African population were organized around this concept. Due to economic constraints in the wake of the Great Depression, the Colonial Office saw the need to reorganize Kenyan agriculture in order to make it more profitable. The political and economic consequences of the Depression led to a reshuffle within this triangle as the interests of all three groups were at stake. As the Colonial Office aspired to the reorganization of the Kenyan agricultural sector, the settlers who dominated this sector were anxious to keep their status. In return they criticized the agricultural practices of Africans in order to defend their own position. Africans, on the other hand, raised a claim on land that the settlers had alienated them from, and began to fight for their rights through unrests.[15]

The political, economic, and social problems colonial administrators saw occurring as a consequence of the land issue were broached by what was to become the typical genre for tackling such kinds of problems: expert commissions and reports. Thus the Colonial Office and several Kenyan administrators commissioned surveys on the land problem. These texts illustrate the "triumph of the expert"[16] as well as the importance of knowledge production through so-called fact-finding missions that were the signatures of the new colonial agenda.[17] Three of them are well known and frequently cited: the *Kenya Land Commission Report* (1934), the pamphlet *The Kikuyu Lands* (1945) and the *East African Royal Commission Report* (1953). These reports attracted a lot of scholarly attention, and important and revealing interpretations were made.[18] Yet, as some of the points already made are relevant to the story told in this chapter, they are worthy of being repeated. These texts are of concern here because they can be situated at the interface of problem diagnoses and political solutions. Thus, they fulfilled three functions: they were the first texts describing the African population in terms of surplus and growth; they were important multipliers of demographic data; and they connected problem diagnoses and solutions through political recommendations.

The first priority of the aforementioned texts and reports was coming to terms with the question of land. They tried to include the most current demographic information, as they considered population an important factor in relation to land; therefore it is revealing to look at how these data were presented and received. As their production was constantly problematized, their reliability was challenged. This assessment had its roots in a controversy over demographic methodology, as a case in point. The demographic findings cited in the *Kenya Land Commission Report* were based on tax registers; Robert René Kuczynski, one of the leading professional statisticians of that time, challenged their validity because he insisted that accuracy can only be reached through countrywide enumerations.[19]

In the 1930s and 1940s, statements and reflections on the unreliability of data seemed to be a matter of good form for everyone participating in this debate. Norman Humphrey, the author of the pamphlet *The Kikuyu Lands* conceded that "statistical data, where the native lands are concerned is apt to be limited and of doubtful accuracy, so much so that one tends to regard it as of little value."[20] Nevertheless, statements where people showed themselves convinced that changes were beginning to occur became more frequent as this example of the Director of Medical Services in Kenya from 1946 illustrates: "I know of course that all census enumerations in Africa are exceedingly unreliable but there have been a number of small scale investigations which seem to be of value."[21]

The East African Population Census of 1948 can be seen as reaction to this growing debate on the unreliability of data. It was the first census in which the African population was explicitly the focus. Yet, even after the census had taken place, debate continued as this reaction from the British High Commission to the demographic data in the report of the East Africa Royal Commission highlights:

> Without disputing the conclusions on population growth arrived at by the Royal Commission, it is worth noting ... that the basic data available for the examination of the problem were meagre. The first full population census ever taken in East Africa was held in 1948. For a variety of reasons it has not been possible to take a full population census of Africans since then. It is hoped to carry this out ... probably in Kenya in 1959. Much further information should then become available.[22]

This second census was finally carried out in 1962.

In summary, one can say that the advocates of both narratives, that of population decline as well as that of surplus, were equally convinced that the data with which they tried to legitimize their premises were meager and unreliable. Thus, the coexistence of both narratives can be explained firstly by the fact that the data aimed to visualize the shift in African population growth, and the methods by which they were produced were constantly criticized. Secondly, the political circumstances, namely the Mau-Mau uprising between 1952 and 1957 might have contributed to the fact that no proper population policy measures were discussed or introduced before Kenyan independence in 1963. They might simply have seemed too delicate.[23] Finally, it can be stated that the perception of

African population in the Kenyan colony was the result of the different weighting of three factors: data, ideologies, and political practices.[24]

Transferring Models: The Nexus between Population and Economy

The new interventionist agenda adopted by the Colonial Office since the 1930s can be regarded as a major catalyst for the transformed perspective on Kenyan population. At the same time, it echoed an increasing international tendency to orient political strategies and actions towards the categories of planning, social engineering, and development.[25] The United States especially acted as a much-cited archetype for a variety of actors in this period. When Norman Humphrey in his aforementioned pamphlet on *The Kikuyu Lands* wrote about the deterioration of the soil and possibilities for intervention to stop it, he themed his demonstrations under a motto of David E. Lilienthal's book on the Tennessee Valley Authority project, *TVA: Democracy on the March* (1944), which was often treated in the scholarly literature as the epitome of social engineering.[26] The motto went as follows: "A thousand valleys over the globe and our valley here are in this way the same: everywhere what happens to the land, the forests, and the water determines what happens to the people."[27] It is revealing for its promulgation of a universal approach, saying that there are comparable phenomena all over the world from which basic principles can be deduced.

When the concept to which population was mostly referred changed in the 1940s from "land" to "economy," the principle of universality remained a prominent feature of the perception of population as well as the interlacement of empire-wide and international concerns and approaches. This can be exemplified in a text by the Director of Medical Services in Kenya, A.R. Paterson, who was one of the earliest advocates of a narrative of African population growth, presented to the Rotary Club in Nairobi and published in 1947. It was a follow-up to a talk he gave a year before, in which he had problematized the growth of African population due to colonial medical practices helping to treat disease and curb the mortality rate without exerting influences on the fertility rate.[28] In his second talk, he considered possible outcomes of this situation leading, according to him, to unprecedented and problematic population growth within Kenya and the whole of colonized Africa.[29] He proposed an "integrated program of modernization" that he derived from the U.S. publication *Policy in Areas of Heavy Population Pressure* authored by Frank W. Notestein in 1944.[30] In this publication, Notestein outlined an early version of the demographic transition, the model for which the director of the Office of Population Research and later director of the U.S.-based private Population Council became famous. The demographic transition model to which Paterson alluded represented a meta-narrative that should describe and explain the transformation of the Euro-Atlantic societies during the nineteenth and twentieth centuries, and which was also used as a forecasting tool to predict a similar change in the postcolonial world. It thus aimed at universal validity, classifying every society into one of three stages and assuming that every society would pass through every stage. While the first phase postulated the equilibrium of fertility and mortality on a high level, the second phase of transition marked a high fertility with a parallel decline of mortality. The third phase would eventually lead to a new equilibrium between fertility and mortality, this time on a low level. It was assumed that the Western nations had reached the third phase in the mid-twentieth century. Yet, the newly independent developing countries were considered as being on the edge of transition, which was understood as being indicative of a dramatic increase in birth rates in these areas. The reason for the demographic change through the decline of fertility in industrialized countries was located in the fact that a comprehensive modernization process through which these societies ran questioned the so-called traditional model of the extended family. Thus, practices of reproduction adapted themselves to the capitalist modes of economy and a changed lifestyle.[31]

In this early formulation of 1944, Notestein understood fertility as a cultural factor that could only be changed through a transformation of the whole context in which it was embedded. He was convinced that every effort to intervene into the fertility behavior of people in developing countries needed a "whole process of modernization in all its economic and cultural aspects as the necessary precondition for the emergence of the appropriate motivational context for systematic, mass fertility control to appear in any society."[32] It was this process to which Paterson alluded and deemed necessary to initiate in Kenya. With this opinion he embodied an early pioneer, as he emphasized himself, from an international perspective. Africa was still considered as "not only a continent of open and empty spaces but one where the population may even be declining."[33] He thus made it clear that the model of demographic transition was not devised with Africa in mind. Nevertheless, as he understood it as a model representing basic principles and universal laws, he saw no barriers in applying it to conditions in Kenya.[34] This perception of an empty African continent with a declining population seemed to have been kept alive due to the alleged absence of data proving the contrary.

In the meantime, the demographic transition model was transformed from an abstract model into a concrete development strategy. For this, the events in postcolonial Kenya serve as a good example. In April 1965, the Kenyan government communicated in a letter to the Population Council its decision "to pursue vigorously policies designed to reduce the rate of population growth."[35] Written just two years after Kenyan independence, this aim might astonish. Here, the reaction of the British colonial regime against the Mau-Mau uprising can be seen as influential for Kenyan politics after independence. While the conflict took the shape of a civil war and divided Kenyans into "rebels" and "moderates" or "loyalists," the British government made certain that political responsibility after independence would only be entrusted to the latter.³⁶ As a result, the transition between colonial and postcolonial times appears to be relatively smooth, facilitating the continuity of capitalist economic structures. This continuity is striking when it comes to the invitation of the Population Council.

The place where all threads ran together was the Kenyan Ministry of Economic Planning and Development, where three parties were instrumental in their attempt to set the issue of population growth on the agenda of the young Kenyan republic. First of all, the former colonial government demographer, John Blacker, chief interpreter of the census of 1962, tried to spread awareness of a problematic development of population in the Ministry of Economic Planning and Development.³⁷ Secondly, Edgar O. Edwards, the Ford Foundation funded advisor in the Kenyan Ministry of Planning and Development, played an important role.³⁸ And thirdly, the Minister of Economic Planning and Development himself, Tom Mboya. Because of his Oxford education and the way he led his ministry, he gained a reputation for being pro-Western through and through. Politically, in these first years after independence, his ministry succeeded in taking the lead and defining the roads to be taken.³⁹ These three parties, representing the old colonial power, the new foreign aid regime, and the independent Kenyan government, emerge as a knowledge community, sharing basic assumptions regarding Kenya's future.

Within this shared knowledge universe, the signposts pointing the route to follow announce "development," "economic growth," and "modernization." Here, the entity of population comes into play. In 1958, Ansley J. Coale, Frank W. Notestein's student and a demographer at the renowned Office for Population Research in Princeton, initiated an empirical study in order to evaluate the economic consequences of rapid population growth. Together with the economist Edgar Hoover, he published the much-cited paper "Population Growth and Economic Development in Low-Income Countries." It was based on the universal and abstract assumptions of the demographic transition model and confirmed, taking India as an example, its basic hypothesis that a country's economy and the individual life standard of its people can be significantly improved through a reduction of rapid population growth.⁴⁰ This established link between population growth and economic development made rapid population growth endanger Mboya's ambitious prospects for the young Kenyan nation. Mboya's absolute priority in the economic sphere⁴¹ becomes obvious in a memorandum, drafted by Edgar O. Edwards and presented by the minister himself to the country's Development Committee in January 1965, which was entitled "Population Growth and Economic Development." Based on the census results of the years 1948 and 1962, the text posited a population growth rate of three percent per year. Linking the rising fertility to a declining mortality, Edwards and Mboya derived from these data that Kenya had a population problem. To emphasize the evidence, they correlated their findings with the Coale-Hoover results for India: "The Coale-Hoover analysis suggests that there is much to be gained in both total and per capita incomes and therefore in economic influence, prestige, and power from a reduction in the rate of population growth."[42]

Shortly afterwards, in the name of the Kenyan government, Titus K. Mbathi, Permanent Secretary in the Ministry of Economic Planning and Development, addressed a letter of invitation to the Population Council, again under the heading "Population Growth and Economic Development." Mbathi "made it clear that the council was asked to send a mission because [the Kenyans] understood [the council] were interested not merely in birth control but would consider population in the context of its relationship to economic development."[43] Thus, driven by economic arguments, the knowledge community in the Ministry of Economic Planning and Development invited the Population Council, as they shared the motive of problematizing rapid population growth, believing that it would be a hindrance to economic development.

The expectations for the Population Council were twofold: to "study the population problem in Kenya" and "to recommend a suitable program for effecting the ideal rate of [population] growth."[44] Answering favorably to Kenya's request, the organization sent an "Advisory Mission" of four experts who traveled around the country for three weeks. Richmond K. Anderson, the Population Council's Director of Technical Aid, guided the mission, which was completed by two Ford Foundation members and Ansley J. Coale, the aforementioned author of the study "Population Growth and Economic Development in Low-Income Countries." This being said, on the level of demographic knowledge, the mission's final report followed the assumptions of the demographic transition model, which apparently prefigured the experts' perception of the Kenyan "reality." An analysis of the main categories used in the report may illustrate this. First of all, Kenya was defined as a developing country and thus compared to other developing countries that "share ... the problems associated with rapid (three percent or over) rate of population increase and the prospect of further acceleration with the further reductions in mortality which are certain to take place."[45] Secondly, while it was acknowledged that "to persons unaccustomed to dealing with population data, an annual rate of increase of three percent may seem moderate," the mission members used techniques to give the abstract issue a more concrete shape. For one thing, they introduced a comparison. With regard to the category of density, they postulated that "nearly three-quarters of the population lives in districts ... approaching the average population density of India."[46] In this context, India signified the epitome of an overpopulated country. Furthermore, they problematized the issue through displacing the whole scenario into the future, stating that at three percent the population would double "every 23 years, so that in 92 years it is multiplied by 16."[47] The last step to further concretion of the problem is its relation to the rate of economic growth: "a reduced rate of population growth which permitted high levels of investment in education and in economic and social development would result in a more vigorous, better educated and more highly modernized nation."[48]

Thus, to reveal the extent of the population problem, the experts strictly related the rate of economic growth to the rate of population growth. Here, it is worth paying attention to how the text dealt with the question of data. During their trip, the mission members were mainly preoccupied with the collection of existing material and data on population. The population figures, however, stem mainly from the censuses taken in 1948 and 1962, which were—according to the report—"the only information available from which to estimate [birth and death] rates and the rate of increase of the Kenya population."[49] While there is complete absence of economic data, the report's estimates indicating consequences of population growth in different fields of economic and social development, like education or employment, were wholly based on the population figures. Daniel Speich has hinted at the pitfalls of comparing national accounting categories, because the "normative instances for the national accounting framework were in this case the structures of the Australian, British, and American economies of the interwar period."[50] The attempt to apply these norms in different contexts must necessarily fail, because they don't match with different realities. The same can be stated for the demographic transition model, which dealt with similar abstractions on the macro level. Thus census data on the one hand and GDP on the other were both based on the infrastructures of industrialized nations. The link between these two categories, carried out in the demographic transition model, was now transferred by the Population Council experts to the developing world. Consequently, this perspective overshadowed the perception of an area for which reliable data were lacking. On the level of demographic knowledge, the experts' findings reflect their own categories and abstractions on the basis of an alleged universal model.

The Advisory Mission experts, however, seemed to be aware that their view on Kenya originated from a bird's-eye perspective. Hence, Richmond Anderson mentioned in his log notes during the trip that he asked Mwai Kibaki, then Assistant Minister of Economic Planning and Development, "how much detail regarding organization, administration and cost he would like in the report, saying that we did not have enough knowledge of Kenya to be confident about making detailed recommendations."[51] Here, it becomes clear that the mission's report furnished a textbook analysis for what they saw as a typical developing country at the brink of modernization.

From the Transfer of Solutions to the Transfer of a Problem

The abstract model of demographic transition took shape in the practice of family planning. A family planning program seemed thus to make the realization of this transition possible in Kenya. It was the Population Council who epitomized the link between demographic transition and family planning. As Frank W. Notestein and some of his colleagues from the Office of Population Research in Princeton joined the Population Council, they brought in their demographic background based on the assumptions of demographic transition theory. At the same time, the New York-based organization pioneered an active approach in supporting developing countries to overcome their alleged population problems. Thus, the fertility rate was discovered as the key variable to be controlled in order to accelerate the modernization process. Frank Notestein drew this consequence when he considered the integration of family planning into programs of public health.[52] Treating overpopulation as a disease seemed to facilitate the Population Council's advocacy for a fertility decline in developing countries for two reasons. Firstly, it suggested the incorporation of family planning into the field of development assistance, to which health initiatives had been strongly associated since the malaria eradication campaigns of the 1950s.[53] Secondly, in view of the reservations with which population politics were often received due to their association with birth control, the Population Council envisaged integrating family planning measures with infrastructures of maternal and child health care. Hence, family planning passed as the ideal solution, because it promised to link the reduction of population growth deemed detrimental to economic growth with already existing and accepted developing aid structures in the field of public health. It might not surprise that the Advisory Mission also recommended in their report to the Kenyan government that this modernization formula be the core of the Population Council agenda.[54] Yet this "standard choreography"[55] of population politics had to be embedded into a Kenyan context, which from the Population Council expert's view turned out to be more challenging than the alleged universality of their approach suggested.

In reaction to the report of the Population Council Advisory Mission, the Kenyan government accepted the establishment of a National Family Planning Program, which was implemented and received with ambivalence. The National Family Planning Program started in 1967 under the responsibility of the Kenyan Ministry of Health. According to the Advisory Mission report, the recommended solution to the alleged population problem should be "to make every pregnancy the result of a voluntary choice."[56] Inspired by this aim, the declared program objective consisted in making contraceptives and family planning information available for every woman or at least in every clinic and maternal and child health care institution. To get the program off the ground, the Population Council sent two external advisors, a gynecologist and a nurse. They were followed by many other experts delegated by a variety of institutions committed to population policies.

Critics accompanied the measures from their inception. Their voices were compiled and bequeathed in surveys of and correspondences by Kenyan and foreign commentators. An inventory of the most common objections reveals that they are intimately bound to the Kenyan social and political climate of that time. In terms of content, three groups of criticism can be differentiated. Firstly, people denied the existence of an overpopulation problem. They argued that efforts to implement population policies in Kenya had their roots in racist or ethnic plots either by foreigners or by influential Kenyan groups such as the Kikuyu.[57] When Kenya became independent in 1963, it was a deeply divided country, looking back on the brutal Mau-Mau uprising, which at some point took the shape of a civil war, against a racist and oppressing settler regime.[58] Against this background, skepticism towards expatriates dominating the program characterized the second group of criticisms. Hence, Kenyans commented that "as long as foreigners continue to be so heavily involved, there will be never be a stronger local commitment."[59] Assumptions that the implementation of family planning measures chiefly represented the interests of foreign donors leads to the third group, uniting those critical voices that were not denying a population problem but argued that it would not be solved through family planning. Here, a prominent claim stated that the rather simple availability of foreign donor money for family planning was part of a strategy to divert attention from the deeper causes of the poverty problem.[60] In public, Kenyan government officials emphasized and propagated the health benefits of the program for mother and child while disassociating it completely from targets to reduce the population growth rate.[61] In sum, it can be said that the realities of the national family planning program caused a dissolution of the modernization package that experts intended to transfer to Kenya: family planning, population growth reduction, and economic benefits were not necessarily conceived as a unity.

To expatriates in charge of transferring population policy infrastructures to Kenya, observations suggesting that the national family planning program exerted no influence on Kenyan birth rates at all presented itself as a paradox. For though "over the last years, the Kenyan government has received . . . in per capita terms . . . more population assistance than other countries in the world including India and Bangladesh," the country was considered since the early 1980s to have the highest population growth rate in the world.[62] The author of these lines, Ford Foundation representative Goran Hyden, along with his colleagues, found a threefold paradoxical situation which for some of them had announced itself since the 1970s. Firstly, they were related to data. The aforementioned topos of their unreliability was replenished by the topos of the irrelevance of data. Hence, during a Ford Foundation-organized workshop on "Needed Research in Eastern Africa on Family Planning," it was stated that "there are insufficient research data upon which to base certain program decisions or that research that has already been carried out does not answer the most pressing questions."[63] As the data did not fulfill the function that was expected from them, namely to provide the actors with orientation in the field, they were replaced through models and experiences from other countries. Yet, in the 1980s, officials from the World Bank and the Ford Foundation blamed the "tendency to readily borrow insights gained from the demographic transition in other parts of the world"[64] for having led to the formulation of "unrealistic [program] targets."[65] Instead, Hyden insisted, "the peculiarities of the situation in a country like Kenya" should have been "more closely examin[ed]."[66]

Some studies, conducted in the period between 1967 and 1978, however, have tried to integrate a Kenyan perspective into the knowledge framework of population planning. The findings of the Knowledge Attitude Practice (KAP) surveys and the Kenyan Fertility Survey in 1977 assumed a high so-called ideal family size of Kenyan women of between six and seven children.[67] On the basis of these results and in "striking contrast to those [results] found in a number of developing countries," a journal digest from 1980 appraising the Fertility Survey attested that Kenya was "a very pro-natalist culture."[68] This assumption served as a second explanation in the discourse trying to explain the alleged failure of family planning measures. Thirdly, a controversial debate over the aims of Kenyan population policy was started already in the 1970s mainly by expatriates, as can be seen from a report of a World Bank evaluation mission from 1971. It postulated that "there is no firm commitment by the government to develop the program to a stage where it has a significant impact on the population growth rate. It is essentially a health program."[69]

In sum, three strategies crystallize that were used to explain why the program had not shown any visible effect in the 1980s, notwithstanding the huge amount of expert personnel and foreign aid money involved: blaming the lack of relevant data as well as the organization of the program, and turning the alleged failure to realize a population decline into a cultural phenomenon under the label of the "high fertility aspirations" of Kenyans.[70] The function of these strategies can be seen in the fact that the advising foreign organizations did not see a reason to question their own approach. Instead, they drew the conclusion that the majority of Kenyans did not yet fully grasp the scale and seriousness of their country's population problem, and thus propagated the necessity to not only transfer solutions but also create an awareness of the problem itself.

The appropriate mediator for the propagation of the problem was found in a Population Studies and Research Institute (PSRI) which should be established at the interface between the production of population knowledge and its application. This project of institution building has already been pursued since the early 1970s,[71] but was not realized before 1977. In the period between 28 March 1977 and 15 September 1984, the United States Agency for International

Development (USAID) awarded funding to the Population Council, who delivered technical assistance for building up the Institute at the University of Nairobi. The PSRI's tasks were defined by the funding agencies and can be read as a reaction to what the foreign experts had identified as shortcomings of Kenyan population policies. Thus, the PSRI was intended to generate population knowledge through the production and interpretation of data, educate young Kenyan scholars in demography, and influence political practices through a close cooperation with a whole range of ministries.[72] The combination and bringing together of data, practices, and its promulgation within one Kenyan institution was seen as a successful way to create and transport a Kenyan population problem. This seemed necessary because of the increasingly observed dissolution of the modernization formula that the Population Council and many organizations in its wake aspired to transfer. The link between the demographic transition model, family planning practices and data proving its dependency did not seem to work in the Kenyan context. This frame of reference eroded increasingly due to complaints about unreliable or irrelevant data on the one hand, and practices alienated from their envisaged purpose, a population decline, on the other, which contributed to undermine the model. The PSRI was therefore seen as a chance to reunite data and practices within a Kenyan frame. Hence, high priority was set on the "Kenyanization" of the institute.[73]

The evaluations of the institute's performance varied widely and were dependent on the textual genre in which they took place as well as on the interests of the evaluation institution or author. Yet, while at some point research interests "in mortality [rather] than in fertility"[74] were criticized as well as "a lethargic performance,"[75] other voices emphasized situations in which the institute proved to be instrumental. Thus, some of the institute's policy-oriented papers published in the late 1970s were deemed to have "established for the first time that Kenya has one of the highest rates of population growth in the world"[76] as well as having contributed to bring about a "shift ... [in] Kenya's family planning program from a health orientation to a development perspective."[77] Here, of course, the institute's activities did not take place in a vacuum. They must rather be understood in the context of a momentous economic crisis in 1979, which introduced a phase in which the World Bank began to exert a strong influence on Kenya's political agenda.[78] As the Kenyan government was in urgent need of money, it agreed to a structural adjustment program.[79] The World Bank officials insisted on integrating population policy measures into these structures, which led to a new strengthening of family planning measures as well as a revaluation of the population problem, which was again emphasized as one of Kenya's foremost impediments to development. This overshadowing of the institute's activities by the general political background must be taken into account when the instrumental role of the institute in putting the population problem to the foreground is underlined in foreign organizations' evaluation reports.

Conclusion

The perception of Kenya as an overpopulated country established itself in the long term from the 1960s. It was manifested in a number of reports, newspaper articles, and also books, such as Daniel Branch's recently published history of postcolonial Kenya made clear: "The story of Kenyan politics after independence is the story of politics in a time of demographic explosion."[80] Yet, as this chapter has shown, this perception of problematic population growth has a history in itself, which influenced Kenyan politics and even more so governmental structures, because foreign aid organizations interfered in a significant way in Kenyan infrastructures, agendas, and programs. It is remarkable, though, that numbers and population data played only a minor role in this history. Much more important were the concepts to which population was related such as labor, land, or economy, as well as demographic models. While the data were constantly qualified as meager, unreliable, or irrelevant, in the 1960s, the model of demographic transition stood in as a compensating and influential tool for the perception of population and the orientation of politics alike.

In the Kenyan context, however, this developmentally turned modernization formula, which conceived of a population growth reduction through family planning in order to stimulate economic growth, eroded and dissolved increasingly. While some influential politicians and technocrats in the Kenyan government during the 1960s shared economic priorities with the population experts, disagreements predominated over the implementation of family planning practices. Yet the only way to substantiate the abstract nexus of population and economy, related to each other within the demographic transition framework in a Kenyan context, was the transfer of solutions within the concrete object and practice of family planning. As many experts agreed since the 1970s that this transfer had not had the expected effect of being able to illustrate demographic transition, efforts to transport the whole problem context were initiated. Thus, the parameters of the original constellation continued to play a role, but transition and family planning were not exclusively linked to each other anymore. This implied that the inherent dimension of this link, the promise of modernization under the sign of economic development, dwindled as well. At the same time, the establishment of the Population Studies and Research Institute took place when the context and conditions in which population policies were embedded changed with the structural adjustment agenda of the World Bank, beginning in the 1980s. When family planning programs became part of the financial conditions of the World Bank, the Kenyan government lost a part of its scope of interpretation of population and policies.

Acknowledgments

My thanks go to Julia Angster whose feedback on an early draft helped me develop my argument. I am grateful to the anonymous reviewers and especially to Corinna Unger and Heinrich Hartmann for their valuable comments on the manuscript. The staff at the various archives provided me with generous advice and help.

Notes

1. Population Council to Agency for International Development. 28 March 1977–15 September 1984. *Final Report. Population Studies and Research Institute Project*, PD-AAT-805, USAID, 4.
2. See T. Robertson, *The Malthusian Moment: Global Population Growth and the Birth of American Environmentalism* (New Brunswick, 2012), 66–72.
3. See M. Connelly, *Fatal Misconception. The Struggle to Control World Population* (Cambridge, Mass., 2008); M. Frey, "Neo-Malthusianism and Development: Shifting Interpretations of a Contested Paradigm," *Journal of Global History* 6 (2011): 75–97; J. Sharpless, "World Population Growth, Family Planning and American Foreign Policy," *Journal of Policy History* 7 (1995): 72–102.
4. See L.M. Thomas, *Politics of the Womb: Women, Reproduction, and the State in Kenya* (Berkeley, 2003), 4–5.
5. See T. Etzemüller, *Ein ewigwährender Untergang. Der apokalyptische Bevölkerungsdiskurs im 20. Jahrhundert* (Bielefeld, 2007), 42.
6. See J. Krige and H. Rausch, "Introduction – Tracing the Knowledge: Power Nexus of American Philanthropy," in *American Foundations and the Coproduction of World Order in the Twentieth Century*, J. Krige and H. Rausch eds. (Göttingen, 2012), 21.
7. J. Ferguson, *Global Shadows: Africa in the Neoliberal World Order* (Durham, 2006), 42.
8. M.L. Pratt, *Imperial Eyes: Travel Writing and Transculturation* (London, 1992).
9. See M. Pesek, "Die Kunst des Reisens. Die Begegnung von europäischen Forschungsreisenden und Ostafrikanern in den Kontaktzonen des 19. Jahrhunderts," in *Kommunikationsräume – Erinnerungsräume. Beiträge zur transkulturellen Begegnung in Afrika*, W. Speitkamp ed. (München, 2005), 67.
10. See R.L. Tignor, *The Colonial Transformation of Kenya: The Kamba, Kikuyu and Maasai from 1900 to 1939* (Princeton, 1976), 22.
11. See Thomas, *Politics of the Womb*, 12, 28.
12. See R.M.A. Zwanenberg and A. King, *An Economic History of Kenya and Uganda, 1800–1970* (Plymouth, 1975), 7.
13. Thomas, *Politics of the Womb*, 24.
14. See K. Ittmann "'Where Nature Dominates Man.' Demographic Ideas and Policy in British Colonial Africa," in *The Demographics of Empire: The Colonial Order and the Creation of Knowledge*, K. Ittmann, D.D. Cordell and G.H. Maddox eds. (Athens, 2010), 64–65.
15. See D. Anderson, *Histories of the Hanged: The Dirty War in Kenya and the End of Empire* (New York and London, 2005), 22–23.
16. J. Hodge, *Triumph of the Expert: Agrarian Doctrines of Development and the Legacies of British Colonialism* (Athens, 2007).
17. See J. Lewis, *Empire State-Building: War and Welfare in Kenya, 1925–52* (Oxford, 2000), 29.

18. See for example D. Anderson, "Depression, Dust Bowl, Demography, and Drought: The Colonial State and Soil Conservation in East Africa During the 1930s," *African Affairs* 83 (1984): 321–341; B.A. Ogot, "The Decisive Years 1956-63," in *Decolonization and Independence in Kenya*, B.A. Ogot and W.R. Ochieng' eds. (London, 1995), 49–50; L.M. Thomas, *Regulating Reproduction: State Interventions into Fertility and Sexuality in Rural Kenya, ca. 1920–1970* (Ph.D. diss., University of Michigan, 1997).
19. See Thomas, *Regulating Reproduction*, 192–193.
20. N. Humphrey. 1945. *The Kikuyu Lands*, Nairobi: Government Printer, CO 852/662/8, The National Archives, Kew [TNA], 1.
21. A.R. Paterson to Lord Hailey. 18 September 1946. CO 1018/29, TNA.
22. A.M.B. Hutt to A.T. Lennox-Boyd. 10 February 1956. *East Africa High Commission*, CO 822/1118, TNA.
23. See Thomas, *Regulating Reproduction*, 261.
24. See Ittmann, *Where Nature Dominates Man*, 59.
25. See on the change of colonial policies in this period Lewis, *Empire State-Building*, 10–35; furthermore Hodge, *Triumph of the Expert*, 8.
26. See J.M. Jordan, *Machine-Age Ideology: Social Engineering and American Liberalism, 1911–1939* (Chapel Hill and London 1994), 243–247; M. Hochgeschwender, "The Noblest Philosophy and Its Most Efficient Use: Zur Geschichte des Social Engineering in den USA, 1910–1965," in *Die Ordnung der Moderne. Social Engineering im 20. Jahrhundert*, T. Etzemüller ed. (Bielefeld, 2009), 171–197.
27. Cited after Humphrey, *The Kikuyu Lands*, 17.
28. See A.R. Paterson, "The Human Situation in East Africa, Part I: On the Increase of the People," *East African Medical Journal* 24 (1947): 83.
29. Thomas, *Regulating Reproduction*, 220–221.
30. A.R. Paterson, "The Human Situation in East Africa, Part II: Towards a Population Policy," *East African Medical Journal* 24, no. 4 (1947): 148.
31. On the model of demographic transition theory see S. Szreter, "The Idea of Demographic Transition and the Study of Fertility Change: A Critical Intellectual History," *Population and Development Review* 19, no. 4 (1993): 659–701; S. Greenhalgh, "The Social Construction of Population Science: An Intellectual, Institutional, and Political History of Twentieth-Century Demography," *Comparative Studies in Society and History* 38, no. 19 (1996): 26–66; D. Hodgson, "Demography as Social Science and Policy Science," *Population and Development Review* 9, no. 1 (1983): 1–34.
32. S. Szreter, *Fertility, Class and Gender in Britain, 1860–1940* (Cambridge, 1996), 17–18.
33. Paterson, "Towards a Population Policy," 148.
34. See ibid.
35. T.K.B. Mbathi to J.F. Kantner. 8 April 1965. *Population Growth and Economic Development*, RG IV3B4.3a, Series T65.86, box 65, folder 1137, Rockefeller Archives Center [RAC].
36. See Anderson, *Histories of the Hanged*, 333–335.
37. See A. Ayorinde and J. Kekovole, "Kenya's Population Policy: From Apathy to Effectiveness," in *Do Population Policies Matter? Fertility and Politics in Egypt, India, Kenya, and Mexico*, A.K. Jain ed. (New York, 1998), 114–115.
38. C.A. Nelson to D.J. Kingsley. 7 June 1967. *Family Planning in Kenya. The Ford Foundation: Inter-Office Memorandum*, Reel 1151, Ford Foundation Archives [FFA].
39. See D. Goldsworthy, *Tom Mboya: The Man Kenya Wanted to Forget* (Nairobi and London, 1982), 250–259.
40. See A.J. Coale and E.M. Hoover, *Population Growth and Economic Development in Low-Income Countries: A Case Study of India's Prospects* (Princeton, 1958); Szreter, *Fertility, Class and Gender*, 24.

41. See D. Speich, "Der Entwicklungsautomatismus. Ökonomisches Wissen als Heilsversprechen in der ostafrikanischen Dekolonisation," *Archiv für Sozialgeschichte* 48 (2008), 185, 205.
42. T. Mboya. 14 January 1965. *Population Growth and Economic Development. Memorandum by the Minister for Economic Planning and Development T.J. Mboya to Cabinet Development Committee*, RG IV3B4.3a, Series T65.86, box 65, folder 1137, RAC, 6; E.O. Edwards. 5 January 1965, File No. C/305, AMB 1/4, Kenya National Archives [KNA].
43. R.K. Anderson. June/July 1965. *Diary*, RG IV3B4.3a, box 65, folder 1138, RAC, 26.
44. Mbathi to Kantner, *Population Growth and Economic Development*.
45. F.W. Notestein to T.K. Mbathi. 13 August 1965. *Report of the Advisory Group*, RG IV3B4.3a, Series T65.86, box 65, folder 1137, RAC.
46. Ibid., 2.
47. Ibid., 25.
48. Ibid., 2.
49. Ibid., 24.
50. D. Speich, "The Use of Global Abstractions. National Income Accounting in the Period of Imperial Decline," *Journal of Global History* 6 (2011): 19.
51. Anderson, *Diary*, 26.
52. See Szreter, "The Idea of Demographic Transition," 679.
53. See R. Packard, "Visions of Postwar Health and Development and Their Impact on Public Health Interventions in the Developing World," in *International Development and the Social Sciences. Essays in the History and Politics of Knowledge*, F. Cooper and R. Packard eds. (Berkeley, 1997), 103–108.
54. See *The Population Council: A Chronicle of the First Twenty-Five Years, 1952–1977* (New York, 1978), 23; Notestein to Mbathi, *Report of the Advisory Group*.
55. C. Chimbweteàà, E. Zulu and S. Cotts Watkins, "The Evolution of Population Policies in Kenya and Malawi," *Working Paper* 27, Nairobi: African Population and Health Research Centre [http://www.aphrc.org], 3.
56. Notestein to Mbathi, *Report of the Advisory Group*, 3. For the influence of rational choice theories on the Population Council see C. Unger's chapter in this volume.
57. See Anderson, *Diary*, 5, 30; G. Shepherd. 1984. *Responding to the Contraceptive Needs of Rural People. A Report to OXFAM on Kenya*, London N5 1AT, SA/POP/C/2/2, Wellcome Library.
58. See Anderson, *Histories of the Hanged*, 4; Lewis, *Empire State-Building*.
59. K. Ndeti and C. Ndeti, *Cultural Values and Population Policy in Kenya* (Nairobi, 1977), 141–142.
60. Ndeti, *Cultural Values*, 62–63; U. Olin. 18 May 1972. *A Population Policy for Kenya*, PC Acc. II AD 61, RAC, 23.
61. L. Laurenti to P. Ndegwa. 23 April 1971. *Whither the Family Planning Programme?* Ministry of Economic Planning and Development 1970–71, AMB 6/99, KNA; Ndeti, *Cultural Values*, 133.
62. G. Hyden to R.S. McNamara. 6 May 1983. *The Population Scene in Kenya*, Reel 4165, FFA.
63. Workshop on Needed Research in Eastern Africa on Family Planning: Medical Research and Programme Trials. 23–25 July 1970. *Statement of Purpose*, PC Acc II AD 61, RAC, 1.
64. Hyden, *The Population Scene*.
65. D. Radel to K. Kanagaratnam. 22 February 1980. *Kenya Briefing Note*, ID 805611, World Bank Group Archives [WBGA].
66. Hyden, *The Population Scene*.
67. See the documentation on KAP studies T.E. Dow "Attitudes Toward Family Size and Family Planning in Nairobi," *Demography* 4, no. 2 (1967): 780–797; D.F. Heisel, "Attitudes and Practice of Contraception in Kenya," *Demography* 5, no. 1 (1968): 632–641; A. Molnos, *Attitudes toward Family Planning in East Africa* (München, 1968). On the KAP surveys see H. Hartmann's chapter in this volume.

68. "Kenya WFS: Fertility High, Contraceptive Practice Low; Most Women Say That They Want Large Families," *International Family Planning Perspectives* 4, no. 2 (1980), 78.
69. IBRD/IDA. 18 June 1971. *Economic Development in Eastern Africa*, vol. 3 annex 1, AMB 18/18, KNA, 19.
70. IBRD/IDA, *Economic Development*, 9.
71. 13 April 1971. *Informal Co-Ordination Meeting on Population and Family Planning Programmes in Kenya*, PC Acc. II AD 61, RAC, 7.
72. Population Council, *Final Report*.
73. This corresponded with general schemes of U.S. or international organizations to "Africanize" research institutions founded and funded by them through the education of elites. See E.H. Berman, *The Ideology of Philanthropy: The Influence of the Carnegie, Ford and Rockefeller Foundations on American Foreign Policy* (Albany, 1983), 77–78; C.R. Unger, "The United States, Decolonization, and the Education of Third World Elites," in *Elites and Decolonisation in the Twentieth Century*, J. Dülffer and M. Frey eds. (Basingstoke, 2011), 246–253.
74. Hyden, *The Population Scene*.
75. W.D. Carmichael to F.A. Thomas. 8 December 1988. *Population Studies and Research Centre*, Reel 6338, FFA, 1.
76. Population Council, *Final Report*.
77. M. Bangser to C. Bailey. 27 May 1993. *Final Evaluation: University of Nairobi Population Studies and Research Institute for Support for Diploma Training and Staff Development of the Institute*, Reel 6338, FFA, 1.
78. See P. Mosley, "Kenya," in *Aid and Power: The World Bank and Policy-based Lending, Volume 2: Case Studies*, P. Mosley, J. Harrigan and J. Toye eds. (London, 1991), 274.
79. See on these programs J. Ferguson, *Global Shadows*, 100–102; Hodge, *Triumph of the Expert*, 273.
80. D. Branch, *Kenya Between Hope and Despair, 1963–2011* (New Haven and London, 2011), 17.

Bibliography

Anderson, D., *Histories of the Hanged: The Dirty War in Kenya and the End of Empire* (New York and London, 2005).

Anderson, D., "Depression, Dust Bowl, Demography, and Drought: The Colonial State and Soil Conservation in East Africa During the 1930s," *African Affairs* 83 (1984): 321–341.

Ayorinde, A., and Kekovole, J., "Kenya's Population Policy: From Apathy to Effectiveness," in *Do Population Policies Matter? Fertility and Politics in Egypt, India, Kenya, and Mexico*, A.K. Jain ed. (New York, 1998).

Berman, E.H., *The Ideology of Philanthropy: The Influence of the Carnegie, Ford and Rockefeller Foundations on American Foreign Policy* (Albany, 1983).

Branch, D., *Kenya Between Hope and Despair, 1963–2011* (New Haven and London, 2011).

Chimbweteàà, C., Zulu, E., and Cotts Watkins, S., "The Evolution of Population Policies in Kenya and Malawi," *Working Paper* 27, Nairobi: African Population and Health Research Centre [http://www.aphrc.org].

Coale, A.J., and Hoover, E.M., *Population Growth and Economic Development in Low-Income Countries: A Case Study of India's Prospects* (Princeton, 1958).

Connelly, M., *Fatal Misconception. The Struggle to Control World Population* (Cambridge, Mass., 2008).

Dow, T.E., "Attitudes toward Family Size and Family Planning in Nairobi," *Demography* 4, no. 2 (1967): 780–797.

Etzemüller, T., *Ein ewigwährender Untergang. Der apokalyptische Bevölkerungsdiskurs im 20. Jahrhundert* (Bielefeld, 2007).
Ferguson, J., *Global Shadows: Africa in the Neoliberal World Order* (Durham, 2006).
Frey, M., "Neo-Malthusianism and Development: Shifting Interpretations of a Contested Paradigm," *Journal of Global History* 6 (2011): 75–97.
Goldsworthy, D., *Tom Mboya: The Man Kenya Wanted to Forget* (Nairobi and London, 1982).
Greenhalgh, S., "The Social Construction of Population Science: An Intellectual, Institutional, and Political History of Twentieth-Century Demography," *Comparative Studies in Society and History* 38, no. 19 (1996): 26–66.
Heisel, D.F., "Attitudes and Practice of Contraception in Kenya," *Demography* 5, no. 1 (1968): 632–641.
Hochgeschwender, M., "The Noblest Philosophy and Its Most Efficient Use: Zur Geschichte des Social Engineering in den USA, 1910–1965," in *Die Ordnung der Moderne. Social Engineering im 20. Jahrhundert*, T. Etzemüller ed. (Bielefeld, 2009), 171–197.
Hodge, J., *Triumph of the Expert: Agrarian Doctrines of Development and the Legacies of British Colonialism* (Athens, 2007).
Hodgson, D., "Demography as Social Science and Policy Science," *Population and Development Review* 9, no. 1 (1983): 1–34.
Ittmann, K., "'Where Nature Dominates Man': Demographic Ideas and Policy in British Colonial Africa," in *The Demographics of Empire: The Colonial Order and the Creation of Knowledge*, K. Ittmann, D.D. Cordell and G.H. Maddox eds. (Athens, 2010).
Jordan, J.M., *Machine-Age Ideology: Social Engineering and American Liberalism, 1911–1939* (Chapel Hill and London 1994).
"Kenya WFS: Fertility High, Contraceptive Practice Low; Most Women Say That They Want Large Families," *International Family Planning Perspectives* 4, no. 2 (1980): 78.
Krige, J., and Rausch, H., "Introduction – Tracing the Knowledge: Power Nexus of American Philanthropy," in *American Foundations and the Coproduction of World Order in the Twentieth Century*, J. Krige and H. Rausch eds. (Göttingen, 2012).
Lewis, J., *Empire State-Building: War and Welfare in Kenya, 1925–52* (Oxford, 2000).
Molnos, A., *Attitudes toward Family Planning in East Africa* (München, 1968).
Mosley, P., "Kenya," in *Aid and Power: The World Bank and Policy-based Lending, Volume 2: Case Studies*, P. Mosley, J. Harrigan and J. Toye eds. (London, 1991), 274.
Ndeti, K., and Ndeti, C., *Cultural Values and Population Policy in Kenya* (Nairobi, 1977).
Ogot, B.A. "The Decisive Years 1956-63," in *Decolonization and Independence in Kenya*, B.A. Ogot and W.R. Ochieng' eds. (London, 1995), 48–79.
Packard, R., "Visions of Postwar Health and Development and Their Impact on Public Health Interventions in the Developing World," in *International Development and the Social Sciences: Essays in the History and Politics of Knowledge*, F. Cooper and R. Packard eds. (Berkeley, 1997), 93–115.
Paterson, A.R., "The Human Situation in East Africa, Part I: On the Increase of the People," *East African Medical Journal* 24 (1947): 83.
Paterson, A.R., "The Human Situation in East Africa, Part II: Towards a Population Policy," *East African Medical Journal* 24, no. 4 (1947): 148.
Pesek, M., "Die Kunst des Reisens. Die Begegnung von europäischen Forschungsreisenden und Ostafrikanern in den Kontaktzonen des 19. Jahrhunderts," in *Kommunikationsräume – Erinnerungsräume. Beiträge zur transkulturellen Begegnung in Afrika*, W. Speitkamp ed. (München, 2005).
The Population Council: A Chronicle of the First Twenty-Five Years, 1952–1977 (New York, 1978).
Pratt, M.L., *Imperial Eyes: Travel Writing and Transculturation* (London, 1992).

Robertson, T., *The Malthusian Moment: Global Population Growth and the Birth of American Environmentalism* (New Brunswick, 2012).

Sharpless, J., "World Population Growth, Family Planning and American Foreign Policy," *Journal of Policy History* 7 (1995): 72–102.

Speich, D., "Der Entwicklungsautomatismus. Ökonomisches Wissen als Heilsversprechen in der ostafrikanischen Dekolonisation," *Archiv für Sozialgeschichte* 48 (2008): 183–212.

Speich, D., "The Use of Global Abstractions. National Income Accounting in the Period of Imperial Decline," *Journal of Global History* 6 (2011): 7–28.

Szreter, S., *Fertility, Class and Gender in Britain, 1860–1940* (Cambridge, 1996).

Szreter, S., "The Idea of Demographic Transition and the Study of Fertility Change: A Critical Intellectual History," *Population and Development Review* 19, no. 4 (1993): 659–701.

Thomas, L.M., *Politics of the Womb: Women, Reproduction, and the State in Kenya* (Berkeley, 2003), 4–5.

Thomas, L.M., *Regulating Reproduction: State Interventions into Fertility and Sexuality in Rural Kenya, ca. 1920–1970* (Ph.D. diss., University of Michigan, 1997).

Tignor, R.L., *The Colonial Transformation of Kenya: The Kamba, Kikuyu and Maasai from 1900 to 1939* (Princeton, 1976).

Unger, C.R., "The United States, Decolonization, and the Education of Third World Elites," in *Elites and Decolonisation in the Twentieth Century*, J. Dülffer and M. Frey eds. (Basingstoke, 2011), 246–253.

Zwanenberg, R.M.A., and King, A., *An Economic History of Kenya and Uganda, 1800–1970* (Plymouth, 1975).

10

FILTERING DEMOGRAPHY AND BIOMEDICAL TECHNOLOGIES
Melanesian Nurses and Global Population Concerns

Alexandra Widmer

Introduction

One of the most tantalizing aspects of demographic knowledge is its promise for predicting the future of a particular population and providing a basis on which institutions can plan social and economic projects. A related and rather astounding characteristic of demography, notes Michelle Murphy, is the way that "when taking the large aggregate view—the lives of individuals wink out of visibility."[1] This is all the more troubling, she continues, because the knowledge is used to develop policies and programs that attempt to "alter some of the most intimate and emotion laden aspects of human life"[2] such as sexuality, fertility, pregnancy, and birth. This transformation of numbers and graphs into an applicable science entails the transfer of knowledge and technology whereby people become numbers plotted on growth curves. This transformation also articulates with cultural and geographical factors and local social change. My aim in this chapter is to trace certain assemblages of demographic thinking and global concern for population size as they intersected with Melanesian lives during the transition from village to hospital birth and the introduction of biomedical birth control in a village in the New Hebrides (now Vanuatu). My hope is to flesh out the complex social worlds that can all too easily be subsumed in the notion of "population." Population, Duden writes, is an epistemic object of demographic discourse that migrates to policy and popular use as "statistical driftwood"[3] and reduces "persons to bloodless entities that can be managed as characterless classes that reproduce, pollute, produce, or consume, and for the common good, call for control."[4]

I approach this topic as an anthropologist using historical and ethnographic methods to understand changes to knowledge and governance of reproduction in the New Hebrides in relation to the twentieth century history of demography.

Analyzing how demographic knowledge filtered into a particular colonial project, and how that particular place filtered into global debates about population, is one way to bring people—both the counted and the counters, both the policy makers and those who deliver the policy—into visibility. This means adding to those scholars who have attempted to combine anthropological and demographic perspectives,[5] who consider cultural and political aspects of fertility[6] and the particular historical genealogies of demography in their analysis.[7] Here, I emphasize the epistemic place of Melanesian populations in the history of demography, and how this history articulated with the transfer of technologies for the regulation of reproduction for people living under the Condominium of the New Hebrides. In 2010,[8] I conducted oral histories with retired ni-Vanuatu[9] nurses because I see them as crucial agents in the making of modern Vanuatu, especially where reproduction is concerned. They were among the first women educated in a Western education system and they acted as intermediaries between indigenous and biomedical paradigms of birth, fertility, and health. To further understand changes in knowledge and ritual pertaining to birth, I also interviewed the oldest women from Pango, a peri-urban village just outside the capital of Port Vila, about giving birth at the mission hospital (1950s–1972) and mothers of children under the age of one about their recent birth experiences in the government hospital. To situate these changes in the context of colonial governance, I conducted research in the New Hebrides British Service (NHBS) archives. Finally, to understand the scientific entanglements of colonial and international organizations' attempts to regulate population, I looked at the production of demographic knowledge of populations in the New Hebrides and the significance of Melanesia in knowledge of global population.

The history of population politics in China,[10] India,[11] as well as European nations[12] are obviously significant objects of analysis for the sheer scale of how numbers of people are transformed into forecasts and policies, and the resulting technology transfer for intimate interventions of the state or NGOs in kinship relations and fertility management. In this chapter, I look at the opposite end of the scale: a group of small islands in the southwestern Pacific. Though small—in some ways because they are small—these islands were part of the assemblage of how the scientific study of the quantity and quality of global populations between the 1920s and 1970s was developed. The islands are also important for what they can tell us about how demographic knowledge was filtered in the absence of a strong state. Although there were no large-scale population control projects of states or NGOs, demographic thinking had effects nevertheless in association with existing social and cultural conditions. The filtering of demography took place in spite of the supposedly culture-neutral behaviorist underpinnings of family planning programs associated with demographic knowledge and projects during the 1950s and 1960s.[13]

In many colonial projects, the relationship between global and local demographic knowledge was entangled with anxieties about population size and quality, the transfer of knowledge of medical childbirth, and the scientific management of fertility control. In the New Hebrides, this knowledge transfer was implicated in the training for ni-Vanuatu women to become nurses, the shift from home to hospital birth, and the eventual introduction of biomedical birth control. I focus on the transfer of knowledge via the particular technologies that were introduced to improve and standardize the course of maternal and infant health care and, by extension, the size and quality of the population. These technologies became part of networks of Christian service, civilizing ideologies, indigenous social forms, and gender relations. These assemblages include birthing women as well as multiple experts and kinds of knowledge and tools. By describing how nurses were selected and trained to implement biomedical hospital birthing as a process of knowledge and technology transfer that sifted through locally meaningful frameworks, I show how demographic knowledge was filtered in the New Hebrides.

A few words on the metaphor of "filter." I chose this device to complicate understandings that characterize the impact of demography as one of knowledge that is transferred from scientific and policy arenas to local contexts. This is a question of how to analyze encounters between actors and discourses of demography, colonial regimes, and indigenous people and their knowledge. Rather than emphasize the colonial state's power over women's bodies or the loss of traditional practices through the introduction of biomedical birth techniques and fertility control, Lynn Thomas prefers to focus on how changes in population politics entailed debate, negotiation, and "the uneven mixing of the indigenous and the imperial."[14] Additionally, I would add, in the New Hebrides, the demographic knowledge and, more powerfully, biomedical technologies were metaphorically "filtered" through the sediments of ancestral knowledge and Christian values by ni-Vanuatu nurses and the women they cared for. Filtering implies a process of categorization, letting through what is relevant, and obstructing what is not. And finally, on the one hand, the incorporation of demographic knowledge and biomedical technology can be an active process with clear intentions, yet on the other, it can happen by passive sifting without draconian measures.

The New Hebrides is a significant place to explore the circulation of demographic knowledge as population there has been in both dramatic decline and increase over the last century. In the twentieth century, researchers began studying the depopulation that missionaries had already been reporting for decades.[15] By the early 1970s, significant population pressures in urban areas were on the minds of researchers and planners.[16] This chapter spans this demographic shift, discussing how the Pacific islands, especially the Melanesian region, filter into global concerns of population size—first as a "race" or "primitive population" in decline in the 1920s, and later as an "undeveloped" place with a precarious relationship to modernity in the 1960s. I tack between this narrative of how global populations were subdivided and that of how knowledge of population size was filtered in Pango village during the same period.

"Primitive Peoples" and Global "Problems of Population"

During the interwar period, demography had not yet emerged as a formal discipline, but through the collaborations of birth control activists, biologists, geneticists, geographers, eugenicists, and physical anthropologists and others, population had emerged as an issue of global significance. The "world population" was understood as an entity that could (and should) be controlled for quality and quantity.[17] At the 1927 World Population Conference in Geneva that established the "International Union for the Scientific Study of Population" and the organization's subsequent meeting in 1932, both overpopulation and depopulation were identified as phenomena of global scope. These conferences, and many others,[18] brought together researchers of many stripes and political leanings who were not always in agreement about either the causes of global population problems or the measures to be taken.

The depopulation of the Pacific islands figured in global scientific conversations in ways that reflected the scientific spectrum of debates about population size, which were framed by concerns of culture and heredity. Physical anthropologist Pitt-Rivers[19] focused on imbalanced sex ratios in the Pacific Islands (then a "racial" concern) as indicators for "racial" survival. The British demographer Alexander Morris Carr-Saunders, in his treatise *World Population: Past Growth and Present Trends* (1936), developed his analysis by dividing humanity into "Europeans," "Non-Europeans," and "Primitive Peoples," and then analyzed the different migration, health, and cultural value issues affecting mortality and fertility in each group. Though Pacific islanders accounted for a very small proportion of the world population, Carr-Saunders argued that they were scientifically significant "for the peculiar features of the population situation among all the primitive peoples reach their fullest development in the Pacific Islands."[20] These were identified as: introduced diseases, violent conflict with Europeans, the disintegration of tribal organization, customs of abortion and infanticide and lack of parental care, the abolition of polygamy, and the temporary removal of men as plantation laborers.[21] Finally, W.H.R Rivers, famous by then for his work on veterans and shell shock, saw psychological factors as the most important consideration for population decline.[22]

The population decline of the Pacific islands was of scientific interest at this time for what supposedly laboratory-like isolated populations could reveal about racial concerns like heredity and adaptation. The scientific understanding of the depopulation of Melanesia brought together many significant strands of ongoing racial debates on the environment and heritability in respect to a population's viability, and Melanesians' experiences were taken as evidence of the significance of the relationship between culture, the environment, and the mind for the reproduction and survival of a population.[23] In the 1920s, as racial mixing became an important scientific topic in physical anthropology and population genetics,[24] the region had become significant for studying this theme,[25] particularly because "racial crosses" between Europeans, Asians, and Pacific islanders were understood as a recent phenomenon. The biological thinking of the day, Warwick Anderson demonstrates, entailed the ambiguous co-existence of arguments that race mixing could at once mean white triumph in Australia and the invigoration of Pacific peoples through hybridization.[26] Yet, as I have noted elsewhere,[27] racial mixing was only favorable for Polynesians whose features could be absorbed into European populations, while between "Europeans and Melanesians or Papuans, the barrier is impassable: the union unwise or, to use the phraseology of the race-specialist, 'disharmonious.'"[28]

Colonial Infrastructures of Biomedical Birth

The scientific concept of a "world population" ultimately entailed the transfer of many population programs, technologies, and practices and forms of expert knowledge throughout the world. In contexts where fertility was low, a common line of thinking was to improve maternal and child health care by standardizing the course of maternity care, while also eliminating indigenous customs deemed unsanitary or unsafe.[29] This transfer of technologies to many parts of empire was carried out through the often pre-existing colonial infrastructure and missionary values. Such interventions took the form of "maternal and child health programs erected on the basis of the understandings of the role of women in reproduction (with respect to biological, social and daily reproduction), assuming that some women, by virtue of class and race were able to undertake these roles 'naturally."[30]

In British imperial projects in Africa, colonists joined forces with missionaries, training local women—selected for their cultural knowledge—to be birth attendants.[31] In Sudan in the 1920s,[32] it was hoped that biomedically-trained local midwives would stop indigenous practices like female genital mutilation partially in the name of improving fertility. In 1930, as part of the attempt to solve the problem of depopulation in the British sphere of influence in the Western Pacific, a senior British administrator in London wrote to the High

Commissioner stationed in Fiji and the resident commissioners in the British Solomon Islands Protectorate, as well as the Gilbert and Ellice Islands and the New Hebrides, to ask whether this practice in initiation rites was a factor in depopulation in the region.[33] The British Resident Commissioner replied that this practice was not a factor, but early marriage was to be considered.[34] Other indigenous customs deemed problematic for public health and depopulation in the New Hebrides during the interwar period included: sleeping on *pandanus* mats on the ground, communal feasts, pigs, dogs and general lack of sanitation,[35] abortion, as well as the high bride price.[36] When local men were educated in the 1940s to be assistant doctors in Suva, Fiji, they were trained to enforce colonial regulations about public sanitation and to deliver primary health care. Eventually the Anglican and Presbyterian missions founded their own formalized nurse training programs, beginning in the 1950s.

Senior women in Pango told me in oral history interviews that in the 1940s, the mission doctor at the Paton Memorial Hospital (PMH), Dr. Alexander Frater, sent word to Reverend Mackenzie, the Presbyterian missionary living at Pango. Dr. Frater invited the missionary to suggest women who could train as nurse midwives through apprenticeship. Mackenzie, who knew the village well, named three women who were already attending births in the village. These women were part of prominent matrilineages that possessed knowledge of plants and medicines. In Pango, as in other places in Vanuatu, such knowledge is kept in lineages or clans (*naflak*), passed from mothers to their daughters. Women with special knowledge about pregnancy, birth, and infant care routinely attended to a woman during late pregnancy and birth in their homes until the early 1950s. According to oral histories in Pango, these were women who typically had ancestral knowledge and several, though not all, of the first nursing trainees had prior knowledge and status in the village. The women would do some prenatal care, generally from approximately the sixth month onward. These experts would massage the sore bodies of pregnant women, and monitor that the fetus was positioned with its head down. They would attend the last part of the labor and the birth and care for the mother during the first post-partum days. After this, the new mother's female relatives would care for her and the newborn infant, while the mother remained at home for the first month. Once it was established that the mother and baby were healthy, after five days or so, the expert would leave and the new mother would thank her by giving mats, bundles of calico or other important gifts suitable for ceremonial payments. This ritual exchange was important to "clean the face:"[37] that is, to make the relationship between the mother and midwife strong again because the midwife had seen the "taboo parts" of the woman during birth. Such perceptions of the female body were part of larger ancestral cosmologies that required seclusion during birth and the post-partum period and gender segregation during menstruation as these were times when feminine potencies were understood as damaging to masculinities.[38]

Remarkable Islands: Isolation, Health, and the History of the New Hebrides

The stories of the New Hebrides that the Presbyterians and Anglicans published depicted the islands as among the most heathen and savage places in the world and thus rendered the New Hebrides a missionary destination almost without equal in the mid-1800s Protestant imagination.[39] This classification of remarkable difference would have far reaching consequences for ni-Vanuatu. Supported by the pennies of school children and the finances of their congregations in Canada, Australia, New Zealand, and Scotland, Presbyterian and Anglican missionaries set up biomedical clinics in the second half of the nineteenth century to keep their own families alive and to demonstrate what they believed to be a civilizing Christian ethic of service by administering to the sick.[40] The missionaries brought new microbes and encouraged new settlement patterns, leading to catastrophic levels of illness and death.[41] Though the conversion process was not uniform,[42] within a century of the missionaries' arrival, many ni-Vanuatu would develop a Christian worldview.[43]

The islands of the New Hebrides were also of interest to scientists for their isolation and remarkable cultural and biological diversity. Beginning in the early 1900s, anthropologists like Felix Speiser, W.H.R. Rivers, John Layard, Arthur Deacon, biologist John Randall Baker and public health physicians Dr. Patrick Buxton and Sylvester Lambert published on the alarming levels of death and disease they witnessed. Missionaries, anthropologists, and public health doctors alike were deeply concerned about the declining population, which might have decreased from over 500,000 inhabitants prior to the arrival of Europeans to possibly as low as 30,000 inhabitants in the 1920s. Throughout the 1920s, the researchers wrote numerous reports to the British-French Condominium admonishing the lack of colonial efforts to improve the health of the local population.[44] From 1906–1980, the British Resident Commissioner (BRC), and his French counterpart (FRC), presided over the British-French condominium called the New Hebrides, an archipelago of over eighty islands in the southwestern Pacific. The New Hebrides was "a joint sphere of influence" rather than a formal colony of either empire.[45] The efforts of the Condominium to increase the indigenous population were quite modest, and more frequently based on the efforts of individual agents, rather than a concerted effort of a colonial state, as was the case in nearby Fiji.[46] While the French did run a meager state system of clinics, for most of the seventy-four years of colonial presence, the British chose to support the clinics and hospitals that the missionaries operated. Since their arrival in the mid-nineteenth century, the Anglican and Presbyterian missionaries ran basic hospitals and primary health care clinics, and advocated basic village sanitation. Chief among their priorities was the belief that they were educating mothers about infant care. The Melanesian Mission on Aoba (now Ambae) founded the Godden Memorial Hospital, where Sister Betty Pyatt ran the Mothercraft house. Ni-Vanuatu had been informal assistants in the clinics since the beginning of the missions but formal biomedical training began in the 1940s when indigenous men were trained in Fiji to work as assistant doctors.[47] Recognizing the need for formally trained nurses, by the 1950s, two nursing schools were established in the New Hebrides. An Anglican sister from New Zealand, Sister Betty Pyatt headed one at Godden Memorial Hospital on the island of Ambae, and Presbyterians from Australia Sisters Heard and Edgar ran the other at Paton Memorial Hospital in Port Vila. Because my ethnographic and oral history work is situated in Pango, where the nurse training and maternal and child health care were delivered primarily through the Presbyterian mission with British support, I focus on Presbyterian and British institutions in this chapter.

The interplay of colonial, Christian, and capitalist social forms has long intersected with gendered social experiences for women in all parts of the archipelago. Right from their arrival in the mid-nineteenth century, the work of female Presbyterian missionaries in the southern islands focused on converting women in a manner that made Christian virtues visible in the formation of nuclear families and the performance of feminine homemaking in newly shaped spaces where "domestic" activities were undertaken.[48] Indigenous practices surrounding birth and child care were considered profoundly primitive by missionaries[49] who "promoted a model of motherhood based on ideals of bourgeois domesticity back home, typically accorded the status of 'nature,' where biological and social maternity were normatively fused."[50] With respect to improving the population growth rate through an attempt to alter fertility rates, the British administration focused on regulating the bride price, which they hoped would reduce the marriage age of men, thereby encouraging more fertility within monogamous marriages. This method of demographic intervention would also further the missionaries' attempts to inculcate values about nuclear families.[51] Such assumptions that naturalized the woman-child dyads made mothers, together with their infants, targets of intervention by missionaries and doctors. This shift was particularly problematic in a context where indigenous cosmologies often included important responsibilities for men in child nurturance and fertility.[52] By the 1950s and 1960s, nurses would go to the villages surrounding Port Vila, like Pango, on a weekly basis to weigh infants and offer advice on infant care. Despite the civilizing agenda attached to birth and mothering activities, the meanings that women in Pango attach to place of birth in colonial and postcolonial hospitals are neither that of straightforward acceptance nor an outright rejection of the biomedical and Christian practice.

Because of their proximity to Port Vila, women and men in Pango were implicated in the colonial agenda earlier and more profoundly than many other villages[53] and they have had different experiences than women in *kastom*[54] communities. Leaders in *kastom* villages actively kept out mission schools and other Western influences, particularly for women.[55] Women and men who lived close to town could see the ever increasing variety of imported consumer goods, and the potential for wage labor, especially during the 1960s and 1970s. This was a time of remarkable growth for Port Vila, with rising "government spending, economic expansion, and the introduction of a tax haven."[56] Of importance for thinking about how demographic knowledge was filtered, the British government and the Presbyterian hospital employed many of the oldest generation now living in Pango as groundskeepers, nurses, cleaning/cooking staff, telegraph operators, and police during the 1950s and 1960s. Being near to Port Vila also made giving birth in hospital routinely possible. The ongoing Christian ethos in the village (which officially started in 1845) likely furthered this shift.

Ni-Vanuatu Nurses and Indigenous Modernities

For women in Pango village, practices of prenatal, birth, and post-natal care began to change more rapidly in the early 1950s, when truck transport for the roughly five kilometer trip to the wharf to catch the launch to the Paton Memorial Hospital on the island of Iririki became more commonly available, and they did not have to walk the inland track to the wharf. It was also at this time that women began to be recruited by the doctor from Pango and Ifira to be trained as nurses. All of these factors were part of larger processes of social change, and although the change might appear to be driven by the transfer of knowledge and practice from overseas, the nurses would filter these tools through local worlds.

These first medically trained nurses are no longer alive, but I spoke with the next generation about their training at nursing school in the 1950s. The program was a forum whereby they learned to use new technologies and comfort measures for assisting birthing women and their infants. Learning to make a bed was absolutely prominent in their memories, which included smooth white sheets with the corners tightly tucked under the mattress. Though far from luxurious, the beds at the mission hospital were part of the transfer of knowledge and technology of medical care for childbirth. The next aspect of the curriculum the women typically recalled was learning to bathe patients, an important skill as the new mothers would typically stay in hospital for a week after birth. The nurses would also learn English vocabulary necessary for their work. In the mid-1960s, the trainees were given technical English training from an Australian volunteer, Anne Naupa, who taught English to all variety of ni-Vanuatu colonial employees, and their lessons were all based on practical contexts. For example, Naupa told me, "The policemen would learn vocabulary to give traffic tickets and the nurses would learn bandages, forceps, and thermometers." As well, the doctor in charge recalled in his memoir that throughout the nursing training, the

Christian values of "love, peace, patience, stoicism, discipline, tolerance were promoted."[57] After birth, the nurses would bring the baby to the mother every four hours to be nursed. When I spoke with women who had their babies at the Paton Memorial Hospital, they remember the kindness of the ni-Vanuatu nurses and the sisters from Australia and New Zealand. They speak with affection about how much the staff cared for them and give evidence by referring to how the nurses bathed them and the baby. The women were glad to stay a whole week at the hospital and remember the sheets and the beds that were different from the *pandanus* mats they slept on at home. They laugh at the exercises the sisters made them do from their beds where they lay with the other sick people admitted to the hospital and fondly remember that every morning began with devotion, prayer, and hymn singing.

In addition to assisting in the hospital, the nurses had other duties. One told me that she would accompany the doctor to the village when he gave his talks about the importance of giving birth in the hospital. She would try to put the women's minds at ease by telling them that the doctor saw the private parts of many women as part of his work, so they did not need to worry about it. Almost without exception, when I spoke with women about giving birth in the Paton Memorial Hospital, they recalled giving birth alone with the nurse and sometimes the doctor at the very end. Their husbands and other family members waited outside. They did not mind this arrangement, perhaps as it incorporated aspects of traditional practices of gendered seclusion at birth.

The attempts to stabilize the population growth at the Paton Memorial Hospital in the 1950s were carried out through a complex assemblage of technology transfer practices and knowledge. There were technologies that people needed to be trained to use properly: beds, clean sheets, scales, and thermometers. There were new practices: in-hospital birthing during which women were attended by biomedically trained attendants (who were not necessarily from their village), week-long stays in hospital, bathing babies and women after birth, weighing babies, and routinized infant feeding. New linguistic and technological vocabularies needed to be taught in order to facilitate the work of the attendants. The direct interventions of a state or NGO were less important than the work of the Presbyterian mission. Furthermore, though knowledge of demographic growth and decline circulated, concrete numbers of population size were scarce until the first census took place in 1967.

"Undeveloped Countries," "Demographic Transition," and the "Population Bomb" (1950–1970)

By the late 1960s, scientific anxieties about world population growth were framed less in terms of racial issues and more in terms of demographic transitions and ecological issues. In these paradigms, population growth would slow as the result of economic development, Western education and overall social modernization.[58] Traditional societies, as the theory went, entailed many births and high rates of infant mortality, as well as poor maternal health. Defusing the "population bomb"[59] that could cause global famine and conflict was considered a problem of global consequence to be accomplished by advocating for one of "mankind's inalienable rights," that of "the right to limit families."[60] Frederick Osborne, another prominent postwar population expert wrote that: "The planning of family size should be part of a new concept of man's dignity, an integral aspect of moral progress in response to new opportunities and obligations created by the progress of science."[61] The large families of so-called traditional societies were identified as barriers to health and happiness and were understood as objects for intervention in demographic transitions to modernity. For example:

> In a primitive society with abundant resources the rearing of children may be relatively simple. . . . The conditions of tribal and communal life ease the burdens of parents with large families. . . . But as a general rule it must be recognized that for most people in areas where birth rates are high and incomes are low, large families make it difficult to improve the care and education of children and handicap all efforts to improve the quality of family life.[62]

The disciplines of social demography and population ecology in particular stressed economic and ecological prosperity through the achievement of an optimal "carrying capacity." According to Sabine Hoehler, population ecologists who wrote about optimal carrying capacities of populations:

> explicitly distanced themselves from hereditary theories to ameliorate and optimize population, stressing instead overall economical and ecological prosperity. Nevertheless, their propositions followed similar principles of classification, designation and evaluation. Aggregating and disaggregating human beings on the scale of the world, their taxonomies identified certain regions and populations less valuable and more threatening to the well being of the human collective than others.[63]

In the global population accounting of the 1950s and 1960s, the demography of the Pacific islands was an important context through which to understand social change and the unique cultural adaptations that varied so widely across the region. For example, in *The Study of Population: An Inventory and Appraisal*, Hauser and Duncan write:

> The miracles of public health were brought to the islands and death rates were reduced to very low levels. Population increase is replacing population decline as the welfare problem for administering powers. The balances that preserved the people of the islands in the indigenous cultures must have indeed been delicate

ones. Or perhaps there were alternating periods of growth and decimation, with disappearance the fate of those whose fertility was inadequate or superabundant for the fragile economic development permitted by the islands. The major demographic research interest in the island populations lies in the plasticity of the cultural forms and processes that condition marriage, family, child bearing mortality and migration.[64]

Anxieties about Demographic Growth in the New Hebrides

Already in 1935, Tom Harrison, a maverick researcher who had a short-lived career as a colonial administrator, raised the possibility of impending difficulties of a recovered population. He wrote:

> Important in connection with the probable increase in population is the question—where are the natives to expand to? ... Almost all the land in the islands [the Maskelines off Malakula] and a lot that is under the sea—is claimed by companies and individuals. Anyone who knows native custom re land tenure and sale must be appalled by the absurdity."[65]

The French anthropologist Jean Guiart also reported to the Condominium, "The moment when this begins to cause problems, especially with land tenure, is possibly not very far off."[66] By the early 1970s, the growing urban population was considered a problem[67] that would undoubtedly be exacerbated if measures were not taken, such as the creation of housing in Melanesian style (not simplified copies of European dwellings), as well as gardening land near each house as a source of building materials, food, and medicine, but also for its cultural importance.[68] People in Pango were differently positioned in this urban growth than the many migrants coming from other islands as their village predated the colonial settlement. Urban growth meant new pressures on land and resources, which hitherto had been used for subsistence agriculture.

After bringing birth and, to a lesser extent infant care, under the purview of biomedicine and the mission, and having witnessed the proliferation of large families in the late 1940s into the 1960s, employees at the mission hospitals started distributing birth control in the late 1960s. This was not an organized public awareness project of the missions at either an international or a national scale, or an official stance, but rather the localized work of their front line workers who were concerned about public health and the health of mothers and children in particular. Public health campaigns spearheaded by organizations other than the Condominium were organized throughout the archipelago since the 1920s, beginning with the Rockefeller Foundation-funded anti-hookworm campaign followed by anti-malarial campaigns of the U.S. military during the war.[69] The WHO organized an anti-Yaws campaign in 1958, an anti-TB campaign in 1967–1968 (together with UNICEF), and an anti-malarial effort from 1971–1973. Maternal and child health (MCH) were consistently mentioned in the communication and reports from these campaigns, but the 1962 study of maternal and child health, jointly undertaken by the WHO and the South Pacific Commission (SPC),[70] was the first (and only during that time period) project undertaken by international organizations for prenatal and postnatal care and infant health. With respect to family planning in the region, the SPC organized a seminar for MCH workers from across the South Pacific on MCH and family planning, including the topics: "Population problems in the world, with special reference to the South Pacific," "Socio-psychological factors and program acceptance," and IUD insertion demonstrations.[71] But no one attended from the New Hebrides since the British Resident Commissioner indicated "the territory is not vitally interested in family planning at this stage."[72] The International Planned Parenthood Federation designed posters for distribution throughout Southeast Asia and Oceania proclaiming "To improve the Quality is to Plan the Quantity" and "the Happy Family is a Planned Family" with space for local offices to write the location of the nearest family planning clinic.[73] However, there were no family planning clinics or IPPF offices in the New Hebrides during the 1950s and 1960s.[74] Despite the growing international organizations' concern for population growth, in the New Hebrides there was a relative dearth of international presence concerned for MCH in general and virtually no concern for family planning in an institutionalized form. Yet concern for Western technologies of family planning filtered into the New Hebrides by the late 1960s and early 1970s.

Sister Betty Pyatt, who dedicated over twenty years of her life to nursing in the New Hebrides, frequently told me in oral history interviews that when she arrived in 1944, women asked her advice on how to have more children. By Pyatt's last years nursing in the early 1970s, women had begun asking her for birth control. She worked at the Godden Memorial Hospital on Ambae and started a nursing school there. With depopulation no longer a concern, Australian Dr. Freeman and New Zealander Dr. Mackereth, working at the main mission hospitals, independently decided to start offering birth control, in the form of the combined oral contraceptive pill, and most often IUDs, referred to by the nurse-midwives I interviewed as "the loop." Dr. Mackereth, the doctor in charge at the Godden Memorial Hospital, would offer the pill to married women with four or more children. In his memoir, Dr. Freeman recounts that while the British administration were not actively involved in providing clinical care, "one of the major drives of the British administration was an attempt to limit population growth."[75] Freeman recounts his pragmatic approach to introducing birth control as follows: "It was obviously impractical to supply birth control pills to New Hebrideans ... I had just learned about the intro-uterine contraceptive device (IUCD) and, as it appeared to be a very inexpensive and effective method of birth control, I ordered some from the manufacturers in Australia."[76] Tubal ligations were also performed. All of these methods of birth control were almost exclusively provided to married women with children with the intent of reducing the stress of childbearing on the mother's body. The standard procedure was that husbands were consulted, and if need be, convinced by the doctor that it would be best for his wife and existing children that his wife undergo the operation. Furthermore, it was incorporated into (still recalled by women in Pango in 2010) existing relationships and networks that the Presbyterian Church had established over decades. Mrs. Freeman made visits to the villages, weighed babies, and taught women about the importance of spacing children, or "family planning." These visits, Dr. Freeman writes in hindsight, were "a long established tradition. They had been a means of getting to know the New Hebridean women and of providing them with both knowledge and confidence in the hospital and the mission, as well as a means of checking on the health of the babies."[77]

This transfer of knowledge and technology about cosmopolitan birth and fertility occurred in a context with a very recent history of dramatic population decline, but also one where ni-Vanuatu women possessed knowledge of fertility control that was passed on from matrilineal kin that included knowledge of herbal contraceptives and abortifacients available on their ancestral land. There were existing indigenous practices that worked to limit fertility, now remembered in terms of "spacing children." In addition to the use of herbs, these practices involved prolonged breastfeeding and sexual abstinence. Many older women and men in Pango told me that once your child can walk, only then should you get pregnant again, otherwise the fetus takes power from the nursing baby. A prime consideration in Pango for family size was that both male and female children were needed for families to be considered ideal and complete.[78]

Conclusion

Between the 1920s and the 1970s, concerns about population size, both globally and of the Pacific islands more specifically, shifted from debates on "racial" decline of "primitive" people in the 1920s to concerns emphasizing the importance of balancing population growth, economic development, and modernization by the late 1960s. These agendas entailed the transfer of technologies that local nurses and birthing women filtered to render them meaningful in local cultural practices. During the 1960s and early 1970s, the worldwide institutional relationships of demography to family planning programs and population policies were being negotiated, and thus the relationships between local contexts and global networks reveal a great deal to historians, as the process was neither exclusively from the top down nor from the bottom up.

Disturbing accounts of population politics understandably focus on technologies that are invasive and directly intervene in women's bodies, like experimental hormonal methods, the Dalkon shield (an IUD)[79] and mass sterilizations.[80] I hope to have shown that when speaking of knowledge and technology transfer in the interest of population, what counts as technology—beds with clean sheets, for example—needs to be interpreted broadly with respect to local context. Ni-Vanuatu nurses, who would have been among the women with the most European education at the time, were crucial agents in being trained to use new technologies, which played a central role in the transformation of birth from an event taking place in the village to a medicalized event staged in a hospital. Population technologies articulate with local gender relations, kinship formations, ancestral beliefs and religious ethics. Analyzing the transfer of population technology in this particular corner of the British and French empires shows that strong states or development organizations were not always part of how the demographic knowledge and technologies circulated, but rather the knowledge was filtered by local agents and social worlds. Finally, local contexts mattered for the production of demographic knowledge about global populations, as islands are unique and limited environments.

Acknowledgments

The research for this chapter was conducted during a postdoctoral fellowship at the Max Planck Institute for the History of Science. I extend my thanks to Veronika Lipphardt and Corinna Unger for the invitation to participate in the conference session in 2010, and to Sarah Blacker, Heinrich Hartmann, Ricky Heinitz, Jean Mitchell, and especially to the women in Pango who shared stories with me.

Notes

1. M. Murphy, "Technology, Governmentality, and Population Control," *History and Technology* 26, no. 1 (2010): 69–76, 73.
2. Ibid., 73.
3. B. Duden, "Population," in *The Development Dictionary*, W. Sachs ed. (Boulder, 1990), 146.
4. Ibid., 149.
5. E.g. *Anthropological Demography: Toward a New Synthesis*, D. Kertzer and T. Fricke eds. (Chicago, 1997).
6. E.g. *Situating Fertility: Anthropology and Demographic Inquiry*, S. Greenhalgh ed. (Cambridge, 1995).
7. N. Riley and J. McCarthy, *Demography in the Age of the Postmodern* (Cambridge, 2003).
8. This builds on previous fieldtrips in 2001, 2003, and 2004.

9. Ni-Vanuatu is the post independence term for indigenous citizens in Vanuatu. Using this term to refer to people in the New Hebrides is an anachronism but a common one in the historiography of the Condominium, e.g. M. Meyerhoff, "A Vanishing Act: Tonkinese Migrant Labour in Vanuatu in the Early 20th Century," *The Journal of Pacific History* 37, no. 1 (2002): 45–56; M. Jolly, "Other Mothers: Maternal 'Insouciance' and the Depopulation Debate in Fiji and Vanuatu, 1890–1930," in *Maternities and Modernities: Colonial and Post Colonial Experiences in Asia and the Pacific*, K. Ram and M. Jolly eds. (Cambridge, 1998), 177–212.
10. S. Greenhalgh, *Just One Child: Science and Policy in Deng's China* (Berkeley, 2008); S. Greenhalgh, *Cultivating Global Citizens: Population in the Rise of China*, (Cambridge, Mass., 2010).
11. E.g. J. Olszynko-Gryn, C. Unger in this volume.
12. E.g. M. Quine, *Population Politics in Twentieth-Century Europe: Fascist Dictatorships and Liberal Democracies* (New York, 1996).
13. C. Unger, in this volume.
14. L. Thomas, *Politics of the Womb: Women, Reproduction and the State in Kenya* (Berkeley, 2003), 175.
15. J.R. Baker, "Depopulation in Espiritu Santo, New Hebrides," *Journal of the Royal Anthropological Institute of Great Britain and Ireland* 58, no. 1 (1928): 279–303; P.A. Buxton, "The Depopulation of the New Hebrides and Other Parts of Melanesia," *Transactions of the Royal Society of Tropical Medicine and Hygiene* 19, no. 8 (1926): 420–458; W.H.R. Rivers, "The Psychological factor," in 84–113; F. Speiser, "Decadence and Preservation in the New Hebrides," in *Essays on the Depopulation of Melanesia*, W.H.R. Rivers ed. (Cambridge, 1922), 25–61.
16. R. Bedford, *New Hebridean Mobility: A Study in Circular Migration* (Canberra, 1973); J. Bonnemaison "Circular Migration and Uncontrolled Migration in the New Hebrides: Proposals for an Effective Urban Migration Policy," *South Pacific Bulletin* 26, no. 4 (1976): 7–13.
17. A. Bashford, "Nation, Empire, Globe: the Spaces of Population Debate in the Interwar Years," *Comparative Studies in Society and History* 49, no. 1 (2007): 1–32; M. Connelly, *Fatal Misconception: The Struggle to Control World Population* (Cambridge, Mass., 2008).
18. Ibid.
19. G.H.L.F. Pitt-Rivers, *Problems of Population* (London, 1932); G.H.L.F. Pitt-Rivers, "Depopulation in Melanesia," *Man* 28, no. 12 (1928): 213–215; G.H.L.F. Pitt-Rivers, "Sex Ratios and Cultural Contact," *Man* 27, no. 3 (1927): 59–60.
20. A. Carr-Saunders, *World Population: Past Growth and Present Trends* (Oxford, 1936), 299–300.
21. Ibid., 297–299.
22. Rivers, *The Psychological Factor*.
23. A. Widmer, "Of Field Encounters and Metropolitan Debates: Research and the Making and Meaning of the Melanesian 'Race' During Demographic Decline," *Paideuma* 58 (2012): 69–93.
24. V. Lipphardt, "Isolates and Crosses in Human Population Genetics, or: A Contextualisation of German Race Science," *Current Anthropology* 53, no. 5 (2012): 69–82.
25. W. Anderson, "Ambiguities of Race: Science on the Reproductive Frontier of Australia and the Pacific Between the Wars," *Australian Historical Studies* 40, no. 2 (2009): 143–160.
26. Anderson, "Ambiguities of Race."
27. Widmer, *Of Field Encounters*.
28. S.H. Roberts, *Population Problems of the Pacific* (London, 1927), 366.
29. L. Manderson, *Sickness and the State: Health and Illness in Colonial Malaya, 1870–1940* (Cambridge, 1996); J. Boddy, *Civilizing Women: British Crusades in Colonial Sudan* (Princeton, 2007).
30. Manderson, *Sickness and the State*, 228.

31. E.g. N. Hunt, *A Colonial Lexicon of Birth Ritual, Medicalization, and Mobility in the Congo* (Durham, 1999); N. Thomas, "Sanitation and Seeing: The Creation of State Power in Early Colonial Fiji," *Comparative Studies in Society and History* 32, no. 1 (1990): 149–170.
32. Boddy, *Civilizing Women*.
33. Passfield to Fletcher, Letter 8th March, 1930. Decrease in Numbers and Physique of Indigenous Population NHBS 246/1930 Western Pacific Archives, Special Collections, University of Auckland Library.
34. B.R.C. Joy to High Commissioner, Report on Depopulation. 15th July, 1930. Decrease in Numbers and Physique of Indigenous Population NHBS 246/1930 Western Pacific Archives, Special Collections, University of Auckland Library.
35. A. Widmer, "Native Medical Practitioners, Temporality and Nascent Biomedical Citizenship in the New Hebrides," *Political and Legal Anthropology Review* 30, no. 1 (2010): 57–80.
36. A. Widmer, "The Imbalanced Sex Ratio and the High Bride Price: Watermarks of Race in Demography, Census, and the Colonial Regulation of Reproduction," *Science, Technology and Human Values*. Published online on March 18, 2014 as doi:10.1177/0162243914523509.
37. This is an expression rendered from the Bislama, *klinim fes*. Bislama is the lingua franca of Vanuatu.
38. M. Jolly, "From Darkness to Light? Epidemiologies and Ethnographies of Motherhood in Vanuatu," in *Birthing in the Pacific: Beyond Tradition and Modernity?*, V. Lukere and M. Jolly eds. (Honolulu, 2001), 148–177.
39. M. Jolly, "'To Save the Girls for Brighter and Better Lives': Presbyterian Missions and Women in the South of Vanuatu: 1848–1870," *Journal of Pacific History* 26, no. 1 (1991): 27–48.
40. A. Widmer, "The Effects of Elusive Knowledge: Census, Health Laws and Inconsistently Modern Subjects in Early Colonial Vanuatu," *Journal of Legal Anthropology* 1, no. 1 (2008): 92–116.
41. N. McArthur, *Population and Prehistory: The Late Phase on Aneityum* (Ph.D. diss., Australian National University, 1974).
42. E.g. M.J. Mitchell, "Objects of Expert Knowledge: On Time and the Materialities of Conversion in the southern New Hebrides," *Anthropologica* 55, no. 2 (2013): 291–302; A. Eriksen, *Gender, Christianity and Change in Vanuatu: An Analysis of Social Movements in North Ambrym* (Burlington, 2008).
43. B. Douglas, "Christian Citizens: Women and Negotiations of Modernity in Vanuatu," *Contemporary Pacific* 14, no. 1 (2002): 1–38.
44. E.g. Baker, *Depopulation in Espiritu Santo*. Buxton, *Depopulation of the New Hebrides*. Sylvester Lambert, "Health Survey of the New Hebrides," Western Pacific Archives (WPA), University of Auckland, New Zealand, New Hebrides British Service (NHBS) 105/1924, 1924. Rivers, *Psychological Factor*, Speiser, *Decadence*.
45. For more on the Condominium see M. Rodman, *Houses Far from Home: British Colonial Space in the New Hebrides* (Honolulu, 2001); K. Woodward, "Historical Note," in *Tufala Gavman: Reminiscences from the Anglo-French Condominium of the New Hebrides*, B.J. Bresnihan and K. Woodward eds. (Suva, 2002), 16–72.
46. Thomas, *Sanitation and Seeing*.
47. Widmer, *Native Medical Practitioners*.
48. Jolly, *To Save the Girls*.
49. Jolly, *From Darkness to Light*, 148–151.
50. Ibid., 157.
51. Widmer, *Watermarks of Race*.
52. M. Jolly, "Infertile States: Person and Collectivity, Region and Nation in the Rhetoric of Pacific Population," in *Borders of Being: Citizenship, Fertility and Sexuality in Asia and the Pacific*, M. Jolly and K. Ram eds. (Ann Arbor, 2001), 262–306.

53. G. Rawlings, "Foundations of Urbanization: Port Vila Town and Pango Village, Vanuatu," *Oceania* 70, no. 1 (1999), 84.
54. *Kastom* is the Bislama (the local lingua Franca) word that refers to indigenous knowledge and practice. As many anthropologists have noted it is a complex term that has been part of postcolonial nation building, cultural revitalization, as well as gendered and generational exclusionary practices. E.g. M.J. Mitchell, "Engaging Feminist Anthropology in Vanuatu : Local Knowledge and Universal Claims," *Anthropology in Action* 18, no. 1 (2011): 29–41; L. Bolton, *Unfolding the Moon: Enacting Women's Kastom in Vanuatu* (Honolulu, 2003); J. Taylor, "Janus and the Siren's Call: Kava and the Articulation of Gender and Modernity in Vanuatu," *Journal of the Royal Anthropological Institute* (N.S.) 16 (2010): 279–296.
55. M. Jolly, "The Forgotten Women: A History of Migrant Labour and Gender Relations in Vanuatu," *Oceania* 58, no. 2 (1987): 119–139.
56. Rawlings, *Foundations of Urbanization*, 84.
57. T. Freeman, *Doctor in Vanuatu: A Memoir* (Suva, 2006), 47.
58. F.W. Notestein, "Some Economic Aspects of Population Change in the Developing Countries," in *Population Dilemmas in Latin America*, J.M. Stycos and J. Blois eds. (Washington, 1966), 86–100.
59. P. Ehrlich, *The Population Bomb* (New York, 1968).
60. Ibid., back cover.
61. F. Osborn, "Population: An International Dilemma," in *On Population: Three Essays*, T. Malthus, J. Huxley, and F. Osborn eds. (New York, 1960), 116.
62. Osborn, *Population*, 93.
63. S. Hoehler, "The Law of Growth. How Ecology Accounted for World Population in the 20th Century," *Distinktion: Scandinavian Journal of Social Theory* 8, no. 1 (2007): 57–58.
64. P. Hauser and O. Duncan, *The Study of Population: An Inventory and Appraisal* (Chicago, 1959), 273.
65. Harrison to BRC. Anthropological: Ethnological & Tribal survey of Malekula. 1935. NHBS 83/1935 Western Pacific Archives, Special Collections, University of Auckland Library.
66. "Le moment où cela commence à poser des problèmes, en particulier de tenure des terres, n'est peut-être pas très éloigné." J. Guiart, 1953. "Commentaire" 5. mai, "Native Census" New Hebrides British Service 12/2/3 Western Pacific Archives, Special Collections, University of Auckland Library.
67. Bedford, *New Hebridean Mobility*.
68. Bonnemaison, *Circular Migration*, 12.
69. J. Bennett, "Malaria, Medicine, and Melanesians: Contested Hybrid Spaces in World War II," *Health and History* 8, no. 1 (2006): 27–55.
70. The South Pacific Commission was founded by six governments who administered "dependent" territories in 1947 to restore stability after the Second World War. It became the intergovernmental Secretariat of the Pacific Community in 1997. The SPC supervised a significant amount of demographic and health research in the region.
71. South Pacific Commission. 1966. "Seminar on Maternal and Child Health (including family planning)." December 3. SPC Projects, Maternity and Child Health Project 1967. NHBS 354/28. Western Pacific Archives, Special Collections, University of Auckland Library.
72. C. Allan, Letter from British Resident Commissioner to UK Commissioner. September 4, 1967. SPC Projects, Maternity and Child Health Project. NHBS 354/28, Western Pacific Archives, Special Collections, University of Auckland Library.
73. Connelly, *Fatal Misconception*, 164.
74. I know from ethnographic research that the Port Vila office of Planned Parenthood did print posters in 2003 stating that families should only have as many children as they could care for, and that smaller families were happier families.

75. Freeman, *Doctor in Vanuatu*, 122.
76. Ibid.
77. Freeman, *Doctor in Vanuatu*, 124.
78. It bears mention that today, public health workers and development planners are worried about rapid demographic growth in urban areas, e.g. H. Ware, "Demography, Migration and Conflict in the Pacific," *Journal of Peace Research* 42, no. 4 (2005): 435–454. Women have access to tubal ligations with the written consent of their husbands. Abortion of any kind is officially illegal, outlawed by the first Prime Minister of Vanuatu Walter Lini, a ni-Vanuatu Anglican minister at independence in 1980.
79. E.g. B. Hartmann, *Reproductive Rights and Wrongs: The Global Politics of Population Control* (Boston, 1995).
80. E.g. J. Olszynko-Gryn, in this volume.

Bibliography

Anderson, W., "Ambiguities of Race: Science on the Reproductive Frontier of Australia and the Pacific Between the Wars," *Australian Historical Studies* 40, no. 2 (2009): 143–160.
Baker, J.R., "Depopulation in Espiritu Santo, New Hebrides," *Journal of the Royal Anthropological Institute of Great Britain and Ireland* 58, no. 1 (1928): 279–303.
Bashford, A., "Nation, Empire, Globe: the Spaces of Population Debate in the Interwar Years," *Comparative Studies in Society and History* 49, no. 1 (2007): 1–32.
Bedford, R., *New Hebridean Mobility: A Study in Circular Migration* (Canberra, 1973).
Bennett, J., "Malaria, Medicine, and Melanesians: Contested Hybrid Spaces in World War II," *Health and History* 8, no. 1 (2006): 27–55.
Boddy, J., *Civilizing Women: British Crusades in Colonial Sudan* (Princeton, 2007).
Bolton, L., *Unfolding the Moon: Enacting Women's Kastom in Vanuatu* (Honolulu, 2003).
Bonnemaison, J., "Circular Migration and Uncontrolled Migration in the New Hebrides: Proposals for an Effective Urban Migration Policy," *South Pacific Bulletin* 26, no. 4 (1976): 7–13.
Buxton, P.A., "The Depopulation of the New Hebrides and Other Parts of Melanesia," *Transactions of the Royal Society of Tropical Medicine and Hygiene* 19, no. 8 (1926): 420–458.
Carr-Saunders, A., *World Population: Past Growth and Present Trends* (Oxford, 1936).
Connelly, M., *Fatal Misconception: The Struggle to Control World Population* (Cambridge, Mass., 2008).
Douglas, B., "Christian Citizens: Women and Negotiations of Modernity in Vanuatu," *Contemporary Pacific* 14, no. 1 (2002): 1–38.
Duden, B., "Population," in *The Development Dictionary*, W. Sachs ed. (Boulder, 1990).
Ehrlich, P., *The Population Bomb* (New York, 1968).
Eriksen, A., *Gender, Christianity and Change in Vanuatu: An Analysis of Social Movements in North Ambrym* (Burlington, 2008).
Freeman, T., *Doctor in Vanuatu: A Memoir* (Suva, 2006).
Greenhalgh, S., *Cultivating Global Citizens: Population in the Rise of China*, (Cambridge, Mass., 2010).
Greenhalgh, S., *Just One Child: Science and Policy in Deng's China* (Berkeley, 2008).
Greenhalgh, S., ed., *Situating Fertility: Anthropology and Demographic Inquiry* (Cambridge, 1995).
Hartmann, B., *Reproductive Rights and Wrongs: The Global Politics of Population Control* (Boston, 1995).
Hauser, P., and Duncan, O., *The Study of Population: An Inventory and Appraisal* (Chicago, 1959).
Hoehler, S., "The Law of Growth. How Ecology Accounted for World Population in the 20th Century," *Distinktion: Scandinavian Journal of Social Theory* 8, no. 1 (2007): 45–64.

Hunt, N., *A Colonial Lexicon of Birth Ritual, Medicalization, and Mobility in the Congo* (Durham, 1999).
Jolly, M., "The Forgotten Women: A History of Migrant Labour and Gender Relations in Vanuatu," *Oceania* 58, no. 2 (1987): 119–139.
Jolly, M., "From Darkness to Light? Epidemiologies and Ethnographies of Motherhood in Vanuatu," in *Birthing in the Pacific: Beyond Tradition and Modernity?*, V. Lukere and M. Jolly eds. (Honolulu, 2001), 148–177.
Jolly, M., "Infertile States: Person and Collectivity, Region and Nation in the Rhetoric of Pacific Population," in *Borders of Being: Citizenship, Fertility and Sexuality in Asia and the Pacific*, M. Jolly and K. Ram eds. (Ann Arbor, 2001), 262–306.
Jolly, M., "Other Mothers: Maternal 'Insouciance' and the Depopulation Debate in Fiji and Vanuatu, 1890–1930," in *Maternities and Modernities: Colonial and Post Colonial Experiences in Asia and the Pacific*, K. Ram and M. Jolly eds. (Cambridge, 1998), 177–212.
Jolly, M., "'To Save the Girls for Brighter and Better Lives': Presbyterian Missions and Women in the South of Vanuatu: 1848–1870," *Journal of Pacific History* 26, no. 1 (1991): 27–48.
Kertzer, D., and Fricke, T., eds., *Anthropological Demography: Toward a New Synthesis*, eds. (Chicago, 1997).
Lipphardt, V., "Isolates and Crosses in Human Population Genetics, or: A Contextualisation of German Race Science," *Current Anthropology* 53, no. 5 (2012): 69–82.
Manderson, L., *Sickness and the State: Health and Illness in Colonial Malaya, 1870–1940* (Cambridge, 1996).
McArthur, N., *Population and Prehistory: The Late Phase on Aneityum* (Ph.D. diss., Australian National University, 1974).
Meyerhoff, M., "A Vanishing Act: Tonkinese Migrant Labour in Vanuatu in the Early 20th Century," *The Journal of Pacific History* 37, no. 1 (2002): 45–56.
Mitchell, M.J., "Engaging Feminist Anthropology in Vanuatu : Local Knowledge and Universal Claims" *Anthropology in Action* 18, no. 1 (2011): 29–41.
Mitchell, M.J., "Objects of Expert Knowledge: On Time and the Materialities of Conversion in the southern New Hebrides," *Anthropologica* 55, no. 2 (2013): 291–302.
Murphy, M., "Technology, Governmentality, and Population Control," *History and Technology* 26, no. 1 (2010): 69–76.
Notestein, F.W., "Some Economic Aspects of Population Change in the Developing Countries," in *Population Dilemmas in Latin America*, J. M. Stycos and J. Blois eds. (Washington, 1966), 86–100.
Osborn, F., "Population: An International Dilemma," in *On Population: Three Essays*, T. Malthus, J. Huxley, and F. Osborn eds. (New York, 1960).
Pitt-Rivers, G.H.L.F., "Depopulation in Melanesia," *Man* 28, no. 12 (1928): 213–215.
Pitt-Rivers, G.H.L.F., *Problems of Population* (London, 1932).
Pitt-Rivers, G.H.L.F., "Sex Ratios and Cultural Contact," *Man* 27, no. 3 (1927): 59–60.
Quine, M., *Population Politics in Twentieth-Century Europe: Fascist Dictatorships and Liberal Democracies* (New York, 1996).
Rawlings, G., "Foundations of Urbanization: Port Vila Town and Pango Village, Vanuatu," *Oceania* 70, no. 1 (1999).
Riley, N., and McCarthy, J., *Demography in the Age of the Postmodern* (Cambridge, 2003).
Rivers, W.H.R., "The Psychological Factor," in *Essays on the Depopulation of Melanesia*, W.H.R. Rivers ed. (Cambridge, 1922), 25–61, 84–113.
Roberts, S.H., *Population Problems of the Pacific* (London, 1927).
Rodman, M., *Houses Far from Home: British Colonial Space in the New Hebrides* (Honolulu, 2001).
Speiser, F., "Decadence and Preservation in the New Hebrides," in *Essays on the Depopulation of Melanesia*, W.H.R. Rivers ed. (Cambridge, 1922), 25–61.

Taylor, J., "Janus and the Siren's Call: Kava and the Articulation of Gender and Modernity in Vanuatu," *Journal of the Royal Anthropological Institute* (N.S.) 16 (2010): 279–296.

Thomas, L., *Politics of the Womb: Women, Reproduction and the State in Kenya* (Berkeley, 2003).

Thomas, N., "Sanitation and Seeing: The Creation of State Power in Early Colonial Fiji," *Comparative Studies in Society and History* 32, no. 1 (1990): 149–170.

Ware, H., "Demography, Migration and Conflict in the Pacific," *Journal of Peace Research* 42, no. 4 (2005): 435–454.

Widmer, A., "The Effects of Elusive Knowledge: Census, Health Laws and Inconsistently Modern Subjects in Early Colonial Vanuatu," *Journal of Legal Anthropology* 1, no. 1 (2008): 92–116.

Widmer, A., "Of Field Encounters and Metropolitan Debates: Research and the Making and Meaning of the Melanesian 'Race' During Demographic Decline," *Paideuma* 58 (2012): 69–93.

Widmer, A., "Native Medical Practitioners, Temporality and Nascent Biomedical Citizenship in the New Hebrides," *Political and Legal Anthropology Review* 30, no. 1 (2010): 57–80.

Widmer, A., "The Imbalanced Sex Ratio and the High Bride Price: Watermarks of Race in Demography, Census, and the Colonial Regulation of Reproduction," *Science, Technology and Human Values*. Published online on March 18, 2014 as doi:10.1177/0162243914523509.

Woodward, K., "Historical Note," in *Tufala Gavman: Reminiscences from the Anglo-French Condominium of the New Hebrides*, B.J. Bresnihan and K. Woodward eds. (Suva, 2002), 16–72.

Notes on Contributors

Maria Dörnemann is a research associate at the Seminar für Zeitgeschichte, University of Tübingen, Germany. She is working on the project "'Plan Your Family-Plan Your Nation': International Population Policies in Kenya," funded by the Deutsche Forschungsgemeinschaft (DFG).

Heinrich Hartmann is Assistant Professor of History at the University of Basel, Switzerland. Currently he is also a research fellow at Boğaziçi University, Istanbul, and at Princeton University. His book, *Der Volkskörper bei der Musterung. Militärstatistik und Demographie in Europa vor dem Ersten Weltkrieg* (Wallstein, 2011), received the Henry E. Sigerist Award in 2012. His research focuses on the history of nineteenth and twentieth century demography in Europe and on the history of Turkish modernization from a transnational perspective.

Morgane Labbé is Assistant Professor of History in population statistics and population policies in Eastern and Central Europe at the Ecole des Hautes Etudes en Sciences Sociales (EHESS) of Paris. Recent publications include: "Institutionalizing the Statistics of Nationality in Prussia in the 19th Century" (*Centaurus*, 2007); "Internationalisme statistique et statistique des nationalités au 19e siècle" (*Courrier des Statistiques*, 2009); "La statistique d'une minorité sans nom: les 'Tutejsi' dans la Pologne de l'entre-deux-guerres," in *Minorités nationales en Europe centrale* (CEFRES, 2011).

John P. DiMoia is Assistant Professor of History at the National University of Singapore, where he teaches courses about the history of Korea, as well as the broader history of science, technology, and medicine. He holds a Ph.D. in the History of Science (2007) with a dissertation on the formation of South Korean scientific institutions and practices. He recently published his first book, *Reconstructing Bodies: Biomedicine, Health, and Nation-Building in South Korea since 1945* (Stanford University Press, Columbia University Press—WEAI). Related interests include the history of disease, the comparative history of statistics, demography and epidemiological practice, and energy issues in Asia since the mid to late nineteenth century.

Jesse Olszynko-Gryn is a research associate in the Department of History and Philosophy of Science at the University of Cambridge. His main project is a history of pregnancy testing in twentieth-century Britain. Supported by the Wellcome Trust Strategic Award, "Generation to Reproduction," it recovers a lost world of laboratory services and the transition of women from patients to consumers of this now ubiquitous diagnostic technology. With George Weisz (McGill University) he has also worked on Abdel Omran's theory of epidemiologic transition and, with Patrick Ellis (Berkeley), he is currently working on overpopulation in Hollywood cinema and popular culture.

Jadwiga E. Pieper Mooney is Associate Professor of History at the University of Arizona, teaching and researching Latin America, gender, and comparative, global, and world history. She has explored histories of gender and citizenship rights in *The Politics of Motherhood: Maternity and Women's Rights in Twentieth-Century Chile* and has also written about forced sterilization campaigns and human rights violations in Peru and North Carolina. Her ongoing research projects include transnational women's activism and the forging of global feminisms in the post World War II era. Currently, she is working on a study of the politics of public health in the twentieth century, told through a biographical lens, through the life of Chilean physician Dr. Benjamin Viel. She is also writing a book titled *Roads they Traveled: The Politics of Chilean Exile in the Cold War*.

Thomas Robertson is Associate Professor of History at Worcester Polytechnic Institute in Worcester, Massachusetts. He is author of *The Malthusian Moment: Global Population Growth and the Birth of American Environmentalism* (Rutgers University Press, 2012). His new research uses archival and ethnographic data to illuminate the environmental history of U.S. development projects, including population programs, in Nepal during the Cold War.

Paul Schor is Associate Professor of American history and American studies at the Université Paris Diderot. His book *Compter et classer. Histoire des recensements américains*, published in French in 2009 (Ed. de l'EHESS), received the 2011 Willi Paul Adams Award from the Organization of American Historians. An English version will be published by Oxford University Press in 2015. He has published extensively on the history of immigration, race, and racism in the United States.

Corinna R. Unger is Associate Professor of Modern European History at Jacobs University, Bremen. Her research focuses on European, North American, and international history of the twentieth century, with an emphasis on the history of knowledge. Together with Heinrich Hartmann, she has edited a thematic journal issue on the history of population studies in the twentieth century (*Berichte zur Wissenschaftsgeschichte* 33.3 (2010)).

Alexandra Widmer teaches in the anthropology department at York University, Toronto. Prior to this she held a research scholar appointment at the Max Planck Institute for the History of Science. Her recent publications include "Of Temporal Politics and Demographic Anxieties: 'Young Mothers' in Demographic Predictions and Social Life in Vanuatu" in the special collection she edited (with Jean Mitchell) called "Time and the Expert: Temporalities and the Social Life of Expertise" in *Anthropologica* (2013). Other publications concerning demography and population appear in *Anthropology and Medicine* (2013) and *Paideuma* (2012).

Index

A

abortion, 7, 86–99, 101nn26–27, 101n30, 104n66, 104n82, 225, 227, 240n78
Allende, Salvador, 98
American Association of Gynecological Laparoscopists (AAGL), 154–57
American Cytoscope Makers, Inc., 150
Asociación Chilena de Protección de la Familia (APROFA), 95–98, 104n73
Asociación Peruana de Protección Familiar (APPF), 93
Association for Voluntary Sterilization (AVS), 153
Atatürk, Mustafa Kemal, 181, 185
atomic weapons, 84, 109–19

B

Back, Kurt W., 67
Balfour, Marshall C., 129, 182
behavioralism, 8, 59–73
behaviorism, 63–64
Belaúnde, Fernando, 92–93
Berelson, Bernard, 69–72, 178, 182–91, 196n33
biopolitics, 59–60
birth control, 2, 6, 39–40, 69, 71, 75n32, 83–84, 86–99, 99n2, 104n66, 109, 114, 119–20, 137–39, 181–84, 191–93, 209, 211, 222, 224–25, 233–35. See also contraceptive pill, condom, contraception
Buxton, Patrick, 228

C

Carnegie Endowment for International Peace, 38
Carr-Saunders, Alexander Morris, 225
Carson, Rachel, 111, 122n5
census, 3, 5, 7, 19–33, 33n4, 33n7, 34n13, 34n16, 24n21, 36, 44, 47, 50, 88–92, 102n46, 131–32, 144n9, 194, 205, 208, 210, 231
Center for Population and Development Studies (CEPD), 92–93, 96
Christian, 95–97, 224, 228–31. See also missionaries
class, 28–33, 43, 45, 87–90, 93, 120, 157, 164, 226
Coale, Ansley, 61, 208–9
Cold War, 6, 63–64, 72, 83–84, 114, 119, 132, 179
colonialism, 2, 5, 9, 88, 90, 130–33, 136–39, 144n9, 203–4, 206–8, 223–24, 226–30, 233
Comilla, 67–68
Commoner, Barry, 8, 108–12, 116–21, 122nn4–5, 123n27
community development, 65–67, 183
condom, 97, 151–52, 157, 164, 169n78. See also birth control, contraception, contraceptive pill
Condominium, 223, 228, 233, 237n9
consumption, 58, 110–22

contraception, 43, 67–72, 75n32, 83, 86–99, 99n2, 104n83, 115, 120, 147–53, 155, 157, 165, 178, 181, 183–87, 189, 191, 197n41, 211, 234–35. *See also* birth control, contraceptive pill, condom
contraceptive pill, 75n32, 83, 87, 96–97, 99n2, 148, 151–52, 157, 169n78, 234. *See also* birth control, condom, contraception
Corsa Jr., Leslie, 182
cybernetics, 6, 58–65, 76n44

D
Darwinian Synthesis, 113
DDT (Dichlorodiphenyltrichloroethane), 110, 114
decolonization, 6, 60
Demographic Transition Theory, 6, 59, 74n8, 211
depopulation, 88, 224–34
Dhanraj, Deepa, 163
Donayre, José, 85, 91–93
Draper Report, 84
Draper, William H., 83–84
Du Bois, W.E.B, 26

E
ecology, 59, 108–21, 123n27, 232
Ecuador, 152
Ehrlich, Paul, 8, 109–21, 122nn4–5, 123n27, 149, 163
El Salvador, 152
Encina, Francisco, 90
environmentalism, 58, 109–21, 122nn4–5, 123n27, 149
Erenus, Necedet, 185
ethnicity, 7, 20–33, 33n7, 43, 185, 191, 212
Etimesgut, 185
eugenics, 5, 7, 37, 43, 53, 89–90, 149, 225

F
family planning, 2, 6–7, 9, 59–73, 74n8, 85–99, 130, 132, 136–44, 144n11, 145n25, 148–51, 157, 160–63, 178–94, 201, 211–15, 224, 234–35
fertility rates, 40, 46–51, 72, 143, 206, 211
Fişek, Nusret H., 182, 184, 186, 189, 197n41
Fishlock, Trevor, 147
Foerster, Heinz von, 62
Ford Foundation, 63, 65, 69, 70, 84–86, 92, 94, 103n63, 132, 151, 155, 188, 208–9, 212–13
Forrester, Jay W., 59
Frangenheim, Hans, 149, 154
Frei Montalva, Eduardo, 96

G
game theory, 64
Giri, Kanti, 151
Gordon, John E., 58–59
Green Revolution, 114

H
Hoagland, Hudson, 63, 75n32
Hoover, Edgar, 61, 209
Hulka, Jaroslav, 155–56
Humanae Vitae, 94, 97, 109

I
India, 58, 61, 65, 69–71, 114–16, 121, 147–65, 182, 208–9, 212, 223
indigenous, 66, 89–90, 223–36; knowledge, 239n54
Indonesia, 191
International Conference on Population (Bucharest, 1974), 98
International Planned Parenthood Federation (IPPF), 6, 84, 92–98, 101n27, 189, 234
International Population Congress, 40, 45, 48
International Union for the Scientific Investigation of Population Problems (IUSIPS), 40–41, 43, 45, 47, 53
Islam, 179, 180, 196n33
IUD, 97, 148, 160, 234, 236. *See also* Lippes loop

J

Japan Organization for International Cooperation in Family Planning (JOICP), 132
Johnson, Lyndon B., 84, 111, 113–15, 119

K

KAP Surveys (Family Planning Knowledge Attitude and Practices Surveys), 66–67, 139, 183–89, 192, 213
Karl Storz GmbH & Co., 149
Keith, Louis, 157
Kerrins, Joseph, 96–97
Khanna Study, 58, 73n2
Kirk, Dudley, 60, 74n11, 185
KLI, Inc., 157
Koseki, 131, 134, 144
Kuczynski, Robert René, 8, 37, 39, 49–53, 56n52, 205
Kwon, E. Hyock, 138–39

L

Lambert, Sylvester, 228
laparotomy, 148, 154
League of Mental Hygiene, 90
Lebanon, 153
Lewin, Kurt, 65, 67
Limits to Growth, 58–59, 72
Lippes loop, 160. *See also* IUD
Lotka, Alfred J., 8, 37, 49–53, 56n52

M

Malaysia, 152
Malthus, Thomas, 3, 37–39, 42, 113. *See also* Malthusian
Malthusian, 37–39, 58, 60–61, 72, 85, 91, 98, 108, 110, 113, 116–20
Marcuse, Herbert, 61
Maternal/Child Health (MCH), 191, 234. *See also* Program for Family Planning based on Maternal/Child Health Services
Mauldin, C. Parker, 182
Mead, Margaret, 62
Medical Technologies International, Inc., 151
Mehta, Pravin, 147, 161–63
midwives, 9, 139, 185–86, 191, 226–27, 234
Milbank Memorial Fund, 40, 84
Ministry of Health in India, 160; Kenya, 211; Peru, 99; Turkey, 179, 182, 185, 187, 191, 193
missionaries, 224–29. *See also* Christian
mixing, 21–26, 224, 226. *See also* race
modernization, 6, 66–67, 74n8, 91, 179, 181, 183, 188, 190, 192–93, 206–15, 232–35
Morgenstern, Oskar, 64

N

Nehru, Jawaharlal, 61
Nepal, 151–52
Neumann, John von, 62–64
Notestein, Frank W., 86, 129, 181–82, 206–8, 211
nurses, 9, 97, 162, 211, 223–36

O

Office of Population Research (OPR), 60, 129, 140, 206, 208, 211
Organization for Economic Co-operation and Development (OECD), 181, 192
Ortho Pharmaceutical Corporation, 153
Osborn, Fairfield, 108, 112, 115, 119
overpopulation, 1, 8, 37–39, 52, 54n9, 58–60, 63, 84–85, 87, 91, 98, 116, 119, 179, 211–12, 225, 244
Özbay, Ferhunde, 188

P

Pakistan, 67–68, 152, 182
Palacios, Nicolás, 90
Pan American Health Organization (PAHO), 92
Panama, 152
Pathfinder Fund, 97, 153, 189
Pavlov, Ivan, 63
Pearl, Raymond, 41

Philippines, 155, 191
Pitt-Rivers, G.H.L.F., 225
Planned Parenthood Federation of Korea (PPFK), 137
Poland, 7–8, 27, 36–53, 55n26, 55n29, 55n33
Pope Paul VI, 94, 109
population bomb, 84, 109–10, 114, 149, 164, 231–33
Population Council, 6, 9, 60, 68–69, 84, 86, 91, 94, 99, 151, 160, 178, 182–94, 195n5, 196n33, 201–2, 206–11, 214
post-partum approach, 68–69, 187, 189, 191, 227
prejudice, 26, 28, 30
Program for Family Planning based on Maternal/Child Health Services, 191. *See also* Maternal/Child Health (MCH)
Program for International Education in Gynecology and Obstetrics (PIEGO), 153–54
Puerto Rico, 75n32, 83, 155, 164

R
race, 7, 19–33, 33n7, 33n9, 90, 120, 212, 225–26. *See also* mixing
RAND Corporation, 64
rational choice, 59–73, 115
Ravenholt, Reimert T., 60, 151–52, 157–58
Requena, Mariano, 86, 103n63
Richard Wolf GmbH, 149–50, 155
Riley, John, 71
Rivers, W.H.R., 225, 228
Rockefeller Foundation, 38–39, 58, 85, 93, 99, 103n63, 129, 132, 144n3, 151, 182, 233
Rockefeller III, John D., 84–86, 94, 144n3
Rocket Medical PLC, 156
Ross, John, 186–87

S
Schramm, Wilbur, 71
Seeger, Pete, 121

Sen, Amartya, 163–64
Shepard, Bonnie, 87
Shorter, Frederick, 188
Singapore, 155
Skinner, B.F., 63
social engineering, 4–5, 65, 72, 202, 206
social eugenics, 89–90
South Korea, 8, 129–44, 145nn12–13, 152, 155, 184
South Pacific Commission (SPC), 234, 239n70
State Planning Organization (Turkish) (SPO), 187–88, 194
Steptoe, Patrick, 154
sterilization, 9, 71, 97, 115–16, 147–65, 236
systems analysis, 59–65

T
Taeuber, Irene, 129–33, 144nn3–4
Taiwan, 8, 71, 132, 134, 137, 139, 144n11, 152, 184
Takeshita, John Y., 137
Tarsus, 186, 188–93, 198n75
Taylor, Howard C., 69, 182, 184, 186–92
technology transfer, 223–24, 231, 236
Tekce, Belgin, 192
Thailand, 152, 155
Toros, Aykut, 188–89, 194
Treadway, Roy, 189–90
Turkish Development Foundation (TDF), 188–90, 198n71

U
United Nations Conference on the Environment (Stockholm, 1972), 109
United Nations Fund for Population Activities (UNFPA), 6, 91–92, 151, 192–93
United Nations International Children's Emergency Fund (UNICEF), 189, 234
United States Agency for International Development (USAID), 85–86, 151–61, 183–84, 192, 214

United States Food and Drug
  Administration (FDA), 157

V
vasectomy, 148, 152, 154, 161–63
Velasco Alvarado, Juan, 93, 98
Viel, Benjamin, 85–87, 91, 103n49, 103n63
Vogt, William 108, 112, 115, 119

W
Wheeless, Clifford, 149–55
Wiener, Norbert, 62, 65, 75n25

Wilcox, W.F., 26
World Bank, 213–15
World Health Organization (WHO), 151, 189, 233–34

Y
Yang, Jae-Mo, 138–40
Yoon, In Bae, 155

Z
Zero Population Growth (ZPG), 71, 113–14, 121, 149
Zipper, Jaime, 85, 103n63

www.ingramcontent.com/pod-product-compliance
Lightning Source LLC
Chambersburg PA
CBHW072149100526
44589CB00015B/2150